Marx, Engels, and Marxisms

Series Editors

Terrell Carver
University of Bristol
Bristol, United Kingdom

Marcello Musto
York University
Toronto, Ontario, Canada

The volumes of this series challenge the 'Marxist' intellectual traditions to date by making use of scholarly discoveries of the *Marx-Engels Gesamtausgabe* since the 1990s, taking on board interdisciplinary and other new critical perspectives, and incorporating 'reception studies'. Authors and editors in the series resist oversimplification of ideas and reinscription of traditions. Moreover, their very diversity in terms of language, local context, political engagement and scholarly practice mark the series out from any other in the field. Involving scholars from different fields and cultural backgrounds, the series editors ensure tolerance for differences within and between provocative monographs and edited volumes. Running contrary to 20th century practices of simplification, the books in this innovative series revitalize Marxist intellectual traditions.

More information about this series at:
http://www.springer.com/series/14812

Domenico Losurdo

Translated by Gregory Elliott

Class Struggle

A Political and Philosophical History

Domenico Losurdo
University of Urbino
Colbordolo, Vallefoglia
Pesaro-Urbino, Italy

Translated by Gregory Elliott

Translation from the Italian language edition: La lotta di classe: Una storia politica e filosofica by Domenico Losurdo, © Editori Laterza, 2013. All Rights reserved.
© Domenico Losurdo, 2016.

Marx, Engels, and Marxisms
ISBN 978-1-137-52387-7 (hardcover)   ISBN 978-1-349-70660-0 (eBook)
ISBN 978-1-349-70662-4 (softcover)
DOI 10.1057/978-1-349-70660-0

Library of Congress Control Number: 2016940579

© The Editor(s) (if applicable) and The Author(s) 2016, First softcover printing 2018
This work is subject to copyright. All rights are solely and exclusively licensed by the Publisher, whether the whole or part of the material is concerned, specifically the rights of translation, reprinting, reuse of illustrations, recitation, broadcasting, reproduction on microfilms or in any other physical way, and transmission or information storage and retrieval, electronic adaptation, computer software, or by similar or dissimilar methodology now known or hereafter developed.
The use of general descriptive names, registered names, trademarks, service marks, etc. in this publication does not imply, even in the absence of a specific statement, that such names are exempt from the relevant protective laws and regulations and therefore free for general use.
The publisher, the authors and the editors are safe to assume that the advice and information in this book are believed to be true and accurate at the date of publication. Neither the publisher nor the authors or the editors give a warranty, express or implied, with respect to the material contained herein or for any errors or omissions that may have been made.

Cover illustration: © bgwalker / Getty Images
Cover design by Oscar Spigolon

Printed on acid-free paper

This Palgrave Macmillan imprint is published by Springer Nature
The registered company is Nature America Inc. New York
The registered company address is: 1 New York Plaza, New York, NY 10004, U.S.A.

Series Foreword

The Marx Revival

The Marx renaissance is underway on a global scale. Whether the puzzle is the economic boom in China or the economic bust in 'the West', there is no doubt that Marx appears regularly in the media nowadays as a guru, and not a threat, as he used to be. The literature dealing with Marxism, which all but dried up twenty-five years ago, is reviving in the global context. Academic and popular journals and even newspapers and on-line journalism are increasingly open to contributions on Marxism, just as there are now many international conferences, university courses and seminars on related themes. In all parts of the world, leading daily and weekly papers are featuring the contemporary relevance of Marx's thought. From Latin America to Europe, and wherever the critique to capitalism is remerging, there is an intellectual and political demand for a new critical encounter with Marxism.

Types of Publications

This series bring together reflections on Marx, Engels and Marxisms from perspectives that are varied in terms of political outlook, geographical base, academic methodologies and subject-matter, thus challenging many preconceptions as to what 'Marxist' thought can be like, as opposed to what it has been. The series will appeal internationally to intellectual communities that are increasingly interested in rediscovering the most powerful critical analysis of capitalism: Marxism. The series editors will ensure that authors and editors in the series are producing overall an eclectic and stimulating yet synoptic and informative vision that will draw a very wide and diverse audience. This series will embrace a much wider range of scholarly interests and academic approaches than any previous 'family' of books in the area.

This innovative series will present monographs, edited volumes and critical editions, including translations, to Anglophone readers. The books in this series will work through three main categories:

Studies on Marx and Engels

The series will include titles focusing on the *oeuvre* of Marx and Engels which utilize the scholarly achievements of the on-going *Marx-Engels Gesamtausgabe*, a project that has strongly revivified the research on these two authors in the past decade.

Critical Studies on Marxisms

Volumes will awaken readers to the overarching issues and world-changing encounters that shelter within the broad categorisation 'Marxist'. Particular attention will be given to authors such as Gramsci and Benjamin, who are very popular and widely translated nowadays all over the world, but also to authors who are less known in the English-speaking countries, such as Mariátegui.

Reception Studies and Marxist National Traditions

Political projects have necessarily required oversimplifications in the 20th century, and Marx and Engels have found themselves 'made over' numerous times and in quite contradictory ways. Taking a national perspective on 'reception' will be a global revelation and the volumes of this series will enable the worldwide Anglophone community to understand the variety of intellectual and political traditions through which Marx and Engels have been received in local contexts.

Titles Published

1. Terrell Carver and Daniel Blank, *A Political History of the Editions of Marx and Engels's "German Ideology" Manuscripts*, 2014.
2. Terrell Carver and Daniel Blank, *Marx and Engels's "German Ideology" Manuscripts*, 2014.
3. Alfonso Maurizio Iacono, *The History and Theory of Fetishism*, 2015.
4. Paresh Chattopadhyay, *Marx's Associated Mode of Production*, 2016.
5. Domenico Losurdo, *Class Struggle: A Political and Philosophical History*, 2016.
6. Frederick Harry Pitts, *Critiquing Capitalism Today: New Ways to Read Marx*, 2017.
7. Ranabir Samaddar, *Karl Marx and the Postcolonial Age*, 2017.
8. George Comninel, *Alienation and Emancipation in the Work of Karl Marx*, 2018.
9. Jean-Numa Ducange and Razmig Keucheyan (Eds.), *The End of the Democratic State: Nicos Poulantzas, a Marxism for the 21st Century*, 2018.
10. Robert Ware, *Marx on Emancipation and the Socialist Transition*.
11. Xavier LaFrance and Charles Post (Eds.), *Case Studies in the Origins of Capitalism*.

Titles Forthcoming

Vladimir Puzone and Luis Felipe Miguel (Eds.), *The Brazilian Left in the 21st Century: Conflict and Conciliation in Peripheral Capitalism*

John Gregson, *Marxism, Ethics, and Politics: The Work of Alasdair MacIntyre*

James Muldoon, *The German Revolution and Political Theory*

Michael Brie, *Rediscovering Lenin: Dialectics of Revolution and Metaphysics of Domination*

Kaan Kangal, *Friedrich Engels and the* Dialectics of Nature

Acknowledgements

For their help in reading the manuscript and correcting the proofs, I am grateful to Stefano Azzarà, Paolo Ercolani, Giorgio Grimaldi, and Emanuela Susca.

CONTENTS

1 Introduction: The Return of Class Struggle? 1

2 The Different Forms of Class Struggle 7

3 A Protracted, Positive-Sum Struggle 53

4 Class Struggles and Struggles for Recognition 73

5 Overcoming Binary Logic: A Difficult, Unfinished Process 101

6 The Multiplicity of Struggles for Recognition and the Conflict of Liberties 121

7 The South-East Passage 139

8 Lenin in 1919: 'The Class Struggle is Continuing—It has Merely Changed its Forms' 175

9	After the Revolution: The Ambiguities of Class Struggle	199
10	After the Revolution: Discovering the Limits of Class Struggle	227
11	Class Struggle at the 'End of History'	247
12	Class Struggle between Exorcism and Fragmentation	267
13	The Class Struggle Poised between Marxism and Populism	309

Bibliography 345

Index 357

CHAPTER 1

Introduction: The Return of Class Struggle?

Amid an economic crisis that is exacerbating social polarization and rekindling memories of the 1930s Great Depression, condemning millions of people to unemployment, insecurity, constant anxiety about getting by, and even hunger, essays, and articles making reference to the 'return of class struggle' have become more frequent. So had it disappeared?

In the mid-twentieth century, sharply criticizing the 'dogma' of Marx's theory of class struggle, Ralf Dahrendorf summarized the achievements of the capitalist system: '[t]oday the allocation of social positions is increasingly the task of the educational system'. Property had lost any influence and been replaced by merit, 'making a person's social position dependent on his educational achievement'. And that was not all: 'the social situation of people [has] bec[o]me increasingly similar' and there was undoubtedly a tendency to a 'levelling [of] social differences'. The painter of this rosy picture was nevertheless obliged to criticize other sociologists for whom the world was spontaneously heading towards 'a state in which there are no classes and no class conflicts, because there is simply nothing to quarrel about'.[1]

These were years when an enormous number of men, women, and children from the global South and the countryside began to abandon their birthplace to seek their fortune elsewhere. This was also a mass phenomenon in Italy, where, hailing for the most part from the *Mezzogiorno*, immigrants crossed the Alps or stopped this side of them. Working conditions in north Italian factories can be illustrated in detail. In 1955, in order to suppress strikes and working-class militancy, hundreds of thousands of militants and activists from the CGIL—a trade union accused of unacceptable radicalism—were sacked.[2] Such practices were not confined to underdeveloped countries. In fact, the model was furnished by the USA, long characterized by yellow dog contracts, whereby, on being hired, workers and employees pledged (were forced to pledge) not to join any trade union organization. Was it really class struggle that had disappeared? Or was it substantive union freedoms, confirming the reality of class struggle?

Subsequent years witnessed the 'economic miracle'. But let us see what was happening in 1969 in the West's model country, giving the floor to a US periodical with an international diffusion ('Reader's Digest Selection'), engaged in propaganda on behalf of the 'American way of life'. 'Hunger in America' was the eloquent title of an article that had this to say:

> In Washington, the federal capital, 70 per cent of patients in the paediatric hospital suffer from malnutrition.... In America, food aid programmes cover only about 6 of the 27 million in need.... Having undertaken a tour of inspection in the Mississippi countryside, a group of doctors stated before a Senate sub-committee: 'the children we saw are obviously lacking in health, energy and vivacity. They are hungry and sick; and these are direct and indirect causes of death'.

According to Dahrendorf, what determined individuals' social position was solely or predominantly educational merit. But the US magazine drew attention to an obvious but wrongly ignored fact: '[d]octors are convinced that malnutrition impacts on the growth and development of the brain'.[3] Once again, the indicated question is, did such terrible poverty in a country of capitalist opulence have something to do with class struggle?

Subsequently, abandoning his illusory observations-predictions of the mid-twentieth century, Dahrendorf noted 'an increase in the percentage of the poor (often working poor)' in the USA.[4] The most interesting and disturbing observation was consigned to an inconspicuous parenthesis: even a job was insufficient to avert the risk of poverty! Long forgotten, the figure of the working poor reappeared and, with it, the spectre of class struggle, which seemed to have been exorcized for good. Even so, a famous philosopher—Jürgen Habermas—reiterated the positions now abandoned by the famous sociologist. What refuted Marx and his theory of class struggle was something obvious to everyone: the 'pacification of class conflict' by the welfare state, which had developed in the West 'since 1945', thanks to 'a reformism relying on the instruments of Keynesian economics'.[5] What is immediately striking here is an initial inaccuracy: while this might apply to Western Europe, it certainly does not to the USA, where the welfare state never flourished, as is confirmed by the distressing picture just seen.

But that is not the main thing. Above all, Habermas's claim is marked by the absence of a question that should be obvious: was the advent of the welfare state the inevitable result of a tendency inherent in capitalism? Or was it the result of political and social mobilization by the subaltern classes—in the final analysis, of a class struggle? Had the German philosopher posed this question, perhaps he would have avoided assuming the permanence of the welfare state, whose precariousness and progressive dismantlement are now obvious to everyone. Who knows whether Habermas had subsequently had his doubts. In the West, the welfare state emerged not in the USA but Europe, where the trade union and labour movement is traditionally more deep-rooted; and it emerged when that movement was at its strongest, because of the discredit which two world wars, the Great Depression, and fascism had brought upon capitalism. But is this refutation or confirmation of Marx's theory of class struggle?

Habermas points to 1945 as the starting point for the construction of the welfare state in the West and the attenuation and disappearance of class struggle. The previous year, visiting the USA, the Swedish sociologist, Gunnar Myrdal, reached a dramatic conclusion: 'segregation is now becoming so complete that the white Southerner practically never sees a Negro except as his servant and in other standardized and formalized caste situations'.[6] Two decades later, the slave-master relationship between blacks and whites had far from disappeared: '[i]n the 1960s, more than 400 men of colour in Alabama were used as human guinea pigs by the government. Suffering from syphilis, they were not treated because the authorities wished to study the effects of the disease on a "population sample"'.[7] Historically, the decades from the end of the Second World War to the successful 'pacification of class conflict' also witnessed the explosion of the anti-colonial revolution. The peoples of Asia, Africa, and Latin America threw off the yoke of colonialism or semi-colonialism, while the USA saw the development of the struggle by African-Americans to end the regime of racial segregation and discrimination, which continued to oppress and degrade them, relegate them to the bottom rungs of the labour market and even treat them as guinea pigs. Did this massive revolutionary wave, which profoundly altered the division of labour globally and did not even leave it untouched in the USA, have something to do with class struggle? Or is the latter limited to the conflict pitting proletarians and capitalists, dependent labour, and haute bourgeoisie, against one another in a single country?

Such is clearly the opinion of a bestselling contemporary British historian, Niall Ferguson. In the major historical crisis of the first half of the twentieth century, 'class struggle'—'the supposed struggle between proletariat and bourgeoisie'—played a very modest role. Decisive, instead, was what Hermann Göring, with his main focus on the conflict between the Third Reich and the Soviet Union, defined as the 'great racial war' (see Chap. 5, Sect. 8). Does Nazi Germany's attempt to reduce Slavs to the condition of black slaves in the service of the master race, and the epic resistance to this war of colonial subjugation and actual enslavement— the 'great racial war' undertaken by the Third Reich—mounted by entire peoples, have nothing to do with class struggle?

For Dahrendorf, Habermas, and Ferguson (but also, as we shall see, for distinguished scholars of a Marxist or post-Marxist persuasion), class struggle refers exclusively to the conflict between proletariat and bourgeoisie— in fact, to a conflict between proletariat and bourgeoisie that has become acute and of which both parties are conscious. But was this Marx and Engels' view? As is well known, having evoked 'the spectre of communism' 'haunting Europe', and even before analysing the 'existing class struggle' between proletariat and bourgeoisie, the *Communist Manifesto* opened with a statement that was destined to become famous and play a prominent role in nineteenth- and twentieth-century revolutionary movements: 'the history of all hitherto existing society is the history of class struggles'(*Klassenkämpfe*).[8] The transition from the singular to the plural clearly signals that the conflict between proletariat and bourgeoisie is but one class struggle among others and the latter, running throughout world history, are by no means a feature exclusively of bourgeois, industrial society. Should any doubts remain, some pages later the *Manifesto* reiterates: 'the history of all past society has consisted in the development of class antagonisms, antagonisms that assumed different forms at different epochs.'[9] Not only 'class struggles' but also the 'forms' they take in different historical epochs, different societies, and different concrete situations are declined in the plural. But what are the multiple class struggles or the multiple configurations of class struggle?

To answer this question, we must reconstruct the significance of a theory, as well as the alterations and oscillations it has undergone, philologically and logically. But textual history is insufficient; we must also refer to real history. What is required is a double reinterpretation of a historico-theoretical kind. On the one hand, we need to throw light on the theory of class struggle formulated by Marx and Engels, integrating it into the history of their development as philosophers and revolutionary militants and their active engagement in the political struggles of their time. On the other, we must determine whether this theory is capable of shedding light on the rich, tormented history that starts out from the *Communist Manifesto*.

Hence, the first reinterpretation concerns the theme of class struggle in 'Marx and Engels'. But is this conjunction legitimate? I shall rapidly clarify the reasons for my approach. In the context of a division of labour and distribution of tasks that was jointly conceived and agreed, the authors of the *Manifesto* were in a relationship of constant collaboration and intellectual cross-fertilization. At least as regards politics proper and class struggle, they regarded themselves as members or leaders of a single 'party'. In a letter to Engels of 8 October 1858, after having raised an important theoretical and political problem (could an anti-capitalist revolution occur in Europe while capitalism remained in the ascendant in most of the world?), Marx exclaimed that '[f]or us, this is the difficult question'.[10] The indicated respondent is not an individual intellectual, however brilliant, but the leadership group of a political party in the process of being formed. In fact, the followers of this 'party' referred to Marx and Engels as an indissoluble intellectual and political partnership, as the leading group of a party that thought and worked in unison. The same was true of opponents, starting with Mikhail Bakunin, who in his criticism repeatedly conjoined 'Marx and Engels' or 'Messrs.Marx and Engels', or picked out 'Mr. Engels' as Marx's 'alter ego'.[11] Other opponents warned against the 'Marx and Engels clique' or waxed ironic over 'Mr. Engels, Marx's Prime Minister'.[12] So intimate was the association between the two that reference was sometimes made to 'Marx and Engels' in the singular, as if they were a single author and person (this was noticed by the first in a letter to the second of 1 August 1856).[13]

Obviously, we are dealing with two individuals, and the differences that inevitably arise between two distinct personalities must be borne in mind and, where necessary, indicated, but without thereby introducing a kind of posthumous split in a 'party' or party leadership group which proved capable of facing the countless challenges of the time united. So what did Marx and Engels understand by class struggle?

Notes

1. Ralf Dahrendorf, *Class and Class Conflict in Industrial Society*, Stanford, CA: Stanford University Press, 1959, pp. 59, 63–4.
2. Sergio Turone, *Storia del sindacato in Italia (1943–1969)*, Rome and Bari: Laterza, 1973, p. 259.
3. C.T. Rowan and D.M. Mazie, 'Fame in America', *Selezione dal Reader's Digest*, March 1969, pp. 100–2.
4. Ralf Dahrendorf, *Per un nuovoliberalismo*, Rome and Bari: Laterza, 1988, p. 122.
5. Jürgen Habermas, *Theory of Communicative Action*, trans. Thomas McCarthy, Boston: Beacon Press, 1987, Vol. 2, p. 348.
6. Gunnar Myrdal, *An American Dilemma: The Negro Problem and Modern Democracy*, New York and London: Harper & Brothers, 1944, p. 41.
7. R.E., 'Clinton: "Usammoinericomecavieumane. Unavergognaamericana"', *Corrieredella Sera*, 10 April 1997.
8. Karl Marx and Frederick Engels, *Collected Works*, London: Lawrence &Wishart, 1975–2004, Vol. 6, pp. 498, 481–2.
9. Ibid., p. 504.
10. Ibid., Vol. 40, p. 347.
11. See Hans Magnus Enzensberger (ed.), *Colloqui con Marx e Engels*, Turin: Einaudi, 1973, pp. 401, 356, 354.
12. Ibid., pp. 167, 296, 312.
13. Marx and Engels, *Collected Works*, Vol. 40, p. 64.

CHAPTER 2

The Different Forms of Class Struggle

1 'Emancipation of the Working Class' and 'National Liberation'

Marx and Engels did not systematically expound and clarify a thesis central to their thought. However, to appreciate how reductive and misleading the habitual interpretation of the theory of class struggle is, it suffices to glance at the theoretical and political platform to be found in Marx (and Engels) from their early writings onwards. The starting point is well-known: although it had secured important results, the overthrow of the *ancien régime*, and abolition of monarchical despotism and feudal relations of production, was not the terminus of the requisite process of radical political and social transformation. It was necessary to go well beyond the 'political emancipation' that was the outcome of the bourgeois revolution, achieving 'human emancipation', 'universal emancipation'.[1] A new revolution was on the horizon, but what were its objectives?

The power of the bourgeoisie had to be overthrown to break the 'chains' imposed by it—the chains of 'the present enslavement of the worker' or 'wage-slavery'.[2] The 'emancipation of the working class', its 'economical emancipation', was to be achieved in and through 'the abolition of all class rule'.[3] Marx and Engels' attention to struggle that the proletariat was enjoined to wage against the bourgeoisie was constant. But is the struggle for 'human emancipation', 'universal emancipation', exhausted by it?

© The Editor(s) (if applicable) and The Author(s) 2016
D. Losurdo, *Class Struggle*, Marx, Engels, and Marxisms,
DOI 10.1057/978-1-349-70660-0_2

Shortly before launching its final appeal for the 'communist revolution' and 'the forcible overthrow of all existing conditions', the *Communist Manifesto* invokes the 'national emancipation' of Poland.[4] Here we find a new watchword emerging. From his earliest writings and interventions, Engels supported the 'liberation of Ireland', or 'the conquest of national independence' by a people that had suffered 'five centuries of oppression'.[5] In his turn, having demanded the 'liberation' of 'oppressed nations' in late 1847, Marx never tired of calling for a struggle for 'the national emancipation of Ireland'.[6]

Let us take stock: the radical revolution invoked by Marx and Engels was geared not only to the emancipation of the oppressed class (the proletariat) but also to the liberation of oppressed nations. Having mentioned the problem of Poland's 'national liberation', the *Manifesto* closed with the exhortation: 'Working Men of All Countries, Unite!' This celebrated appeal also concludes the *Inaugural Address* of the International Working Men's Association, founded in 1864. But in that text ample space is devoted to a 'foreign policy' that would prevent 'heroic Poland', as well as Ireland and other oppressed nations, 'being assassinated', which was committed to the abolition of Black slavery in the USA, and which would put an end to Western Europe's 'piratical wars' in the colonies.[7]

The struggle for the liberation of oppressed nations is no less important than the struggle for the emancipation of the proletariat. The two struggles were followed and promoted with the self-same passion. In August 1844, Marx wrote to Feuerbach: 'You would have to attend one of the meetings of the French workers to appreciate the pure freshness, the nobility which burst forth from these toil-worn men. …But in any case it is among these "barbarians" of our civilized society that history is preparing the practical element for the emancipation of mankind'.[8] Four years later, in an article of 3 September 1848, Engels drew attention to the dismemberment and partition of Poland, carried out by Russia, Austria, and Prussia. In the nation that experienced it, this tragedy elicited a well-nigh unanimous response. A liberation movement emerged in which the nobility itself participated. To put an end to national oppression and humiliation, that class was ready to renounce its feudal privileges and 'supported the democratic-agrarian revolution with quite unprecedented selflessness'.[9] The enthusiasm evident from this text should not be attributed to the ingenuousness and over-simplification for which Engels is often criticised. Marx expressed himself in even more emphatic terms in this connection: 'world history does not know another example of such nobility of soul'.[10] The 'nobility'

celebrated in French workers was now attributed to the Polish nobility and, indirectly, to a great national liberation struggle as such.
Yet we must not lose sight of the differences. While the proletariat is the agency of the emancipatory process that breaks the chains of capitalist rule, the alliance required to break the shackles of national oppression is broader. We have seen this in the case of Poland, but it also applies to Ireland. In a long letter of April 1870, Marx supported a union whose heterogeneous features stand out: it would have as its protagonists, British workers, on the one hand, and the Irish nation as such, on the other. The former were called on to support the 'Irish national struggle' and reject the policy pursued 'against Ireland' as a whole by 'aristocrats and capitalists'. The oppression by the British ruling classes was harsh and ruthless. Fortunately, however, the 'revolutionary character of the Irish',[11] taken as a whole, could be depended on. And such revolutionary enthusiasm was summoned to find an initial outlet in the national liberation struggle. While the oppressed nation was enjoined to wage its struggle on the widest possible national basis, the task of the proletariat in the oppressor nation was to nurture its antagonism towards the ruling class, thereby furthering its own 'human' emancipation and, at the same time, contributing to the emancipation of the oppressed nation.

Marx and Engels did not arrive at this theoretical platform without fluctuations: 'Ireland may be regarded as the earliest English colony', wrote the latter to the former in a letter of May 1856.[12] We are thus led to the non-European colonial world and, in particular, India, which three years earlier had been defined by Marx as 'the Ireland of the East'.[13] India's tragic situation had already been invoked in *The Poverty of Philosophy*, which drew attention to a reality generally ignored by bourgeois economists intent on demonstrating capitalism's capacity for improving the condition of the working class. They lost sight of 'the millions of workers who had to perish in the East Indies so as to procure for the million and a half workers employed in the same industry in England three years' prosperity out of ten'.[14] Here the clash is between workers and workers; and it hinges on the difference in conditions between capitalist metropolis and colony. And now let us see the picture that emerges from an article by Marx dating from July 1853. Having described the tragic condition of India and the unrest in it following the encounter-clash with European culture (represented by British colonialists), the text continues: 'the Indians will not reap the fruits of the new elements of society scattered among them by the British bourgeoisie, till in Great Britain itself the new ruling classes shall have been supplanted by the industrial proletariat, or till the Hindoos themselves shall have grown strong enough to throw off the English yoke altogether'.[15]

Two different revolutionary scenarios are envisaged here: the first (in Britain) casts the 'industrial proletariat' as the protagonist of anti-capitalist revolution; the second (in the subject colony) has as its protagonist the 'Hindoos'. Every time 'national emancipation' or 'national liberation' is at stake, the subject is the oppressed nation as such: the Poles, Irish, and Indians. Has the concern with class struggle vanished?

2 A DISTRACTION FROM CLASS STRUGGLE?

There has been no lack of interpreters who answer in the affirmative. The author of a very well-documented book on *Marx, Engels et la politique internationale* argues that, in the years immediately following the *Communist Manifesto*, 'foreign policy and the battle between nations took precedence over class struggle'. Indeed, 'Marx not only analysed political intrigues [of an international kind] in detail, but did so without any reference to economic and social forces and factors'. To take but one example, the articles published in the *Neue Rheinische Zeitung* 'seem completely disconnected from the body of his doctrine'.[16] The impression is that, where 'foreign policy' and the diplomatic and military 'intrigues' bound up with it begin, class struggle ends, and the 'doctrine' of historical materialism falls silent.

At this point a disconcerting conclusion might dictate itself: while they stress that 'every society' is shot through with class struggle throughout the course of its development, and that all historical struggles are class struggles, Marx and Engels resort to their theory only intermittently. But is this how things really stand? It is worth noting the testimony (dated summer 1872) of the French socialist Charles Longuet, who, having paid tribute to the 'martyrs' of the Paris Commune, proceeded thus when reporting from the 'temple of historical materialism', or the Marx household (which he knew well, being Marx's son-in-law): 'the Polish insurrection of 1863, the Irish rebellions of the Fenians in 1869, the Land League and Home Rulers in 1874: these movements of oppressed nationalities were followed from the battlements of this fortress of the International with no less interest than the rising tide of the socialist movement in both hemispheres'.[17] So interest in the 'movements of oppressed nationalities' was no less lively and constant than that reserved for the agitation of the proletariat and subaltern classes. It would be difficult to challenge the reliability of this evidence: it is enough to leaf through editions of the collected works of Marx and Engels to realize just how many texts are devoted to the struggle of the Irish and Polish peoples and to denunciation of the policy of national oppression pursued by Britain and Russia, respectively.

The interest was intellectual and political, but with an emotional charge. On 23 November 1867, three Irish revolutionaries were hanged in Manchester, convicted of having orchestrated the armed liberation of two leaders of the independent movement, in an action that involved the death of a police officer. Some days later, Marx wrote to Engels referring to the reaction of his eldest daughter: 'Jenny goes in black since the Manchester execution, and wears her Polish cross on a green ribbon'.[18] The symbol of the national liberation struggle of the Polish people (the cross) was thus married with the green of the Irish cause. On receipt of his friend's letter, Engels answered immediately on 29 November: 'I need hardly tell you that black and green are the prevailing colours in my house, too'[19]—the colours of the mourning into which the Irish people's national liberation movement was thrown by the British executioner.

Marx and Engels compared the Mancunian victims to John Brown, the abolitionist who sought to spark a slave revolt in the Deep South of the USA and faced the gallows courageously.[20] And this comparison between the Irish independence fighters and the champion of abolitionism confirms the passion with which Marx and Engels followed the 'movements of oppressed nationalities' and the key role played by these uprisings in the process of human emancipation in their view.

Not only hostility but also indifference towards oppressed nations was harshly condemned politically and morally. The *Inaugural Address* reproved the 'upper classes of Europe' and, in particular, Britain for their anti-labour policy, but also for their support for the secessionist American South, as well as 'the shameful approval, mock sympathy, or idiotic indifference' with which they viewed the tragedy of the Polish nation.[21] Affecting an air of superiority towards this tragedy, Pierre-Joseph Proudhon merely exhibited 'cynicism' in Marx's view—and cynicism that was quite the reverse of intelligence (see Chap. 5, Sect. 1).

Does an interest in 'foreign policy' have nothing to do with class struggle? Is it in fact a distraction from the latter? In reality, according to Longuet's testimony, passionate sympathy for the 'movements of oppressed nationalities' burned in the 'temple of historical materialism'—the doctrine that construed history as the history of class struggles. In any event, as early as July 1848, the same year as the publication of the *Communist Manifesto*, Engels evoked and invoked 'a democratic foreign policy'.[22] Sixteen years later, via Marx's pen, the newly founded International Working Men's Association stressed that a 'political economy of labour' was imperative, but insufficient. The 'working classes' had to be taught 'the duty to master … the mysteries of international politics; to watch the diplomatic acts of their respective Governments; to counteract them, if necessary, by all the means in their power'. They must realize that the struggle for a 'foreign policy' supportive of oppressed nations was an integral part of 'the general struggle for the emancipation of the working classes'.[23] How is so exacting an assertion to be explained?

3 'Class Struggles and National Struggles': 'Genus' and 'Species'

In addition to the 'direct exploitation (*Ausbeutung*) of labour', condemning workers to 'present enslavement' in any particular country, *The Poverty of Philosophy*, the *Communist Manifesto* and contemporaneous texts denounce 'the exploitation (*Exploitation*) of one nation by another' or 'the exploitation of some nations by others'.[24] In the case of Ireland, it must be remembered that 'the exploitation (*Ausbeutung*) of this country' was 'one of the main sources of [Britain's] material wealth'.[25] Was the exploitation that occurs in a single country the sole cause of class struggle? In the same year as the *Communist Manifesto*, Marx issued an authoritative warning: those who 'cannot understand how one nation can grow rich at the expense of another' were even less well-equipped 'to understand how in the same country one class can enrich itself at the expense of another'.[26] Far from being of minor relevance from the standpoint of class struggle, the exploitation and oppression that obtain internationally are a precondition, at least methodologically, for understanding social conflict and class struggle at a national level.

As we know, along with the 'liberation' or 'economic emancipation of the proletariat', Marx and Engels demanded the 'liberation' or 'emancipation' of oppressed nations. Is the struggle for the liberation/emancipation of exploited classes a class struggle—but not the struggle for the liberation/emancipation of exploited (and oppressed) nations? Is the struggle whose protagonist is a class that has achieved its political emancipation, but not its economic and social emancipation, a class struggle, whereas the struggle waged by a nation, yet to achieve its political emancipation, is not a class struggle?

Not having secured economic and social emancipation, the proletariat is currently subjected to 'enslavement'. This is a phrase that immediately puts us in mind of slavery in the strict sense. And once again a question is tabled: is the struggle whose protagonists are subject to 'present enslavement', 'emancipated slavery', or 'wage slavery', to 'the indirect slavery of the white man in England', a class struggle, whereas the struggle whose protagonists are subject to 'real slavery'—'the direct slavery of the Black men on the other side of the Atlantic'—is not a class struggle?[27] Is the struggle whose subject is defined by the *Grundrisse*, in an unusual phrase, as 'free labour' a class struggle, whereas the struggle whose subjects (in the words of *The German Ideology*) are 'the insurgent Negroes of Haiti and the fugitive Negroes [slaves] of all the colonies', is not?[28]

Take the terms in which Marx condemns bourgeois society. First of all, let us attend to *The Poverty of Philosophy*: '[m]odern nations have been able only to disguise slavery in their own countries, but they have imposed it without disguise upon the New World'.[29] Some years later, with the colonial rule imposed on India by Britain in mind, Marx reiterated: 'the profound hypocrisy and inherent barbarism of bourgeois civilization lies unveiled before our eyes, turning from its home, where it assumes respectable forms, to the colonies, where it goes naked'.[30] Is it only the struggle challenging masked slavery and camouflaged barbarism that is tantamount to class struggle? I think it would be absurd to answer in the affirmative and decline to apply the category of class struggle precisely where exploitation and oppression are most overt and brutal.

But let us return to Longuet's testimony. Having referred to Marx's interest in and passion for the 'movements of oppressed nationalities', he continued: '[h]is philosophy was not casuistry: he would never have taken refuge in ambiguous quibbling when the clear, frank theory of class struggle was at stake'.[31] The nexus between national struggles and class struggles is clear. Is this interpretation correct?

In 1849, in *Wage Labour and Capital*, Marx investigated 'the *economic relations* which constitute the material foundation of the present class struggles and national struggles' (*Klassenkämpfe und Nationalkämpfe*); and stated his intention 'to trace the class struggle [*den Klassenkampf*] in current history'.[32] Judging from this passage, it would seem that 'national struggles' are to be subsumed under the category of 'class struggle' broadly construed. Comparison with another passage, from the aforementioned letter of April 1870, where Marx proceeds to a more in-depth analysis of the Irish question, is in order. Let us read the conclusion: '[i]n Ireland, the *land question* has, so far, been the *exclusive form* of the social question; it is a question of existence, a *question of life or death* for the immense majority of the Irish people; at the same time, it is inseparable from the *national* question'.[33]

In Ireland, there was no 'social question' apart from the 'national question'. A *de facto* identity existed between the two, at least for a whole historical period, as long as independence had not been gained. The 'social question' is the more general category here—the genus—which, in the concrete situation of the unhappy island exploited and oppressed by Britain for centuries, takes the specific form of the 'national question'. For anyone who has not grasped the point, Marx reiterates it: the 'social significance of the Irish question' should never be lost from view.[34] The species cannot be understood if it is detached from the genus. We can argue similarly in connection with the passage from *Wage Labour and Capital* referring to 'class struggles and national struggles': class struggle is the genus which, in determinate circumstances, takes the specific form of 'national struggle'.

If classes and class struggle are formed and develop on the 'material base' of the production and distribution of the resources and means that ensure life, on the basis of 'social relations' and 'actual relations of life',[35] it is clear that we must bear in mind the 'division of labour' not only nationally but also internationally, never losing sight of the 'world market'.[36]

For peoples stripped of their independence, and especially for peoples subject to colonial rule and despoliation, the existing order reserves a particularly revolting division of labour. In the colonies (observed Marx in summer 1853 with reference to India), capitalism drags 'individuals and people through blood and dirt, through misery and degradation'.[37] We know that Ireland too was a 'colony' and in it (observed Engels) there was not a trace of 'the English citizen's so-called freedom'; '[i]n no other country have I seen so many gendarmes'.[38] To be precise, Marx went further in an article of January 1859, what was involved was oppression evincing genocidal tendencies: 'the [British] landlords of Ireland are federated for a fiendish war of extermination against the cotters; or, as they call it, they combine for the economical experiment of clearing the land of useless mouths'.[39] The specific difference that characterized the social question and class struggle in the colonies by comparison with the capitalist metropolis has to be registered. There the international division of labour converted the subject peoples into a mass of serfs or slaves over whom a *de facto* power of life and death could be wielded. Secondly, the victim of this condition was a whole people, the nation as such. Hence Britain, the country that had 'hitherto ruled the world market', imposed 'slavery' on Ireland and represented the 'dominant nation', was one thing; Ireland, reduced to 'simple pastureland to provide meat and wool at the cheapest possible price for the English market', and whose population had been drastically reduced 'through eviction and forced emigration', was quite another.[40]

Perhaps the meaning of the expression 'class struggles' (*Klassenkämpfe*) used in the *Communist Manifesto* is now becoming clearer. The plural is not employed to denote repetition of the identical, the continual recurrence of the same class struggle in the same form. It refers to the multiplicity of shapes and forms that class struggle can assume.

We may conclude on this point. Marx did not define the relationship between class struggle and national struggle, social question and national question, clearly and unequivocally; and only in fits and starts did he arrive at the more mature formulation which distinguishes between genus and species. But the interest and passion with which he followed the 'movements of oppressed nationalities' were an expression not of distraction from the class struggle and social question, but of an attempt to grasp their concrete manifestations. Oppressed nations are summoned to be the protagonists of the second great class struggle for emancipation.

4 The Condition of Women and the 'First Class Oppression'

The genus of emancipatory class struggles includes a third species. There is another social group that is so numerous as to form (or exceed) half the population; a social group that suffers 'autocracy' and awaits its 'emancipation' (*Befreiung*): women. Weighing on them is the domestic oppression exercised by the male.[41] I am citing a text (*The Origin of the Family, Private Property and the State*) published by Engels in 1884. It is true that Marx had died the previous year, but as early as 1845–6 *The German Ideology*—a text to which Engels explicitly refers—observed that in the patriarchal family 'wife and children are slaves of the husband'.[42] In its turn the *Communist Manifesto*, which criticizes the bourgeoisie for reducing the proletarian to the condition of a machine and instrument of labour, observes that 'the bourgeois sees in his wife a mere instrument of production', so 'the real point aimed at is to do away with the status of women as mere instruments of production'.[43] The category used to define the condition of the worker in the capitalist factory is now applied to the social condition of woman in the patriarchal family.

Taken as a whole, the capitalist system presents itself as a set of more or less servile relations imposed by one people on another internationally, by one class on another in an individual country, and by men on women within one and the same class. We can now understand the thesis formulated by Engels drawing on Fourier, which was also maintained by Marx—namely, that women's emancipation was 'the natural measure of the general emancipation'.[44] For better or worse, the relationship between men and women is a kind of microcosm reflecting the total social order. In largely pre-modern Russia, subject to ruthless repression by their masters, the peasants (Marx observed) proceeded in their turn to 'awful beating-to-death of their wives'.[45] Or take the capitalist factory. While it affected all workers, the owner's despotic power was experienced by women (stressed Engels) in especially degrading fashion: 'his mill is also his harem'.[46]

It is not difficult to find voices denouncing the oppressive character of the female condition in the culture of the time. In 1790, Condorcet defined the exclusion of women from political rights as an 'act of tyranny'.[47] The following year, the *Declaration of the Rights of Woman and the Female Citizen*, whose author was Olympe de Gouges, drew attention in article 4 to the 'perpetual tyranny' imposed by man on woman. More than half a century later, John Stuart Mill in Britain referred to the 'slavery of the woman', 'domestic tyranny' and legally sanctioned 'actual bondage'.[48]

But what were the causes of this oppression and of the widespread indifference to it? Condorcet condemned the 'power of habit', which dulled the sense of justice even in 'enlightened men'.[49] Mill argued in a similar vein, referring to the set of 'customs', 'prejudices', and 'superstitions' that needed to be overcome or neutralized through a 'sound psychology'. Although alluding to social relations, these were confined to 'social relations between the two sexes', which sanctioned the slavery or subaltern status of woman on account of 'inferiority in muscular strength' and the survival in this context of the 'law of the strongest'.[50]

The connection between the condition of women and other forms of oppression was not investigated. In fact, in Mill's view, the man/woman relationship was portrayed as a kind of island where the logic of subjugation, which had largely disappeared in other contexts, persisted: '[w]e now live—that is to say, one or two of the most advanced nations of the world now live—in a state in which the law of the strongest seems to be entirely abandoned as the regulating principle of the world's affairs'.[51] From Marx and Engels' standpoint, by contrast, the relationship between capitalist metropolis ('the most advanced nations of the world') and colonies was more than ever one of domination and subjugation; and in the capitalist metropolis itself, economic (but not now legal) coercion continued to govern relations between capital and labour.

It was Mary Wollstonecraft who combined denunciation of the 'slavish dependence' reserved for woman with indictment of the existing social order.[52] Male domination seemed to go hand in hand with the *ancien régime*. While champions of the struggle for the abolition of slavery singled out the 'aristocracy of the epidermis' or the 'nobility of the skin',[53] the feminist militant targeted what, in her view, took the form of the aristocratic power of males. Denunciation of it was combined with condemnation of hereditary 'riches and inherited honours', with condemnation of 'preposterous distinctions of rank'. In any event, women would not be 'freed' 'till ranks are confounded' and 'till more equality be established in society'.[54]

At times, the British feminist and Jacobin seemed to challenge capitalist society itself. Women 'ought to have representatives, instead of being arbitrarily governed without having any direct share allowed them in the deliberations of the government'. But it should not be forgotten that in Britain workers too were excluded from political rights: 'as the whole system of representation is now, in this country, only a convenient handle for despotism, [women] need not complain, for they are as well represented as a numerous class of hard-working mechanics, who pay for the support of royalty when they can scarcely stop their children's mouths with bread'.[55] The condition of workers and the condition of women had things in common. As was the case for members of the working class, 'the few employments open to women, so far from being liberal, are menial'. Ultimately, in this wide-ranging critique of the relations of domination characteristic of the existing social order, women themselves (in particular, the better-off) must learn to question things. Instead, they displayed 'folly' in 'the manner in which they treat servants in the presence of children, permitting them to suppose that they ought to wait on them, and bear their humours'.[56]

The 'English Jacobin', who constitutes a brilliant exception, seems in a way to anticipate Marx and Engels, who established a link between the division of labour in the family and the division of labour in society. Engels, in particular, formulated the thesis that 'the modern individual family is based on the overt or covert domestic slavery of the woman'. In any event, the man 'is the bourgeois; the wife represents the proletariat'.[57]

Of Marx and Engels' contemporaries, the one who developed an analysis that might be compared with theirs, albeit with a converse value judgement, was not Mill but Nietzsche. The implacable critic of revolution as such, including the feminist revolution, compared the condition of woman to that of 'sufferers of the lower classes', 'slave laborers [*Arbeitssklaven*] or prisoners';[58] and indirectly equated the feminist movement, the workers' movement and the abolitionist movement. All three were on the look-out for 'everything slave-like and serf-like', in order to indignantly denounce it, as if registering its existence did not serve to confirm that slavery was 'a condition of every higher culture'.[59]

Obviously, the theme of the link between the subjection of women and social oppression as a whole was developed much more amply and organically by Engels, with reference to *The German Ideology*, co-written by him with Marx and long unpublished: 'the first class oppression coincides with that of the female sex by the male'. This was a state of affairs with a long history behind it that had not yet arrived at its terminus:

> The overthrow of mother right was the *world-historic defeat of the female sex*. The man seized the reins in the house too; the woman was degraded, enthralled, became the slave of the man's lust, a mere instrument for breeding children [*Werkzeug der Kinderzeugung*]. This humiliated position of women ... has become gradually embellished and dissembled and, in part, clothed in milder form, but by no means abolished.[60]

5   THE CLASS STRUGGLES OF THE EXPLOITING CLASSES

I have hitherto been concerned with the three major emancipatory class struggles, which are set to radically alter the division of labour and the relations of exploitation and oppression that obtain internationally, in a single country, and within the family. But we must not lose sight of the struggles whose protagonists are the exploiting classes.

Let us see how, in November 1848, Marx summarized the key events of that year: '[i]n Naples the *lazzaroni* are leagued with the monarchy against the bourgeoisie. In Paris, the greatest struggle ever known in history is taking place. The bourgeoisie is leagued with the *lazzaroni* against the working class'.[61] The struggle whereby feudal reaction, availing itself of the support of lumpen elements, suppressed the democratic-bourgeois revolution in Naples is likewise class struggle; and so is the ruthless repression with which the French bourgeoisie, thanks again to the support of the urban lumpen-proletariat, quelled the desperation and rebellion of Parisian workers in the June days.

Finally, let us return one last time to Longuet's testimony. In confirmation of the 'clear, frank theory of class struggle' professed by Marx and his family circle, he added a further detail: '[i]n this house people never hesitate to take sides in conflicts where "different fractions of the bourgeoisie" can be recognized'.[62] As we can see, 'class struggle' is mentioned even in connection with conflicts between 'different fractions of the bourgeoisie'—that is, conflicts pitting exploiting classes, or fractions of them, against one another. As the *Manifesto* stresses, 'the bourgeoisie finds itself involved in a constant battle. At first with the aristocracy; later on, with those portions of the bourgeoisie itself, whose interests have become antagonistic to the progress of industry; at all times, with the bourgeoisie of foreign countries'. Where the struggle against the aristocracy prompted the revolutions heralding the collapse of the *ancien régime*, economic competition between the bourgeoisies of different capitalist countries can issue in an 'industrial war of extermination between nations'.[63] Reference is probably being made here to the wars of the Napoleonic era, whose main protagonists were two countries—Britain and France—that had left behind the *ancien régime* and fought on several continents for control of the world market. However, while it outlines a historical balance-sheet of the past, the 'extermination' in which the class struggle between opposing capitalist bourgeoisies results calls to mind the carnage of the First World War, which occurred more than 60 years after the publication of the *Manifesto*.

6   1848–9: A 'Class Struggle in Colossal Political Forms'

The intricate picture of class struggles, which is beginning to emerge, is not yet complete. We have seen them in operation in abstraction from one another. However, a concrete historical situation, especially a major historical crisis, is characterized by the conjunction of multiple, contradictory class struggles.

We may take a look at the major historical crises witnessed by the authors of the *Communist Manifesto*. We possess two balance-sheets of the revolutionary years 1848–9, both written on the spur of the moment by Marx. The first, from April 1849, is contained in *Wage Labour and Capital*, which, to judge from its title, should deal with a more strictly economic and trade union subject. In reality, Marx situates everyday 'class struggle' in the context of the upheavals underway: the 'defeat of the revolutionary workers'(who had risen in Paris in June 1848); the 'heroic wars of independence' and 'the desperate exertions of Poland, Italy, and Hungary'; the emergence on the horizon of a possible 'world war', which would see 'the proletarian revolution and the feudalistic counter-revolution' ranged against one another; the 'starving of Ireland' (the terrible famine that decimated the island's inhabitants, and which was greeted by distinguished representatives of the British ruling class as an act of Providence); the contribution made in their different ways by Britain and Russia to the crushing of the revolutionary movement, and hence, the relapse of Europe 'into its old double slavery, the Anglo-Russian slavery', with 'the commercial subjugation and exploitation of the bourgeois classes of the various European nations by the despot of the world market—England'. Thus, the world had seen 'the class struggle develop in colossal political forms in 1848'; nothing was alien to 'the class struggle [and] the European revolution'.[64] Rather than presenting itself in directly economic guise, the class struggle had assumed the most varied political forms (working-class and popular revolts, national insurrections, repression unleashed by domestic and international reaction with recourse to military or economic tools). Far from disappearing, it had become more acuter.

The second historical balance-sheet is drawn up in *Class Struggles in France*. The date was 1850 and in Marx's view the crisis had not yet reached a conclusion and might, in fact, open up new, grandiose revolutionary prospects:

> The defeat of June [of the Parisian workers] divulged to the despotic powers of Europe the secret that France must maintain peace abroad at any price in order to be able to wage civil war at home. Thus the peoples who had begun to fight for their national independence were abandoned to the superior power of Russia, Austria and Prussia, but, at the same time, the fate of these national revolutions was made subject to the fate of the proletarian revolution, and they were robbed of their apparent autonomy, their independence

of the great social revolution. The Hungarian shall not be free, nor the Pole, nor the Italian, as long as the worker remains a slave.

Finally, with the victories of the Holy Alliance, Europe has taken on a form in which every fresh proletarian upheaval in France directly involves a *world war*. The new French revolution is forced to leave its national soil forthwith and *conquer the European terrain*, on which alone the social revolution of the nineteenth century can be accomplished.[65]

An intervention by the counter-revolutionary powers similar to that of 1792 was to be anticipated. Consequently, 'the class war within French society turns into a world war, in which the nations confront one another'.[66]

Here revolutionary impatience tends imaginatively to run ahead of a long (and highly complex) historical process. But I would mainly like to examine the theoretical and categorial aspect: what is configured as a 'class war' is 'world war', a nexus of revolutions and international conflicts.

Clearly, 1848–9 reminded Marx of the historical crisis that began in 1789. Starting from the invasion of France by powers committed to defending the *ancien régime*, it too saw revolutions and international conflicts intersect and converge in a global or European war. The most relevant novel factor in the new crisis was that its protagonists were no longer two social subjects, but three: in addition to the aristocracy and bourgeoisie, there was now the proletariat which (Marx hoped) might play a decisive role in reversing, over and above the *ancien régime*, capitalism itself. At all events, in both historical crises, assuming a different form each time, class struggle exploded in 'colossal political forms' (to borrow the terminology of *Wage Labour and Capital*), and 'class war' ended up taking the form of a 'world war' (to quote *Class Struggles in France*).

Class struggle almost never presents itself in the pure state, almost never confines itself to involving directly antagonistic subjects. Above all, it is precisely thanks to this lack of 'purity' that it can issue in a victorious social revolution. Marx envisaged a 'proletarian insurrection' occurring in the most developed capitalist country. Counter-revolutionary intervention would then target Britain, where, however, the weight of the working class was menacing from the perspective of powers determined to preserve the existing order at any cost. In the course of 'world war', or the novel conjunction of revolutions and wars that would detonate it, conditions would thus be created conducive to an event that was destined to signal a turning-point in world history: 'the proletariat is pushed to the fore in the nation which dominates the world market, to the forefront in England. The revolution, which finds here not its end, but its organisational beginning, is no short-lived revolution'.[67] In its time, the feudal powers' intervention against revolutionary France had prompted the Jacobin radicalization, had presaged the arrival in power of a political and ideological stratum not organically connected to the bourgeoisie, and which in fact (as stressed by *The German Ideology*) the bourgeoisie only managed to reabsorb later and with difficulty (see Chap. 9, Sect. 2). A potential counter-revolutionary intervention against Britain while it was immersed in a revolutionary crisis could end up setting in motion a similar process, requiring socialists in that eventuality to direct their energies to the defence of both social conquests and national independence.

While the occasionally fantastic character of the scenario sketched by Marx in 1850 is evident, what is undeniable is the almost prophetic foresight it displays. During major historical crises, which are characterized by a conjunction of domestic and international conflicts, the class struggle intensifies and becomes a revolutionary struggle in a country invested by an unprecedented national crisis. This was a scenario also evoked by the late Engels. In a letter of 13 October 1895 to August Bebel, he underscored the growing dangers of war. What would happen if Germany, where the strongest socialist party was active, were to be attacked by tsarist Russia (supported in the West by its allies) and the 'nation's existence' threatened? 'It might happen that, in contrast to the cowardice of the bourgeoisie and Junkers, who want to save their property, *we* should turn out to be the only vigorous war party. Of course, it might also happen that we should have to take the helm and do a 1794 in order to chuck out the Russians and their allies'.[68]

This is a passage which was invoked by German social-democracy in 1914 to justify its support for imperialist war: a decidedly bizarre reference, which indirectly compared the Germany of Wilhelm II with the France of Robespierre! But it is the case that a key aspect of the twentieth century was the blossoming of national liberation movements that ended up being hegemonized by communist or communist-inspired parties. And the development of these movements was precisely punctuated by two world wars wherein the aspect of counter-revolutionary intervention was more or less massively present. The intervention of the Entente against Soviet Russia was followed, more than twenty years later, by the aggression of Hitlerite Germany, which simultaneously aimed to liquidate the socialist movement and build a colonial empire in the East, as a result of which defeat of this project provoked an immense wave of anti-colonial revolutions on a global scale. Once again, to adopt Marx's terminology, we witness 'the class war develop in colossal political forms' and 'class war' configured as 'world war'.

7   1861–5: A 'Crusade of Property against Labour'

More than two decades after the revolutionary crisis of 1848–9, Marx and Engels were witnesses of the tragedy of the Paris Commune. In this instance, however, the clash between bourgeoisie and proletariat was obvious to everyone, if only on account of the execution squads mobilized by the former against the latter. We must concern ourselves with a more complex historical sequence, which they followed from an observation post located thousands of miles away. I am referring to the American Civil War, which Volume One of *Capital*, published in 1867, characterized as 'the one great event of contemporary history'.[69] This phrase recalls that used in connection with the Parisian workers' 'June insurrection' of 1848, characterized as 'the most colossal event [*kolossalstesEreignis*]in the history of European civil wars'.[70]

Capital establishes a parallel between the Civil War and the struggle (in Britain and France) against working conditions that effectively force workers to 'work to death'. If the abolition of slavery was the result of the American Civil War, analogously, 'the legal limitation and regulation [of the working day] had been wrung step by step after a civil war of half a century'.[71] While the Emancipation Proclamation banned the purchase and sale of Black slaves in the USA, in Europe legal regulation of the working day prevented workers from 'selling, by voluntary contract with capital, themselves and their families into slavery and death'.[72] If, across the Atlantic, the election of Lincoln, suspected of being an abolitionist, was followed by the secession of the slaveholding states, British capitalists reacted to the reduction and regulation of working hours with a 'proslavery rebellion in miniature', agitating in defence of the maintenance of wage slavery in its pure form.[73]

In both instances, we are dealing with a class struggle waged at once from below and from above. In the USA, especially in the final phase of the war, the ranks of the Union were swollen by an influx of slaves or ex-slaves, who abandoned their masters or ex-masters to help defeat the pro-slavery secession, while in Britain working-class agitation went back a long way. In both countries, the reformist bourgeoisie played an important role. We are dealing with an emancipatory class struggle that does not present itself in the pure state as a clash between exploited and exploiter, oppressed and oppressor.

The 'impure' character of the American Civil War was even more marked and manifest—and not only because the contestants were not (at least at first sight) a ruling class and an oppressed class. Furthermore, the North was far from being motivated by pure abolitionist zeal. Lincoln himself guaranteed slaveholding states peaceful enjoyment of self-government (and private property in human livestock) if they were prepared to display loyalty to the union. To justify their sympathy for the South, sizeable sections of the British bourgeoisie invoked this, arguing as follows: the Union was fighting primarily for protectionist customs tariffs (necessary to promote autonomous industrial development), and to defend its territorial integrity (and the vast national market required by the US bourgeoisie). Prominent figures in the socialist movement adopted a not dissimilar position (see Chap. 5, Sect. 2). Was a bloodbath justified merely to indulge the industrial bourgeoisie of the North against the landowning aristocracy of the South, or to replace one exploiting class with another and spread wage slavery by removing classical slavery? What was at stake seemed all the more vile given that the material conditions of wage slaves were no better than those of slaves proper at the time. Capping it all was the hypocrisy for which substantial sections of the British working class criticized abolitionists in their country. The latter were moved by the lot of Black slaves across the Atlantic, but remained impervious in the face of the tragedy of White slaves in their own backyard.

Marx was well aware of the limitations of British abolitionism. In *Capital*, he expressed utter contempt for the ideal-typical figure of the Duchess of Southerland. The noble lady 'entertained Mrs. Beecher Stowe, authoress of *Uncle Tom's Cabin*, with great magnificence in London, to show her sympathy for the Negro slaves of the American republic'. At the same time, however, she was ruthless towards her own 'slaves', who were 'systematically hunted and rooted out' of their land, condemned to die of hunger, and sometimes swept away along with the villages inhabited by them.[74]

Nevertheless, from his first article in the *New York Daily Tribune*, which appeared on 11 October 1861, Marx sharply rejected such arguments. It was true that Lincoln had confirmed that he sought only to preserve the territorial integrity of the USA, but 'the South, on its part, inaugurated the war by loudly proclaiming "the peculiar institution" as the only and main end of the rebellion'. Besides, the Constitution of the Confederacy 'had recognized for the first time Slavery as a thing good in itself, a bulwark of civilization, and a divine institution. If the North professed to fight for the Union, the South gloried in rebellion for the supremacy of Slavery'. Hence, what was at stake was clear: the defence or abolition of the 'Southern slaveocracy'.[75]

As we can see, we are witness to a surprising inversion of positions. Resorting to ideology-critique (of an economistic and reductionist kind) were the pro-South sectors of the British ruling class (habitually inclined to celebrate the purity of spiritual values), while highlighting the abolitionist significance and virtues of the North's war was Marx, the great and caustic critic of ideology. For what reasons? I shall try to summarize why for Marx the Union's war to suppress the slaveholding secession took the form of a gigantic, emancipatory class struggle.

1. A society dominated by 'an oligarchy', 'where all productive labour devolves on the *niggers*',[76] had to be defeated. As has been justly observed, '[f]or most of human history the expression "free labor" was an oxymoron'.[77] This contradiction in terms was especially crying in the years before the Civil War in the American Deep South where, in Tocqueville's words, 'labor is confounded with the idea of slavery'.[78] Breaking with this tradition entailed conferring dignity on the very idea of labour and achieving an important ideological victory. Above all, emancipating the labour 'branded ... in the black [skin]'of slavery proper, the Union's 'Abolitionist war' on the slaveholding, secessionist South had created more conditions more propitious for the emancipation of labour 'in the white skin'.[79] All the more so because 'the slaveholders' rebellion was to sound the tocsin for a general holy crusade of property against labour'.[80] With this observation, Marx hit the nail on the head. In the very midst of the Civil War, one of the South's most distinguished theorists, George Fitzhugh, although legitimating the subjection of Blacks and regarding it as necessary and beneficial, criticized the idea of 'confin[ing] the justification of slavery to that race'. In Europe, meanwhile, echoing these themes and situating them in the framework of a developed philosophy of history, Nietzsche celebrated slavery as such, not necessarily racial slavery, as the ineliminable foundation of civilization.[81]

2. When he maintained that the institution of slavery was required to regulate the relationship between capital and labour as such, Fitzhugh probably had in mind the expeditions of the 'filibusters' who set out from the South to export slavery to the countries of Central America—expeditions aimed at the 'conquest of new territory for the spread of slavery and of the slaveholders' rule'.[82] In fact, in the years leading up to the Civil War William Walker had set out at the head of a small army of adventurers to conquer Nicaragua, reintroduce Black slavery there, restart the slave

trade and impose forced labour, on the Nicaraguans themselves.[83] We can now understand the message of congratulations drafted by Marx in January 1865 and sent by the International to Lincoln on the occasion of his re-election: '[f]rom the commencement of the Titanic-American strife the working men of Europe felt instinctively that the star-spangled banner carried the destiny of their class'; they realized that 'their hopes for the future, even their past conquests were at stake in the tremendous conflict on the other side of the Atlantic'.[84]

3. With the abolition of Black slavery, the Civil War ended in the emancipation, albeit partial, of an oppressed 'race' or nationality. And from this standpoint too it took the form of a major class struggle. In the final phase of its existence, the Confederacy was obliged to retreat from its original position and 'treat Negro soldiers as "prisoners of war"',[85] rather than shooting them as rebel slaves and barbarians excluded from the *jus publicum europaeum*. In addition, Marx stressed that bound up with the abolition of slavery in the USA was recognition by Washington of the 'independence of the Negro republics of Liberia and Haiti'.[86] Of particular significance was the recognition of Haiti, which was born in the wake of the great Black slave revolution led by Toussaint L'Ouverture and long subject to diplomatic isolation and economic strangulation by the USA and the West.

For all these reasons, Marx regarded the Civil War as among the most important chapters in the class struggle of his time. The slave-owners' bid to assert or reassert the identity between labour and slavery, the 'crusade of property against labour', suffered a defeat whose significance transcended the borders of the USA and the Black 'race'.

Unfortunately, the defeat of the pro-slavery counter-revolution was only partial and attempts to stage a come-back under sign of 'white supremacy' were soon forthcoming. But for Marx this was further confirmation that the gigantic class struggle which exploded between 1861 and 1865 was far from over.

8 Class Struggle and Other Paradigms

As we can see, the theory of class struggle seeks to shed light on the historical process as such. It is a type of explanation that is opposed to other kinds of explanation. We can understand the latter and, as a result, arrive at a better understanding of the former, if we take a look at the theoretical challenges which nineteenth-century culture had to face. What particularly stood in need of investigation was the reasons for the irresistible rise of the West. To put it in the enthusiastic terms employed at the start of the first Opium War by de Tocqueville, it was a question of clarifying the 'multitude of events of the same kind that are gradually impelling the European race beyond its borders and subjecting all the other races in succession to its dominion and influence', the 'reasons for the subjugation of four-fifths of the world by the remaining fifth'.[87] What was this triumphal march to be attributed to? Secondly, it was necessary to explain France's differential political development compared with Britain and the USA. In France, revolution had been followed by counter-revolution, which in its turn paved the way for a subsequent revolution. A succession of political regimes followed one another: absolute monarchy, constitutional monarchy, Jacobin Terror, military dictatorship, empire, democratic republic, Bonapartism, and so forth. And no end to these convulsions, with the advent of an orderly regime of liberty and the rule of law, was in sight. In fact, on closer inspection, with the exception of brief intervals, absolute power presented itself as a destiny or a curse: divine right monarchy was followed by the Jacobin Terror, which in its turn paved the way for Bonapartist dictatorship. What a striking contrast with the gradual, constructive evolution of the other two countries, characterized by liberty and the rule of law! So what were the reasons for the interminable historical crisis engulfing France? Thirdly, even as it engaged in its colonial expansion, the West anxiously observed the irruption at home of shocking mass movements which, in the shape first of Jacobinism and then of socialism, seemed to be attacking the very foundations of civilization. What was happening?

Let us now glance in broad terms at the paradigms employed by the culture of the time to confront these three major theoretical and political cruces. In 1883, the year Marx died, a book appeared in Austria by Ludwig Gumplowicz which, in its very title (*Der Rassenkampf*, 'The Race Struggle'), was counter-posed to the thesis of the class struggle as the key to interpreting history. Three decades before Gumplowicz, Arthur de Gobineau in France began to send to the printers his *Essay on the Inequality of the Human Races*—a work whose title once again speaks for itself. At the same time, a similar line of argument was advanced in Britain by Benjamin Disraeli, who formulated the thesis that race was 'the key of history'—'[a]ll is race; there is no other truth'. Furthermore, 'there is only one thing which makes a race, and that is blood'. The whole historical cycle from the discovery-conquest of America to the Opium Wars, and the rise and triumph of the British Empire, perfectly illustrated the decisive character of the racial factor. Only thus could it be understood how, though few in number, the Spanish *conquistadores* had triumphed in America and the British in China.

The racial or ethnologico-racial paradigm can be presented in diluted form and refer primarily to what, in contemporary terminology, would be called the 'clash of civilizations'. Obviously, civilizations genuinely exist and are not to be confused with 'races'. But if, rather than being construed on the basis of historically determinate contexts and conflicts, they are regarded as expressions of a tendentially eternal spirit or soul, there is a danger of a naturalistic slippage. The civilizations contrasted by Tocqueville with Western civilization, or the 'Christian world', all seem incomparably inferior in value and immobile in time, and are therefore destined by Providence to disappear. At this point, there is a strong tendency to abandon the terrain of history. The slippage into naturalism proves unstoppable when the discourse focuses on 'semi-civilized tribes' and 'savages': 'the European race has received from heaven, or acquired by its own efforts, such incontestable superiority over the other races that make up the great human family that the man placed by us, on account of his vices and ignorance, on the bottom rung of the social scale is still first among savages'. We can readily understand the French liberal's horror at something that had occurred in Australia: transported White European prisoners had escaped into the forests, married the daughters of Aborigine 'savages', proceeding to a miscegenation that generated a 'race of halfcastes' dangerous to the existing social and racial order.[88]

Twelve years after Marx, Engels died. The date was 1895, the year in which Gustave Le Bon published *Crowd Psychology*. The book's main thesis is well-known: the prolonged crisis from 1789 to 1871, from the outbreak of the Great Revolution to the Paris Commune, was ultimately the product of mental illness. Here, then, nineteenth-century bourgeois culture tackled the second theoretical and political challenge (France's differential development) by recourse to the psychopathological paradigm. In the country stamped by an interminable revolutionary cycle, 'a virus of a new and unknown kind' raged, which had attacked the mental faculties of generations of intellectuals and political agitators: such was the view of Tocqueville, as of Hippolyte Taine and Le Bon himself.

But why did this virus rage in one country rather than another? The fact was, lamented Tocqueville, that the French were lacking in the stable morality, strong common sense, and love of liberty and individual dignity exhibited by Anglo-Saxons—in particular, Americans. The French frequently succumbed to the delirium of ideological abstractions and exhibited a morbid attachment to equality and even homogenization. They were 'afraid of isolation' and harboured a 'desire to be in the crowd', feeling themselves members of 'a nation that marches to the same step in perfect alignment'. They regarded liberty as 'the least important of their possessions, and thus are always ready to offer it up with reason at moments of danger'. These were characteristics whose disappearance was difficult to imagine, given a people whose 'basic characteristics are so constant that we can recognise the France we know in portraits made of it two or three thousand years ago'.

As we can see, the psychopathological paradigm tends to intersect with the ethnological or ethnologico-racial paradigm. This applies to Taine as well as Le Bon, who, to explain the insanity, delirium and convulsions of revolutionary France, adverted to morbid 'crowd psychology', but more exactly the morbid crowd psychology of 'Latins', who were wanting in 'that sentiment of the independence of the individual so powerful in the Anglo Saxons'.[89]

Such stereotypes became even more widely diffused across the Channel and can even be found in John Stuart Mill. He contrasted the orderly liberty and economic development of the Anglo-Saxon world with the 'submission', 'endurance' and statism peculiar to the 'continental nations' of Europe, which, moreover, were rotten with 'bureaucracy' and envious egalitarian impulses. Thus, even in liberal Britain, albeit in less crudely naturalistic form, we find a conjunction of the psychopathological paradigm (which attributed a protracted historical crisis to a sick psyche) and the ethnological paradigm (which detected this sick psyche in specific peoples).

In Tocqueville, the naturalistic slippage of the psychopathological paradigm is more pronounced. Having died in 1859, he did not live to see the American Civil War, but had sensed its advent. What were the causes of the impending cataclysm? Ideological fanaticism, which had had such devastating effects in the country of radical Enlightenment and Jacobinism, was absent across the Atlantic. So what was the cause of the looming civil war? The French liberal was in no doubt: it was the 'rapid introduction into the United States of men who were foreign to the English race'; it was the sudden arrival of 'so many alien elements', who disastrously altered the 'nature' (*naturel*) and 'economy and health' of the original 'social body'.

Finally, to explain the irruption of the subaltern classes onto the historical stage, and the emergence of the Jacobin-socialist movement, nineteenth-century culture employed the same admixture of psychopathological paradigm and ethnological paradigm. In Tocqueville's view, socialism was the 'natural disease' of the French; and this was Le Bon's position too.[90] At the same time, it availed itself of the racial paradigm to brand the subaltern classes who rebelled against the existing order as barbaric and savage. What was occurring was a 'new barbarian invasion', this time originating from within the civilized world. Indeed, wrote Nietzsche, commenting on the Paris Commune and condemning it, a 'barbaric slave class' was at work that threatened to visit horrendous destruction on civilization.[91] Or, to put the point in the words of Jeremy Bentham this time, nothing good was to be expected of the 'savage' that was the poor man.[92]

As we can see, the main paradigms employed by bourgeois culture especially in the second half of the nineteenth century (following the failure of the 1848 revolution, Hegel became a dead dog) allotted very little space to history. This explains some extraordinary slips. Tocqueville counterposed the USA to a France incapable of ridding itself of absolute power. We are in a period that predates the American Civil War: the country where Black slavery remained alive and well was celebrated as a champion of the cause of liberty, while deafness to that cause was embodied by a country that had abolished slavery in its colonies decades earlier.

It was in disputing these paradigms that Marx and Engels developed the theory of class struggle.

9 THE FORMATION OF THE THEORY OF CLASS STRUGGLE

Tackling the issue of the working class on the terrain of historical and social analysis, the 27-year-old Marx not only ridiculed cries of alarm at the 'new barbarian invasion', but turned them back against those who uttered them. It was precisely from these 'barbarians' that emancipation was to be anticipated. The 'barbaric slave class' warned against by Nietzsche (and the culture of the time) was the working class which, breaking the chains of 'present enslavement' to which it was subject, made a decisive contribution to constructing a society and civilization no longer based on exploitation and oppression. The racial and civilizational clash paradigms were refuted in advance, on the grounds that concrete socio-historical analysis disclosed the fluidity of the boundaries between civilization and barbarism. This did not only apply to class relations within the capitalist metropolis. The latter claimed to export civilization to the colonial world. In reality, it was precisely there that the 'inherent barbarism of bourgeois civilization' clearly manifested itself (see Sect. 3). During the 'civilizing war' represented by the Opium War (according to the dominant ideology in the West and Tocqueville and Mill as well), it was the 'semi-barbarian' China which showed respect for 'the principle of morality'.[93] In any event, colonial expansion was not the triumph, ordained and consecrated by Providence, of the superior civilization and 'European race' about which Tocqueville, among others, fantasized. Rather, it was a key moment in the formation of the world market by the bourgeoisie, which had emerged 'dripping from head to toe, from every pore, with blood and dirt'. With its class struggle, the Western bourgeoisie had imposed an international division of labour based on the enslavement of Blacks and the expropriation, deportation and even annihilation of Native Americans.[94] The class struggle of oppressed peoples did not fail to respond to all this.

As regards interpretation of the major historical crisis that began in 1789, from the outset Marx developed an analysis in which race, the stereotypical characteristics attributed to this or that people, and madness played no role. In 1850, he published *Class Struggles in France from 1848 to 1850*. The methodology clearly formulated in the title also forms the guiding thread of a book published two years later, *The Eighteenth Brumaire of Louis Bonaparte*. It was devoted to explaining why the revolutionary crisis, after having variously invested 'all classes and parties', resulted in the dictatorship of Bonaparte, that 'chief of the lumpen-proletariat', 'a princely lumpen-proletarian'.[95] It made no sense to counter-pose Britain and the USA to a France supposedly incurably deaf to the value of liberty. Britain distinguished itself by the 'indecent haste' with which, prior to anyone else, it recognized the France issuing from Louis Bonaparte's coup d'état, whose author was 'deified' by the Conservative press.[96] As for the North American republic, even were Black slavery to be ignored, it must be remembered that across the Atlantic 'the class contradictions are but incompletely developed; every clash between the classes is concealed by the outflow of the surplus proletarian population to the west'[97]—an emigration presupposing the expropriation and deportation of the natives and hence a ferocious dictatorship over them.

Departure from naturalistic paradigms was an essential moment in the process of developing the theory of class struggle. Already in his early writings, Engels criticized Thomas Carlyle, 'with his prejudice in favour of the Teutonic character', for his 'exaggerated and one-sided condemnation of the Irish national character'. Rather than drawing attention to 'the shameless oppression inflicted by the English', the great writer had wrongly stigmatized the inhabitants of the subjugated island 'Latins' and 'Celts', members of a 'race robbed of all humanity', starkly inferior to the 'Germanic' or 'Saxon' race of which the English formed an integral part.[98] It is also the context wherein to locate Marx's critique of the dominant ideology, which claimed to attribute the tragedy of a people to the '"aboriginal faults of the Celtic race"'.[99] What should be put on trial was not some putative 'Irish nature' but 'British misrule' and hence the responsibility of the dominant classes.[100]

These were the years when the Irish, who occupied the bottom rungs of the labour market in England, seemed to Carlyle to be not only 'Latins' and 'Celts', but also—worse—'negroes', members of the race whose slavery the British writer, with his focus in particular on the USA, justified.[101] Unfortunately, this view was also widespread among British workers, who (Marx observed in 1870) tended to adopt towards the Irish a similar attitude to that displayed in the American South by poor Whites towards the 'niggers' they despised and hated.[102] But all this had little or nothing to do with 'race'. In a society of the kind to be found in the Deep South, where, even after the formal abolition of the institution of slavery, the ruling oligarchy proudly displayed its *otium* and saddled Blacks with 'all the productive labour', social arrogance manifested itself as racial arrogance and contempt for 'productive labour' was, at the same time, contempt for the servile or semi-servile race forced to supply it.

Along with Carlyle, Marx and Engels' polemic targeted François Guizot, who, after the workers' revolt of June 1848, like Tocqueville, and probably in his wake, contrasted England and France. The first knew how to combine love of liberty with a robust pragmatism; the second was prey to fanatical subversiveness and lacked any sense of limits. Hence (ironized Marx) everything was to be explained by 'the superior intelligence of the English'. Class struggle—conflict that was always historically determinate—ceded to a mythical, more or less eternal nature of peoples possessing a different degree of pragmatism and sense of reality. Those who argued thus took no account of the radicalism and civil war that marked the first English revolution, the Puritan revolution. The latter, however, was attributed by Guizot to 'a few ambitious, fanatic and evil-minded people', not content with 'moderate freedom'.[103] Directed at the French, the ethnological paradigm gives way to the psychopathological paradigm, which sets off in search of fanatics and lunatics. The terrain of an 'understanding of history'[104] is abandoned here too. This way of arguing seemed so ridiculous to Marx and Engels that they pointed to adhesion to the ethnological and psychopathological paradigm as evidence of a decline in *'les capacités de la bourgeoisie'*. Terrified by the spectre of proletarian revolution, it was no longer capable of interpreting social conflict in historical terms.[105]

Whether directly or indirectly, the polemic of the theoreticians of the class struggle ended up encompassing a fair number of the major authors of the nineteenth century. According to Tocqueville, the vehicle of the 'virus of a new and unknown kind' was a 'new race of revolutionaries': 'we are still dealing with the same men, but the circumstances are different'.[106] One has the impression that Engels was replying to the French liberal when, in 1851, he waxed ironic about 'that superstition which attribute[s] revolutions to the ill-will of a few agitators'.[107]

In denouncing an eruption of revolutionary insanity, nineteenth-century liberals had France in particular in their sights. In the conviction that the revolutionary cycle afflicting the West went back a long way, Nietzsche called for a settlement of accounts with 'the madhouse-world of entire millennia' and the mental illness originating with Christianity.[108] Although taking the psychopathological paradigm to extremes, Nietzsche acknowledged his debt to the tradition behind him and declared that he had 'passed through the school of Tocqueville and Taine'.[109] On the other side, Engels mocked 'Taine and Tocqueville, those idols of the philistines'.[110]

The various representatives of the dominant nineteenth-century culture were therefore in agreement in identifying France, with its protracted revolutionary cycle, as the clearest example of the horrors in which revolutionary madness could result. In 1885, Engels, by contrast, asserted that France was 'the land where, more than anywhere else, historical class struggles were each time fought out to a decision'.[111] For his part, Marx expressed utter contempt for the psychopathological paradigm, noting in 1867 that autocratic, feudal Russia employed it: Nicholas I explained the spread of the 1848 revolutionary crisis in Europe by the diffusion of the 'French plague' and French revolutionary 'madness', with the metastasis of the 'cancer of a sacrilegious philosophy' attacking the healthy organs of the European social body.[112]

10 CLASS STRUGGLE AND IDEOLOGICAL STRUGGLE

Class struggle not only encompasses different social relations, but is also played out at an ideological level, not sparing religion. The latter claims to be a sacred space that transcends conflict. In reality, it often acts as an 'opium of the people', facilitating the task of the ruling class.[113] It is worth dwelling on this point because Marx's discourse on religion has been confused with Enlightenment discourse, which risks compromising an understanding of the Marxian critique of ideology. For Marx religion is one of the ideologies, not ideology as such. The concrete role played by religion in the context of the class struggle in its various configurations has to be examined. Let us take a glance at history.

In the late eighteenth century, Poland was still formally a sovereign state. Frederick II of Prussia exploited the anti-Catholic sentiments of Enlightenment *philosophes* to justify the annexation of Polish territory, presenting it as a contribution to the diffusion of Enlightenment and defence of the cause of religious tolerance. In a letter sent to him, D'Alembert celebrated the 'delicious verses' of the enlightened sovereign which, in a felicitous blend of 'imagination' and 'reason', mocked the Poles and the 'Holy Virgin Mary', in whom they reposed their hopes of 'liberation'.[114] Something similar occurred in connection with Ireland, a colony of Protestant and Anglican Great Britain. Here too the struggle against national oppression was fuelled by religious themes and mobilized watchwords of a religious (Roman Catholic) kind. In this instance, it was John Locke who seized on the spirit of Enlightenment to combat the rebels, a manifestation of the 'ignorant and zealous world' of Popery, led astray by 'the art and industry of their clergy'. They were incited by 'priests' who 'everywhere', to secure their empire, 'hav[e] excluded reason from having anything to do in religion'.[115] There could be no toleration of papists. In addition to looking to a foreign, hostile power, they harboured 'dangerous opinions, which are absolutely destructive to all governments but the pope's'; '[t]hose opinions and whoever shall spread or publish any of them the magistrate is bound to suppress'.[116] In both cases, the alleged struggle against clerical obscurantism was, at the same time, repression of the national aspirations of the Polish and Irish peoples. Proudhon may be regarded as the inheritor of such Enlightenment ideology. In him we find a combination of the posture of a free thinker and derision of independence movements, for which defence of national identity (and liberation) also took the form of defence of religious identity.

Marx and Engels' attitude was very different. From the outset, commitment to the struggle for the emancipation of subaltern classes, often stupefied and paralyzed by religious 'opium', was conjoined with support for independence movements which, precisely thanks to religion, achieved initial awareness of the national question. In the eyes of the Irish (noted the young Engels), the 'Protestant intruders' were one and the same as the 'landlords' and, in a way, an integral part of the machine subjugating the people, who had been invaded and subjected to the 'most brutal plundering'.[117] Digging beneath the surface of the religious clash between Catholics and Protestants, we uncover the clash between Irish farm hands, whose land was often expropriated, and the expropriating British colonists; we witness the emergence of the reality of class struggle in its concrete configuration. Religious affiliation can be experienced very intensely and mobilized effectively in political and historical upheaval. But it is not the primary cause of such conflict.

In the case of Poland, immediately after the (rapidly repressed) rebellion of January 1863, Marx, reconstructing the history of the partitioned, oppressed country, observed that tsarist Russia had not hesitated to use the pretext of the 'exclusion of (non-Catholic) dissidents from political rights' to justify its policy of intervention and expansion at Poland's expense.[118] This is a theme subsequently developed by Engels. At the time of the country's first partition (he observed), there was 'an enlightened "public opinion" in Europe', under 'the immense influence of Diderot, Voltaire, Rousseau and the other French writers of the eighteenth century'. In its expansionist march, tsarist Russia exploited it. Although engaged in ferocious persecution of Jewry, it 'came soon upon Poland in the name of religious toleration' and the rights of Orthodox Christians infringed by a Catholic, obscurantist country and government. In so doing, Russia could count on the support and benevolence of the *philosophes*:

> The Court of Catherine II was made the head-quarters of the enlightened men of the day, especially Frenchmen; the most enlightened principle was professed by the Empress and her Court, and so well did she succeed in deceiving them that Voltaire and many others sang the praise of the 'Semiramis of the North', and proclaimed Russia the most progressive country in the world, the home of liberal principles, the champion of religious toleration.[119]

The date was 1866. The following year, we have seen Marx telling Engels about his daughter Jenny paying tribute to the Irish patriots, who had just been hanged, and associating them with the Polish patriots who were also fighting for their independence. This was not prompted by some fleeting emotion. In 1869, Marx returned to the issue. He sent a photo of Jenny first to Engels, and then to Ludwig Kugelmann, and explained in the accompanying letter that the cross she was wearing round her neck was 'the Polish 1864 Insurrection Cross'.[120] In the house of the philosopher, revolutionary and scourge of the 'opium of the people', there was no hesitation in expressing solidarity with the liberation struggle of an oppressed people to the extent of displaying its religious symbols.

Attention to the concrete significance of religion in a concrete historical situation, and in the context of a specific conflict, was a constant in Marx and Engels' thinking. During the American Civil War, Marx warmly stressed the vanguard role played by Christian abolitionists like William L. Garrison and Wendell Phillips. The latter, in particular, '[f]or 30 years ... has without intermission and at the risk of his life proclaimed the emancipation of the slaves as his battle-cry, regardless alike of the persiflage of the press, the enraged howls of paid rowdies and the conciliatory representations of solicitous friends'. Indeed, he did not hesitate to criticize Lincoln, reproving him for relying mainly on negotiations from above with the leaders of states situated on the border between North and South, and uncertain about what position to adopt, rather than on mobilization from below of Blacks determined to break the chains of slavery. 'Lincoln is waging a political war': such was the condemnation by Phillips, who wanted to transform the military showdown between the two sections of the Union into a kind of abolitionist revolution, for which Marx likewise hoped.[121]

The great opponent of Christian abolitionism was John C. Calhoun, who thundered against 'the rabid fanatics, who regard slavery as a sin, and thus regarding it, deem it their highest duty to destroy it, even should it involve the destruction of the constitution and the Union'. For them, abolition was a conscientious duty. Only thus, they thought, could they free themselves from the agonizing sense of being complicit with the unforgivable 'sin' allegedly represented by slavery, against which they proclaimed a 'general crusade'.[122] Despite his hatred, or perhaps precisely because of it, Calhoun hit home. In Christian abolitionism, quasi-fundamentalist accents were not lacking, with which the major theorist of the slave-holding South liked to contrast a secular attitude that was 'enlightened' in its way. Yet Marx came down in favour of Garrison and Phillips, celebrating them as champions of the cause of liberty. In the gigantic class struggle that unfolded before and during the Civil War, it was Christian abolitionism, often echoing with fundamentalist accents, which embodied resistance to the 'general crusade of property against labour' and the revolutionary cause of the emancipation of labour.

Not only as militants required to take a position on the conflicts of their time, but also as historians analysing conflicts that now lay in the past, the remote past even, Marx and Engels carefully avoided indiscriminate liquidation of movements inspired by religion in one way or another. In its time, the Spanish uprising against Napoleon's army had been directed against the invading country's cultural tradition as well as its military occupation. Hence, it had denounced the French Enlightenment and Revolution and, against these more or less 'satanic' ideas, appealed to the religion of its ancestors and the Holy Faith. But all this did not prevent Marx from formulating a balanced judgement in 1854 that, in the Napoleonic era, '[a]ll the wars of independence waged against France bear in common the stamp of regeneration, mixed up with reaction'.[123] 'Regeneration' was represented by the mass struggle for national independence, while 'reaction' consisted in the obscurantist ideology informing the struggle.

Immediately after the failure of the 1848 revolution, rejecting tendencies to discouragement and escapism, Engels engaged in reconstructing the German 'revolutionary tradition',[124] and thus wrote a book on the 'peasants' war', the great anti-feudal revolt that had erupted more than three centuries earlier, in the wake of the Protestant Reformation, with slogans drawn from the Old and New Testaments.

Later, at the end of his life in 1895, Engels had no hesitation comparing the irresistible rise of socialism with the triumph of Christianity, notwithstanding Diocletian's persecution and thanks to Constantine's conversion.[125] This stance was all the more significant because it occurred at the same time as Nietzsche's equation and condemnation of Christianity and socialism in the name, first, of 'Enlightenment' proper and then, in the final phase of his development, of a 'new Enlightenment'.[126]

Finally, it is worth remembering that very early on, Marx polemicized against Gustav Hugo, who, posturing as a 'complete sceptic' even more consistent than 'the other Enlighteners', ridiculed the ideal of the emancipation of slaves, not infrequently fostered (as we have seen) by Christian abolitionists.[127]

In Marx and Engels, then, religion was represented as an 'opium of the people' in as much as it claims to transcend conflict, thereby impeding attainment of revolutionary consciousness and strengthening the chains of oppression. But it may be that religion is the terrain where rudimentary consciousness of the conflict, of class struggle in its various configurations, emerges. This is the case, in particular, with the national question. In such instances, religious representations, which explain the conflict on the basis of a clash between Irish Catholics and British Protestants, or between Polish Catholics and Russian Orthodox Christians, is much less idealistic and much less mystificatory than the view that sees Enlightenment and obscurantism at grips in Ireland and Poland. Transfiguring domination into an expression of the light of reason, such 'illuminism', dear to Frederick II (and, in part, D'Alembert), as to Hugo, Calhoun, and Nietzsche, might well be defined as court Enlightenment. And we must then never lose sight of the fact that the critique of religion cannot be separated in Marx and Engels from the critique of court Enlightenment.

11 From Religion to 'Rustic Idyll'

Recourse can also be had to art as an illusory escape from conflict. In reality, 'social conflicts' clearly emerge from the masterpieces of Aeschylus, Aristophanes, Dante, and Cervantes.[128] In fact, this sometimes happens against the wishes of the author. Balzac ended up mercilessly describing the inevitable eclipse of a class (the aristocracy) for which he felt sympathy and pining nostalgia.[129] Attempts to escape social reality and its contradictions can assume different forms, but all alike are inane.

After the failure of the 1848 revolution, criticizing a now forgotten author (Georg Friedrich Daumer) who expressed disdain for 'abstract, exclusive politics', and who counter-opposed to its miseries the beauty and warmth of nature, Marx and Engels mocked the widespread tendency to 'flee before the historical tragedy that is threatening … to alleged nature, i.e. to a stupid rustic idyll'.[130]

In Feuerbach too, disillusion and disgust were so strong in these years that he was led to repeat Cicero's exclamation about the 'politics of his time': '*sunt omnia omnium miseriarum plenissima*' ('everything is full of every misery'). It remained only to practice 'indifference towards political parties and chatter', seeking refuge and consolation in the arms of nature: 'nature alone is not concerned with politics, but is the direct opposite of politics'.[131] Rather than religion, evasion or escape from the conflict now seeks safety in nature. Marx had already cautioned against this attitude five years before the 1848 revolution, when he observed that Feuerbach referred 'too much to nature and too little to politics'.[132]

What has been said of escape into religion also broadly applies to escape into nature. Far from expressing a genuine transcendence of social conflict, it is an immature, often mystifying, expression of that conflict. We are dealing with a spiritual attitude that tends to manifest itself every time the hopes reposed in politics and political change fade or vanish. This is what happened after 1789, when the extreme complexity of the revolutionary process seemed to have definitively mocked the enthusiasm initially elicited in German culture by the fall of the *ancien régime* in France. In 1803, Friedrich Schiller had sung: 'only on mountains is liberty to be found!' Only where nature was as yet uncontaminated by man 'is the world perfect'. As a result, only he who lived 'in the silence of the countryside', suckling with childish abandon on the 'breast of nature', could be regarded as happy; or she who lived 'in the peaceful convent cell', where likewise the 'sad figure of humanity' did not intrude—that is, where one was similarly far removed from the ephemeral din of historico-political upheavals. Hegel argued against Schiller and his 'invocation of nature'. Rejecting any consolatory escape from the contradictions and conflicts of the political world (whether into nature or religion), he stressed that '[w]hat is created by human reason must possess at least the same dignity as what is created by nature'; in this sense, 'the most banal Berlin wisecrack' was no less worthy of admiration than a magnificent natural spectacle.[133]

This was a lesson which must have profoundly influenced Marx. According to the authoritative testimony of Paul Lafargue (the philosopher's son-in-law, having married his daughter Laura), he loved to repeat 'the saying by Hegel, the philosophy master of his youth: "Even the criminal thought of a malefactor is more grandiose and sublime than the marvels of the heavens"'.[134] In his turn, in a letter of 1893 Engels wrote: 'Nature is wonderful. I have always liked going back to her as a change from the movement of History, but History, after all, seems even more wonderful than Nature to me'. Contact with nature should serve to revive energies, enabling a return with renewed vigour to observing the historical and political world and participating in building a society based on solidarity and an awareness of common humanity, rather than exploitation and oppression—'this approaching accomplishment of a thing never before attained in the history of our earth'.[135]

We have seen Marx wax ironic about the 'alleged nature' where the philistine disgusted with historical and political developments thinks to find refuge. Such 'nature' is 'alleged' in two senses. Firstly, it is not, in fact, uncontaminated by political and social conflict: conservative circles appeal to it to reprove the irrational agitation of the city. Secondly, observes *The German Ideology*, in the planet inhabited by humanity, 'the nature that preceded human history', which is precisely conceived in contrast to human history, 'today no longer exists anywhere (except perhaps on a few Australian coral islands of recent origin)'.[136] The countryside where Schiller, Daumer, and Feuerbach sought refuge had behind it a long, tormented history as well as a gigantic revolution—the Neolithic Revolution—which involved the introduction of agriculture and animal husbandry and the domestication of animals. In practice, everything celebrated as eternal nature, under the sign of order and regularity, and hence in contrast to the class struggles, agitation, and convulsions of the historical and political world is the product of a major historical upheaval.

Contrary to Schiller's claim, even mountains are not uncontaminated by the 'sad figure of humanity'. It is enough to think of shepherds and livestock, which pertain to the history just invoked. In any event, to scale heights that are not easily accessible, it is necessary to employ what has been produced by human labour, starting with clothes to protect against cold and storms. The 'nature' evoked and dreamed of by Schiller, Daumer, and Feuerbach is nothing but 'the mental expression of a pious wish about human affairs', a fantasy projection of 'ideas' that people 'would like to see realized in human society'.[137] Thus, it is a 'nature' from which the 'dichotomy of life and happiness' bemoaned in human society has vanished. In reality (to continue to cite *The German Ideology*), 'Hobbes had much better reasons for invoking nature as proof of his *bellum omnium contra omnes*, and Hegel ... for perceiving in nature cleavage'.[138] The only thing that can overcome 'the dichotomy of life and happiness' is political action: class struggle.

12 'Nature' between Escape and Class Struggle

Marx and Engels ironized about attempts to seek shelter from the conflict in a nature uncontaminated by human history and celebrated in opposition to it. They criticized the evasion implicit in the 'cult of nature', as in religion in the strict sense.[139] But all this did not prevent them being among the first to draw attention to what would today be called the ecological question.

From the outset, Marx stressed that 'man lives on nature';[140] 'the first premise of all human history is, of course, the existence of living human individuals', whose 'physical organization' and 'consequent relation to the rest of nature' cannot be ignored.[141] Almost 30 years later, the *Critique of the Gotha Programme* opens with a caution that sounds prophetic today: however great and growing labour productivity might be, '[l]abour is *not the source* of all wealth'. A key point must never be neglected: '*Nature* is just as much the source of use values (and it is surely of such that material wealth consists!) as labour, which itself is only the manifestation of a force of nature, human labour power'.[142]

We are immediately directed back to class struggle. While capitalism has the merit of promoting an unprecedented growth of the productive forces, it risks doubly jeopardizing 'real wealth'. Firstly, with its ruthless pursuit of maximum profit and periodic crises, capitalism involves an enormous dissipation of the 'natural power' that is 'human labour-power', already sacrificed without scruple in children condemned to death from toil and hardship. It could be said that Volume One of *Capital* is, in large part, a critical analysis of 'the incessant human sacrifices from among the working class' and 'the most reckless squandering of [natural] labour power'.[143]

But that is not all. *Capital* elsewhere underscores that 'all progress in capitalistic agriculture is a progress in the art, not only of robbing the labourer, but of robbing the soil', thereby 'ruining the sources of [its] fertility'.[144] In any event, applied to the relationship between humanity and nature as a whole, the idea of private property on which bourgeois society is based proves even more devastating. The more absolute such an idea, the more serious the consequences for nature. In the American Deep South, slave-holding society was also characterized by 'brutal spoliation of the soil'.[145] As regards Ireland, 'the potato blight resulted from the exhaustion of the soil, it was a product of English colonial rule' and the policy of colonial despoliation pursued by the London government.[146]

We may draw a general conclusion: '[e]ven a whole society, a nation, or even all simultaneously existing societies taken together, are not the owners of the globe. They are only its possessors, its usufructuaries, and, like *boni patres familias*, they must hand it down to succeeding generations in an improved condition'. In future, '[f]rom the standpoint of higher economic form of society, private ownership of the globe by single individuals will appear quite as absurd as private ownership of one man by another'—that is, the relationship of slavery.[147]

We can now understand Engels' warning in *Dialectics of Nature*: 'we by no means rule over nature like a conqueror over a foreign people, like someone standing outside nature—but … we, with flesh, blood and brain, belong to nature, and exist in its midst'.[148] To safeguard nature, which makes the continuation and development of human history possible, politico-social conflict, from which the religious 'cult of nature' recommends escape, must be confronted and resolved. Appeals to look to nature for a place that transcends societal disagreements and contradictions are a distorting, mystificatory expression of the very conflict they vainly seek to repress.

But let us nevertheless try to take such appeals seriously. We should first of all remember that the worker 'never gets the slightest glimpse of Nature in his large town with his long working-hours'.[149] Besides, the 'nature' present in the 'working-people's quarters' of urban centres affords a desolate spectacle: they have been constructed 'without the slightest reference to ventilation, with reference solely to the profit [*Gewinn*]secured by the contractor', and abandoned to 'the most miserable and filthy condition' and 'a shocking stench, with filth and swarms of vermin'.[150] Furnishing one of the very first analyses of the ecological and environmental question, Engels noted how the logic of profit explained the pollution of the atmosphere (witness a city 'enveloped in a grey cloud of coal smoke'), of waterways (here we have a 'coal-black, foul-smelling stream' and there a 'dark-coloured body of water, which leaves the beholder in doubt whether it is a brook or a long string of stagnant puddles').[151]

The text just quoted dates from 1845. Two years earlier, Herbert Spencer had ironized as follows: if the state is to be assigned the task of intervening against industry's polluting discharges, why deny it competence as regards 'the spiritual sanity of the nation'?[152] Some decades later, the English liberal had a rethink and felt obliged to come to terms with the problem of air pollution: he made some very modern-sounding observations about the foul air people were sometimes forced to breathe on trains. But it is always and only individuals who appear on stage; and the problem is treated without any reference to factories and industrial locations or rivers, lakes and the natural environment. The conflict emerges when gentlemen or, rather, 'men who think themselves gentlemen smoke in other places than those provided for smokers'.[153] Classes and class struggle are as absent as ever.

13 A GENERAL THEORY OF SOCIAL CONFLICT

We can draw some conclusions. Firstly, by virtue of its ambition to encompass the whole historical process, the theory of class struggle is configured as a general theory of social conflict. According to the *Communist Manifesto*, it is 'the history of *all* [*aller*]hitherto existing society', 'the history of *all* [*ganzen*] past society', which is characterized by 'class struggles' and 'class antagonisms'.[154] Decades later, in 1885, Engels reverted to the theme: '[i]t was ... Marx who had first discovered the great law of motion of history, the law according to which *all* [*alle*]historical struggles ... are in fact only the more or less clear expression of struggles between social classes'.[155] I have emphasized the keyword which identifies social conflict as such with class struggle, whoever its protagonists are and whatever form it takes.

Secondly, effecting a radical epistemological break with naturalistic ideologies, the Marxian theory of class struggle situates *social conflict* on the terrain of history.

Thirdly, precisely because it seeks to supply an interpretative key to the historical process, it strives to take into account the multiplicity of forms in which *social* conflict manifests itself. With this italic I intend to signal a preliminary problem. Obviously, existence is marked by an infinity of conflicts that develop between individuals for a whole variety of reasons. But what is involved here is analysing conflicts whose protagonists are not single individuals, but social subjects who, directly or indirectly, pertain to the social order, to some essential articulation of the division of labour and the social order.

This is how the object of Marx's theory of 'class struggles' is defined. We are dealing with a general category—a genus—which can subsume different species. We may venture a typology starting, obviously, not from world history, but from the historical time in which the authors of the *Communist Manifesto* lived. An initial distinction is indicated. On the one hand, there are conflicts that oppose exploiting classes—class struggles that see the bourgeoisies of different countries rise up against the landed aristocracy and the *ancien régime*, and then confront one another in more or less fierce competition liable to result in war. On the other hand, we have struggles for emancipation, which are class struggles from the standpoints of the social subjects engaged in achieving it and of those intent on preventing or impeding it. At this point we must make a second distinction—to be exact, a tripartite distinction—between the struggle whose protagonists are peoples in colonial or semi-colonial conditions; the struggle waged by the working class in the capitalist metropolis (the one on which Marx and Engels were particularly focused); and the struggle of women against 'domestic slavery'. Each of these three struggles challenges the prevailing division of labour internationally, nationally, and within the family. A 'relation of compulsion' (*Zwangsverhältniß*) obtains between capital and labour in bourgeois society.[156] But the same is true of the other two relations. The three struggles for emancipation challenge the three fundamental 'relations of compulsion' constitutive of the capitalist system as a whole.

Benedetto Croce took no account of all this when, in September 1917, with reference to the war that was raging, he declared: 'the concept of power and struggle, which Marx transported from states to social classes, now seems to have reverted from classes to states'.[157] It is true that, at least in the early stages of the patriotic *union sacrée*, the gigantic conflict was regarded and theorized by not a few European intellectuals as further confirmation of the crisis of historical materialism or as 'an instrument to abolish class structure'.[158] However, only a few weeks after the class struggle had been declared dead by Croce, the October Revolution and the insurrection of the popular masses against the war, and the privileged classes who ruled the country and army, occurred in Russia. But that is not the only reason why the terrible trial of strength between the great powers which erupted in 1914 was far from being the termination or suspension of class struggle.

We should take special note of the observation made by an eminent contemporary historian, Arno J. Mayer: no war has ever been so ardently invoked as 'prophylaxis', as 'an instrument of domestic politics', as a lifeline for a political and social order that felt ever more imperilled by the rise of the labour and socialist movement. To cite the example of a figure not far removed from Croce's circle, ten years before its outbreak, the war was invoked and summoned by Vilfredo Pareto to set socialism back 'for at least half a century'. In a similar vein, in Germany, Admiral Alfred von Tirpitz also justified his policy of naval rearmament by the need to discover an antidote to 'Marxism and the political radicalization of the masses'. And this is not to mention the conviction, widespread among the dominant classes and their ideologues, that colonial expansion alone could defuse the social question in the metropolis and weaken or contain the socialist movement.[159]

On closer inspection, the First World War was not merely an expression of the class struggle, but was so in a triple sense. It pertained (a) to the struggle for hegemony between the capitalist bourgeoisies of the great powers; (b) to the social conflict in the metropolis which the dominant class hoped to neutralize and deflect via international confrontation and colonial conquest; and (c) to the oppression and exploitation of peoples in colonial or semi-colonial conditions for whom (to adopt Marx's terminology on the subject of Ireland) the 'social question' was posed as the 'national question'.

In each individual country, the ruling class certainly seized the opportunity to commend or impose social peace and national unity, to suppress strikes and, if need be, extend working hours. However, far from betokening its end, such behaviour was a manifestation of the class struggle waged by the bourgeoisie, which subsequently, with the intensification of the sacrifices required by the war and the progressive loss in credibility of patriotic rhetoric, the proletariat countered with a class struggle that could even take revolutionary forms.

In the light of such considerations, Karl Popper's summary cannot but raise a smile. He expounds as follows the thesis that fascism and communism share an evil, obviously German father: 'the left wing [represented by Marx] replaces the war of nations which appears in Hegel's historicist scheme by the war of classes, the extreme right replaces it by the war of races'.[160] In fact, social and class conflict is very much present in Hegel, who constantly referred to it to explain the fall of the monarchy in ancient Rome, overthrown by an aristocracy determined to strengthen its hold over the plebs; or to shed light on the modern process that saw the absolutist monarchy progressively limit the power and privileges of a feudal aristocracy stubbornly attached to its privileges and the serfdom and exploitation imposed on the peasant mass. With the advent of the modern representative state derived from the French Revolution, social conflict had far from disappeared for Hegel: the proletarian who was unemployed or incapable of working, or the poor man who risked dying of starvation, was in a similar condition to the slave and hence fully entitled to rebel.[161] On the other hand, the 'war of nations' (a reality obvious to everyone) features prominently in Marx and Engels: capitalism was also condemned by them because it secreted an 'industrial war of extermination between nations' and waged piratical wars against colonial peoples, who responded with legitimate wars of resistance and national liberation.

As for the 'war of races', Marx and Engels certainly rejected interpreting history in racial terms. In so doing, they were compelled to argue not only against the phantom Hegelian 'extreme right' fantasized by Popper, himself a prisoner of the ethnological paradigm in a way (he pointed to Germany as the source of all evil), but also against figures and newspapers in liberal America and Britain. However, what at first sight presents itself as a 'racial war' is, in reality, a class struggle. For example, it is clear that in the USA of Black slavery and white supremacy the fate of African Americans was sealed primarily by 'racial' affiliation. In such circumstances, to raise the 'racial' (or national) question did not in fact mean repressing social conflict, but confronting it in the concrete, particular terms in which it manifested itself.

Only if we appreciate this can we understand the twentieth century, which (as we shall see) was marked by epic class struggles and national resistance struggles against attempts by the Third Reich and the Empire of the Rising Sun to revive the colonial and even slave-holding tradition in Eastern Europe and Asia, respectively.

In short, what escapes Croce, Popper, and Ferguson is the role played by class struggle in contradictions, clashes, and confrontations that seem purely national and racial in character. None of them appreciates that Marx and Engels' theory of class struggle is a general theory of social conflict, even if it is not organically and systematically expounded. We may proceed to a comparison. Likewise benefiting from the extraordinary cultural season that witnessed the blossoming of German classical philosophy, Carl von Clausewitz wrote his celebrated book *On War*, which encompassed the most varied armed conflicts, interpreting them as the continuation of politics by other means. Marx and Engels in principle composed a treatise *On Social and Political Conflict* which, rising to a higher level of generalization and abstraction, on the basis of the division of labour into antagonistic classes and class struggle, interprets the various forms of social conflict, including wars and different types of war, in a unitary key. It should at once be added that, while Clausewitz adopted an at least partially objectivist attitude, the two philosophers and revolutionary militants explicitly declared that they did not seek to rise *au-dessus de la mêlée*, confining themselves to observing it with detachment, but were actively engaged in changing the world in a very precise direction.

NOTES

1. Karl Marx and Frederick Engels, *Collected Works*, London: Lawrence & Wishart, 1975–2004, Vol. 3, pp. 149, 168, 186.
2. Ibid., Vol. 6, pp. 519, 125; Vol. 22, p. 335.
3. Ibid., Vol. 20, pp. 110, 14.
4. Ibid., Vol. 6, pp. 518–19.
5. Ibid., Vol. 6, p. 449; Vol. 4, p. 561; Vol. 3, p. 390.
6. Ibid., Vol. 6, p. 388; Vol. 43, p. 475.
7. Ibid., Vol. 20, p. 13.
8. Ibid., Vol. 3, p. 355. It should in fact be noted that while the terms *Arbeiter* (worker) and *Arbeiterklasse* (working class) refer to the industrial proletariat in the strict sense in the early writings of Marx and Engels, they subsequently tend to assume a broader meaning, to the point of ultimately becoming synonymous with dependent labour.
9. Ibid., Vol. 7, p. 373.
10. Karl Marx, *Manuskripte über die polnische Frage (1863–4)*, ed. W. Conze and D. Hertz-Eichenrode, 'S-Gravenhage, 1961, p. 124.
11. Ibid., Vol. 43, pp. 473–4.
12. Ibid., Vol. 40, p. 49.
13. Ibid., Vol. 12, p. 125.
14. Ibid., Vol. 4, p. 160.
15. Ibid., Vol. 12, p. 221.
16. Miklos Molnár, *Marx, Engels et la politique internationale*, Paris: Gallimard, 1975, pp. 122, 114, 20.
17. Quoted in Hans Magnus Enzensberger (ed.), *Colloqui con Marx e Engels*, Turin: Einaudi, 1977, pp. 327–8.
18. Marx and Engels, *Collected Works*, Vol. 42, p. 479.
19. Ibid., Vol. 42, p. 483.
20. Ibid., Vol. 42, p. 474; Vol. 21, p. 189.
21. Ibid., Vol. 20, p. 13.
22. Ibid., Vol. 7, p. 167.
23. Ibid., Vol. 20, pp. 11, 13.
24. Ibid., Vol. 6, pp. 196, 125, 503, 388.
25. Ibid., Vol. 43, p. 473.
26. Ibid., Vol. 6, pp. 464–5.
27. Ibid., Vol. 4, p. 122; Vol. 22, p. 335; Vol. 19, p. 20.
28. Ibid., Vol. 29, p. 121; Vol. 5, p. 309.
29. Ibid., Vol. 6, p. 168.
30. Ibid., Vol. 12, p. 221.
31. Enzensberger, *Colloqui con Marx*, pp. 328–9.
32. Marx and Engels, *Collected Works*, Vol. 9, p. 197.

33. Ibid., Vol. 43, p. 474.
34. Ibid., Vol. 43, p. 476.
35. Ibid., Vol. 35, p. 375 n.
36. Ibid., Vol. 38, p. 98.
37. Ibid., Vol. 12, p. 221.
38. Ibid., Vol. 40, p. 49.
39. Ibid., Vol. 16, p. 137.
40. Ibid., Vol. 43, pp. 474–5.
41. See ibid., Vol. 26, p. 262.
42. Ibid., Vol. 5, p. 46.
43. Ibid., Vol. 6, p. 502.
44. Ibid., Vol. 25, p. 248; Vol. 43, p. 185.
45. Ibid., Vol. 43, p. 424.
46. Ibid., Vol. 4, p. 442.
47. Marie-Jean-Antoine Condorcet, *Oeuvres*, ed. A. Condorcet O'Connor and M.F. Arago, Stuttgart and Bad Cannstatt: Frommann-Holzboog, 1968, Vol. 10, p. 121.
48. John Stuart Mill, 'The Subjection of Women', in *Collected Works*, ed. J.M. Robson, Toronto and London: Toronto University Press and Routledge & Kegan Paul, 1963–91, Vol. 21, pp. 264, 288, 323.
49. Condorcet, *Oeuvres*, Vol. 10, p. 121.
50. Mill, 'The Subjection of Women' pp. 263–4.
51. Ibid., pp. 264–5.
52. Mary Wollstonecraft, *A Vindication of the Rights of Woman*, London: Everyman's Library, 1992, p. 3.
53. See Domenico Losurdo, *Liberalism: A Counter-History*, trans. Gregory Elliott, London and New York: Verso, 2011, Chapter 5, §6.
54. Wollstonecraft, *A Vindication of the Rights of Woman*, pp. 155–6, 209.
55. Ibid., p. 158–9.
56. Ibid., pp. 160, 208.
57. Marx and Engels, *Collected Works*, Vol. 26, p. 181.
58. Friedrich Nietzsche, 'On the Genealogy of Morality', III, 18, in *Beyond Good and Evil/On the Genealogy of Morality*, trans. Adrian Del Caro, Stanford, CA: Stanford University Press, 2014, p. 323.
59. Nietzsche, 'Beyond Good and Evil', 239, p. 142.
60. Marx and Engels, *Collected Works*, Vol. 26, pp. 173, 165.
61. Ibid., Vol. 8, p. 17.
62. Enzensberger (ed.), *Colloqui con Marx*, pp. 328–9.
63. Marx and Engels, *Collected Works*, Vol. 6, pp. 493, 509.
64. Ibid., Vol. 9, pp. 197–8.
65. Ibid., Vol. 10, p. 70.
66. Ibid., Vol. 10, p. 117.

67. Ibid., Vol. 10, p. 117.
68. Ibid., Vol. 49, p. 258.
69. Ibid., Vol. 35, p. 262 n.
70. Ibid., Vol. 11, p. 110.
71. Ibid., Vol. 35, pp. 262 n, 300.
72. Ibid., Vol. 35, p. 306.
73. Ibid., Vol. 35, pp. 290, 293.
74. Ibid., Vol. 35, p. 720 and n.
75. Ibid., Vol. 19, pp. 8, 12.
76. Ibid., Vol. 41, p. 416.
77. Seymour Drescher, *From Slavery to Freedom: Comparative Studies in the Rise and Fall of Atlantic Slavery*, London: Macmillan, 1999, p. 401.
78. Alexis de Tocqueville, *Democracy in America*, London: Everyman's Library, 1994, Vol. I, Chapter 18, pp. 363, 394–5.
79. Marx and Engels, *Collected Works*, Vol. 19, p. 14; Vol. 35, p. 305.
80. Ibid., Vol. 20, p. 20.
81. See Domenico Losurdo, *Nietzsche, il ribelle aristocratico. Biografia intellettuale e bilancio critic*, Turin: Bollati Boringhieri, 2002, Chapter 12, §8.
82. Marx and Engels, *Collected Works*, Vol. 19, p. 37.
83. See Richard Slotkin, *The Fatal Environment: The Myth of the Frontier in the Age of Industrialization 1800–1890*, New York: Harper Perennial, 1994, pp. 245–61.
84. Marx and Engels, *Collected Works*, Vol. 20, pp. 19–20.
85. Ibid., Vol. 41, p. 562.
86. Ibid., Vol. 19, p. 229.
87. Alexis de Tocqueville, *Oeuvres complètes*, ed. Jacob-Peter Mayer, Paris: Gallimard, 1951–, Vol. 6, part 1, p. 58.
88. Ibid., Vol. 4, part 1, pp. 271–2.
89. Gustave Le Bon, *The Crowd: A Study of the Popular Mind*, New York: Dover Publications, 2002, pp. 13, 25.
90. In this section, I have summarized analyses elaborated in one of my earlier books, to which readers are referred for more detailed documentation: see Losurdo, *Liberalism*, Chapter 8, §2 (for J.S. Mill), §6 (for the contrast between French and Anglo-Saxons, in particular in Tocqueville), §8 (for Tocqueville's denunciation of the influx into the USA of immigrants 'foreign to the English race'), §10 (for Gobineau and Disraeli).
91. Friedrich Nietzsche, *The Birth of Tragedy*, ed. Michael Tanner and trans. Shaun Whiteside, London: Penguin, 1993, p. 87.
92. Jeremy Bentham, *The Works*, ed. John Bowring, Edinburgh: Tait, 1838–43, Vol. 1, p. 309.
93. Marx and Engels, *Collected Works*, Vol. 16, pp. 517, 16.
94. Ibid., Vol. 35, Part VIII, Chapter 31.

95. Ibid., Vol. 11, pp. 111, 149, 157.
96. Ibid., Vol. 22, p. 269.
97. Ibid., Vol. 10, p. 333.
98. Ibid., Vol. 4, pp. 364, 390, 559–60.
99. Ibid., Vol. 12, pp. 158–9.
100. Ibid., Vol. 16, p. 489.
101. Thomas Carlyle, *Latter-Day Pamphlets*, ed. M.K. Goldberg and J.P. Seigel, Ottawa: Canadian Federation for the Humanities, 1983, pp. 463–5.
102. Marx and Engels, *Collected Works*, Vol. 43, pp. 474–5.
103. Ibid., Vol. 10, p. 254.
104. Ibid., Vol. 10, p. 251.
105. Ibid., Vol. 10, pp. 256, 301.
106. Tocqueville, *Oeuvres complètes*, Vol. 13, pt. 2, p. 337; Vol. 2, pt. 2, p. 337.
107. Marx and Engels, *Collected Works*, Vol. 11, p. 5.
108. Friedrich Nietzsche, *Twilight of the Idols and The Anti-Christ*, ed. Michael Tanner and trans. R.J. Hollingdale, London: Penguin, 1990, p. 123.
109. See Losurdo, *Nietzsche, il ribelle aristocratico*, Chapter 28, §2.
110. Marx and Engels, *Collected Works*, Vol. 48, p. 266.
111. Ibid., Vol. 26, p. 302.
112. Ibid., Vol. 20, p. 197.
113. Ibid., Vol. 3, p. 175.
114. Fréderic II Roi de Prusse, *Oeuvres posthumes*, Vol. 20, *Correspondance de Monsieur D'Alembert avec Fréderic II Roi de Prusse*, Berlin, 1791, pp. 169–70.
115. John Locke, *Political Writings*, ed. David Wooton, London and New York: Penguin, 1993, p. 203; *The Reasonableness of Christianity as Delivered in the Scriptures*, London: Rivington, 1824, p. 135.
116. Locke, *Political Writings*, p. 202.
117. Marx and Engels, *Collected Works*, Vol. 4, p. 560.
118. Marx, *Manuskripte über die polnische Frage (1863–4)*, p. 108.
119. Ibid., Vol. 20, p. 160.
120. Ibid., Vol. 43, pp. 206, 214.
121. Ibid., Vol. 19, pp. 233–4.
122. See Losurdo, *Liberalism*, Chapter 5, §11.
123. Marx and Engels, *Collected Works*, Vol. 13, p. 403.
124. Ibid., Vol. 10, p. 399.
125. Ibid., Vol. 27, pp. 523–4.
126. See Losurdo, *Nietzsche, il ribelle aristocratico*, Chapters 7–8 and Chapter 28, §4.
127. Marx and Engels, *Collected Works*, Vol. 1, pp. 205–6.
128. Ibid., Vol. 47, p. 357.
129. Ibid., Vol. 48, pp. 167–8.
130. Ibid., Vol. 10, pp. 243–4.

131. Ludwig Feuerbach, 'Die Naturwissenschaft und die Revolution', in *Feuerbach, Antrophologischer Materialismus. Ausgewählte Schriften*, ed. Alfred Schmidt, Frankfurt am Main and Vienna: Europäische Verlagsanstalt, 1967, Vol. 2, pp. 213–14.
132. Marx and Engels, *Collected Works*, Vol. 1, p. 400.
133. See Domenico Losurdo, *Hegel e la Germania. Filosofia e questione nazionale tra rivoluzione e reazione*, Milan: Guerini/Istituto Italiano per gli Studi Filosofici, 1997, Chapter 10, §5.
134. Quoted in Enzensberger (ed.), *Colloqui con Marx*, p. 246.
135. Marx and Engels, *Collected Works*, Vol. 50, p. 134.
136. Ibid., Vol. 5, p. 40.
137. Ibid., Vol. 5, pp. 473, 475.
138. Ibid., Vol. 5, p. 473.
139. Ibid., Vol. 10, p. 245.
140. Ibid., Vol. 3, p. 276.
141. Ibid., Vol. 5, p. 31.
142. Ibid., Vol. 24, p. 81.
143. Ibid., Vol. 35, p. 490.
144. Ibid., Vol. 35, p. 507.
145. Ibid., Vol. 37, p. 613.
146. Ibid., Vol. 21, p. 318.
147. Ibid., Vol. 37, p. 763.
148. Ibid., Vol. 25, p. 461.
149. Ibid., Vol. 4, p. 527.
150. Ibid., Vol. 4, pp. 364, 339.
151. Ibid., Vol. 4, pp. 343, 345.
152. Herbert Spencer, 'The Proper Sphere of Government', in *The Man versus the State*, Indianapolis: Liberty Classics, 1981, p. 244.
153. See Herbert Spencer, *The Principles of Ethics*, 2 vols, ed. T.R. Machan, Indianapolis: Liberty Classics, 1978, Vol. 2, pp. 99–100.
154. Marx and Engels, *Collected Works*, Vol. 6, pp. 484, 504.
155. Ibid., Vol. 26, p. 303.
156. Ibid., Vol. 34, p. 426.
157. Benedetto Croce, Preface to 3rd edition, *Materialismo storico ed economia marxista*, Bari: Laterza, 1973, p. xiv.
158. George L. Mosse, *Fallen Soldiers: Reshaping the Memory of the World Wars*, New York: Oxford University Press, 1994, p. 65.
159. See Domenico Losurdo, *War and Revolution: Rethinking the 20th Century*, London and New York: Verso, 2015, Chapter 3, §3.
160. Karl Popper, *The Open Society and its Enemies*, London and New York: Routledge, 2003, Vol. 2, p. 33.
161. See Domenico Losurdo, *Hegel and the Freedom of the Moderns*, trans. Marella and Jon Morris, Durham, NC: Duke University Press, 2004, Chapter 7 and *passim*.

CHAPTER 3

A Protracted, Positive-Sum Struggle

1   'UNIVERSAL LEVELLING' OR 'GREAT DIVERGENCE'?

The *Communist Manifesto* theorizes class struggle on the basis of an analysis of the bourgeois society that was increasingly becoming established in the West. But had such a view not already been refuted by the disappearance of the *ancien régime*, organized as it was into stable, naturally fixed estates and its replacement by a social order characterized by social mobility? In Tocqueville's view, the advent of industrial, democratic society rendered struggles belonging to a superseded social stage obsolete. *Democracy in America* asserts that 'castes disappear and the classes of society draw together'. In fact, 'so to speak, there are no longer any classes'. At least as regards the West, they belonged to the past; and in any event, societies where 'the members of a community are divided into castes and classes' were destined to fade away.[1]

This was not a prediction formulated solely with a view to the USA—a country without a long feudal past behind it. In fact, we are dealing with a sociological analysis conjoined with a discourse in the philosophy of history. According to the French liberal, from the eleventh century onwards 'a two-fold revolution … in the state of society' had been underway in the West. Indeed, '[t]he noble has gone down the social ladder, and the commoner has gone up; the one descends as the other rises. Every half-century brings them nearer to each other, and they will soon meet'. Everything

© The Editor(s) (if applicable) and The Author(s) 2016
D. Losurdo, *Class Struggle*, Marx, Engels, and Marxisms,
DOI 10.1057/978-1-349-70660-0_3

was working in concert to this end. Now, not only landed wealth but also 'personal property' could 'confer influence and power'. This already served to undermine the privileges and domination of the aristocracy. Along with property in its various forms, 'the exercise of the intellect became a source of strength and of wealth', so that 'every discovery in the arts, every improvement in commerce [and] manufactures, created so many new elements of equality among men'. All the various factors of the modern world 'seemed to co-operate to enrich the poor and impoverish the rich'. In conclusion, the tendency towards 'universal levelling' was irreversible; it could not be blocked or even slowed down, especially given that the wealthy were 'few and powerless' and therefore incapable of mounting effective resistance. There was no doubt that a higher will was presiding over this: 'the gradual development of the principle of equality is ... a providential fact. It has all the chief characteristics of such a fact: it is universal, it is lasting, it constantly eludes all human interference, and all events, as well as all men contribute to its progress'.[2]

The passages I have just cited are from Volumes One and Two of *Democracy in America* and thus date from 1835 and 1840, respectively. In subsequent years, with his focus on France and Britain, Tocqueville drew a significantly different picture: 'equality is gradually extending its dominion everywhere except industry, which is organized in an ever more aristocratic [and hierarchical] form'; a relationship of 'strict dependency' bound the wage worker to the employer. As regards both power relations and the distribution of social wealth, equality was far off: 'the organized forces of a multitude produce for the benefit of one man'. In sum, '[h]ere the slave, there the master; here the wealth of a few, there the poverty of the overwhelming majority'. Lying in wait were 'slave wars'.[3] Initially ignored, the reality of social classes, and social classes ready to square up in a trial of strength, makes its abrupt appearance. Now, it is no longer equality, but precisely inequality, that has been sanctioned by a higher will, as emerges from the polemic against the 'economic and political theories' which would have us 'believe that human misfortunes are the effects of laws and not of Providence and that poverty can be abolished by changing the social order'.[4]

However, publishing the twelfth edition of *Democracy in America* immediately after the 1848 revolution, Tocqueville reiterated the viewpoint expressed 'fifteen years' earlier about the irresistible and providential character of the march of equality in the USA and the West as a whole.[5] But how can the thesis of the impoverishment of the wealthy and enrichment of the poor be reconciled with the warning against social polarization so stark as to elicit fears about the eruption of 'slave wars'? It remains the case that the French liberal refused to query the view that 'universal levelling' was impending in the West. Initially ignored, and then occasionally conceded, the reality of classes and class struggle was now in a sense repressed. In fact, this repression, manifestly prompted by a political concern to cushion and contain the resentment of the subaltern classes, sounds like an involuntary confirmation.

The surviving power of wealth, notwithstanding the eclipse of the *ancien régime*, was also clearly underestimated by J.S. Mill, who in 1861 expressed concern that seems very strange today. He feared that with the extension of the suffrage the 'working classes', much more widespread and numerous in Britain (and Europe) than the USA (at the time still scarcely industrialized), might win an electoral majority and utilize it for the purposes of 'substituting the class ascendancy of the poor for that of the rich'. The government of the 'numerical majority' would end up enacting 'class legislation', in the sense that it would sanction 'collective despotism', or the uncontested power of a majority of the poor over a minority of the wealthy.[6] To avert this danger, Mill recommended plural voting by those deemed more intelligent and those who performed more demanding tasks—for example, entrepreneurs. This would enable the rich to preserve a presence, albeit an exiguous one, in representative bodies. The English liberal reached the same conclusion as Tocqueville: the wealthy person was now isolated and impotent. Hence, the class struggle of the proletariat was either superfluous or a harbinger of disaster.

Although entangling himself in serious contradictions, Tocqueville prophesied the advent of 'universal levelling' in the West. At the same time, he registered and rejoiced at the gulf being created between the West and the rest of the world. The relationship that made 'a few million men'—Westerners—'the rulers of their whole species' was 'manifestly preordained in the provisions of Providence'.[7] Similarly, while he cautioned against a process of democratization so far advanced in the West as to condemn wealth to isolation and impotence, Mill celebrated the 'vigorous despotism' exercised internationally by the West (and its dominant classes). Far from being negative, this relationship of extreme inequality must be extended to embrace the whole globe; 'it is already common, and is rapidly tending to become the universal, condition of the more backward populations, to be held ... in direct subjection by the more advanced'.[8]

The extremely unequal relationship prevailing internationally did not only concern the distribution of political and military power. Tocqueville wrote: 'the discovery of America opened a thousand new paths to fortune and led obscure adventurers to wealth and power'.[9] The same motivation might impel French citizens to transfer to the colonies and, in particular, Algeria: 'to get inhabitants to come to such a country, it is first of all necessary to offer them great opportunities to make their fortune'; 'the most fertile and best irrigated land' must be reserved for them.[10] In this way, colonial expansion (in America and Algeria) generated remarkable social mobility, opening up access to wealth even to individuals of popular extraction, thereby confirming the process of 'universal levelling'. But this was only one side of the coin. It was the French liberal himself who acknowledged that as a result of the process of colonization, the Arab population in Algeria was 'literally dying of hunger' while the Native Americans were on the point of being wiped off the face of the earth.[11] That is, if it reduced inequalities in the metropolis and within the white community, the enrichment of 'adventurers' and colonists created an ever wider gulf between conquistadors and subject peoples. Constantly, and exclusively, adopting the standpoint of the 'Christian world' or the West, Tocqueville did not appreciate the nexus between these contradictory aspects of a single phenomenon and was never induced to problematize his view of the irresistible march of equality of conditions and the disappearance not only of 'castes', but also of 'classes'.

The *Communist Manifesto* seems to answer the two liberal authors: 'the modern bourgeois society that has sprouted from the ruins of feudal society has not done away with class antagonisms. It has but established new classes, new conditions of oppression, new forms of struggle in place of the old ones'.[12] Indeed, with voting rights having been obtained by the popular masses and the abolition of censitary discrimination, wealth lost its immediate political significance, but could henceforth precisely celebrate its triumph: mass poverty now pertained to a private sphere where public power had no right to intervene. This was a triumph which the capitalist bourgeoisie could also celebrate internationally, giving impetus to colonial expansion and enslaving and decimating entire populations.

By way of confirmation of the irresistible tendency to 'universal levelling' and equality between 'commoner' and 'noble', Tocqueville asserted that 'literature became an arsenal open to all'.[13] *The German Ideology* argues very differently: 'the class which has the means of material production at its disposal, consequently also controls the means of mental production, so that the ideas of those who lack the means of mental production are on the whole subject to it'.[14]

Far from being synonymous with 'universal levelling', the bourgeois revolution involved the accentuation of inequalities at many levels. Internationally, what has been called the 'great divergence' between the prosperous West and the rest of the planet derived from it.[15] In 1820 China, for centuries or millennia eminently placed in the development of human civilization, still boasted a GDP amounting to 32.4 % of the world GDP, while 'Chinese life expectancy (and thus nutrition) was at roughly English levels (and so above Continental ones) even in the late 1700s. At the time of its foundation, the People's Republic of China was the poorest country in the world or among the poorest. The history of India is not very different. In 1820, it still accounted for 15.7 % of global GDP, before likewise succumbing to desperate poverty.[16] This is a process that can be understood starting from Marx (and the section of *Capital* devoted to 'primitive accumulation'), but which is far beyond the range of Tocqueville, who tended to offer an apologetic description of the world he inhabited.

In any event, far from rendering class struggle obsolete through 'universal levelling', bourgeois society aggravates national and international inequalities, which can only be contested through class struggle.

2 OBSOLESCENCE OF WAR?

With the advent of industrial democracy, is the phenomenon of war destined to disappear along with class struggle? Kant's hopes that the end of the *ancien régime* and the patrimonial conception of the state would lead to an international order marked by peace were dashed by the post-Thermidorian and Napoleonic Wars. But they seemed to enjoy a new lease of life after the July Revolution, with the fading of the antagonism between France and Britain and the consolidation of the Pax Britannica. This is the context in which to locate Tocqueville's thesis that modern democratic society lacks the objective basis for war, even if the ambition of military men of modest social origin, eager to forge a career by distinguishing themselves on the battlefield, invariably played a role.[17] Other authors, rather than assigning it to the representative regime, entrusted the realization of the ideal of perpetual peace to the development of industrial and commercial society. The world market supposedly rendered state and national borders less significant and bound peoples in ever closer, ultimately indissoluble links of interest, mutual respect, and friendship. Such was the argument of Benjamin Constant and, above all, Herbert Spencer.

At times, the *Communist Manifesto* betrays the influence of this discourse: '[n]ational differences and antagonisms are daily more and more vanishing, owing to the development of the bourgeoisie, to freedom of commerce, to the world market, to uniformity in the mode of production and in the conditions of life corresponding thereto'. It seems to attest to a waning of the phenomenon of war in the wake of the development of capitalism, without having to wait for communism: '[i]n proportion as the antagonism between classes within the nation vanishes, the hostility of one nation to another will come to an end'.[18] On the other hand, it is the *Manifesto* which, as we know, rejects the harmonious vision of what would today be called the process of globalization.

A similar oscillation runs through a speech made by Marx in Brussels in January 1848. Free trade '[tears] down the few national barriers which still restrict the free development of capital', leaving space for nothing but the 'antagonism of proletariat and bourgeoisie', which paves the way for the 'social revolution'.[19] However, the same speech contains the assertion that free trade accentuates contradictions internationally as well:

> We have shown what sort of fraternity Free Trade begets between the different classes of one and the same nation. The fraternity which Free Trade would establish between the nations of the earth would not be more real[;] to call cosmopolitan exploitation universal brotherhood is an idea that could only be engendered in the brain of the bourgeoisie.[20]

This became Marx and Engels' settled view. Only a few months later, the *Neue Rheinische Zeitung* criticized Arnold Ruge for not having understood that the phenomenon of war did not, in fact, disappear with the feudal regime. Rather than being 'natural allies', countries, where the bourgeoisie was dominant were divided by ruthless competition, the outcome of which could be war.[21] Such competition also aimed at despoliation of colonial peoples. Notwithstanding Spencer's contrary opinion, the advent of industrial capitalist society did not betoken the disappearance of war as a tool of enrichment. It sufficed to glance at 'piratical wars' and 'piratical expeditions against China, Cochin-China, and so forth'.[22]

Far from being synonymous with peaceful development, *Capital* subsequently stressed, the capitalist system involved 'brute force'. Conjoined with wars (of enslavement and even extermination) against 'barbarians' were rivalry and conflict in the 'civilized world' between the great powers, who were the protagonists and beneficiaries of colonial expansion and despoliation. Overall, what characterized capitalism was 'the commercial war of the European nations, with the globe for a theatre'. It 'begins with the revolt of the Netherlands from Spain, assumes giant dimension in England's Anti-Jacobin War, and is still going on in the opium wars against China, etc'.[23] The 'commercial war of the European nations' recalls the 'industrial war of extermination between nations' alluded to by the *Manifesto*. In any event, the historical period from the emergence of Holland (the first country to shake off the yoke of the *ancien régime*) to the rise of liberal (and imperial) Great Britain was quite the reverse of a prelude to the advent of perpetual peace.

For war to be eradicated, it was not enough for one exploiting class to replace another, as in the bourgeois revolution: the system of exploitation and oppression, domestic and global, must be eliminated in its entirety. This is the sense in which, in July 1870, taking a position on the Franco-German war that had just broken out, a text written by Marx for the International Working Men's Association called for a struggle for 'a new society ... whose International rule will be *Peace*, because its national ruler will everywhere be the same—*Labour*!'.[24]

This analysis is virtually contemporaneous with that of J.S. Mill, who celebrated the British Empire as 'a step ... towards universal peace, and general friendly co-operation among nations'. In support of this thesis, a peculiar argument is advanced. The gigantic (albeit 'unequal') 'federation' that was the British Empire embodied the cause of 'liberty' and international 'morality' to a greater extent 'than any other great nation seems to conceive as possible or recognise as desirable'. Hence, backward populations had an interest in becoming part of it, so as to avoid 'being absorbed into a foreign state, and becoming a source of additional aggressive strength to some rival power'.[25] Homage to 'universal peace' fails to conceal the reality of colonial wars, set to 'absorb' this or that colony, and the rivalry which was a harbinger of larger-scale wars between Great Britain, celebrated as the embodiment of the cause of peace, and 'some rival power', suspected of the worrying design of seeking to enhance its 'aggressive strength'.

While Mill sought to demonstrate the disappearance of war on the basis of the imperialist rivalry actually priming it, Tocqueville, in the very title of a key chapter of Volume Two of *Democracy in America*, claimed that

'Great Revolutions Will Become More Rare'. In the event, the century and a half since such predictions were ventured represent what is perhaps the historical period richest in wars and revolutions. And now let us read Marx. A few years after the publication of the text just cited, in a letter of 28 December 1846, starting from 'the conflict between the productive forces already acquired by man, and his social relations, which no longer correspond to those productive forces', he evoked 'the terrible wars now imminent between the various classes of a nation and between the various nations'.[26] Shortly thereafter, the *Communist Manifesto* discerned on the horizon either proletarian revolutions (or 'bourgeois revolutions' liable to be transformed into 'proletarian revolutions'), or 'agrarian revolutions' as a precondition of 'national emancipation',[27] against an order that exuded violence not only because it was based on social and national oppression, but also because it secreted the danger of competition between the various capitalist bourgeoisies issuing in a catastrophic confrontation. On the basis of the theory of class struggle, Marx was in a sense able to foresee the upheavals of the twentieth century.

3 An Eternal Conflict between Masters and Slaves?

Adequately to understand Marx's theory of class struggle, it is not enough to distinguish it from the thesis of those who regard the end of the *ancien régime* as the start of the disappearance, or dramatic reduction, of socio-political conflict at home and abroad. In a famous letter of 5 March 1852, Marx observed: 'as for myself, I do not claim to have discovered either the existence of classes in modern society or the struggle between them'. In their different ways, bourgeois historians and economists had spoken of it long before him. The true novelty of historical materialism lay in its assertion of the historically determinate and transient character of societies based on class struggle and class domination.[28]

The date is the mid-nineteenth century. In the light of subsequent developments, we might undertake a comparison with other authors. While the *Communist Manifesto* referred to 'class struggles', Nietzsche likewise saw a 'struggle between estates and classes' (*Stände- und Classenkampf*) unfolding in history.[29] While the authors of the *Manifesto* repeatedly compared and juxtaposed modern wage slavery with black slavery, on several occasions both Nietzsche and, across the Atlantic, the ideologues of the slave-holding South argued in a similar vein, with a view to demonstrating the inanity of the abolitionist project. If, in Marx and Engels' view, capitalist society had substituted modern slavery for mediaeval serfdom, which had in its time supplanted the slavery proper of classical antiquity, for Nietzsche in Europe and the southern ideologues in the USA the servile subjection of labour was an essential, ineliminable foundation of civilization. In the words of arguably the most illustrious of them, John C. Calhoun, 'I hold then, that there never has yet existed a wealthy and civilized society in which one portion of the community did not, in point of fact, live on the labor of the other.... There is and always has been, in an advanced stage of wealth and civilization, a conflict between labor and capital'.[30]

'Struggle between estates and classes'; the permanence of 'slavery' even in a social order that has formally abolished it; 'conflict between labour and capital'—the conceptual analogies do not stop there. In Nietzsche, we find two more key categories of Marxian discourse. He refers to the 'surplus labour' (*Mehrarbeit*) extracted from slaves and workers, who are thereby subject to 'exploitation' (*Ausbeutung*).[31] Where, then, are the differences?

In the theorist of 'aristocratic radicalism', the extortion of 'surplus labour' and 'exploitation' are the expression of a general, irrepressible tendency of natural and social reality, of life as such. It should be added that in Marx and Engels not only can slavery in all its forms be overcome, but these forms are not equivalent. Already in an early writing (*The Holy Family*), they criticized the Jacobins for having confused the 'real slavery' (*wirkliches Sklaventum*) of the ancient world with the 'emancipated slavery' (*emanzipiertes Sklaventum*) of the modern world.[32] The adjective certainly does not cancel the substantive and yet is not devoid of significance either. We subsequently saw *The Poverty of Philosophy* denouncing the as it were masked slavery prevalent in Europe. The 'mask' referred to here is like the 'appearance' (*Schein*) referred to in Hegel's logic,[33] which expresses a level of reality, albeit a superficial one.

We can now understand why, on the outbreak of the American Civil War, Marx and Engels took a clear position in favour of the Union. From the outset they urged it to wage a revolutionary war against the South to abolish black slavery. And yet in the North the slavery to which wage-labour was subjected was alive and well—the slavery to which *Capital*, taking up the Declaration of the General Congress of Labour at Baltimore, defined as 'capitalistic slavery'.[34] The fact is that the 'indirect slavery' (*indirekte Sklaverei*) of whites in Britain was not the same thing as the 'direct slavery [*direkte Sklaverei*] of the black men on the other side of the

Atlantic'.[35] The 'direct forced labour' imposed on the slave could not be equated with the indirect economic coercion to which the wage worker, the at least formally 'free labourer', was subject.[36] In fact, when the Civil War exploded in the USA, and there was no shortage of sympathizers with the South in Europe, Marx was concerned to avoid any ambiguity. Shelving traditional denunciation of the 'indirect slavery' inherent in the capitalist system, he repeatedly called for a struggle to defend 'the system of free labour' against 'the system of slavery'.[37]

Certainly, Engels observed in 1885, with the end of the Civil War an attempt was made to replace 'open Negro slavery'(formally abolished) with the 'disguised slavery of Indian and Chinese coolies'.[38] Here, in the context of a discussion of the slavery affecting labour to different degrees, we find a dual differentiation. On the one hand, there is a distinction between 'open' and 'disguised' forms of slavery, respectively imposed on blacks and Indians and Chinese, but always on colonial populations or populations with colonial origins. On the other, in the capitalist metropolis, the struggle for the reduction and regulation of the working day seemed to have attenuated what remained slave-like in the condition of labour in capitalist society, and be capable of further attenuating it.

Hence, in Nietzsche (as in Calhoun) we can indeed find key categories of Marx's discourse. In the latter, however, analysis of the conflict between capital and labour is a history of the progressive emancipation of labour which, albeit partially, does occur and which it is possible to achieve through class struggle in the framework of existing society. In Nietzsche, by contrast, the conflict is schematically reduced—sometimes in a heavily naturalistically sense, outside any concrete historical dialectic—to the antagonism eternally pitting masters and slaves against one another. Consequently, the class struggle of those who are subject to slavery in its ancient or modern, open or disguised, form—the revolt of a 'barbaric caste of slaves'—cannot accomplish any real emancipation, but only mean disaster for civilization.

4 The Proletariat, Class Interest, and its Transcendence

In Marx and Engels, not only is there no eternal clash between masters and slaves, but the latter, definitively abolishing social relations based on domination and exploitation, create an order which, from a strategic perspective, yields richer, more fulfilling forms of existence for the ex-masters as well.

Let us first see what happens to the development of the productive forces. By terminating the crises of the over-production characteristic of bourgeois society, the socialist revolution promotes the development of the productive forces. The proletarian is the first, most direct beneficiary of the supersession of a system that seeks to transform him or her into an 'ascetic but productive slave'.[39] But she is not the sole beneficiary of the overall growth in social wealth.

Of particular importance is what occurs intellectually and morally. The *Economic and Philosophical Manuscripts* of 1844 stress that the capitalist system involves the dehumanization of the agents of the exploitation of labour: '[p]roduction does not simply produce man as a commodity, the human commodity, man in the role of commodity; it produces him in keeping with this role as a *mentally* and physically *dehumanised* being.— Immorality, deformity, and dulling of the workers and capitalists'.[40] Along with the exploited, the process of stupefaction and commodification ends up engulfing the exploiters themselves. This is a thesis reiterated in *The Holy Family*:

> The propertied class and the class of the proletariat present the same human self-estrangement. But the former class feels at ease and strengthened in this self-estrangement, it recognises estrangement as *its own power* and has in it the *semblance* of a human existence. The latter feels annihilated in estrangement; it sees in it its own powerlessness and the reality of an inhuman existence.[41]

Although primarily and especially afflicting the worker, who 'is less than a human being to the bourgeois', and who is exploited and 'used as mere material, a mere chattel', the processes of impoverishment of social relations and reification invest capitalist society as a whole: 'people regard each other only as useful objects'.[42] No one—not even the bourgeois—is spared.

It is not a thesis restricted to the early works. In describing the horror of primitive capitalist accumulation, *Capital* invites readers 'to see what the bourgeoisie makes of itself and of the labourer, wherever it can, without restraint, model the world after its own image'.[43] The capitalist master 'is rooted in that alienation process and finds in it his absolute satisfaction, whereas the worker, as its victim, stands from the outset in a relation of rebellion towards it and perceives it as a process of enslavement' (*Knechtungsproceß*).[44] Once victory has been obtained, however, the workers' 'rebellion' ends up liberating the capitalist boss himself from alienation.

This also applies to individual reforms imposed by the workers' class struggle in bourgeois society. In some respects, the reduction of the working day may prove beneficial for those who do everything in their power to prevent it. Let us read *Capital*: '[w]ith suppressed irony, and in very well weighed words, the Factory Inspectors hint that the actual law also frees the capitalist from some of the brutality natural to a man who is a mere embodiment of capital, and that it has given him time for a little "culture"'.[45] In other words, if the proletariat has a material interest, as well as an intellectual and moral one, in overthrowing capitalist class rule, individuals and sections of the exploiting class itself could develop an intellectual and moral interest in being rid of the existing order. This is a point stressed above all by Engels, who was himself a 'capitalist'. To be precise, he suggested that the more farsighted bourgeois could have an interest in the transformation of society that goes beyond the intellectual and moral level proper. Take the consequences in England of the terrible degradation of working-class and popular districts, which were structured like ghettos. Attempts were made 'to conceal from the eyes of the wealthy men and women of strong stomachs and weak nerves the misery and grime which form the complement of their wealth'. But however sophisticated this 'hypocritical plan', this 'shameful method of construction', it could not erase the disfigurement of the urban landscape, which remained an eyesore for everyone.[46]

Working-class and popular districts-ghettos were also repugnant when it came to hygiene and hence, were liable to epidemics. With the spread of cholera in Manchester, 'a universal terror seized the bourgeoisie of the city. People remembered the unwholesome dwellings of the poor, and trembled before the certainty that each of these slums would become a centre for the plague, whence it would spread desolation in all directions through the houses of the propertied classes'.[47] Although reserving its most serious consequences for the workers massed and confined in factories and unhealthy districts, the logic of capitalist profit wreaked general devastation.

This also applied to other aspects of social existence. No one should be indifferent to the polarization of wealth and poverty inherent in bourgeois society. It was the source of 'the social war, the war of each against all' and general insecurity, which placed 'every man's house in a state of siege'.[48] In this case too, the existing social order involved negative consequences for the dominant class itself.

But to what extent could individual members of the capitalist bourgeoisie be held responsible? Having drawn attention to the ruinous consequences for the proletariat of the unbridled hunt for 'profit' ('premature death', 'torture of overwork', etc.), *Capital* feels the need to add: 'looking at things as a whole, all this does not, indeed, depend on the good or ill will of the individual capitalist. Free competition brings out the inherent laws of capitalist production, in the shape of "external coercive laws" having power over every individual capitalist'.[49] While it mainly impacted upon the proletarian, the 'relation of compulsion' between capital and labour did not spare the individual capitalist, likewise subject to a 'coercive law' imposed on him from without.[50] He was 'but one of the wheels ... of the social mechanism'.[51] Going yet further, the young Engels wrote that socialism/communism applies the principle of 'the irresponsibility of the individual' when analysing the modus operandi of the social order. For this very reason, 'the more the English workers absorb communistic ideas, the more superfluous becomes their present bitterness' towards their oppressors as individuals (with a commensurate reduction in the violent charge of the anti-capitalist revolution).[52]

For Marx and Engels it was a question of abolishing not only class exploitation in a single country, but also national oppression. And we once again encounter the base line with which we are already familiar: while they primarily and directly addressed the oppressed, they not only called upon the proletariat of the oppressor country not to make common cause with the privileged classes, but did not even close the door to the most enlightened members of those classes. We shall find the thesis that a people which oppresses another people is not free repeatedly formulated. Like the 'social war' inside a country, *a fortiori* the latent or open state of war between peoples induces a more or less general 'state of emergency' and hence, a restriction of liberty for the oppressor too.

So it is the overwhelming majority of humanity that has an interest in the impending social revolution. The sections and members of the exploiting class and oppressor nation most inclined to theoretical study and moral reflection are invited not to lose sight of the grave practical drawbacks and general human devastation created by the social system, of which they are nevertheless beneficiaries in immediate material terms. Being a communist certainly means appealing to the class struggle waged by the oppressed (internationally, nationally, and within the family). But it also means having developed the capacity to see things in the round. In this sense, the young Engels asserted that '[c]ommunism stands above the strife between bourgeoisie and proletariat' and thus was different from 'purely proletarian Chartism', which contained residues of corporatism.[53]

5 Marx 'against' Nietzsche (and Foucault)

Something remarkable has emerged: on the one hand, there is no escaping the class struggle; on the other, it has a tendency to transcend itself, pursuing and realizing objectives liable to be universally welcomed. How is this possible? The authors of the *Communist Manifesto* evinced an ethos of reason and science throughout their careers: 'truth is general, it does not belong to me alone, it belongs to all, it owns me'.[54] When he expressed himself thus, in manifestly Hegelian accents, Marx was only 24 years old, but he remained loyal to this view to the end. *Capital* forcefully asserts that the 'outward appearance' or 'delusive appearance' of a phenomenon does not coincide with its 'essence'; and hence, a prolonged, laborious intellectual engagement was required to achieve 'science', 'scientific truth'.[55]

Has conflict disappeared? That is not the point. The ethos of reason and scientific truth does not prevent Marx from stressing that in bourgeois society science is pressed into 'the service of capital'. The history and critique of 'the capitalist employment of machinery' in *Capital* are precisely the history and critique of the capitalist use of science.[56] In 1854, Engels declared that he sought to respect 'the principle that military science, like mathematics or geography, has no particular political opinion'.[57] Obviously, in saying this, he was not unaware that 'military science' played a key role in the class struggle, be it in wars between opposed capitalist bourgeoisies or civil wars and colonial wars. But those capable of analysing and evaluating the logic, internal consistency and efficacy of the various sciences could also condemn their utilization in the service of capitalism and colonialism (or other causes).

This is a discourse that does not only hold good for the applied sciences. As is clear from their critique of what I have characterized as court Enlightenment, Marx and Engels were perfectly well aware that reason and the light of reason can be employed to justify domination and oppression. However, this can be highlighted and refuted only through a new, more cogent and compelling recourse to reason and the light of reason. In other words, we are dealing with a critique of Enlightenment very different from that which has found expression in our day in Hans-Georg Gadamer. He writes: 'the fundamental prejudice of the Enlightenment is the prejudice against prejudice itself, which denies tradition its power'.[58] In this way, Gadamer equates two very different attitudes. Appealing to reason and submitting to its control, Enlightenment 'prejudice' is capable of challenging itself; not so anti-Enlightenment prejudice. Reason can understand what is rational in prejudice and how much prejudice there is in the historically and socially determinate forms taken by reason. Prejudice is incapable of an analogous operation: it refuses to submit itself, and the tradition to which it pertains, to the authority of reason.

While for Gadamer everything is affected by 'prejudice', for Nietzsche everything is profoundly marked by conflict. No cultural expression can claim an even relative and partial autonomy. Take the science of physics: the attempt to discover in nature regularity, law, equality, the alleged 'conformity of nature to law', goes hand in hand with alleged 'equality before the law' (which governs the judicial order deriving from the fall of the *ancien régime*). This is 'a nice example of ulterior motives, disguising once again the plebeian hostility against everything privileged and aristocratic'. Ultimately, to cry 'long live natural law!' in the manner of physicists, is merely another way of crying '*Ni Dieu, ni maître*', in the manner of anarchists. Indeed, modernity and the reason cherished by it are characterized by 'resistance to every special claim, special right and privilege'.[59]

The interpretation of philosophical and scientific arguments in an anti-aristocratic key is thus not as new as it might first seem. Let us glance at the intellectual tradition behind Marx. It was Kant who noted that 'rigorous universality', peculiar to reason, precluded 'any exception'.[60] In his turn, Hegel asserted that philosophy, '*as the science of reason*, on account of the universal mode of its being and in accordance with its nature, is a science for everyone'.[61] Granted the different (opposite) value judgement, Nietzsche concurred with this thesis. He was not wrong to stress that the 'syllogism' dear to Socrates is apparently merely a formal rule of discourse that does not pursue particular political objectives. In reality, however, inherent in recourse to the 'syllogism', to logical-rational discourse in which all human beings can participate, and which is thereby distinguished from the esoteric, aristocratic revelation of a sapient truth, is the lethal plebeian 'knife-thrust'.[62] That is to say, the 'syllogism', or logical-rational discourse, is not politically more pure than sapient discourse. A comparison of these two types of discourse yields the same result as emerged from the contrast between two different types of 'prejudice' (Enlightenment and anti-Enlightenment): logical-rational discourse is capable of refuting itself and understanding what might be valid in another kind of discourse; sapient discourse is incapable of any such operation. Not coincidentally, in order to measure up to Socrates polemically, Nietzsche lapses into a performative contradiction. He seeks to demonstrate the beneficent character of aristocratic privilege by himself resorting to logical argument, which by definition places all interlocutors on the same level and excludes any privilege. Availing himself of logical-rational arguments, the champion of 'aristocratic radicalism' in a sense discredits sapient discourse and makes the plebeian 'knife-thrust' he condemns in Socrates.

If Nietzsche runs into a blatant performative contradiction, how can Marx and Engels combine an ethos of class struggle with an ethos of reason and science? Reason can certainly be employed to justify privilege, domination and oppression. Yet, as Nietzsche recognizes, inherent in it is the tendency to assert relations of equality, and hence, to delegitimize privilege, domination, and oppression. Emancipatory class struggle and reason have a tendency to converge.

In addition, far from being the eternal clash between masters and slaves referred to by Nietzsche and Calhoun, class struggle involves constant developments and mutations. The result of this is what might be defined as processes of objectification. Although manifestly 'bound up with certain forms of social development' (observes Marx), 'Greek art and epic poetry … still give us aesthetic pleasure and are in certain respects regarded as a standard and unattainable model'.[63] The political and social conflicts that inspired these masterpieces are now in the past. Not only does aesthetic enjoyment remain, however, but men and women from the most diverse social backgrounds and political positions partake of it or tend to. A process of objectification has occurred.

This does not apply only to art. The Ptolemaic vision of the universe was refuted and defeated during a bitter ideological confrontation. Yet even the heirs of those who condemned Galileo some centuries ago wound up identifying with heliocentrism. What has just been observed of the Ptolemaic system might easily be extended to the so-called 'Donation of Constantine'. The alleged testament of the Roman Emperor, which legitimized the temporal power of the Catholic Church, is no longer taken seriously even by those most loyal to the Catholic Church. We might argue in similar fashion for the Socratic syllogism and science of physics targeted by Nietzsche. In our day, however aristocratic, and however great its admiration for the philosopher of 'aristocratic radicalism', a political movement or government may affect an air of superiority towards the plebeianism of the syllogism, but it will find it difficult to banish physical science as anarchical. We might sum up Marx's viewpoint thus: everything is prey to conflict, but not in the same way and, in any event, not in a way that is immutable over time.

However, we must go further if we wish to understand the relationship between reason and power established by the champion of 'aristocratic radicalism', on the one hand, and the theorist of emancipatory class struggle, on the other. Over and above reason, the former sought to challenge the concept of man as such. There is not, and cannot be, a community of the concept and reason because there is not, and cannot be, a human community in the true sense. The condemnation of the plebeianism inherent in logical science, as in physical science, goes hand in hand in Nietzsche with a nominalist deconstruction of the universal concept of man, with a critique of 'the bloodless abstraction "man"', that 'general pale fiction',[64] with affirmation of the thesis that 'most are *no one*', and cannot be subsumed under the category of man or the individual, given that they are 'bearers, tools of transmission', exactly like Aristotle's slaves.[65] The opposite is true for Marx: the ethos of the community of the concept and reason goes hand in hand with the ethos of human community, which is the inspiration for emancipatory class struggle.

Those (one thinks particularly of Michel Foucault) who have discovered a more radical critique of domination in Nietzsche than Marx, who supposedly stopped half-way, as demonstrated by his genuflection to reason and science, argue in mistaken and misleading fashion. In reality, in the theorist of aristocratic radicalism, the non-transcendability of conflict through reason ultimately refers to the irreparable naturalistic rift splitting the human community into masters and slaves, successes and failures.

Marx and Engels' attitude to the relationship between class struggle and reason proves all the more persuasive if we glance at the history of the political movement inspired by them. In the course of that history, prompted by horror at the carnage of the First World War and the need to break radically with the past, a kind of spontaneous Foucaultianism *avant la lettre* emerged, which set off in search of power relations to unmask and condemn in any and every context. The result was far from positive. The direct identification of reason with domination encouraged the emergence of a hermeneutic of universal suspicion and greatly compromised the space of inter-subjective communication. Ignoring its argumentative basis and logical structure, it interpreted any proposition as an expression of class struggle. Furthermore, the construction of post-capitalist society was rendered even more difficult by a 'microphysics of power' that denounced the advent of new forms of power and domination in the regulation of any relationship or institution, in the judicial order as such. This basically anarchistic attitude created an enormous void, without rules, which could only be filled by direct violence and the indefinite continuation of the direct violence contained in the revolution.

Notes

1. Alexis de Tocqueville, *Democracy in America*, London: Everyman's Library, 1994, Vol. 2, pp. 32, 4, 282 n.
2. Ibid., Vol. 1, pp. 5–6; Vol. 2, p. 252.
3. Alexis de Tocqueville, *Oeuvres complètes*, ed. Jacob-Peter Mayer, Paris: Gallimard, 1951–, Vol. 5, pt. 2, pp. 80–82; Vol. 3, pt. 2, p. 727.
4. Ibid., Vol. 12, pp. 92–4, 84.
5. Tocqueville, *Democracy in America*, Vol. 1, p. lxiii.
6. John Stuart Mill, *Utilitarianism, Liberty, Representative Government*, ed. Harry B. Acton, London: Dent, 1972, p. 269.
7. Tocqueville, *Oeuvres complètes*, Vol. 9, pp. 243–4.
8. Mill, *Utilitarianism, Liberty, Representative Government*, p. 382.
9. Tocqueville, *Democracy in America*, Vol. 1, p. 6.
10. Tocqueville, *Oeuvres complètes*, Vol. 3, pt. 1, pp. 259, 321–2.
11. Ibid., Vol. 15, pt. 1, pp. 224–5; *Democracy in America*, Vol. 1, pp. 339, 355.
12. Karl Marx and Frederick Engels, *Collected Works*, London: Lawrence & Wishart, 1975–2004, Vol. 6, p. 485.
13. Tocqueville, *Democracy in America*, Vol. 1, p. 5.
14. Marx and Engels, *Collected Works*, Vol. 5, p. 59.
15. See Kenneth Pomeranz, *The Great Divergence: China, Europe, and the Making of the Modern World Economy*, Princeton and Woodstock: Princeton University Press, 2000.
16. Mike Davis, *Late Victorian Holocausts: El Nino Famines and the Making of the Third World*, London and New York: Verso, 2001, p. 293.
17. Tocqueville, *Democracy in America*, Vol. 2, p. 264ff.
18. Marx and Engels, *Collected Works*, Vol. 6, p. 503.
19. Ibid., Vol. 6, pp. 463, 465.
20. Ibid., Vol. 6, p. 464.
21. Ibid., Vol. 7, pp. 372–6.
22. Ibid., Vol. 20, p. 13; Vol. 19, p. 30.
23. Ibid., Vol. 35, p. 739.
24. Ibid., Vol. 22, p. 7.
25. Mill, *Utilitarianism, Liberty, Representative Government*, p. 380.
26. Marx and Engels, *Collected Works*, Vol. 38, p. 103.
27. Ibid., Vol. 6, pp. 518–19.
28. Ibid., Vol. 39, pp. 62, 65.
29. Friedrich Nietzsche, *Sämtliche Werke, Kritische Studienausgabe*, ed., Giorgio Colli and Mazzino Montinari, Munich: DTV-de Gruyter, 1988, Vol. 12, p. 493.
30. John C. Calhoun, *Union and Liberty*, ed. R.M. Lence, Indianapolis: Liberty Classics, 1992, pp. 474–5.
31. See Domenico Losurdo, *Nietzsche, il ribelle aristocratico. Biografia intellettuale e bilancio critico*, Turin: Bollatti Boringhieri, 2002, Chapter 12, §7 and Chapter 20, §8.

32. Marx and Engels, *Collected Works*, Vol. 4, p. 122.
33. G.W.F. Hegel, *Werke in zwanzig Bänden*, ed. E. Moldenhauer and K.M. Michel, Frankfurt am Main: Suhrkamp, 1969–79, Vol. 6, pp. 17–24.
34. Marx and Engels, *Collected Works*, Vol. 35, p. 305.
35. Ibid., Vol. 19, p. 20.
36. Ibid., Vol. 28, pp. 176, 522.
37. Ibid., Vol. 19, pp. 44, 50.
38. Ibid., Vol. 6, p. 168 n.
39. Ibid., Vol. 3, p. 309.
40. Ibid., Vol. 3, p. 284.
41. Ibid., Vol. 4, p. 36.
42. Ibid., Vol. 4, pp. 420, 355, 329.
43. Ibid., Vol. 35, p. 740 n.
44. Ibid., Vol. 34, p. 399.
45. Ibid., Vol. 35, p. 307 n.
46. Ibid., Vol. 4, pp. 348–9.
47. Ibid., Vol. 4, p. 365.
48. Ibid., Vol. 4, pp. 329–30.
49. Ibid., Vol. 35, pp. 275–6.
50. Ibid., Vol. 34, p. 426.
51. Ibid., Vol. 35, p. 588.
52. Ibid., Vol. 4, p. 582.
53. Ibid., Vol. 4, p. 582.
54. Ibid., Vol. 1, p. 112.
55. Ibid., Vol. 37, p. 804; Vol. 20, p. 127.
56. Ibid., Vol. 35, pp. 366, 444.
57. Ibid., Vol. 39, p. 425.
58. Hans-Georg Gadamer, *Truth and Method*, trans. revised by Joel Weinsheimer and Donald G. Marshall, London and New York: Bloomsbury, 2013, p. 283.
59. Friedrich Nietzsche, 'Beyond Good and Evil', in *Beyond Good and Evil/On the Genealogy of Morality*, trans. Adrian Del Caro, Stanford, CA: Stanford University Press, 2014, 22, pp. 24–5 and 202, p. 98.
60. Immanuel Kant, *Gesammelte Schriften*, ed. Academy of Sciences, Berlin and Leipzig, 1900–, Vol. 3, pp. 28–9.
61. Quoted in Johannes Hoffmeister (ed.), *Dokumente zu Hegels Entwicklung*, Stuttgart: Frommann, 1936, p. 242.
62. Friedrich Nietzsche, *Twilight of the Idols and The Anti-Christ*, ed. Michael Tanner and trans. R.J. Hollingdale, London: Penguin, 1990, p. 42.
63. Marx and Engels, *Collected Works*, Vol. 28, p. 47.
64. Friedrich Nietzsche, *Daybreak: Thoughts on the Prejudices of Morality*, ed. Maudemarie Clark and Brian Leiter, Cambridge: Cambridge University Press, 1997, p. 106.
65. Friedrich Nietzsche, *Sämtliche Werke*, Vol. 12, p. 492.

CHAPTER 4

Class Struggles and Struggles for Recognition

1 REDISTRIBUTION OR RECOGNITION?

Emancipatory class struggle tends to transcend the interests of the exploited and oppressed who engage in it. In view of this, the thesis that income redistribution represented the dominant paradigm for '150 years', until the 'demise of communism',[1] proves extremely reductive. Has the movement that set out from the *Communist Manifesto* exclusively, or primarily, raised the banner of redistribution?

In fact, from its inception it engaged on all three fronts of emancipatory class struggle, on a platform that certainly includes economic demands, but which goes far beyond them. When founded, the International Working Men's Association declared itself in favour of the liberation of 'oppressed nations'. As to the political and social emancipation of women, with the defeat of their exclusion from political rights and the liberal professions, and with the end of domestic slavery, I shall confine myself to referring to something that speaks volumes. In a preface to *Woman and Socialism*, August Bebel, interlocutor of Engels and leader of German social-democracy, noted that his book, which had been published 30 years earlier, gone through 50 editions and been translated into 15 languages, had begun its triumphant progress thanks to the clandestine distribution undertaken by members of the socialist party outlawed by Bismarck.[2] The feminist movement was bound by multiple ties to the labour movement.

If we focus on the latter, it is hard to understand its tenacious struggle to abolish censitary discrimination exclusively by reference to the paradigm of redistribution. The latter is likewise of little help when it comes to analysing the commitment of the International Working Men's Association to the emancipation of African-American slaves and Lincoln's war on the slave-holding South. The North's naval blockade of the secessionist South made it impossible to export cotton to Britain, resulting in a serious crisis in the British textile industry, mass redundancies, and reductions in working hours and already meagre wages. Even so, Marx pointed to the workers' determination to counter the measures taken by the industrialists, but especially their support for the Union's struggle to put down the slave-owners' rebellion, and their mass mobilization to prevent the British government supporting the Confederacy militarily or even diplomatically, as an expression of a mature class consciousness and celebrated it.

On closer inspection, the paradigm of redistribution is unable to even adequately explain working-class struggles at the point of production. Along with low wages or hunger, the *Communist Manifesto* denounces the 'despotism' practiced by the boss.[3] And the chains which the workers are summoned to break at the end of that text, are, in the first instance, those of the 'slavery' imposed by bourgeois society.[4] We are dealing with a struggle demanding liberty inside the factory and outside it. One thinks of the agitation, conducted clandestinely, to abolish the anti-socialist legislation enacted by Bismarck, who was targeted even though he was the initiator of the welfare state.

Dissatisfied by the paradigm of redistribution, I happen upon a text by the young Engels, used by Marx as a draft for the *Communist Manifesto*. Indeed, *Principles of Communism*, to which I am referring, suggests an alternative paradigm:

> The slave is sold once and for all, the proletarian has to sell himself by the day and by the hour. Being the property of *one* master, the individual slave has, since it is in the interest of this master, a guaranteed subsistence, however wretched it may be; the individual proletarian, the property, so to speak, of the whole bourgeois *class*, whose labour is only bought from him when someone needs it, has no guaranteed existence. ...The slave is accounted a thing, not a member of civil society; the proletarian is recognised [*anerkannt*] as a person, as a member of civil society. Thus, the slave may have a better subsistence than the proletarian, but the proletarian belongs to a higher stage of development of society and himself stands at a higher stage than the slave.[5]

Applied to the proletarian, the key phrase is '*recognised* as a person'. Although prey to an insecurity not experienced by the slave, making survival difficult, the proletarian does not have to endure the total reification of someone regarded and treated as a commodity like all the rest. The relative economic advantages the slave might enjoy count for little or nothing compared with the first (modest) result achieved by the proletarian in his or her struggle for recognition.

The liberal tradition interprets class struggle in reductionist and vulgarly economistic terms. Relying on the conceptual couple liberty/equality, it has assigned itself jealous, disinterested love of liberty and branded its opponents as vulgar, envious souls, motivated solely by material interest and the pursuit of economic equality. This is an intellectual tradition that issues in Hannah Arendt, according to whom Marx was the theorist of 'the abdication of freedom before the dictate of necessity' and champion of the view that 'the aim of revolution' was material 'abundance', not 'freedom'.[6] Concrete commitment to the emancipation of women and oppressed nations; readiness (during the American Civil War) to support the heaviest material sacrifices to help break the chains imposed on African-Americans; determination to abolish 'modern wage slavery' along with slavery proper; the daily struggle against the bosses' 'despotism' in the factory and Bismarck's legislation suppressing freedoms—all this is forgotten in an interpretation notable more for political and ideological passion (these were the years of the Cold War) than philological and philosophical rigour.

2 A Widespread Demand for Recognition

The summons to comprehensive class struggle issued by Marx and Engels came at a historical moment when the request—the demand—for recognition advanced by those who, in one way or another, felt themselves subject to exclusion clauses injurious to their human dignity became ever more widespread. A famous cartoon from the abolitionist campaign portrayed a black slave in chains exclaiming: 'Am I not a Man and a Brother?' It was published by the English journal *Punch* in 1844, the same year that Marx wrote the *Economic and Philosophical Manuscripts*, which are profoundly marked by an ethos of humanity and the dignity of man. Lying behind all this was the experience of the Black slave revolution on Santo Domingo in the late eighteenth century, which, in the words of its leader (Toussaint L'Ouverture) invoked 'the absolute acceptance of the principle that no man, born red [i.e. mulatto], black, or white, can be the property of another'. However modest their condition, human beings could not be 'confused with animals', as happened in the slave system.⁷

Even before then, Condorcet had reprehended the fact that the 'American colonist forgets that the Blacks are men; he has no moral relationship with them; for him they are simply objects of profit'.⁸ And, directly addressing the slaves, the French philosopher wrote as follows:

> Dear friends, although I am not the same colour as you, I have always regarded you as my brothers. Nature has fashioned you to have the same spirit, the same reason and the same virtues as White men. I am only speaking here of White men in Europe, for when it comes to those in the colonies, I shall not insult you by comparing them with you ... Were one to set off in search of a man on the islands of America, he would certainly not be found among those with white flesh.⁹

The French philosopher responded to the dehumanization of the Black slave by the White owner by excluding the culprit from the human race in principle. As we can see, the controversy revolves around inclusion, or non-inclusion, in the category of 'man': we are dealing with a struggle for recognition. Engels adopted a not dissimilar attitude when, in 1845, he analysed and denounced *The Condition of the Working Class in England*. Addressing English workers, whom he was 'glad and proud' to have frequented, who were 'degrade[d] ... to machines' and 'worse slaves than the Negroes in America' by existing social relations, Engels exclaimed: 'I found you to be Men, members of the great and universal family of mankind', who represented 'the cause of Humanity' trampled underfoot by capitalists engaged in an 'indirect trade in human flesh', in a barely disguised slave trade.¹⁰

The attitude adopted by someone about to become Marx's close and inseparable collaborator affords a kind of historical and theoretical balance-sheet of the struggle underway, whose protagonists were the subaltern classes. They had long been regarded by the dominant ideology with a contempt that was in a sense racial. An illustrious historian has observed that between 1660 and 1760 there developed in England 'an attitude towards the new industrial proletariat noticeably harsher than that general in the first half of the seventeenth century, and which has no modern parallel except in the behaviour of the less reputable of White colonists towards colored labor'.¹¹

In reality, this was a phenomenon extending far beyond the spatial and temporal confines just indicated. It is enough to think of Edmund Burke and Emmanuel-Joseph Sieyès, who defined the wage worker as an *'instrumentum vocale'* or 'bipedal machine'.[12] Such oppressive and explicit dehumanization certainly fell into crisis with the French Revolution and the entry of the putative instruments of labour onto the historical stage. But it did not disappear, so that at each step of the class struggle we find the demand for recognition emerging. In June 1790, Marat had a representative of the 'unfortunates' to whom political citizenship was denied argue thus against the 'aristocracy of the rich': '[i]n your eyes, we are still scum'.[13] Excluding the propertyless from political rights, declared Robespierre in April of the same year, meant seeking to expel them into a 'class of "helots"'. No less than the 'feudal aristocracy', the 'aristocracy of the rich' projected 'a certain idea of inferiority and contempt' onto members of the lower classes.[14] In Paris immediately after the July Revolution, the popular newspapers, indignant at the survival of censitary discrimination and the proscription of trade-union coalitions and organization, accused the 'bourgeois nobles' of insisting on regarding workers not as 'men' but as 'machines', nothing but 'machines' required to produce solely for the 'needs' of their bosses. After the February 1848 revolution, the attainment of political rights by proletarians proved, in their view, that thanks to their struggle they were finally beginning to be elevated to the 'rank of men'.[15]

Finally, similar themes and accents echo in the agitation and struggle of women. In one of the very first feminist texts, Wollstonecraft accused the society of her time of regarding and treating women like 'slaves', who were 'not allowed to breathe the sharp invigorating air of freedom', or, worse, like 'gentle, domestic brutes'. In fact, the dominant culture went so far as to allude to the 'female soul' like 'that of animals'.[16] However, it was 'time to restore to [women] their lost dignity': they must finally be recognized 'as rational creatures', 'as a part of the human species'.[17] In the same year (1792), a French feminist, Pierre Manuel, argued in similar fashion: 'there was a time when human, male society asked itself whether women had a mind'.[18] Once again, the demand for recognition emerges from such indignation. Almost a century later, it was the turn of Marx's daughter Eleanor, in her capacity as a militant in both the labour and feminist movements, to denounce the fact that in bourgeois society women, like workers, were denied 'their rights as human beings'.[19] The struggle for recognition was far from over.

Hence, the summons issued by Marx and Engels had an enormous echo for a very simple reason: they proved capable of registering and elaborating, theoretically and politically, a very widespread request for recognition. The starting point may be identified in Hegel's *Phenomenology of Spirit* and the dialectic of lord and bondsman expounded in it. Over and above explicit references to this text, which must have been profoundly influential in Marx's intellectual formation in particular, its influence makes itself clearly felt terminologically. The *Economic and Philosophical Manuscripts* stress that, '[u]nder the semblance of recognising man' (*Anerkennung des Menschen*), political economy, bourgeois society, 'carries to its logical conclusion the denial of man'.[20] The *Anerkennung*, or recognition, sought by the kind of modern slave represented by the wage worker did not follow the fall of the *ancien régime*. The same applies to the other protagonists of class struggles and struggles for recognition. We can now understand the terms in which the *Manifesto* addresses the bourgeoisie, who pose as champions of the 'person' and her or his dignity: 'by "individual" you mean no person other than the bourgeois, than the middle-class owner of property'.[21]

3 'Positive Humanism' and the Critique of Processes of Reification

The various social and national subjects whom we have seen demanding recognition bemoan the fact that they are not fully subsumed under the category of 'person' and 'human being'. This is the context in which to situate the young Marx's indictment of capitalist society. It inflicted severe mutilation on the proletarian, confining and isolating him in 'the *abstract* existence of man as a mere *workman* who may therefore daily fall from his filled void into the absolute void—into his social, and therefore actual, non-existence'.[22] The wage worker was forced to 'sell himself and his humanity' (*seine Menschheit*), 'reduce[d] ... to a machine', and treated like a 'horse'.[23] The truth was that 'political economy knows the worker only as a working animal—as a beast reduced to the strictest bodily needs'. Notwithstanding magniloquent talk about liberty having finally been attained with the fall of the *ancien régime*, the social order was characterized by the oppression of a 'slave class' (*Sklavenklasse*).[24] The following year, in 1845, Engels expressed himself in similar terms. He too was of the opinion that, along with Blacks in the American Deep

South, the very workers who were free in theory were subject to *de facto* slavery. This signified something very precise: bourgeois society 'publicly proclaimed that proletarians are not human beings, and do not deserve to be treated as such'.²⁵ In any event, the condition they were condemned to was not one 'in which a man or a whole class of men can think, feel, and live as human beings'. Hence, 'the workers must strive to escape from this brutalising condition'. This was only possible in and through class struggle: the worker 'can only save his [humanity] in hatred and rebellion against the bourgeoisie'.²⁶ For the proletarian, 'fight[ing] against the bourgeoisie' ultimately meant 'fight[ing] for his [humanity]'.²⁷ Marx and Engels did not as yet know one another, but were already speaking the same language—a language that blends an ethos of humanity with a powerful demand for recognition.

We can now understand why the young Marx indicted existing society as a negation of 'positive humanism' (*positiver Humanismus*) and 'fully developed humanism' (*vollendeter Humanismus*), of 'real humanism' (*realer Humanismus*).²⁸ He formulated his revolutionary programme articulating 'the categorical imperative to overthrow all relations in which man is a debased, enslaved, forsaken, despicable being'.²⁹ An end had to be put to a social order where man is under 'the rule of inhuman conditions and elements' and 'not yet a *real* species-being'.³⁰ In Louis Althusser's view, these formulations are ideologically naive and fortunately were surpassed by the mature Marx, from roughly 1845 onwards, when an 'epistemological break' supposedly occurred and humanist rhetoric, neglectful of the class struggle, was supplanted by historical materialism or, rather, the science of history.

This is a reading which, philosophically, commits the error of confusing the struggle for recognition, and for the real subsumption of the slave or semi-slave under the category of man, with an edifying humanism that ignores or represses social conflict. In reality, we have seen the young Engels enjoining the worker to 'save his humanity' in and through 'rebellion against the bourgeoisie'—that is, not with generic, vague moral appeals, but with concrete political action, with a challenge to a specific social system. And *The German Ideology* mocks Max Stirner for his view that 'the insurgent Negroes of Haiti and the fugitive Negroes of all the colonies wanted to free not *themselves* but "man"'.³¹ 'Humanism' is 'real' insofar as it can identify and realize universality in specific struggles. To Ruge, who celebrated the 1848 revolution as 'most humane [in] its principles', Engels objected that it was such because 'these principles have arisen as a result of the glossing over of the most contradictory interests' and the conflict between proletariat and bourgeoisie. On the other hand, he repeated (in September of the same year), 'philanthropical fantasies and sentimental phrases about fraternity' served only to wipe the slate clean of 'the ferocious cruelties committed in Paris by the victors of June' and the antagonisms that were continuing to explode.[32] In Marx and Engels, reference to the universal concept of man and the struggle for recognition went hand in glove with a critique of edifying humanism.

Althusser's thesis is also unconvincing in more narrowly philological terms. 'Humanist' rhetoric continues to echo strongly in the speech on free trade made by Marx in Brussels in early 1848, which condemned capitalism because it sought to reduce to a minimum the cost of 'the maintenance of this machine, called workman'.[33] In its turn, the *Communist Manifesto* called for the overthrow of a system that slighted the human dignity of the overwhelming majority of the population. Under attack were socio-economic relations that involved the 'training to act as a machine' of proletarians, who were degraded from childhood into 'simple articles of commerce and instruments of labour', 'an appendage of the machine', of 'capital [which] is independent and has individuality, while the living person is dependent and has no personality'.[34]

It is true that, according to Marx's French interpreter, the *Manifesto* pertains to the 'transitional works', not the fully 'mature works'.[35] Let us now glance at the terms in which, in 1865, *Value, Price and Profit* criticized the capitalist system:

> Time is the room of human development. A man who has no free time to dispose of, whose whole lifetime, apart from the mere physical interruptions by sleep, meals, and so forth, is absorbed by his labour for the capitalist, is less than a beast of burden. He is a mere machine for producing Foreign Wealth, broken in body and brutalised in mind.[36]

We are dealing with a system, *Capital* maintained, which does not hesitate to sacrifice young lives that are incapable of self-defence: witness 'the extensive kidnapping of children, practised by capitalists in the infancy of the factory system, in workhouses and orphanages, by means of which robbery, unresisting material for exploitation was procured'.[37] The human costs of capitalism are terrible. One thinks of the creation of the textile industry in England: the requisite raw material was procured by enclosing, and allocating to pasture, the common land that previously ensured the subsistence of large masses who, now expropriated, were condemned to hunger and desperation, so that (in Thomas More's phrase taken up by Marx) the 'sheep ... eat up ... the very men'.[38]

This was not a closed chapter of history, involving only the process of formation of capitalism. Even in its mature form, the system was marked by a hunt for profit that involved a 'Timur-Tamerlanish prodigality of human life'.[39] Indeed, 'despite all its niggardliness', capitalist production is 'altogether too prodigal with its human material', 'squanders human lives' and destroys 'the life and limbs of labourers'.[40] To summarize, capitalism sanctioned 'the rule of the object over the human',[41] involved the transformation of workers into 'labour-power machines'(*Arbeitskraftmaschinen*), the conversion even of children, of 'immature human beings into mere machines for the fabrication of surplus value', without the least concern about the consequent 'moral degradation' and 'intellectual desolation'.[42] Bourgeois society loved to celebrate itself as 'a very Eden of the innate rights of man', but in it 'human labour', in fact, 'mere man ... [plays] a very shabby part'.[43] No sooner have we turned from the sphere of circulation to the sphere of production than we observe that, far from being recognized in his dignity as a human being, the wage worker 'bring[s] his own hide to market and has nothing to expect but—a hiding'.[44] If, in writing *The Condition of the Working Class in England*, Engels (as we have seen) denounced the 'indirect trade in human flesh' of which capitalists were guilty, *Capital* draws attention to the 'traffic in human flesh', similar to that in Black slaves, which continued to operate in Britain, the then model country of capitalist development and the liberal tradition.[45]

The critique of the dehumanizing processes inherent in capitalism reverberates even more powerfully when Marx refers to the fate of colonial peoples: with 'the rosy dawn of the era of capitalist production', Africa was turned into 'a warren for the commercial hunting of black-skins'.[46] Let us now turn to Asia and the Dutch colonial empire: '[n]othing is more characteristic than their system of stealing men, to get slaves for Java', with 'men stealers [*Menschenstehler*] trained for this purpose'.[47] Still in the mid-nineteenth century, we find the Black slave in the USA so dehumanized by his master as to take the form of mere 'property' like any other, the form of 'human chattel' or 'black chattel'.[48] So consummate was this reduction to the status of commodity that some states specialized in 'the breeding of blacks' (*Negerzucht*), or—a concept that Marx repeats in English—in 'breeding of slaves'.[49] Renouncing traditional 'export articles', these states 'raise[d] slaves' as 'export' commodities.[50] Furthermore, the law on the return of fugitive slaves sanctioned the transformation of northern citizens into 'slave-catchers'.[51] Domestic 'human livestock' was thus transformed into game, in a further escalation of the process of dehumanization.

As we can see, even in the mature writings there is a recurrence of the critical theme that reproves bourgeois society for reducing the overwhelming majority of humanity to 'machines', 'instruments of labour', 'commodities' which can be calmly squandered, to 'articles of commerce' and 'export articles', to 'chattels', to livestock to be raised, or game to be hunted, or hides to be tanned.

Denunciation of the anti-humanism of the capitalist system did not, and could not, disappear because it was at the very heart of Marx's thought. His repeated comparison between modern slavery and ancient slavery, wage slavery and colonial slavery, signifies the permanence in capitalism of the reifying process that manifests itself in all its crudity in connection with the slave proper. Scientific analysis and moral condemnation are intimately linked and this alone can explain the appeal to revolution. However faithful and pitiless, the description of existing society cannot in and of itself stimulate action to overthrow it, except via the mediation of moral condemnation; and such condemnation resounds all the more powerfully because the socio-political order analysed and indicted turns out to be responsible not merely, or not so much, for individual injustices, but for non-recognition of the human dignity of a whole social class and colonial peoples in their entirety—in other words, ultimately, the great majority of humanity.

On this basis, the creation of a new order is experienced as a 'categorical imperative', in the early and mature works alike. If the *Theses on Feuerbach* conclude by criticizing philosophers who are incapable of 'changing' a world where human beings are crushed and humiliated, *Capital* is a 'critique of political economy'—as indicated by the sub-title—in moral terms as well. The 'political economist' is criticized not only for his theoretical errors but also for his 'stoical peace of mind'—his incapacity for moral indignation at the tragedies inflicted by bourgeois society.[52] This is the context in which to situate the denunciation of 'the Pharisees of "political economy"'.[53] In short, it is difficult to imagine a text more charged with moral indignation than Volume One of *Capital*! The continuity in Marx's development is clear, and what Althusser described as an epistemological break is simply the transition to a discourse in which moral condemnation of the reifying processes inherent in bourgeois society, and of its anti-humanism, is expressed more concisely and elliptically.

It is true that the French philosopher concedes the possibility of a 'revolutionary humanism'.[54] But he is very hesitant on this point and thereby precludes understanding class struggles as struggles for recognition. The class struggle waged by slaves (and by colonial peoples or peoples of colonial origins), who represent the social subject prey to the most explicit, radical dehumanization, is a struggle for recognition. The class struggle waged by the proletarians of the capitalist metropolis, themselves long equated by the dominant ideology with instruments of labour or 'bipedal machines', is a struggle for recognition. The class struggle that sees women engaged in challenging, undermining or abolishing the domestic slavery to which the patriarchal family subjects them, is a struggle for recognition.

The inadequate, misleading character of the purely economistic reading of Marx's theory of conflict is now clear. What is at stake in class struggle? Subjugated peoples, the proletariat and subaltern classes, women enduring domestic slavery—these very different subjects can advance the most varied demands: national liberation; abolition of slavery proper and the conquest of the most basic forms of freedom; better living and working conditions; the transformation of property and production relations; an end to domestic segregation. Just as its subjects vary, so does the content of class struggle. However, we can identify a lowest common denominator. On the economico-political level, it comprises the objective of altering the division of labour (internationally, inside the factory or family); on the politico-moral level, that of overcoming the dehumanizing and reifying processes which characterize capitalist society—the objective of achieving recognition.

4 THE CONTRACTUAL PARADIGM AND JUSTIFICATION OF THE EXISTING ORDER

The presence of the paradigm of the struggle for recognition, Hegelian in origin, is tangible. The other philosophical paradigms in circulation proved to be exhausted and inadequate given the contours of socio-political conflict in those years. To popular demands for the right to life and dignified human existence, the ruling classes replied as follows: however low the level of wages, they are the fruit of a freely negotiated contract; as for the unemployed and invalids, no contract requires them to be afforded aid and to claim or invoke it exhibits the mentality of a slave (who expects subsistence from his master), not a free man, who knows how to take responsibility for his free choices and their consequences.[55] In 1845, having underscored that in the factory the capitalist posed as 'absolute lawgiver', and an arbitrary one, Engels referred to the argument with which 'the Justice of the Peace, who is a bourgeois himself', recommended resignation and obedience to the worker: '[y]ou were your own master, no one forced you to agree to such a contract if you did not wish to; but now, when you have freely entered into it, you must be bound by it'.[56] At the heart of *Capital* is precisely the critique of the contractual paradigm: 'the isolated labourer, the labourer as "free" vendor of his labour power, when capitalist production has once attained a certain stage, succumbs without any power of resistance'.[57] That is why Marx regarded legal regulation of working hours as a measure to prevent workers from selling themselves as slaves in a 'voluntary contract with capital' (see Chap. 2, Sect. 7). The tendentially slave-like logic of the contract could be checked only by class struggle, trade-union action, and working-class politics, and state intervention demanded by the working class.

On the other side, capitalists condemned attempts to regulate working hours and practices as a violation of freedom of contract, whether hailing from above (via industrial relations legislation) or below (via trade-union action). Indeed, reference to contract and the free, unimpeded operation of the labour market also served to justify the proscription of coalitions and trade-union organization—'enlarged monopolies', in Adam Smith's definition,[58] which illegitimately prevented free, individual contracting of the terms of labour. From Burke's viewpoint, the only contract that could be regarded as genuinely free and valid was one made in the absence of any 'combination or 'collusion' (the allusion to, and support for, the Combination Acts, which outlawed and penalized working-class coalitions, is manifest).[59]

This was a highly dynamic ideologeme. Passed in the USA in 1890, the Sherman Anti-Trust Act was especially, and very effectively, deployed against workers guilty of combining in union 'monopolies' disrespectful of individual initiative and liberty. By contrast, contracts whereby, on being hired, workers and employees pledged (were compelled to pledge) not to join any trade-union organization, were long regarded as perfectly legal. From the standpoint of legislators and the dominant ideology, the clauses of the contract respected the rules of the market and individual liberty.[60]

To confirm its unsuitability for the emancipatory struggle of the working class, let us glance at the history of the contractualist paradigm. Hugo Grotius employed it to explain and justify the institution of slavery. A prisoner of war at the victor's mercy, or a poor wretch on the point of dying of starvation, was committed to serving his master unremittingly; by virtue of an implicit or explicit contract, both were guaranteed subsistence in exchange. Reference to the contract served to legitimate slavery. In a theorist of contractualism like John Locke, we read that the plantation owners in the West Indies own 'slaves or horses' on the basis of legal 'purchase'—that is, 'by bargain or money'.[61] In the mid-nineteenth century, the slave-owners in the American South argued in the same way—something to which Marx indignantly drew attention in *Capital*: 'the slave-owner buys his labourer as he buys his horse',[62] in accordance with a legal contract.

In addition to legitimizing slavery in the strict sense, the contractualist paradigm was invoked to counter the struggle against more or less servile labour relations. In France, Sieyès proposed to transform the 'slavery of need', afflicting the poor and miserable, into a 'servile engagement' (*engageance serve*), into a 'legally sanctioned slavery', in accordance with the model adopted in America for White indentured servants, who were in fact semi-slaves, often subject to purchase and sale (like black slaves). It might be objected that the servant 'loses part of his liberty'. But Sieyès had a ready reply: '[i]t is more accurate to say that, when the contract is drawn up, far from being impeded in his liberty, he exercises it in the way that best suits him; any agreement is an exchange whereby each likes what he receives more than what he surrenders'. It was true that, for the duration of the contract, the servant could not exercise the liberty ceded by him. But it was a general rule that the liberty of an individual 'never extends to the point of harming others'.[63] Historically, the French author ended up being right in a way. Following the abolition of slavery in the colonies, Britain was concerned to replace the Blacks, ensuring a flow of indentured servants from Africa and Asia: hence, the Indian and Chinese 'coolies', subject to a slavery or semi-slavery that was legitimated and edulcorated by a 'contract'.

As we can see, the idea of the contract can be invoked, and historically has been, to legitimize very different social relations, including those destructive of liberty. Attempts have been made to remedy such formalism by underlining that not everything can be subject to contract or sale and purchase. In Kant's words, 'any pact of servile submission is in and of itself null and void; a man can only lease out his own labour', and only do so in adhering to the 'imprescriptible duty' to safeguard 'his own human determination with respect to the [human] race'. Hence, more or less masked slavery or semi-slavery was precluded, like any social relation that 'degrades humanity'. 'The personality is not alienable' and hence, a social relation in which the servant 'is a thing, not a person' (*est res, non persona*)', was inadmissible.[64] Accordingly, states Hegel's *Philosophy of Right* in its turn, '[t]hose goods, or rather substantial determinations, which constitute my own distinct personality and the universal essence of my self-consciousness are ... *inalienable*'.[65]

In his argument against the economic liberals of the time, T.H. Green, a left-Hegelian, drew on this tradition and lesson in Britain in the second half of the nineteenth century.[66] They condemned state regulation of working hours in factories, and of female and juvenile labour, in the name of 'freedom of contract'—freedom construed exclusively as non-interference in the private sphere by political power. Green was fully aware of this ideological campaign, which witnessed successive interventions by Herbert Spencer, Lord Acton, and others: 'the most pressing political questions of our time are questions of which the settlement, I do not say necessarily involves an interference with freedom of contract, but is sure to be resisted in the sacred name of individual liberty'. Green objected to the liberal ideologues of his time as follows:

> We condemn slavery no less when it arises out of a voluntary agreement on the part of the enslaved person. A contract by which anyone agreed for a certain consideration to become the slave of another we should reckon a void contract. Here, then, is a limitation upon freedom of contract which we all recognise as rightful. No contract is valid in which human persons, willingly or unwillingly, are dealt with as commodities....[67]

The argument previously used to refute contractualist justifications of slavery (and more or less servile labour relations) was now employed to challenge the most odious aspects of what, in Marx and Engels' view, amounted to 'present enslavement'.

However, what might be characterized as the dual formalism of the contractualist paradigm was not thereby overcome. In fact, it was further confirmed. The contract invoked can comprise and legitimize the most diverse and conflicting contents (bearing the stamp of freedom or of serfdom). Above all, it is not clear who the contracting parties are. For centuries the market in the liberal West involved the presence of chattel slavery: in the past, the ancestors of today's Black citizens were commodities to be bought and sold, not autonomous consumers; they were the objects, not the subjects, of purchase contracts.

On the other hand, insistence on the existence of inalienable goods (or determinations), which the individual cannot renounce even should she wish to; insistence on the existence of goods (or determinations) that cannot in any circumstances be subject to purchase and contract, because they are inseparable from the nature or dignity of human beings—all this signals the transition from the contractualist paradigm to the natural law paradigm.

5 THE SHORTCOMINGS OF THE NATURAL LAW PARADIGM

Nor was the natural law paradigm equipped to further the emancipatory 'class struggles' theorized by Marx and Engels. It betrayed its problematic and inadequate character as early as its triumph, when it inspired the Declaration of the Independence of the United States of America in 1776 and, thirteen years later, the Declaration of the Rights of Man and the Citizen in France. The first of these solemn documents proclaimed that 'all men are created equal' and were the bearers of 'unalienable rights'. With even greater eloquence, the second paid tribute to the 'natural, inalienable and sacred rights of man' and affirmed that 'neglect and scorn for the rights of man are the sole cause of public calamities and the corruption of rulers'. But this did not prevent slavery from flourishing in the USA (where the post of President was held by slave-owners for 32 of the country's first 36 years of existence) and in France's colonies.

A violent crisis erupted over slavery in the French colony of Santo Domingoas early as 1791 and the years of Marx and Engels' intellectual formation saw the civil war that eventually erupted in the USA brewing. In both cases, the problem was the same: were Blacks to be counted among the bearers of natural, inalienable rights? The answer was far from self-evident. Grotius, who employed the contractualist paradigm, but who in general is rightly regarded as the father of natural law theory, had no difficulty in justifying the institution of slavery. Although resorting to the natural law paradigm, the principal authors of the Declaration of Independence and the 1787 US Constitution were Thomas Jefferson and James Madison, respectively, both of them slave-owners. The verdict of Engels' *Anti-Dühring* is readily intelligible: 'the American constitution, the first to recognise the rights of man, in the same breath confirms the slavery of the coloured races existing in America'.[68]

What happened in France is especially significant. A particular opponent of the Declaration of the Rights of Man was Pierre-Victor Malouet, a plantation- and slave-owner subsequently in the forefront (with the Massiac club) of the struggle against abolitionist plans. When he spoke in the National Assembly on 2 August 1789, he cautioned against the incendiary impact that the discourse of the rights of man might have on the 'immense multitude of propertyless men', engaged as they were in an arduous struggle for 'subsistence' and inclined to be angered by the 'spectacle of luxury and opulence'.[69] No reference was made to slaves. In other words, for Malouet Black slaves could unquestionably not be included among the bearers of the rights of man; there was a danger that such rights would be invoked by the *menu people* of Paris, not the human livestock of Santo Domingo.

What sparked the second serious critical moment for the natural law paradigm was the feminist movement, which began to take shape in France in wake of the overthrow of the *ancien régime*. Declining in the feminine the rights of man and the citizen proclaimed by the French Revolution, Olympe de Gouges elaborated her *Declaration of the Rights of Woman and the Female Citizen* in 1791, the same year as the Black slave revolt on Santo Domingo. Once again, we are referred to a problem with which we are familiar: is woman to be included among the bearers of natural, inalienable rights? Here too the answer was far from self-evident, as demonstrated by the tragic fate of Gouges, who was guillotined in 1793, at a time when a convinced supporter of the natural law paradigm—Robespierre—was in power. By contrast, the Jacobin leader had no difficulty in appealing to this paradigm when, even before sanctioning the abolition of Black slavery, he proclaimed 'the political rights of men of colour' and demanded respect for the 'rights of humanity' in their case too.[70]

Over and above this exemplary sequence of events, in the liberal tradition the exclusion of women, along with children and minors, from political rights was long regarded as obvious. Both cases involved calmly registering a lack of the maturity required to participate in political life. In Marx and Engels' view, this confirmed that the appeal to natural, inalienable rights in the natural law tradition was not a suitable instrument for genuinely challenging Black slavery, wage slavery, or female domestic slavery, and supersession of the view of its victims as 'mere instruments of production'.

Finally, the third moment in the crisis of the natural law model comprises the labour movement's entry onto the stage of history. Marx dwelt at some length on the French law of June 1791 that outlawed workers' coalitions as an 'attack on liberty and the Declaration of the Rights of Man'. The proposer, Isaac R.G. Le Chapelier, acknowledged that workers in effect found themselves in a 'state of absolute dependence due to the want of the necessities of life, which amounts to slavery'. Yet, he considered the protection of a right of man, which the nascent trade unions sought to obstruct, to be the priority.[71] What emerges ever more clearly is what the natural law banner was raised for by the opposing parties and classes. The popular masses demanded the right to existence, defined by Robespierre as the first of the 'imprescriptible rights of man'.[72] It should be guaranteed by the intervention of political power in existing property relations. However, such intervention was immediately branded as an intolerable violation of the natural right to peaceful enjoyment of property by the affluent classes. On the basis of this final position, we can understand the balance-sheet drawn up by *The Holy Family*: 'the recognition of the rights of man by the modern state has no other meaning than the recognition' of slavery by the state of antiquity had'.[73] Or, to cite *On the Jewish Question*, 'the practical application of man's right to liberty is man's right to private property'; and this in turn was the 'right of man' to 'enjoy [his] property and to dispose of it at [his] discretion ... without regard to other men' (e.g., the slaves or semi-slaves whose existence Le Chapelier himself was compelled to note).[74]

Like the contractualist paradigm, the natural law paradigm suffers from a dual formalism. The category of rights of man can subsume different conflicting contents: the right of the property-owner to enjoy and dispose of his property at will; or, on the contrary, the right to a dignified life or existence, to be realized through the intervention of political power in existing property relations—that is, by means of intervention which is a patent violation of the rights of man in the property-owner's eyes. But the more serious formalism is the second one, which concerns the figure of the bearer of the rights of man: which social subjects are really encompassed by this figure? Locke, a foremost representative of contractualism, raised no objection to the figure of the Black slave, who thus is the object, not the subject, of the contract. Grotius, father of natural law theory, likewise did not challenge the figure of the Black slave, who thus is not included among the bearers of inalienable rights—in fact, can be the object of the inalienable right to property and the untrammelled enjoyment of property by free citizens. An example from history serves to illustrate the problem. In the USA, recently, created in the wake of a rebellion fuelled by ideological motifs derived from contractualism and natural law theory, Virginia and other states rewarded veterans of the War of Independence with land and Black slaves.[75]

Not being a signatory to the contract or the bearer of inalienable rights, the slave aspiring to freedom could not appeal either to contractualism or natural law. In other words, both paradigms wrongly take the main thing for granted, take as read what is in fact the result of a protracted struggle sometimes so bitter as to take the form of armed struggle. This 'presupposition' is the recognition that occurs between the signatories of the contract or the bearers of inalienable rights—more precisely, between those who mutually recognize one another as signatories of the contract or bearers of inalienable rights.

6 HEGEL, MARX AND THE PARADIGM OF THE STRUGGLE FOR RECOGNITION

Hence, we must base ourselves on the struggle for recognition. If we confine ourselves to the capitalist metropolis, the proletarian struggle promoted by Marx and Engels goes far beyond the existing distribution of income, targeting the dehumanizing processes constitutive of capitalist society. Moreover, it is not possible to make a clear distinction between the struggle for redistribution and the struggle for recognition. A man who risks dying of starvation, observes Hegel in *Elements of the Philosophy of Right*, is reduced to a condition of 'forfeit[ing] all his rights',[76] a condition, in other words, which is akin to the slave's; and what defines the figure of the slave is non-subsumption under the universal concept of man, non-recognition as a man.

But is Hegel's influence on Marx and Engels clearly documented? Paradoxically, the presence of the Hegelian paradigm of the struggle for recognition manifests itself with particular clarity in connection with the relationship not between empirical individuals, but between peoples—in connection, that is, with a context which Hegel did not explicitly consider when he developed his analysis of the struggle for recognition. We shall see that on several occasions Marx and Engels asserted that 'a nation cannot be free and at the same time oppress other nations'. We are immediately reminded of the *Phenomenology of Spirit*, which summarizes the result of the dialectic of lord and bondsman thus: 'they recognize themselves as mutually recognizing one another'. Or, in the words of the *Encyclopaedia*

(§431Z), 'I am truly free only when the other is free as well and is recognized as free by me'.[77]

To appreciate the salience in Marx of the theme of the struggle for recognition, we must bear in mind that it is elaborated in Hegel in two different terminologies. We have already encountered the first. We must now examine the second, which is more elliptical and starts out from an important distinction formulated in the *Science of Logic*. It is necessary to distinguish between 'simple negative judgement', which negates a specific, limited predicate of a subject (this rose is not red), and 'negative infinite judgement', which, instead of an individual predicate or predicates, negates the subject as such (this is not a rose). In other words, while the negative infinite judgement negates the genus (the rose as such), the simple negative judgement only negates the species, the specific determination (the red colour of the rose). The logical distinction can also be of help when it comes to analysing social relations. 'Civil litigation', which occurs, for example, during a dispute between the inheritors of a particular property, is one thing, stresses Hegel. The person who goes to law because she has suffered a wrong is the victim of a simple negative judgement: what has been violated is 'only this particular right', not 'right as such', not the 'judicial capacity of a determinate person'. Criminal law, which is the sphere of the application of negative infinite judgement, is very different. Crime in the strict sense also negates the universal, the 'judicial capacity' of the victim, who is not recognized as a rights-bearing subject and, ultimately, is not included in the category of man. The genus negated in the negative infinite judgement represented by crime is the genus 'man', while in the simple negative judgement of civil litigation what is called into question is the species, the specific determination on the basis of which a person is recognized as the owner of a determinate property. Not including the victim in the genus 'man', crime cancels recognition of the other.

In Hegel's view, an 'infinite negative judgement' is pronounced on the slave—an 'infinite negative judgement' in its all its plenitude, in an 'infinity' that is wholly adequate to the 'concept': the negation of recognition has reached its apex. That is why slavery may be regarded as the 'absolute crime', a crime which is in a sense even worse than murder. In the latter instance, the negation of recognition and of the universal concept of man, although it has a fatal result, is nevertheless consummated in an instant. By contrast, slavery represents a negation of recognition and a reification that become an uninterrupted daily practice. In his turn, the hungry man who risks starving to death, and who is reduced to a condition of 'total lack of rights' can be compared to the slave. He too suffers an infinite negative judgement, which cancels his recognition or renders it impossible. This is not a question of isolated or individual cases. Against the mass of those who live in conditions of extreme destitution is 'pronounced the [negative] infinite judgement of crime'. Ultimately, they are no longer recognized as rights-bearing subjects, are no longer recognized as human beings.[78]

Hegel himself juxtaposes the two terminologies. Having observed that an awareness that 'slavery is absolutely contrary to right' is the mandatory starting-point for a correct orientation in the debate on slavery, *Elements of the Philosophy of Right* refers to the pages on the struggle for recognition in the *Phenomenology* and the *Encyclopaedia* on the one hand, while on the other it stresses that the institution of slavery is in contradiction with 'the concept of the human being as spirit'and 'the ineligibility of the human being in and for himself for slavery'.[79] The ethos of the universal concept of man and the struggle for recognition blend into one.

Both these terminologies occur in the young Marx. Let us first look at *On the Jewish Question*, which criticizes bourgeois-civil society in these terms: in it the individual 'regards other men as a means', but in so doing 'degrades himself into a means'.[80] We already know how Hegel's *Encyclopaedia* describes the struggle for recognition: 'I am truly free only when the other is free as well and is recognized as free by me'. In the words of the young Marx, I cease to be a 'means', and am recognized as a man and a free man, only when I refuse to degrade other men to a simple 'means'. The thesis, stated many times by Marx and Engels, that the alienation and reification imposed on the proletariat by the bourgeoisie end up investing the dominant class itself, can be situated in the same context (see Chap. 3, Sect. 4). It is the viewpoint of *The Holy Family*, which also employs the second type of terminology, when it identifies the watchword of *égalité* as 'the French expression for the unity of human essence [*menschliche Wesenseinheit*], for man's consciousness of his species and his attitude towards his species [*Gattungsbewusstsein und Gattungsverhalten*], for the practical identity of man with man, i.e., for the social or human relation of man to man'.[81] Celebration of the human race and its unity is tantamount to condemnation of the non-recognition suffered by a huge mass of human beings in bourgeois society.

The basic thing about the paradigm of recognition, then, is this: it does not take for granted the subject from which the paradigms of the contract and rights of man start out uncritically, as if it were an immediate, incontrovertible datum. And the same might be said of the paradigms of 'praxis' and 'communicative action' favoured by Arendt and Habermas, respectively. There too the main thing is ignored: determination of the subject regarded as signatory to the contract or bearer of human rights, or participant in praxis or communicative action, has been at the centre of centuries-long struggles against exclusion clauses aimed at colonial peoples, subaltern classes, and women. The cancellation of the exclusion clauses is the result of a painful historical process and a protracted struggle for recognition. Social conflict is at the same time a struggle for recognition; the general theory of social conflict is at the same time a general theory of the struggle for recognition.

7   THE STRUGGLE FOR RECOGNITION AND THE CONQUEST OF SELF-ESTEEM

Nevertheless, the Hegelian model undergoes some alteration. In Marx and Engels' view, wage slaves take the first step in the struggle for recognition by forging relations with one another. Nietzsche and Bentham respectively refer to the proletariat and subaltern classes as a 'barbaric caste of slaves' and a tribe of 'savages'. The victims of the capitalist system begin to shake off the sense of culpability, and consequent lack of self-esteem, with which the dominant ideology saddles them, when, overcoming isolation, they engage in a joint struggle and in building organizations to foster it. Regardless of subsequent developments, this merger is a result of decisive importance. Coming into contact with one another, the members of a class that is not only 'oppressed', but also (stresses Engels) 'calumniated', begin to get to know themselves and to shake off the denigration and self-denigration impressed on them by the dominant class.[82] At this point, repeats the young Marx of the *Economic and Philosophical Manuscripts*, there emerges 'a new need—the need for society', so that '[a]ssociation, society and conversation' become an 'end' in themselves.[83] In the words of *The Poverty of Philosophy*, 'the maintenance of association becomes even more necessary to [the workers] than that of wages. It is so true that English economists are amazed to see the workers sacrifice a good part of their wages in favour of associations, which, in the eyes of these economists, are established solely in favour of wages'.[84] Wage demands have become less important than trade-union combination or the workers' political party, and not only because the latter confer regularity and strategic depth on the struggle for wages. Combination as such is an initial major victory won by the workers.

Organization of the struggle and the struggle itself then intervene to consolidate it. Many years later, in two letters to Eduard Bernstein and Laura Lafargue, dated 22 and 29 August 1889 respectively, Engels referred to a strike organized by casual workers on the London docks and explained the reasons for his enthusiasm:

> Hitherto the East End had been in a state of poverty-stricken stagnation, its hallmark being the apathy of men whose spirit had been broken by hunger, and who had abandoned all hope. Anyone who found himself there was lost, physically and morally. ...Because of the lack of organisation and the passively vegetable existence of the real East End workers, the lumpen proletariat has hitherto had last say there, purporting, and indeed being held, to be the prototype and representative of the million starvelings in the East End.

Now, following 'this gigantic strike of the most demoralised elements of the lot', everything had changed:

> They are as you know the most miserable of all the *misérables* of the East End, the broken down ones of all trades, the lowest stratum above the *Lumpenproletariat*. That these poor famished broken-down creatures who bodily fight amongst each other every morning for admission to work, should organise for resistance, turn out 49-50,000 strong, draw after them into the strike all and every trade of the East End in any way connected with shipping, hold out above a week, and terrify the wealthy and powerful Dock Companies—that is a revival I am proud [to have lived to see].[85]

First the coming together of the members of the 'oppressed and calumniated' class, and then their organization for class struggle and the actual class struggle—these preliminary moves altered the picture radically. Poverty was far from having disappeared and material living conditions had not yet improved. But the 'barbarians' and 'savages' had ceased to be such, because they had mutually recognized one another as members of an exploited and oppressed class, called upon to achieve its emancipation through struggle.

8 THE STRUGGLE FOR RECOGNITION: FROM INDIVIDUALS TO PEOPLES

A second alteration occurs in the paradigm of the struggle for recognition: its presence in Marx and Engels emerges with particular clarity in connection with the relations between peoples. We thus witness an extension of the paradigm and its application in a context not explicitly considered by Hegel. In terms of the paradigm of the struggle for recognition, the individual is genuinely free only when he or she recognizes and respects the other as a free individual. The same consideration is reiterated by Engels as regards the relations between peoples. In later 1847, during a London demonstration of solidarity with Poland, he proclaimed: 'a nation cannot become free and at the same time continue to oppress other nations. The liberation of Germany cannot therefore take place without the liberation of Poland from German oppression'.[86] A few months after the outbreak of the revolution, Engels called upon Germany to put an end both to the oppression it suffered at the hands of absolutist monarchy and the *ancien régime* and to the oppression that it inflicted on Poland in particular: 'Germany will liberate herself to the extent to which she sets free neighbouring nations'.[87]

This was not simply an appeal to the German people not to let themselves be engulfed by chauvinism, but to identify their own cause with that of the Polish people. It was also intended to have an analytical significance, as emerges from the position adopted by Marx and Engels in 1875 during another solidarity demonstration with Poland: '[n]o one can enslave a people with impunity'. The consequences for Prussia-Germany, one of the three protagonists in the partitioning of the unhappy country, were manifest: 'we have enemies everywhere, we have encumbered ourselves with debts and taxes in order to maintain countless masses of soldiers who must also serve to suppress the German workers'.[88]

The dialectic also manifested itself in other geographical areas and political contexts. In 1869, Engels observed that 'Irish history shows what a misfortune it is for one nation to subjugate another'.[89] Such is also the recurrent guiding thread of Marx's analysis of the Irish question. The British working class's inability to solidarize with an oppressed people reinforced the rule of the aristocracy and bourgeoisie at home as well: '[a]ny people that oppresses another people forges its own chains'. The 'enslavement of Ireland' prevented 'the emancipation of the English working class' and the 'big standing army' on hand to control and silence the rebel island also impacted on the proletariat of the dominant nation and, in fact, on British society as a whole.[90]

Finally, the dialectic we are referring is graphically illustrated in a famous page of *Capital*. Originating in the East, opium found its way into London and other industrial cities. It served to deaden the hunger pangs of working-class families, to stifle the cries of famished children, and sometimes even became an instrument of 'ill-disguised infanticide'; infants '"shrunk up into little old men" or "wizened like little monkeys"'. Taking these horrific details from official reports, Marx comments: '[w]e here see how India and China avenged themselves on England'.[91] By virtue of a kind of *lex talionis*, non-recognition of the Chinese people ends up having consequences for the country that is the protagonist of colonial oppression and the Opium Wars.

On closer examination, the history of the West as a whole can be interpreted in the light of the principle that a people which oppresses another people is not free. In the twentieth century, the totalitarian domination and genocidal practices running from top to bottom of the colonial tradition erupted in the very continent where this historical sequence started, in the wake of Hitler's attempt to build a continental empire in Eastern Europe, subjugating, decimating and enslaving the 'natives' who inhabited it.

NOTES

1. Nancy Fraser, 'Social Justice in the Age of Identity Politics: Redistribution, Recognition, and Participation', in *Redistribution or Recognition? A Political-Philosophical Exchange*, ed. Fraser and Axel Honneth, London and New York: Verso, 2003, pp. 7–8.
2. August Bebel, *Die Frau und der Sozialismus*, Berlin: Dietz, 1964, pp. 21–2.
3. Karl Marx and Frederick Engels, *Collected Works*, London: Lawrence & Wishart, 1975–2004, Vol. 6, p. 491.
4. Ibid., Vol. 6, pp. 519, 495.
5. Ibid., Vol. 6, pp. 343–4.
6. Hannah Arendt, *On Revolution*, London: Penguin, 2009, pp. 51, 54.
7. Quoted in Laurent Dubois, *Avengers of the New World*, Cambridge and London: Belknap Press of Harvard University Press, 2004, pp. 242, 210.
8. Marie-Jean-Antoine Condorcet, *Oeuvres*, ed. A. Condorcet O'Connor and M.F. Arago, Stuttgart and Bad Cannstatt: Frommann-Holzboog, 1968, Vol. 3, pp. 647–8.
9. Ibid., Vol. 7, p. 63.
10. Marx and Engels, *Collected Works*, Vol. 4, pp. 297, 468–9, 298, 301.
11. R.H. Tawney, *Religion and the Rise of Capitalism: A Historical Study*, New York: Harcourt, Brace and company, 1926, p. 269.
12. See Domenico Losurdo, *Liberalism: A Counter-History*, trans. Gregory Elliott, London and New York: Verso, 2011, Chapter 3, §10
13. Quoted in Henri Guillemin, *La première résurrection de la République*, Paris: Gallimard, 1967, p. 13.
14. Maximilien Robespierre, *Oeuvres*, Paris: Presses Universitaires de France, 1950–67, Vol. 7, pp. 167–8.

15. See Domenico Losurdo, *Democrazia o bonapartismo. Trionfo e decadenza del suffragio universale*, Turin: Bollati Boringhieri, 1993, Chapter 1, §11
16. Mary Wollstonecraft, *A Vindication of the Rights of Woman*, London: Everyman's Library: 1992, pp. 39, 21, 49.
17. Ibid., pp. 49, 156.
18. Quoted in Anne Soprani, *La Révolution et les femmes 1789–1796*, Paris: MA Éditions, 1988, p. 99.
19. Eleanor Marx-Aveling and Edward Aveling, 'The Woman Question', *Marxism Today*, March 1972, p. 83.
20. Marx and Engels, *Collected Works*, Vol. 3, p. 291.
21. Ibid., Vol. 6, p. 500.
22. Ibid., Vol. 3, p. 285.
23. Ibid., Vol. 3, pp. 239–41.
24. Ibid., Vol. 3, pp. 242, 239.
25. Ibid., Vol. 4, p. 578.
26. Ibid., Vol. 4, p. 501.
27. Ibid., Vol. 4, p. 416.
28. Ibid., Vol. 3, pp. 342, 296; Vol. 4, p. 7.
29. Ibid., Vol. 3, p. 182.
30. Ibid., Vol. 3, p. 159.
31. Ibid., Vol. 5, p. 309.
32. Ibid., Vol. 7, 376.
33. Ibid., Vol. 6, p. 458.
34. Ibid., Vol. 6, pp. 501, 502, 490–1, 499.
35. Louis Althusser, *For Marx*, trans. Ben Brewster, London: Allen Lane, 1969, pp. 34–5.
36. Marx and Engels, *Collected Works*, Vol. 20, p. 142.
37. Ibid., Vol. 35, p. 406 n.
38. Quoted in ibid., Vol. 35, p. 710 n.
39. Ibid., Vol. 35, p. 269 n.
40. Ibid., Vol. 37, pp. 90, 92, 94.
41. Ibid., Vol. 34, p. 398.
42. Ibid., Vol. 35, pp. 255, 403.
43. Ibid., Vol. 35, pp. 186, 54.
44. Ibid., Vol. 35, p. 186.
45. Ibid., Vol. 35, p. 273.
46. Ibid., Vol. 35, p. 739.
47. Ibid., Vol. 35, p. 740.
48. Ibid., Vol. 19, p. 36; Vol. 35, p. 272; Vol. 41, p. 420.
49. Ibid., Vol. 35, p. 447; Vol. 41, p. 420.
50. Ibid., Vol. 19, p. 39.
51. Ibid., Vol. 19, p. 37.

52. Ibid., Vol. 35, p. 717.
53. Ibid., Vol. 35, p. 300.
54. Louis Althusser and Étienne Balibar, *Reading Capital*, trans. Ben Brewster, London: New Left Books, 1970, p. 141.
55. See Gertrude Himmelfarb, *The Idea of Poverty: England in the Early Industrial Age*, New York: Vintage, 1985, pp. 162, 183.
56. Marx and Engels, *Collected Works*, Vol. 4, 467.
57. Ibid., Vol. 35, p. 303.
58. Adam Smith, *An Inquiry into the Nature and Causes of the Wealth of Nations*, Indianapolis: Liberty Classics, 1981, Vol. I, Chapter 7, p. 79.
59. Edmund Burke, *The Works: A New Edition*, London: Rivington, 1826, Vol. 7, p. 380.
60. See Losurdo, *Liberalism*, Chapter 6, §10.
61. Ibid., Chapter 2, §3.
62. Marx and Engels, *Collected Works*, Vol. 35, p. 272.
63. Emmanuel-Joseph Sieyès, *Écrits politiques*, ed. Roberto Zapperi, Paris: Editions des Archives contemporaines, 1985, pp. 76, 89, 196.
64. Immanuel Kant, *Gesammelte Schriften*, ed. Academy of Sciences, Berlin and Leipzig: 1900–, Vol. 19, pp. 547, 545.
65. G.W.F. Hegel, *Elements of the Philosophy of Right*, ed. Allen W. Wood and trans. H.B. Nisbet, Cambridge: Cambridge University Press, 1991, §66, p. 95.
66. See Thomas Hill Green, 'Lecture on Liberal Legislation and Freedom of Contract', in *Works*, ed. R.L. Nettleship, London: Longmans Green, 1973, Vol. 3, p. 367.
67. Ibid., pp. 372–3.
68. Marx and Engels, *Collected Works*, Vol. 25, p. 98.
69. Quoted in Charles Fauré (ed.), *Les Déclarations des droits de l'homme de 1789*, Paris; Payot, 1988, p. 162.
70. Robespierre, *Oeuvres*, Vol. 7, pp. 366, 728.
71. Marx and Engels, *Collected Works*, Vol. 35, p. 731.
72. Robespierre, *Oeuvres*, Vol. 8, p. 90; Vol. 9, p. 112.
73. Marx and Engels, *Collected Works*, Vol. 4, p. 113.
74. Ibid., Vol. 3, p. 163.
75. See Losurdo, *Liberalism*, Chapter 2, §6.
76. Hegel, *Elements of the Philosophy of Right*, §127, p. 155.
77. G.W.F. Hegel, *Werke in zwanzig Bänden*, ed. E. Moldenhauer and K.M. Michel, Frankfurt am Main: Suhrkamp, 1969–79, Vol. 3, p. 147; Vol. 10, p. 220.
78. See Domenico Losurdo, *Hegel and the Liberty of the Moderns*, trans. Marella and Jon Morris, Durham, NC: Duke University Press, 2004, Chapter 7, §§ 5 & 7.

79. Hegel, *Elements of the Philosophy of Right*, §57, pp. 87–8.
80. Marx and Engels, *Collected Works*, Vol. 3, p. 154.
81. Ibid., Vol. 4, p. 39.
82. Ibid., Vol. 4, p. 297.
83. Ibid., Vol. 3, p. 313.
84. Ibid., Vol. 6, p. 211.
85. Ibid., Vol. 48, pp. 364–5, 369.
86. Ibid., Vol. 6, p. 389.
87. Ibid., Vol. 7, p. 166.
88. Ibid., Vol. 24, p. 56.
89. Ibid., Vol. 43, p. 363.
90. Ibid., Vol. 21, pp. 120–1.
91. Ibid., Vol. 35, pp. 402 and n, 739.

CHAPTER 5

Overcoming Binary Logic: A Difficult, Unfinished Process

1 MUTILATION OF THE CLASS STRUGGLE

In its most mature formulation, the theory of 'class struggles' takes the form of a general theory of social conflict and theoretically reflects, whilst at the same time encouraging a multiplicity of struggles for recognition. But it is not easy to attain this vantage-point and retain it. Not infrequently, figures and movements engaged on one front do not attend to other fronts or even regard them with disdain. While he had a powerful sense of the social question, Proudhon branded the incipient feminist movement as sheerly synonymous with 'pornocracy',[1] and showed no sympathy for oppressed nations aspiring to shake off the yoke of tsarist autocracy! He was unable to understand the tangled skein of class contradictions: the proletarian exploited by the bourgeoisie might be a participant in the 'first class oppression' affecting woman; the Polish noble who oppressed his own serfs might be involved in the struggle against national oppression.

Proudhon took a very narrow view of the class struggle ranging the subaltern classes against privilege and the ruling power in France. In his eyes, the protagonist of the coup d'état of December 1851 was not the inheritor, however contradictory, of the June 1848 massacre of Parisian workers, was not the one who, on the basis of the bourgeoisie's desire to unsheathe the sword against the insurgent proletariat, ended up

© The Editor(s) (if applicable) and The Author(s) 2016
D. Losurdo, *Class Struggle*, Marx, Engels, and Marxisms,
DOI 10.1057/978-1-349-70660-0_5

unsheathing it against French society as a whole, including the bourgeoisie (see Chap. 9, Sect. 2). Far from sharing Marx's interpretation, Proudhon at times seemed fascinated by Louis Bonaparte, to the extent that immediately after the coup he wrote to a friend and noted in his diary: 'I have reason to believe that I am regarded very favourably at the Élysée ... On this date, I reckon to raise the banner of the social Republic once again, in from two to three months, neither more nor less. This is a magnificent opportunity and success is almost certain'; 'it is said that the Élysée has more than once expressed a desire to address me, and that great pains have been taken to dissuade it'.[2] Marx's verdict was bitter. He denounced Proudhon's two 'basenesses'—that is, '[h]is work on the *coup d'état*, in which he flirts with Louis Bonaparte and, in fact, strives to make him palatable to the French workers, and his last work, written against Poland, in which for the greater glory of the tsar he expresses moronic cynicism'.[3] In any event, the French author, who had the merit of challenging bourgeois private property, performed an anti-educative role, preaching or recommending to the working class 'abstention from the political movement', from the struggle against Bonapartism at home and national oppression abroad, as well as from the struggle for women's emancipation.[4] The binary interpretation of social conflict, which perceives only one contradiction (opposing rich and poor), does not make it possible to understand emancipatory movements, whose social basis is not formed exclusively of poor people. Concentration on the social question in France turns into a prison stamped by insular corporatism.

While Proudhon harboured illusions about Louis Bonaparte, Lassalle cultivated them in Bismarck, whom he hoped to win to his cause. In arguing against the view of the state as a 'night watchman' of property and public order indifferent to the desperate condition of the working class, Lassalle primarily or exclusively targeted the liberal bourgeoisie.[5] Marx was not wrong to reprove him for pursuing an 'alliance with absolutist and feudal opponents against the bourgeoisie',[6] flirting with someone who later promulgated ruthless anti-socialist (and anti-working class) laws.

We may repeat what has already been said in connection with Proudhon. In the case of this great intellectual and charismatic agitator, commitment to the social question—more precisely, the attempt to extract gracious concessions from the existing government in the direction of a welfare state—went hand in hand with neglect of other fronts in the class struggle and a narrowly economistic view of working-class struggle itself. As we shall soon see, Lassalle did not understand the historical importance of the struggle for the abolition of black slavery in the USA. As regards France, he gave vent to odd declarations on Louis Bonaparte's coup d'état. Having attained power, the latter had proceeded to abolish censitary discrimination, already liquidated by the February 1848 revolution, but reintroduced by the liberal bourgeoisie with the law of 30 May 1850. In the circumstances of Bonapartist dictatorship, the return to universal (male) suffrage simply meant that the poorest popular masses could participate in plebiscitary acclamation of the leader. Lassalle did not argue thus. For him, Louis Bonaparte had overthrown not the 'republic', but only 'the bourgeois republic, which sought to impress the seal of the bourgeoisie, of the rule of capital, on the republican state'.[7]

Similar trends to those observed in France and Germany also emerged in other countries. Engels criticized those Russian intellectuals and circles who liked to positively contrast their country (where communal property forms persisted) with France and Britain (where bourgeois private property and capitalist social polarization were now ubiquitous). There was a current of thought that argued as follows: 'the introduction of a better order of things is greatly hindered in Western Europe by the boundless extension of the rights of the individual ... in the West the individual is used to unlimited private rights. ...In the West, a better system of economic relations is bound up with sacrifices, and that is why it is difficult to establish.'[8] The view was not foreign to Alexander Herzen. For him 'there may be a political question for Russia; but the "social question" is already solved as far as Russia is concerned'.[9] We are confronted with a populist current which (Engels observed) liked 'to describe the Russian peasants as the true vehicles of socialism, as born communists, in contrast to the workers of the aging, decayed European West, who would first have to go through the ordeal of acquiring socialism artificially'. Subsequently, '[f]rom Herzen [the] knowledge came to Bakunin, and from Bakunin to Mr. Tkachov' that the Russian people were 'instinctively, traditionally communist'.[10] The underestimation of the task of abolishing an *ancien régime* notable for its oppression of nations and women, as well as the working class, was patent. Once again, the class struggle is heavily mutilated and, even when it comes to engagement on behalf of the subaltern classes, what remains is trifling.

2 'IMPERIAL SOCIALISM'

Mutilation of class struggle can take another form: closing one's eyes to the fate visited by capitalism on colonial peoples or peoples of colonial origin. From the outset, calling attention to the 'millions of workers' forced to die in India, to allow capitalists to make modest concessions to British workers, Marx underlined the connection between the colonial question and the social question in the capitalist metropolis (see Chap. 2, Sect. 3). This was a demanding intellectual perspective. In sharp contrast to Proudhon, Fourier was a champion of the cause of women's emancipation. But it happened that, in the very years when Marx and Engels were expressing their hopes in the proletariat as the agency of universal emancipation with youthful hyperbole, followers of Fourier (and Saint-Simon) planned to construct communities of a more or less socialist kind in Algeria, on land taken from the Arabs in a brutal, sometimes genocidal war.[11]

Later, utopian socialism mostly viewed the abolitionist movement with condescension or suspicion. After the February 1848 revolution, Victor Schoelcher and the new government proceeded to the definitive abolition of black slavery in French colonies, almost half a century after it had been reintroduced by Napoleon, who had thereby cancelled the results of the black revolution on Santo Domingo led by Toussaint L'Ouverture and the laws emancipating blacks enacted by the Jacobin Convention. However, Etienne Cabet, an eminent representative of French utopian socialism, criticized Schoelcher for focusing on a narrow objective—the emancipation of black slaves—rather than committing himself to the universal emancipation of labour.[12] On the outbreak of the Civil War in the USA, Lassalle argued similarly, judging at least from a letter to Engels of 30 July 1862 in which Marx criticized the 'antiquated, mouldering speculative rubbish' of Lassalle, for whom the gigantic clash underway in the USA was 'of no interest whatever'. Rather than developing positive 'ideas' for transforming society, 'the Yankees' confined themselves to mobilizing a 'negative idea' like 'the freedom of the individual'.[13] For the two representatives of socialism cited here, commitment to the abolition of slavery in the colonies or the North American republic distracted attention from the social question, which remained a burning issue in the capitalist metropolis.

To the American Civil War—in Marx's view, an epic event—Lassalle made only distracted, reductive references. Because of the blockade imposed by the Union on the secessionist South, and the consequent shortage of cotton for the textile industry of Britain, and Lancashire in particular, British workers were forced into unemployment and risked having to 'emigrate to the colonies'. It was 'one of the most bloody and horrible wars that history has ever seen'. What was at stake in it was not touched upon. In fact, rather than the institution of slavery, Lassalle indicted 'federalism' and the self-government accorded states as allegedly responsible for the 'absorption in particular interests' and 'mutual hatred' of the contending parties, which were thus put on par.[14]

The economistic or corporatist limitations of representatives of the labour and socialist movement were not unconnected with the initiative of the dominant classes, whose effectiveness was in fact underestimated by Marx and Engels. Having included 'Young England' in the 'spectacle' of 'feudal socialism' staged by 'aristocrats', the *Communist Manifesto* concluded: 'the people, so often as it joined them, saw on their hindquarters the old feudal coats of arms, and deserted with loud and irreverent laughter'.[15] In fact, things turned out rather differently. The historically most important member of Young England was Disraeli. In him (as in the organization he joined) are to be found elements of the transfiguration of the *ancien régime*, but he may be regarded as the inventor of a 'socialism' more appropriately defined as 'imperial' than 'feudal'. Far from meeting with derision from the popular classes, this was socialism that often enchanted and ensnared them.

In the same years as *The Holy Family* and *The German Ideology* proclaimed the irreducible antagonism between proletariat and bourgeoisie, Disraeli published a novel that in its own way dealt with the same themes. We find a Chartist agitator bitterly challenging the existing order and denouncing the reality of the 'two nations' ('rich and poor') into which England is divided. In the *Communist Manifesto*, the Chartists are included among the 'existing working-class parties';[16] and the agitator seems to exhibit the revolutionary consciousness attributed to the proletariat by Marx and Engels. It is interesting to observe Disraeli's response: it made no sense to speak of 'two nations'; a bond of 'fraternity' now united 'the *privileged* and prosperous English people'.[17] The key word is the one emphasized by me: the English aristocracy had shelved the caste, even racial arrogance it traditionally displayed towards the popular classes; and now it was the 'fraternal' national English community as a whole that adopted a pose of supreme aristocratic disdain for other nations, especially colonial populations.

In other words, rather than disappearing, the racialization traditionally suffered by the British popular classes was displaced. It is no accident if Disraeli, who subsequently became the author of the Second Reform Act (which extended political rights beyond the circle of the aristocracy and the bourgeoisie), and of a series of social reforms, was simultaneously the champion of imperialism and the right of the 'superior' races to subjugate 'inferior' ones. In this way, the British statesman proposed to defuse the social question and class struggle in his own country: 'I say with confidence that the great body of the working-class of England [...] are English to the core. They are for maintaining the greatness of the Kingdom and the Empire, and they are proud of being subjects of our Sovereign and members of such an Empire.'[18] These were the years when in France Proudhon adopted the position (according to Marx) of a 'socialist of the Imperial period'—to be precise, the Second Empire.[19]

Thus, we see a new political movement emerge. In the late nineteenth century, alluding to Napoleon III and Bismarck as well as Disraeli, a German observer spoke of an 'imperialist social policy' or 'imperial socialism' (*Imperialsozialismus*).[20] Already brought out by Marx, the connection between the colonial question and the social question in the capitalist metropolis was recognized and put at the centre of a new political project, which proposed a kind of quid pro quo: the popular masses and proletariat were invited to respond to the dominant classes' limited social reforms with patriotism and support for colonial expansionism.

3 'CLASS AGAINST CLASS' ON A GLOBAL SCALE?

The quid pro quo was scornfully rejected by the artisans of the theory of class struggle. But a problem persists. A situation of relatively peaceful development and, *a fortiori*, a major historical crisis is characterized by a tangle of multiple contradictions and various forms of class struggle: there is no pre-established harmony between them. An adequate understanding of a concrete historical situation requires overcoming the habitual binary logic that claims to explain everything on the basis of a single contradiction. In Marx and Engels themselves, this was a difficult, unfinished process.

The Condition of the Working Class in England, published in 1845, ends by evoking the imminent—in fact, already initiated—revolution of the 'workers' against the 'bourgeoisie', or 'open, declared war of the poor against the rich', of the 'cottage' against the 'mansion'.[21] The Irish national question, to which Engels forcefully drew attention, does not seem to play any role in the impending clash. Approximately two years later, in *The Poverty of Philosophy*, Marx issued a kind of watchword: 'the struggle of class against class'.[22] The *Communist Manifesto* clarifies its basis: '[o]ur epoch, the epoch of the bourgeoisie, possesses ... this distinctive feature: it has simplified the class antagonisms. Society as a whole is more and more splitting up into two great hostile camps, into two great classes directly facing each other: Bourgeoisie and Proletariat'.[23] It is true that other social subjects must be taken into account, but the capitalist bourgeoisie—a handful of exploiters—becomes ever more isolated. The prospects for revolution were decidedly encouraging: the proletarians (we read in *The German Ideology*) constitute 'a class which forms the majority of all members of society'.[24] Besides, adds the *Manifesto*, 'entire sections of the ruling classes are, by the advance of industry, precipitated into the proletariat'.[25]

In the (early) writings cited hitherto, the new revolution (set to emancipate, over and above the proletariat, humanity as a whole) ultimately breaks out from a single contradiction, opposing bourgeoisie and working class; and this new revolution is ineluctable because of the progressive, unstoppable expansion of the working-class and pro-working-class front.

There were no pertinent differences between one country and another. In fact, national borders were tending to decline in importance. This is a view that found its most eloquent expression in a speech made by Engels on 9 December 1847, during a demonstration in London in favour of Polish independence. In Britain, 'as a result of modern industry, of the introduction of machinery, all oppressed classes are being merged together into a single great class with common interests, the class of the proletariat', more united than ever thanks to 'this levelling of the living standards of all workers'. '[O]n the opposite side all classes of oppressors have likewise been united into a single class, the bourgeoisie. The struggle has thus been simplified and so it will be possible to decide it by one single heavy blow'. As to the international stage, machinery 'has evened out the position of all workers and daily continues to do so' everywhere, so that 'the workers now have the same interest, which is the overthrow of the class that oppresses them—the bourgeoisie'. In sum, '[b]ecause the condition of the workers of all countries is the same, because their interests are the same, their enemies the same, they must also fight together, they must oppose the brotherhood of the bourgeoisie of all nations with a brotherhood of the workers of all nations'.[26] Not only does everything revolve around a single contradiction, but politics, national peculiarities, and ideological factors seem to play no role.

The binary interpretation of social conflict does not figure only in Engels and is not even limited to the early period. It is enough to think of a very famous passage in Volume One of *Capital*: '[c]entralisation of the means of production and socialisation of labour at last reach a point where they become incompatible with their capitalist integument. This integument is burst asunder. The knell of capitalist private property sounds. The expropriators are expropriated'.[27] Four years later, in the conclusion to *The Civil War in France*, Marx drew up this balance-sheet: the 'cosmopolitan blackleggism' of the Second Empire was countered by authentic internationalism. The Paris Commune, 'as a working men's Government, as the bold champion of the emancipation of labour' (to be achieved in an international framework), was 'emphatically international'. It was no accident if 'the Commune admitted all foreigners to the honour of dying for an immortal cause'.[28]

The picture became even clearer after the repression conducted by the French bourgeoisie (with the complicity of the Prussian army) and the witch hunt (against members of the International) unleashed by the dominant classes throughout Europe: '[w]hile the European Governments thus testify, before Paris, to the international character of class rule, they cry down the International Working Men's Association—the international counter-organization of labour against the cosmopolitan conspiracy of capital—as the head fountain of all these disasters'.[29] The thesis of the 'cosmopolitan conspiracy of capital' errs in forgetting the competition and conflict between the different bourgeoisies to which the *Manifesto* drew attention, and in absolutizing a temporary, short-lived situation. Volume One of *Capital* recalls that 'the June insurrection in Paris' united the different bourgeois countries and 'all fractions of the ruling classes'.[30] The observation dates from 1867. Three years later, the Franco-Prussian War broke out and in its wake emerged the Paris Commune, crushed courtesy of an understanding between the former enemies. But it was an understanding that soon gave way to chauvinistic hatred, destined to result in an 'industrial war of extermination between nations', the First World War. During the struggle against that carnage, the first revolution to identify with Marx and Engels broke out and in its wake there developed an anticolonial movement on a global scale, which targeted the 'exploitation of one nation by another' referred to by the *Manifesto* and contemporaneous texts, but which was totally ignored in 1871 in the wake of the contempt elicited by Franco-German collaboration in repressing the Paris Commune and the well-nigh general applause of the international bourgeoisie for the attendant massacre.

In other circumstances too, a tendency emerges to interpret the revolutionary process with the binary logic of 'class against class'. In the late 1850s, as the peasant agitation that shortly led Tsar Alexander II to abolish serfdom in Russia intensified, premonitory signs of the impending civil war become ever clearer in the USA. On the night of 16–17 October 1859, John Brown, a fervent abolitionist from the North, invaded Virginia in a desperate, failed attempt to incite the slaves of the South to rise up. On 11 January of the following year, Marx wrote to Engels:

> In my view, the most momentous thing happening in the world today is the slave movement—on the one hand, in America, started by the death of Brown, and in Russia, on the other. ...I have just seen in the *Tribune* that there's been another slave revolt in Missouri, which was put down, needless to say. But the signal has now been given. Should the affair grow more serious by and by, what will become of Manchester?[31]

What is intimated here is a scenario of well-nigh global revolution, whose protagonist would be black slaves in the USA, serfs in Russia, and wage slaves or workers in Britain. In all three cases, it would involve revolutions from below and class struggles directly confronting their exploiters and oppressors.

It scarcely needs to be said that the gap between such expectations and the actual unfolding of the historical process was considerable. In Britain, despite the fact that the Union's naval blockade of the slaveholding states occasioned a particularly serious crisis in the textile industry, the workers condemned to unemployment did not allow themselves to be used by those sections of the ruling class which would have liked to urge them onto the streets to demonstrate against Lincoln (and in favour of war against the Union). Marx acknowledged this, although, at the same time the absence of revolution was met with disappointment and even scorn. In a letter to Engels of 17 November 1862, he scoffed at 'the bourgeois and aristocrats [for their] enthusiasm ... for slavery in its most direct form' and at 'the working men [for] their servile Christian nature'.[32]

There was no revolution by wage slaves in the wake of a black slave revolution across the Atlantic; in fact, the latter did not materialize either. The courage and dignity with which Brown faced his trial and execution stirred great emotion in the white community and strengthened the abolitionist party. But the slaves of Virginia and the South did not propel themselves into insurrection, as Brown had hoped and, along with him, Marx and Engels, who followed events from Europe with trepidation. Not only did the desired revolution from below by black slaves not occur, but for a long time, there was no place for them in the conflict waged from above. The call for 'the arming of all slaves as a military measure', made by the most radical (white) officers in the Northern army, and favourably highlighted by Marx, fell on deaf ears.[33] To the serious disappointment of Marx and Engels, the American Civil War mostly took the form of a typical inter-state war, waged by both sides with traditional armies. Only towards the end did the Union proceed to enrol free blacks and black slaves who, escaping their masters in the South, encountered the advancing Northern army. Overall, it may be said the Civil War resulted in a kind of abolitionist revolution, but one conducted chiefly from above and whose protagonists were whites—primarily the statesmen and generals of the industrialized North. Marx and Engels were right to deprecate this outcome. The revolution from above proved wholly incomplete. It abolished slavery, but did not involve genuine emancipation of the blacks, who after a brief interval of inter-racial democracy were subjected to a terroristic regime of white supremacy. The point is that the expectation of a general revolt from below by black slaves, serfs and wage slaves clouded the capacity for historical prediction.

The capacity was restored when Marx and Engels distanced themselves from the binary interpretation of social conflict. Some months before Brown's desperate endeavour, in early 1859, Marx published an article on developments in the situation in Russia, which had just suffered a serious defeat in the Crimean War (against France and Britain) and which, with Alexander II, was to abolish serfdom two years later. There was no reduction in social tension as a result. On the contrary, 'insurrections of serfs' had become 'epidemic' so that, according to the official statistics from the Interior Ministry, around 60 nobles were killed every year. So determined were the serfs that they entertained the idea of exploiting the advance of French troops to unleash a large-scale revolt.[34] Here, as opposed to a general insurrection of the poor against the rich, revolution is anticipated from a conjunction of international war and internal social conflict. We are reminded of October 1917.

4 BINARY LOGIC AND THE 'SELF-EVIDENCE' OF EXPLOITATION

Complementing the binary interpretation of the revolutionary process and social conflict is a theory that seems to derive revolutionary class consciousness from direct sensory self-evidence. Capitalist society, observed *The German Ideology* in 1845–6, presents us with

> a class ... which has to bear all the burdens of society ... and forced into the sharpest contradiction to all other classes; a class which forms the majority of all members of society, and from which emanates the consciousness of the necessity of a fundamental revolution, the communist consciousness, which may, of course, arise among the other classes too through the contemplation [*Anschauung*] of the situation of this class.[35]

So intolerable are the material living conditions forced on the proletariat that they cannot but rebel and, 'contemplating' these, members of other social classes may be induced to challenge the existing order. In other words, sensory self-evidence imposes itself with such force that revolutionary consciousness can, in a way, be taken for granted. In the words of *The Holy Family*,

> Since in the fully-formed proletariat the abstraction of all humanity, even of the *semblance* of humanity, is practically complete ... since man has lost himself in the proletariat, yet at the same time has not only gained theoretical consciousness of that loss, but through urgent, no longer removable, no longer disguisable, absolutely imperative *need*—the practical expression of *necessity*—is driven directly to revolt against this inhumanity. ...It cannot abolish the conditions of its own life without abolishing *all* the inhuman conditions of the life of society today which are summed up in its situation. It is not a question of what this or that proletarian, or even the whole proletariat, at the moment *regards* as its aim. It is a question of *what the proletariat is*, and what, in accordance with this *being*, it will historically be compelled to do.[36]

The strength of sensory perception entails that proletarians are largely immune from the ideological influences of the dominant class. In dedicating *The Condition of the Working Class in England* 'to the working-classes of Great Britain', Engels wrote: '[w]ith the greatest pleasure I observed you to be free from that blasting curse, national prejudice and national pride'. In fact, 'English nationality is annihilated in the working-man'.[37]

In reality, in contradictory fashion, the same text draws attention to the fact that the competition of Irish workers has 'forced down ... the wages' of English workers. The train of recriminations and resentments can be imagined. In any event, Carlyle (a writer hitherto sympathetic to the Chartist movement) took his cue from this to paint a negative picture of the Irish.[38] Three years later, with his focus now on Central and Eastern Europe, Engels summarized the principles adhered to by the dominant classes: they 'employ their skill and efforts to set one nation against another and use one nation to subjugate another, and in this manner to perpetuate absolute rule'.[39] Clearly, the proletariat was not immune from the chauvinist wave. The 'obviousness' of exploitation and, with it, the unity of the exploited class disappears so that a binary interpretation of social conflict becomes unsustainable.

All the more so because the class that is the proletariat's antagonist is far from unified. Having drawn attention to the multiple conflicts in which the bourgeoisie of each country is engaged at home and abroad, the *Manifesto* adds that such conflicts 'further, in many ways, the course of development of the proletariat'. In other words, underlying the emergence and development of revolutionary consciousness is a multiplicity of conflicts; and it cannot be deduced exclusively from the antagonism between working class and bourgeoisie.[40]

Hence, far from deriving from some putative sensory self-evidence, revolutionary consciousness presupposes an understanding of political and social relations extending far beyond the conflict between bourgeoisie and proletariat. Revolutionary consciousness is configured as the product of the direct or indirect action of a multiplicity of social subjects and conflicts: the various factions of the bourgeoisie struggling for power within a single country; the bourgeoisie in power in different countries contesting hegemony internationally; the proletariat, which acquires ideology and political autonomy in resisting the influence and blandishments not only of the new ruling class, but also of the old landed aristocracy, which (as we know) seeks to seduce it with the siren songs of 'feudal socialism'.

The process of acquiring class consciousness is all the more tortuous because, in the absence of robust, stable 'combinations' (far from easy to form and maintain), workers, even those in large-scale industry, constitute 'a crowd of people unknown to one another' and 'an incoherent mass ... broken up by their mutual competition'.[41] This is not simply a matter of competition and conflict between individuals. Later, Engels noted that in Britain unskilled workers were regarded and 'treated with contempt' by skilled workers.[42] Competition can even assume very bitter forms, like the 'literal battles' engaged in 'every morning' by London dockworkers hoping to be hired on a casual basis.[43]

It might be said that the protagonist of such battles is the lumpen-proletariat, rather than the proletariat proper. In reality, Engels speaks of 'poor devils' who are 'in the borderland' between these two classes;'[44] and it is a very fluid border. In fact, on closer inspection, the category of lumpen-proletariat refers to a mutable political function rather than a clearly defined social condition. Depending on the case, it can place itself at the service of the dominant bloc or, more rarely, let itself be drawn into the revolutionary movement. The whites in the USA, who allied with the slave-holding oligarchy, were stigmatized as a 'mob' and 'white trash'— ultimately, as a lumpen-proletariat[45]—on account not of their social condition (which was modest but certainly on the borderline of subsistence), but their political attitude.

Later, in 1870, Engels identified the 'lumpen-proletariat of the cities' (along with the 'petty bourgeois', 'small peasants' and 'farm labourers') as a possible ally of the proletariat, which continued to form a minority of the total population, and hence, could aspire to win power only if, by means of appropriate political action, it succeeded in isolating the ruling class.[46] Here, manifestly, ideological and political maturity and the politics of alliances have taken the place of the decisive role of direct sensory self-evidence and the binary reading of social conflict and the revolutionary process.

5 'CLASS STRUGGLES' OR THE STRUGGLE BETWEEN 'OPPRESSOR AND OPPRESSED'?

The shape of social conflict is extraordinarily variegated, and its protagonists can be very diverse. However, having drawn attention to 'class struggles' (in their various shapes and forms) as the key to interpreting the historical process, the *Communist Manifesto* proceeds:

> Freeman and slave, patrician and plebeian, lord and serf, guild-master and journeyman, *in a word, oppressor and oppressed*, stood in constant opposition to one another, carried on an uninterrupted, now hidden, now open fight, a fight that each time ended, either in a revolutionary re-constitution of society at large, or in the common ruin of the contending classes.[47]

I have italicized the phrase which, 'in a word', equates 'class struggles' (in the plural) with the struggle (in the singular) between 'oppressor and oppressed'. Is this summary correct? To be clearer: does this formula really encapsulate Marx and Engels' vision of history, politics and 'class struggles'?

We should first of all observe that in Marx and Engels conflicts between exploiting classes are the rule, not the exception. They explain the French Revolution primarily on the basis of the contradiction between feudal aristocracy and industrial bourgeoisie. The latter, although not forming part of the ruling bloc in the strict sense before 1789, can scarcely be included in the ranks of the 'oppressed'. Not only did it enjoy increasing wealth and incipient social prestige. But in the factories it already exercised power over an exploited and oppressed class; in the colonies, it had no hesitation in resorting to genocidal practices. Crossing the Atlantic, if we concern ourselves with the 'bourgeois revolution' in America, we see that a decisive role was played in it by slave-owners and, above all, those, at odds with the London government, who were determined to expand beyond the Alleghenies and accelerate the process of expropriation and deportation (and decimation) of the Native Americans. Far from being 'oppressed', the protagonists of this revolt were sometimes more ferocious 'oppressors' than the ruling class overthrown by them. The class struggle which, on Marx and Engels' interpretation, at any rate, determined both the revolutions we are referring to in no way coincides with the struggle between 'oppressor' and 'oppressed'. Similar considerations apply to the fall or end of the *ancien régime* in nineteenth-century Italy and Germany.

Even if we confine ourselves to class struggles of an emancipatory kind, the picture does not change. While it exploited and oppressed workers, when it led the revolution against the *ancien régime*, the bourgeoisie played an essential role in the struggle against the 'oppressor' to be overthrown at that time. The liberation struggles of an oppressed nation or women also witness the participation of social strata that cannot be unequivocally included in the category of 'oppressed'. As regards the proletarian class struggle, it can sometimes count on the support—but more often must reckon with the hostility—of the sub-proletariat, which may be allied with the oppressed or, more often, the oppressor.

The ambiguity is not dispelled if we confine ourselves to the proletariat in the strict sense. Exploited in the factory, the worker (e.g., the English worker) can be indifferent or even sympathetic to the subjugation of Ireland or India, and thus become an accomplice of the oppressor in this respect. Let us then take the Irish or Indian worker, doubly oppressed as a member of an exploited class and, at the same time, an oppressed nation. Yet he is the 'bourgeois' within the family, while it is the woman who represents the proletarian and is subjected to 'domestic slavery'. Let us then take a woman who is working-class and Irish. She is trebly oppressed—in the family, in the factory, and as a member of an oppressed nation. But, within the patriarchal family, she too participates in 'the exploitation of children by their parents' referred to by the *Manifesto*,[48] to which communists are determined to put an end.

In other words, each individual (and even group) is located in a contradictory set of social relations, each of which allocates him or her to a different role in each instance. Far from being based on a single 'relation of coercion', the world capitalist system is a tangle of multiple and contradictory 'relations of coercion'. What determines the ultimate location of an individual (and group) in the camp of the 'oppressor' or of the 'oppressed' is the hierarchical ordering of these social relations in accordance with their political and social relevance in a determinate concrete situation, on the one hand, and the political choice of the single individual (or group), on the other.

6 Exporting Revolution?

The difficult, unfinished process of overcoming the binary interpretation of social conflict also makes itself felt negatively in another respect. What are the tasks of the proletariat, once power has been won? It is enjoined by the *Communist Manifesto* to promote the development of the productive forces and the socialist transformation of the country governed by it. Nearly a quarter of a century later, Marx credited the Commune with being engaged in France in 'uprooting the economical foundations upon which rests the existence of classes, and therefore of class rule'.[49] Are we dealing with a class struggle from above, whose protagonist is the proletariat in power?

This is a picture that contrasts with the passage in the *Manifesto* which, 'in a word', equates class struggle with the clash between 'oppressor and oppressed' and, more exactly, with the insurrection of the latter against the former. On these premises class struggle becomes inconceivable after the conquest of power. The eternal antagonist of the 'oppressor', the victorious proletariat holding political power cannot any longer be included among the 'oppressed'. On the other hand, if we regard proletarians in power as protagonists of a new phase of the class struggle, we shall not only have a class struggle conducted from above but one whose protagonists are not, precisely speaking, the oppressed. Such was the road taken by Lenin, and which Marx himself seems to embark on when he theorizes the 'revolutionary dictatorship of the proletariat'.[50] But there was considerable hesitation. Perhaps because the prospect of the conquest of power was remote, and regularly frustrated by developments, the one-sided view of class struggle as an uprising by the oppressed situated below against the oppressors located above never completely disappeared.

Given this presupposition, if a class struggle can be conducted by the victorious proletariat in a single country, it is the one that sees it rebel against the domination which the capitalist bourgeoisie continues to exercise in every other country and, ultimately, globally. Accordingly, it is no cause for surprise that the lesson drawn by *Class Struggles in France* from the repression of the workers' revolt of June 1848 by the French bourgeoisie, and of national uprisings in Hungary, Poland, and Italy by the Austrian and Russian empires, was that the proletarian revolution would be 'forced to leave its national soil forthwith and conquer the European terrain' (see Chap. 2, Sect. 6). Here the class struggle of the victorious proletariat seems to consist in exporting the revolution. In its way, this resolves the theoretical difficulty mentioned above. When the whole international picture is taken into account, if they have won power in a single (isolated and surrounded) country, proletarians continue to be the 'oppressed' who are called upon to confront the much stronger alliance of 'oppressors'. Still in 1850, deceiving themselves about the approach of a new revolutionary wave, Marx and Engels explained the objectives of the Communist League as follows:

> It is our interest and our task to make the revolution permanent, until all more or less possessing classes have been forced out of their position of dominance, the proletariat has conquered state power, and the association of proletarians, not only in one country but all the dominant countries of the world, has advanced so far that competition among the proletarians in these countries has ceased and that at least the decisive productive forces are concentrated in the hands of the proletarians.[51]

Having prevailed in one country, the struggle of the revolutionary class crosses state and national borders. It might be said that the 'anachronistic and unnatural "Napoleonism"' for which Gramsci reproached Trotsky,[52] can already be glimpsed in Marx. Especially given that, at least in his early writings, he tended to conceive socialist revolution by analogy with the bourgeois revolution. *The German Ideology* credits the Napoleonic occupation of Germany with having delivered powerful blows to the feudal edifice, 'by cleaning out Germany's Augean stables'.[53] *The Holy Family* is even more emphatic, identifying Napoleon as the ultimate expression of 'revolutionary terror'; he 'perfected the [Jacobin] Terror by substituting permanent war for permanent revolution'.[54] Although assuming a new form, the anti-feudal class struggle and liquidation of the *ancien régime* continued and, in fact, assumed a European dimension. Here too the bourgeois revolution is interpreted in a binary logic, as if the only operative contradiction is that between bourgeoisie and feudal aristocracy, and as if Napoleonic expansionism did not generate profound national contradictions. In the early writings, at any rate, Marx tended to conceive the socialist revolution on the model of revolution interpreted thus. In late 1847, he addressed the British Chartists as follows:

> Of all countries, England is the one where the contradiction between the proletariat and the bourgeoisie is most highly developed. The victory of the English proletarians over the English bourgeoisie is, therefore, decisive for the victory of all the oppressed over their oppressors. Hence Poland must be liberated not in Poland but in England.[55]

National emancipation of the less developed countries of Eastern Europe is represented as a product of the initiative of the proletariat that has arrived in power in the most advanced country.

Export of the revolution does not represent a problem, because the export of counter-revolution was underway or on the agenda. This applies to 1848, as to 1871, when the victorious Prussian army backed up the French bourgeoisie in suppressing the Paris Commune. As we know, on the latter occasion Marx saw the world divided in two between a globally unified bourgeoisie and a proletariat urged to create an 'international counter-organization of labour': the different forms of class struggle were, in effect, reduced to a single form.

Notes

1. See Pierre-Joseph Proudhon, *La Pornocratie, ou les femmes dans le monde moderne*, Paris: Librairie Internationale, 1875.
2. Quoted in Mario Albertini, 'Nota biografica', in Pierre-Joseph Proudhon, *La Giustizia nella rivoluzione e nella chiesa* Turin: UTET, 1968, pp. 50–1.

3. Karl Marx and Frederick Engels, *Collected Works*, London: Lawrence & Wishart, 1974–2004, Vol. 20, p. 32.
4. Ibid., Vol. 44, p. 255.
5. See Ferdinand Lassale, 'Arbeiterprogramm', in *Reden und Schriften*, Leipzig: Reclam, 1987, p. 221.
6. Marx and Engels, *Collected Works*, Vol. 24, p. 89.
7. Lassalle, 'Arbeiterprogramm', p. 225.
8. Marx and Engels, *Collected Works*, Vol. 27, p. 423.
9. Ibid., Vol. 27, p. 422.
10. Ibid., Vol. 24, p. 45.
11. I derive this information from a note by André Jardin to Alexis de Tocqueville, *Oeuvres complètes*, ed. Jacob-Peter Mayer, Paris: Gallimard, 1951–, Vol. 3, pt. 1, pp. 250–51.
12. See Seymour Drescher, *From Slavery to Freedom: Comparative Studies in the Rise and Fall of Atlantic Slavery*, London: Macmillan, 1999, p. 193 n. 58.
13. Marx and Engels, *Collected Works*, Vol. 41, p. 390.
14. Lassalle, 'Arbeiterprogramm', pp. 280, 310.
15. Marx and Engels, *Collected Works*, Vol. 6, pp. 507–8.
16. Ibid., Vol. 6, p. 518.
17. Benjamin Disraeli, *Sybil or The Two Nations*, ed. S.M. Smith, Oxford and New York: Oxford University Press, 1988, pp. 65–6, 442.
18. Quoted in William John Wilkinson, *Tory Democracy*, New York: Octagon Books, 1980, p. 52.
19. Marx and Engels, *Collected Works*, Vol. 43, p. 429.
20. See Georg Adler, *Die imperialistische Sozialpolitik. Disraeli, Napoleon III, Bismarck. Eine Skizze*, Tübingen: Laupp'sche Buchhandlung, 1897, pp. 43–4.
21. Marx and Engels, *Collected Works*, Vol. 4, pp. 582–3.
22. Ibid., Vol. 6, p. 211.
23. Ibid., Vol. 6, p. 485.
24. Ibid., Vol. 5, p. 52.
25. Ibid., Vol. 6, p. 493.
26. Ibid., Vol. 6, pp. 389–90.
27. Ibid., Vol. 35, p. 750.
28. Ibid., Vol. 22, p. 338.
29. Ibid., Vol. 22, p. 354.
30. Ibid., Vol. 35, p. 290.
31. Ibid., Vol. 41, pp. 4–5.
32. Ibid., Vol. 41, p. 430.
33. Ibid., Vol. 19, p. 115.
34. Ibid., Vol. 16, p. 147.
35. Ibid., Vol. 5, p. 52.

36. Ibid., Vol. 4, pp. 36–7.
37. Ibid., Vol. 4, pp. 298, 502.
38. Ibid., Vol. 4, pp. 392, 390.
39. Ibid., Vol. 7, p. 165.
40. Ibid., Vol. 6, p. 493.
41. Ibid., Vol. 6, pp. 210, 492.
42. Ibid., Vol. 48, p. 365.
43. Ibid., Vol. 48, pp. 364, 369.
44. Ibid., Vol. 47, p. 403.
45. Ibid., Vol. 41, pp. 307, 416.
46. Ibid., Vol. 21, pp. 98–9.
47. Ibid., Vol. 6, p. 382.
48. Ibid., Vol. 6, p. 501.
49. Ibid., Vol. 22, p. 334.
50. Ibid., Vol. 24, p. 95.
51. Ibid., Vol. 10, p. 281.
52. Antonio Gramsci, *Selections from the Prison Notebooks*, ed. and trans. Quintin Hoare and Geoffrey Nowell Smith, London: Lawrence & Wishart, 1971, p. 241.
53. Marx and Engels, *Collected Works*, Vol. 5, pp. 195–6.
54. Ibid., Vol. 4, p. 123.
55. Ibid., Vol. 6, p. 389.

CHAPTER 6

The Multiplicity of Struggles for Recognition and the Conflict of Liberties

1 THE RANKING OF CLASS STRUGGLES

At their best, when they overcome the binary logic into which, notwithstanding their theoretical premises, they sometimes lapse, Marx and Engels found themselves confronting the problem I have already mentioned. A determinate historical situation is always characterized by a variegated multiplicity of conflicts; and any conflict involves the presence of a multiplicity of social subjects, who express different, opposing interests and ideas. To get one's bearings in this kind of labyrinth, it is necessary to examine not only the internal configuration of each of these conflicts but also how they are articulated and structured in a concrete totality. Mastering a theoretical crisis is a challenge theoretically, as well as politically.

The tangle of political and social, national and international conflicts that erupted in Central-Eastern Europe between 1848 and 1849 represents such a challenge. The Habsburg Empire was shaken to its foundations by a major revolution that radically challenged the *ancien régime*. Metternich managed to suppress it by skilfully exploiting aspirations to autonomy and self-government on the part of various Slav minorities, who did not identify with the government that was being established in Vienna and Budapest. But it was the intervention of tsarist Russia that sealed the defeat of the revolution. We find ourselves facing a set of demands and rights which, taken in isolation, are all legitimate and, in fact, sacrosanct.

It is their conjunction that represents a problem and creates dilemmas. Given their head by Metternich and Nicholas I, the national aspirations of various peoples not only furnished reserves for putting down the revolution in Vienna and Budapest but also reinforced the expansionism of tsarist Russia, which was the bulwark of European reaction.

So how was the situation to be handled? In early November 1848, Marx compared the tragedy being played out in Central and Eastern Europe, at the expense of the democratic movement, with the tragedy that had struck the Parisian proletariat a few months earlier: '[i]n Paris the mobile guard, in Vienna "Croats"—in both cases *lazzaroni*, lumpen proletariat hired and armed—were used against the working and thinking proletarians'.[1] The Slav nations that let themselves be enrolled by the Habsburg Empire were compared to the sub-proletariat, a class which mostly placed itself in the service of reaction, but might be won over to the revolutionary movement. In other words, the issue was not recognizing the right of every nation to self-determination in the abstract. That was incontestable. The problem consisted in the fact that, in a concrete, determinate situation, because of the initiative and political skill of the imperial power, the right of some nations to self-determination could come into conflict with the right of other nations and with the movement struggling against the *ancien régime* and absolutist monarchy, and for the realization of democracy at home and abroad. What is out of the question is the customary binary logic.

In February 1849, Engels believed he could theoretically master this complex situation by branding the 'counter-revolutionary' Slav peoples struggling against 'an alliance of revolutionary peoples' as 'small intercalated states', which 'have never had a history of their own'. The contingent character of the conflict was occasionally recognized: '[h]ow splendid it would be if the Croats, Pandours, and Cossacks formed the vanguard of European democracy'. Unfortunately, for this to transpire, it would be necessary to 'wait' a long time—too long. But it was a scenario that could not be excluded *a priori*. On other occasions, by contrast, Engels not only invoked 'the most determined use of terror' against aspirations to independence or secession on the part of such 'counter-revolutionary' peoples but seemed to definitively condemn them.[2]

The sometimes repugnant language should not lead us to lose sight of the theoretical and political problem confronting us, which Engels tackled in more mature fashion on other occasions. Let us start with an intervention from 1866. The International Working Men's Association, set up two years earlier, demanded independence for Poland. But (objected by Proudhon's followers) this distracted attention from the social question and echoed themes from Napoleon III's propaganda. To further his expansionist plans, Napoleon likewise declared his support for the liberation struggles of oppressed 'nationalities'. Seeking to demarcate himself from Proudhon's national nihilism on the one hand, and pro-Bonapartist agitation on the other, Engels answered this objection by distinguishing between 'nations' and 'nationalities'. The independence struggle of nations such as Poland and Ireland must be supported. On the other hand, it had to be acknowledged that there was no nation in which different 'nationalities' or remnants of 'nationalities' were not present. One thinks of Alsatian Germans and the 'Celtic inhabitants of Brittany' in the case of France, and Francophone ethnic groups as regards Belgium and Switzerland. Hence, there was always some space for the destabilizing and partitioning manoeuvres with which tsarism and Bonapartism sought to further their expansionism and hegemonism.[3] To counter them, Engels observed in an intervention of 1852, that a rule must be followed. The status of a nation could not be assigned to those groups that did not possess a language of their own and 'the very first conditions of national existence, numbers and compactness of territory'.[4]

The dichotomy between nations with a rich history and historyless 'small states' was now replaced by that between nations and nationalities. The picture is not much clearer as a consequence. But the theoretical and political crux emerges unequivocally: affirmation of the principle of self-determination does not necessarily entail support for the agitation of 'small states' or 'nationalities'. Engels' most questionable, or even utterly unacceptable, pages are precisely those that raise a problem of great contemporary relevance: there are countless separatist movements instrumentally encouraged or supported by great powers which are protagonists of national oppression on a large scale (see Chap. 7, Sect. 3). It may even turn out that recognizing a particular people's self-determination strengthens the main enemy of the liberation movement of oppressed peoples as a whole. We must not lose sight of the conflict of liberties that can arise. In other words, the mutilation of class struggles must be rejected. But that does not mean ignoring the problem whereby a historical situation (especially a major historical crisis) can require a ranking of class struggles.

Engels' error was that he sometimes resorted to formulations that involve a slippage—or convey the impression of slipping—from history into nature. The underlying inspiration is in little doubt. In 1848, to confirm the decisive role of history, Engels compared Provence and Poland. With its culture and 'beautiful language', the former long played a vanguard role. But it ended up suffering 'the total obliteration of its nationality' and complete assimilation into France. Historically and socially, there was even an inversion: Provence became the focal point of 'opposition to the progressive classes in the whole of France' and 'the backbone of the French counter-revolution'. The fate of Poland seemed to be the converse. For a very long time, it was the embodiment of the *ancien régime* and the oppression of an overwhelming mass of serfs by a small aristocracy. Now, however, developing the struggle against national oppression and undertaking a 'democratic-agrarian revolution', in which at least part of the nobility generously participated, Poland might be the revolutionary vanguard of the Slav peoples, all the more so in that it represented the quintessential antagonist of that bulwark of reaction, tsarist Russia.[5]

Russia itself was not frozen in time. In 1875, Engels referred optimistically to the social agitation spreading in that immense country:

> The mass of the Russian people, the peasants, have gone on for centuries, from generation to generation, living their dull, unimaginative lives in a sort of ahistorical torpor [*geschichtslose Versumpfung*]; and the only changes that occurred to interrupt this desolate condition were isolated and fruitless uprisings and new waves of repression carried out by nobility and government. The Russian government itself put an end to this ahistorical existence [*Geschichtslosigkeit*] (in 1861) with the abolition of serfdom which could not be delayed any longer and the redemption of the *corvée*.... The very conditions themselves, therefore, which the Russian peasant is now obliged to face, force him into the movement.... [6]

Having endured so long, the 'ahistorical existence' of the peasant masses and the great majority of the Russian population not only came to an end but was on the point of turning into its opposite. In the Preface to the second Russian edition of the *Communist Manifesto*, Marx and Engels expressed the hope that revolution in Russia might represent 'the signal for a proletarian revolution in the West'.[7] This great country could play a vanguard role because active in it (observed Engels in a letter of 23 April 1885 to Vera Zasulich) was 'a party which frankly and unreservedly accepts the great economic and historical theories evolved by Marx'.[8] The bulwark of reaction was on the point of being transformed into a bulwark of revolution. The country long characterized by an 'ahistorical existence' was (to adopt an expression of Marx's) in the process of becoming a 'locomotive of history'.⁹ The ranking of class struggles, dictated in specific circumstances by an especially tangled skein of contradictions and conflicts of liberties, has nothing to do with a naturalistic ranking of nations.

2   THE EMANCIPATION OF SLAVES AND 'DESPOTIC GOVERNMENT'

The conflict of liberties was also brought out by the American Civil War. At the time of its outbreak, Marx invoked the arguments of the pro-southerners on both sides of the Atlantic: 'even if justice is on the side of the North, does it not remain a vain endeavour to want to subjugate eight million Anglo-Saxons by force!'¹⁰ And again: 'the Southern states have the same right to secede from the North as the United States had to separate from England'.¹¹ Here we have a fine example of binary logic! The focus is exclusively on the clash between the two sections of the white community, completely ignoring both the fate of African Americans and the foreign policy of the contending parties. Let us now attend to Marx's response. James Buchanan, the southerner who occupied the post of President of the USA before Lincoln, pursued a policy whose emblem was the export or 'armed spreading of slavery in Mexico, Central and South America'. Indeed, in these years the 'avowed aim' of Washington was the '[a]rmed spreading of slavery abroad'. And that is not all: Buchanan was determined to annex Cuba, possibly buying it from the Spanish or resorting to force of arms, but in any event without consulting the local population.¹² As regards the European supporters of the slaveholding Confederacy, 'it's truly marvellous how *The Times* (which backed all the anti-Irish Coercion Bills with such intense enthusiasm) is now lamenting that "liberty" will be lost should the North tyrannise over the South'.¹³ In other words, even if we ignore the fate of African Americans, Lincoln's American and European enemies were unable to raise the banner of self-government and self-determination with any credibility.

Those enemies advanced a final argument: 'the government [of the Union] has permitted no man to open his mouth for three months. ... The war has many opponents in the North, but they dare not speak. No less than two hundred newspapers have been suppressed or destroyed by the mob'.¹⁴ Once again we see the binary logic at work. With all other aspects of the conflict ignored and repressed, the political regimes in the

South and North are contrasted. The latter seems more illiberal, in as much as it was engaged in neutralizing those who propagandized for capitulation to the secessionists or, at least, for a compromise with them. In response, Marx noted that, long before the outbreak of the war, a climate of insane violence against abolitionists was prevalent, so that 'for thirty years' a leader like Wendell Phillips had not only to face the insults and threats of 'paid rowdies' but also to 'risk his life'.[15] Hence, even if the focus was exclusively on the white community, the secessionists could not be regarded as the champions of liberty.

Obviously, the neglect of the fate of blacks, and the slavery inflicted on them, is glaring and arbitrary. Marx did not regard self-government or press freedom as 'formal' and 'abstract': he devoted significant pages to both causes. In a concrete, determinate situation, however, a choice may be required: permanent black slavery or partial, temporary restriction of the principles of self-government and press freedom? Both options are painful, but not to the same degree: the abolition of slavery is the pre-eminent, priority task. Hence, the decisive support for Lincoln, who suspended *habeas corpus* and introduced conscription, repressing resistance and revolts against this measure and regimenting the adult male population with an iron fist.

In fact, Marx and Engels urged the Union to demonstrate Jacobin willpower, to employ 'revolutionary methods' in the war against the pro-slavery secession.[16] The condemnation of hesitancy was unequivocal: 'what cowardice on the part of the government and Congress! They shrink from conscription ... from everything that is urgently necessary'.[17] Unfortunately, 'the party that is weary of war is growing', thereby hampering resolution of 'an issue as colossal as this'; 'signs of moral prostration are daily more in evidence and the inability to win grows daily greater. Where is the party whose victory and *avènement* would be synonymous with prosecuting the war *à outrance* and with every available means?'[18] Overall, wrote Engels to Marx on 15 November 1862, the Union did not seem to wish to confront the 'great historical dilemma' facing it.[19]

Subsequently, judgement of Lincoln became more balanced, as he displayed unanticipated energy and, not coincidentally, was accused by opponents inclined to compromise with the South of employing Jacobin methods, imposing 'military government' and 'military commissions', and interpreting 'the word "law" as the will of the President' and *habeas corpus* as the 'power of the President to imprison whom he pleases, as long as he pleases'.[20] In the concrete conflict of liberties that had emerged, it was Lincoln who embodied the cause of freedom, not his opponents.

Marx was not the first to query the binary interpretation of social conflict and to raise the problem of the conflict of liberties. In the late eighteenth century, Adam Smith had observed that slavery could more readily be abolished under a 'despotic government' than a 'free government', whose representative bodies were exclusively reserved for white property-owners. There the condition of black slaves was desperate: 'every law is made by their masters, who will never pass anything prejudicial to themselves'. Hence, 'the freedom of the free was the cause of the great oppression of the slaves ... And as they are the most numerous part of mankind, no human person will wish for liberty in a country where this institution is established'.[21] Hegel had argued in similar fashion as regards serfdom. To abolish it, 'the private rights' of the feudal lords must be 'despotically violated' and the 'liberty of the barons', which entailed the 'absolute serfdom' of the 'nation' and prevented 'the emancipation of the serfs', struck down.[22] This is also the line of thinking in which to situate the argument of the *Communist Manifesto* when it demands 'despotic inroads on the rights of property', so as to put an end to the employer's 'despotism' over the wage slave.[23]

To be precise, it is not a question of choosing between 'freedom' and 'despotism', as some of Smith's formulations would seem to have it, but of understanding the conflict of liberties. In the situation described by the great economist, the struggle for freedom took the form of a merciless struggle against slave-owners and the 'free' representative bodies monopolized by them.

3   THE CONFLICT OF LIBERTIES IN THE COLONIES

The condition of African Americans leads us to the more general theme of colonial peoples and peoples of colonial origin. The category that supplies this section with its title ('conflict of liberties') enables us to get our bearings in Marx and Engels' development and oscillations on this subject.

From the outset, Marx and Engels drew attention to the tragedy of countries invested by colonial expansion. Reference to 'the insurgent Negroes of Haiti' in *The German Ideology*, or the highlighting by *The Poverty of Philosophy* of the fact that British capitalism sacrificed the Indian people *en masse* on the altar of welfare or social peace for the metropolis, is not so important. More significant is another consideration. The key categories of the analysis of capitalism developed by the two thinkers involve reference to the colonial question. The masked, camouflaged slavery detected and denounced in the metropolis is explicitly contrasted with the undisguised slavery imposed in the 'New World' (see Chap. 2, Sects. 1 and 3). Even when the discourse is more elliptical, it is clear that, in addition to the slavery of antiquity, 'wage slavery' refers directly to black, colonial slavery.

Colonial expansion was far from being the triumphal march of civilization and progress fantasized by the culture of the time. The pages devoted by Marx in the 1850s to the conquest of Asia are illuminating. Under the shock wave of 'English steam and English free trade', more than even that of the 'British soldier'—i.e., direct military violence—the traditional 'family communities … based on domestic industry' fell irremediably into crisis: 'myriads of industrious patriarchal and inoffensive social organizations' were cast into 'a sea of woes, [with] their individual members losing at the same time their ancient form of civilization and their hereditary means of subsistence'.[24] There was no doubt: 'the devastating effects of British industry, when contemplated with regard to India, a country as vast as Europe, … are palpable and confounding'.[25] What was witnessed in Asia was a fearful regression. In China too, 'the population sank *en masse* into pauperism'.[26] What in our day has been called the 'great divergence' became still more starker.

The tragedy of the peoples invested by colonization went far beyond a deterioration in their material living conditions:

> The misery inflicted by the British on Hindostan is of an essentially different and infinitely more intense kind than all Hindostan had to suffer before. … England has broken down the entire framework of Indian society, without any symptoms of reconstitution yet appearing. This loss of his old world, with no gain of a new one, imparts a particular kind of the melancholy to the present misery of the Hindoo, and separates Hindostan, ruled by Britain, from all its ancient traditions, and from the whole of its past history.[27]

The picture of colonialism painted here is pitiless. However, statements that give us pause for thought are not wanting: 'can mankind fulfil its destiny without a fundamental revolution in the social state of Asia?' Although driven by egotistical and even ignoble motives, in India, Britain the conqueror was undertaking 'the greatest, and to speak the truth, the only *social* revolution ever heard of in Asia'.[28] Hence 'India … could not escape the fate of being conquered'.[29] In terms of the philosophy of history, British conquest and rule were accorded a certain legitimacy.

We can understand this in terms of the conflict of liberties. In the absence of a revolutionary subject, in a colony frozen in a caste order permanently dividing the inhabitants transversally, with a racial kind of rigidity that prevented the formation of a national consciousness and identity and, *a fortiori*, the idea of the unity of the human race, the only spur to alteration of an intolerable situation seemed to hail from without. While it crushed the principle of self-government and entailed grievous social and human costs, colonial rule objectively challenged the caste order and introduced the first elements of social mobility, laying the foundations for subsequent, more radical changes. In effect, the legitimation of Britain's role is partial and problematic: the 'bourgeois period of history', fostering (materially as well as spiritually) the world market and 'universal intercourse founded upon the mutual dependency of mankind' and the 'development of the productive powers of man', created the conditions for a 'great social revolution' set to yield a 'new world'.[30] If colonial rule was the negation of caste society from without, it had its justification in terms of the philosophy of history only in as much as it seeded the negation of the negation, with the supersession of the 'bourgeois period of history' (and colonial rule). What remains clear is Marx's preference for a different resolution of the conflict of liberties: a proletarian revolution in Britain or the development of a national liberation movement in India.[31]

Significantly, very different accents are to be heard in an article devoted to the other great Asian country, published in the *New York Daily Tribune* on 5 June 1857. In this instance, the celebration of the 'national war' waged by China against the 'piratical policy of the British Government' was clear and unconditional. To avert the mortal danger threatening 'Old China', its people were fighting with 'fanaticism', without respecting the rules. However, 'instead of moralizing on the horrible atrocities of the Chinese, as the chivalrous English press does, we had better recognize that this is a war *pro aris et focis*, a popular war for the maintenance of Chinese nationality'.[32] The British attempt to subjugate China was illegitimate. China could avoid the 'fate of being conquered' which, according to the analysis developed four years earlier, seemed inevitable for India. In China, the weight of a caste order was absent and this made possible the development of a formidable resistance and national liberation movement.

In the interim, a 'war of insurrection' had broken out in India too. The Sepoys had stained themselves with horrible crimes, but Britain had responded with even worse crimes: 'torture formed an organic institution of [British] financial policy'; 'the violations of women, the spittings of children, the roastings of whole villages, were ... mere wanton sports', recorded by 'British officers themselves', who arrogated 'power of life and death' to themselves and wielded it unsparingly.[33]

By now, Marx had reached a general conclusion. The colonial power was indeed the more advanced country. But although it persisted, the conflict of liberties, when thought out anew or in the light of the new situation, no longer redounded to the benefit of Britain. The latter should be 'forced by the general pressure of the civilized world to abandon the compulsory opium cultivation in India and the armed opium propaganda to China'.[34]

The immediately ensuing years saw the development of the crisis that issued in the American Civil War. Marx's research yielded results that threw new light on the history of colonialism. In its time, in the *Neue Rheinische Zeitung* Marx edited, an article by Engels had appeared on 15 February 1849 which interpreted the war recently launched by the USA against Mexico as follows. Thanks to 'the bravery of the American volunteers', 'splendid California has been taken away from the lazy Mexicans, who could not do anything with it'. Exploiting the new, gigantic conquests, the 'energetic Yankees' gave new impetus to the production and circulation of wealth, to 'world trade', to the spread of 'civilisation'. Objections of a moral or legal kind were peremptorily silenced by the article's author. Certainly, what had defeated Mexico was an act of aggression, but it represented a 'fact of world-historic significance'.[35] This was a crudely binary interpretation: it confined itself to comparing the different levels of development of the economy and the representative regime in Mexico and the USA, and concluded by celebrating the latter's war as synonymous with the export of 'civilization' and anti-feudal revolution! What was ignored was the fact that slavery had been abolished in the vanquished country, but not the victorious one. Intoxicated by its military triumph, the latter hoisted the flag (manifestly colonialist in character) of the 'manifest destiny', the providential mission, impelling the USA to dominate or control the whole American continent. The studies undertaken by Marx on the eve of the American Civil War and during it revealed further details: the USA had reintroduced slavery into the Texas wrested from Mexico and the southern states of the USA aspired to build a kind of colonial slave empire in Central America.

Published shortly after the end of the Civil War, Volume One of *Capital* painted a memorable picture of the horrors of the West's 'primitive accumulation' and colonial expansion. It was an implicit, renewed appeal to the labour parties to reject the temptations of 'imperial socialism' once and for all.

4   INTERNATIONALISM AND ITS FORMS

Once the binary interpretation of conflict has been superseded, what of internationalism? Its significance is immediately apparent if we start from the hypothesis of an 'international counter-organization of labour' confronting a 'cosmopolitan conspiracy of capital'. If instead, we take account of the multiplicity of forms of class struggle and, in particular, of the national question, then the picture becomes complicated. It is much more difficult to foster internationalist solidarity within a front whose subjects are very different from one another: sometimes a single social class (the proletariat), at others a whole people struggling against 'the exploitation of one nation by another'.

How, then, should we interpret the slogan ('Workers of all countries, unite!'), with which the *Communist Manifesto* ends? Is it intended to evoke a binary type of conflict and a battle front that uniformly divides all countries in two, so that universally, and more or less exclusively, the same social classes—proletariat and bourgeoisie—are ranged against one another? This watchword also concludes the *Inaugural Address* (of the International Working Men's Association), which explicitly calls upon the workers of Britain (and the most advanced industrial countries) to support the 'national liberation' struggle of countries like Ireland and Poland. Not only this. The *Inaugural Address* solemnly states: '[i]t was not the wisdom of the ruling classes, but the heroic resistance to their criminal folly by the working classes of England that saved the West of Europe from plunging headlong into an infamous crusade for the perpetuation and propagation of slavery on the other side of the Atlantic'.[36] Proletarian internationalism can manifest itself in support for national liberation movements, which sometimes witness the participation of such a broad front as to include even the nobility (the case of Poland), and in a bourgeois government (that of Lincoln) engaged in repressing a pro-slavery secession by force of arms.

On the other hand, drying up a key source of the 'material wealth' and 'moral power' of the dominant classes in Britain, the 'Irish national struggle' and the 'national emancipation of Ireland' were a crucial internationalist contribution to the 'social emancipation' of the British working class.[37] Like the class struggle, internationalism can take different forms on different occasions.

An 'internationalism' that ignored this diversity would be ingenuous or dangerous. On the eve of the 1848 revolution, Engels mocked Louis Blanc, who, forgetful of Napoleon's empire and its colonial and semicolonial practices, liked to point to his people as the very embodiment of cosmopolitanism: 'the democrats of other nations … will not be satisfied in the assertion, on the part of the French, that they are cosmopolites by the mere fact that they are French, an assertion which amounts to the demand urged upon all others to become Frenchmen'.[38] Not coincidentally, Blanc would later be branded an 'imperial democrat' posing as a revolutionary.[39] When it avoids the national question and the genuinely internationalist task of support for oppressed nations, putative cosmopolitanism or internationalism turns into an uncritical, fanatical chauvinism.

This was also Marx's view. Having mocked the 'moronic cynicism' exhibited by Proudhon over Poland's ambition to shake off the yoke of the Russian Empire, he dismissed as 'Proudhonised Stirnerianism'the thesis that 'any nationality and even nations' are '*préjugés surannés* (outdated prejudices). The source is a letter to Engels of 20 June 1866, which continues thus:

> The English laughed heartily when I began my speech with the observation that our friend Lafargue, and others, who had abolished nationalities, has addressed us in 'French', i.e., in a language which 9/10 of the audience did not understand. I went on to suggest that by his denial of nationalities he seemed quite unconsciously to imply their absorption by the model French nation.[40]

We are reminded of the irony with which, nearly twenty years earlier, Blanc's cosmopolitan and internationalist declarations had been treated by Engels. The latter went through a final process of maturation. In a text of 1866, he criticized French Enlightenment figures for having allowed themselves to be taken in by Catherine II and tsarism in general. In Poland, Russia elevated itself to protector of Orthodox Christians. The latter were mainly serfs and here was Russia not hesitating to raise the banner of social revolution alongside that of 'religious toleration'. It intervened in the country that was the object of its desires 'in the name of the right of revolution, arming the serfs against their lords'. Here was 'a fine specimen of a class-war' or 'war of class against class'.[41] As we can see, where it ignores or represses the national question, the most revolutionary and internationalist slogan, formulated by Marx himself in *The Poverty of Philosophy* (see Chap. 5, Sect. 3), can be turned into a tool legitimizing chauvinism and expansionism. Engels' analysis hits home. It is only to be added that Frederick II of Prussia adopted a similar posture to Catherine II. Addressing the *philosophes*, he justified his campaign against Poland as follows: 'the masters there practice the cruellest tyranny over the slaves'.[42]

Analysis of Engels' development reveals an interesting fact: a sometimes crude theorist of the export of revolution subsequently became its most radical critic. In 1870, Engels identified the start of the bourgeois revolution in Prussia not from the arrival of Napoleon's troops, but the reform movement that developed in the wake of the national resistance struggle against Napoleon![43] A reversal of positions occurred relative to *The Holy Family* and *The German Ideology*, written with Marx in their youth.

The late Engels thought deeply about the subject. Let us read the letter of 7 February 1882 to Kautsky: 'an international movement of the proletariat is possible only as between independent nations', just as 'international co-operation is possibly only among equals'.[44] This position was forcefully restated ten years later: 'a sincere collaboration of the European nations is possible only if each of these nations is fully autonomous in its own house'. Leading the struggle for national independence, 'Polish workers' also played an international role in as much as this laid the foundations for an otherwise impossible cooperation.[45] Indeed, Engels repeated two years before his death, '[w]ithout restoring autonomy and unity to each nation, it will be impossible to achieve the international union of the proletariat'.[46]

The chauvinist danger did not derive from nations fighting tenaciously for their liberation: 'I am of the opinion that two nations in Europe are not only entitled but duty-bound to be national before they are international—Ireland and Poland. For the best way they can be international is by being well and truly national'.[47] Paradoxically, the chauvinist danger was represented by so-called 'republican internationalism' which, for example, assigned France, by virtue of its revolutionary glories, the 'mission [of] universal liberator'. On closer inspection, 'republican internationalism' proved to be fanatical 'French chauvinism'.[48] This is a general rule: when it ignores the national question, internationalism turns into its opposite. The repression of national particularities in the name of an abstract 'internationalism' facilitates things for a nation intent presenting itself as the embodiment of the universal; and this is precisely what chauvinism—in fact, the most fanatical chauvinism—consists in.

5 The Labour Movement and 'Imperial Socialism'

Drawing attention to the national (and colonial) question was all the more urgent because colonialist ideology was in the process of making massive inroads into working-class parties, which proved increasingly incapable of expressing solidarity and support for colonial peoples engaged in class struggle against the 'exploitation of one nation by another'. In 1858, Engels not only bitterly noted that 'the English proletariat is actually becoming more and more bourgeois', but added: '[i]n the case of a nation which exploits the entire world this is, of course, justified to some extent'.[49] Five years later, he went further: 'the English proletariat's revolutionary energy has all but completely evaporated and the English proletarian has declared himself in full agreement with the dominancy of the bourgeoisie'.[50]

I have cited two letters to Marx, who reached the same conclusions. Far from being in solidarity with the Irish worker, he observed in 1870, the English worker 'feels himself to be a member of the ruling nation.... His attitude towards him is roughly that of poor whites to the niggers in the former slave states of the American Union'.[51] Hence, we are dealing with an ideological involution entailing a slide not only into chauvinism but also racism.

Marx was right to condemn the fact that the British worker's inclination to view his Irish counterpart as a 'nigger' was 'kept artificially alive and intensified by the press, the pulpit, the comic papers, in short by all the means at the disposal of the ruling class'.[52] This campaign succeeded in Britain as in the American Deep South, where (Marx observed) whites of modest means espoused the cause of the slave-owners and often formed the mass social base for attempts to export slavery to Central America. In any event, it was no longer possible to indulge in the illusion derived from the binary reading of conflict and the related credence in the immediate self-evidence of exploitation—an illusion entertained, in particular, by the young Engels—that the 'national prejudices' of the dominant classes were alien to the proletariat.

Very different from such early hopes was the picture that Engels himself drew in a letter of 12 September 1882 to Kautsky. The London government and dominant classes were inclined to co-opt the overseas white settlers: 'the countries occupied by European settlers, such as Canada, the Cape, Australia, will all become independent'. This would not apply to territories inhabited by 'natives', who would continue to be oppressed and exploited. Unfortunately, this policy met with support from British 'workers', who 'cheerfully go snacks in England's monopoly of the world market and colonies', and did not intend to challenge colonialism. Peoples of colour could expect aid only from a proletariat capable of resisting the lures of colonial expansion. What position should be concretely adopted?

> India may, indeed very probably will, start a revolution and, since a proletariat that is effecting its own emancipation cannot wage a colonial war, it would have to be given its head, which would obviously entail a great deal of destruction, but after all that sort of thing is inseparable from any revolution. The same thing could also happen elsewhere, say in Algeria or Egypt, and would certainly suit *us* best.[53]

Compared with the West, the colonies or ex-colonies were at a more backward level of development, were 'semi-civilized'. But it would be senseless to seek to export civilization or revolution: 'a victorious proletariat cannot forcibly confer any boon whatever on another country without undermining its own victory in the process. Which does not, of course, in any way preclude defensive wars of various kinds'.[54] This warning did not succeed in blocking the spread of 'imperial socialism' in the ranks of the working class. It was to the challenge represented by this serious mutilation of the class struggle that Lenin sought to respond.

NOTES

1. Karl Marx and Frederick Engels, *Collected Works*, London: Lawrence & Wishart, 1975–2004, Vol. 7, p. 505.
2. Ibid., Vol. 8, pp. 366–7, 371, 378.
3. Ibid., Vol. 20, pp. 153–8.
4. Ibid., Vol. 11, p. 71.
5. Ibid., Vol. 7, pp. 372–3.
6. Ibid., Vol. 24, p. 104.
7. Ibid., Vol. 24, p. 426.
8. Ibid., Vol. 47, p. 279.
9. Ibid., Vol. 10, p. 122.
10. Ibid., Vol. 19, p. 32.
11. Ibid., Vol. 19, p. 155.
12. Ibid., Vol. 19, pp. 42, 37–8.

13. Ibid., Vol. 41, p. 369.
14. Ibid., Vol. 19, p. 155.
15. Ibid., Vol. 19, p. 233.
16. Ibid., Vol. 41, p. 400.
17. Ibid., Vol. 41, p. 387.
18. Ibid., Vol. 41, pp. 423, 457.
19. Ibid., Vol. 41, p. 428.
20. See Arthur M. Schlesinger Jr., *History of United States Political Parties*, New York and London: Chelsea House & Bawker, 1973, pp. 915–21.
21. Adam Smith, *Lectures on Jurisprudence*, Indianapolis: Liberty Classics, 1982, pp. 452–3, 182.
22. G.W.F. Hegel, *Vorlesungen über die Philosophie der Weltgeschichte*, ed. Georg Lasson, Leipzig: Meiner, 1919–20, pp. 918, 902–03.
23. Marx and Engels, *Collected Works*, Vol. 6, pp. 504, 491.
24. Ibid., Vol. 12, p. 132.
25. Ibid., Vol. 12, p. 222.
26. Ibid., Vol. 10, p. 266.
27. Ibid., Vol. 12, pp. 126–7.
28. Ibid., Vol. 12, p. 132.
29. Ibid., Vol. 12, p. 217.
30. Ibid., Vol. 12, p. 222.
31. Ibid., Vol. 12, p. 221.
32. Ibid., Vol. 15, pp. 281–2.
33. Ibid., Vol. 15, pp. 353–4.
34. Ibid., Vol. 16, p. 13.
35. Ibid., Vol. 8, pp. 365–6.
36. Ibid., Vol. 20, p. 13.
37. Ibid., Vol. 43, pp. 473–5.
38. Ibid., Vol. 6, p. 411.
39. Ibid., Vol. 42, p. 270.
40. Ibid., Vol. 42, p. 287.
41. Ibid., Vol. 20, pp. 160–1.
42. Quoted in Furio Diaz, *Filosofia e politica nel Settecento francese*, Turin: Einaudi, 1962, p. 483 n. 1.
43. Marx and Engels, *Collected Works*, Vol. 23, p. 628.
44. Ibid., Vol. 46, p. 192.
45. Ibid., Vol. 27, p. 274.
46. Ibid., Vol. 27, p. 366.
47. Ibid., Vol. 46, p. 193.
48. Ibid., Vol. 46, p. 192.
49. Ibid., Vol. 40, p. 344.

50. Ibid., Vol. 41, p. 465.
51. Ibid., Vol. 43, pp. 473–5.
52. Ibid., Vol. 43, p. 475.
53. Ibid., Vol. 46, p. 322.
54. Ibid., Vol. 46, pp. 322–3.

CHAPTER 7

The South-East Passage

1 Lenin as a Critic of Mutilation of the Class Struggle

Five years after Engels' death, writing in the *Sozialistische Monatshefte*, Bernstein noted with satisfaction:

> If, in the United States, Canada, South America, and some parts of Australia, etc., several million men find themselves living next to hundreds of thousands from other times, the credit is due to the colonizing advance of European civilization. And if, in England and elsewhere, many nutritious and flavoursome tropical products have become staple items of popular consumption; and if the great American and Australian ranges and fields supply cheap meat and bread to millions of European workers, we must thank the colonial enterprise.... Without the colonial expansion of our economy, the poverty that still exists in Europe today, which we are trying to eradicate, would be much worse and we would have much less hope of eliminating it. Even when counter-balanced by the crimes of colonialism, the benefits derived from colonies always weigh much more heavily in the scales.[1]

Let us focus on the final assertion. It coincided with the consummation of the effacement of Native Americans in the USA and the Aborigines in Australia and New Zealand. These were the years when in South Africa, in the words of Ludwig Gumplowicz, theorist and apologist for 'racial struggle', the 'Christian Boers' regarded and treated 'the jungle men and Hottentots' not like 'humans', but as 'entities' (*Geschöpfe*) whom it was legitimate to exterminate like 'wild game in the forest'.[2]

But for Bernstein colonialism's 'crimes' counted for less than the 'benefits' that could be obtained thanks to it. While Lassalle resolved the class struggle by pursuing a rudimentary welfare state without political democracy, first the British Labourists and then Bernstein resolved it by pursuing political democracy that sought to extract more or less significant social reforms, but which legitimized colonial expansion and, in fact, benefitted from it. 'Imperial socialism' was manifestly also progressing in the most prestigious and authoritative socialist party of the time.

This is the historical context to be borne in mind if we wish to understand *What is to be Done?*, a text by Lenin that appeared two years after Bernstein's article. Two years had also passed since the great powers' expedition to put down the Boxer Rebellion in China. Colonialist violence, Lenin observed in December 1900, had rained down on 'the unarmed Chinese populace, who were drowned or killed, with no holding back from the slaughter of women and children, not to speak of the looting of palaces, homes, and shops'. Russian soldiers, and the invaders generally, had attacked China 'like savage beasts, burning down whole villages, shooting, bayonetting, and drowning in the Amur River unarmed inhabitants, their wives and their children'. Yet, such infamy had been extolled as a 'civilising mission' by the ruling class, 'the press that kowtows to it', and, ultimately, much or even most public opinion.[3] It was an enterprise that also aimed 'to corrupt the political consciousness of the masses'. To try to eliminate 'popular discontent', attempts were made 'to divert [it] from the government to some other object'. This was not a difficult operation:

> For example, hostility is being stirred up against the Jews; the gutter press carries on Jew-baiting campaigns, as if the Jewish workers do not suffer in exactly the same way as the Russian workers from the oppression of capital and the police government. At the present time, the press is conducting a campaign against the Chinese; it is howling about the savage yellow race and its hostility towards civilisation, about Russia's task of enlightenment, about the enthusiasm with which the Russian soldiers go into battle, etc. etc. Journalists who crawl on their bellies before the government and the money-bags are straining every nerve to rouse the hatred of the people against China.[4]

The campaign paid dividends: only 'the voices of the class-conscious workers, of the advanced representatives of the many millions of the working people, are not heard amid this rejoicing'.[5] Even in the case of the proletariat, only a minority resisted the rampant chauvinist contagion.

Lenin could no longer share the illusion harboured by Marx and Engels in their youth. In their view, the process impelling the proletariat to manifest a revolutionary consciousness, and to make a revolution destined to emancipate the whole of humanity, as well as a specific class, was inexorable. The bourgeois revolution had concluded with co-option and fusion between the old ruling class and the new one, so that relations of exploitation and domination remained largely intact. For the social bloc in power in the first half of the nineteenth century, by contrast, it was not possible to co-opt the proletariat, which was irreducibly antithetical to the bourgeoisie. The emancipation of the proletariat would, therefore, be the emancipation of humanity as a whole and the configuration of the proletariat as a conscious revolutionary subject represented by the crucial (impending) turning-point in world history. But now the tendency to co-opt substantial sections of the proletariat of Britain or other countries into colonial adventurism and exploitation was obvious to everyone.

Thus, there lapsed another presupposition in the platform Marx and Engels had developed in their early years, but which they had not repudiated or explicitly problematized subsequently; in the proletariat's conditions of existence, 'the abstraction of all humanity, even of the *semblance* of humanity' was so obvious that, thanks to 'the contemplation of the situation of this class', even individuals socially external to it could partake in its indignation and struggle (see Chap. 5, Sect. 4). On the one hand, the success of 'imperial socialism' ended up inadvertently drawing attention to the revolutionary subject represented by colonial peoples, who were oppressed and forced to pay the price of the policy of co-option of the working class pursued by the bourgeoisie in the capitalist metropolis. On the other, it provoked a crisis in the naïvely sensualist epistemology that attributed an illuminating character to direct perception in and of itself. The new situation dictated the transition to a rational analysis of the totality of political and social relations, national and international, as a precondition for the formation of revolutionary consciousness and participation in the class struggle.

Along with the colonial question, inter-imperialist contradictions militated in the same direction. In a letter of 15 February 1886 to August Bebel, Engels had observed that in Britain, the mass of 'genuine working men' tended to ally with the *Kampfzöllern*—those who, in the name of 'fair trade' and the struggle against the unfair competition for which they criticized other countries (Germany primarily), wanted to shield British industry via protectionism.[6] The ever fiercer competition between the great capitalist powers involved the working class itself, and this was set to become worse in subsequent years. In the preparatory notes for his essay on imperialism, Lenin gleaned information from the book of a German historian that left him shaken and disheartened: 'in August 1893 Italian workers in Aigues Mortes were beaten half dead by their French competitors'.[7] The process of acquiring class consciousness faced an increasing number of obstacles. Corresponding to the political turn, which required particular attention to the devastating effects of imperialism, was an epistemological turn, with an abandonment of the sensualist platform that possibly derived from Feuerbach's influence on Marx and Engels' youth. We can now understand *What is to be Done?*:

> Working-class consciousness cannot be genuine political consciousness unless the workers are trained to respond to *all* cases of tyranny, oppression, violence, and abuse, no matter *what class* is affected—unless they are trained, moreover, to respond from a Social-Democratic point of view and no other. The consciousness of the working masses cannot be genuine classconsciousness, unless the workers learn, from concrete, and above all from topical, facts and events to observe *every* other social class in *all* the manifestations of its intellectual, ethical, and political life; unless they learn to apply in practice and materialist analysis and the materialist estimate of *all* aspects of the life and activity of *all* classes, strata, and groups of the population. Those who concentrate the attention, observation, and consciousness of the working class exclusively, or even mainly, upon itself alone are not Social-Democrats; for the self-knowledge of the working class is indissolubly bound up, not solely with a fully clear theoretical understanding—it would be even truer to say, not so much with the theoretical, as with the practical, understanding—of the relationships between *all* the various classes of modern society, acquired through the experience of political life. ... The sphere from which alone it is possible to obtain this knowledge is the sphere of relationships of *all* classes and strata to the state and the government, the sphere of the interrelations between *all* classes.[8]

Acquisition of class consciousness and participation in revolutionary class struggle presupposed understanding the social totality in all its aspects: the keywords are those emphasized by me. What was required was 'an organisation of revolutionaries capable of guiding the *entire* proletarian struggle for emancipation'.[9] In the case of Russia, the revolutionary party was characterized by 'the political exposure of the autocracy in *all* its aspects'.[10]

The socio-political system to be overthrown did not only comprise the exploitation of workers in factories. The oppression of national minorities (in Russia, Jews in particular), as well as imperialist expansionism intent on subjecting yet more peoples, must not be ignored. The revolutionary party must know how to conduct research and agitate 'on questions of the government's home and foreign policy, on questions of the economic evolution of Russia and of Europe'; must seize every opportunity 'to clarify for *all* and everyone the world-historic significance of the struggle for emancipation of the proletariat'. And a constitutive, crucial part of that struggle was the emancipation of women, as well as the emancipation of colonial slaves, racialized by the liberal bourgeoisie as barbarians external to civilization, and therefore, fated to endure the oppression of white, Western super-men. In this sense, the revolutionary 'tribune of the people' was ranged against the reformist 'trade-union secretary',[11] who often (observed the essay on imperialism, citing an observation by Engels with which we are familiar) behaved as a prop of the ruling class and the uncritical representative of 'a nation which exploits the whole world'.[12]

2 Le Bon's *Crowd Psychology* and Lenin's *What is to be Done?*

Published two years after Bernstein's intervention in favour of colonialism, and the ravages of the 'civilizing mission' in China, *What is to be Done?* appeared seven years after Gustave Le Bon's *Crowd Psychology*. This is not an irrelevant detail. The French author called upon the bourgeoisie to reorganize its propaganda and hegemonic apparatus. It was necessary to register the 'astonishing power of advertising' and promote a political personality or line like a consumer product—for example, a 'chocolate'. This is well-known. Less so are the final considerations of the psychologist of crowds. By definition, the latter were incapable of arguing logically. But this datum, seemingly a drawback, was in fact the precondition for solving the problem: 'the type of hero dear to crowds will always have the semblance of a Caesar. His insignia attracts them, his authority overawes them, and his sword instils them with fear'.[13] In other words, the masses could be controlled at the level of propaganda by employing the seductive techniques peculiar to commercial advertising, and in terms of content by enthusing them with militaristic and bellicose ventures.

Lenin's platform was opposed to Le Bon's on both counts. To counter and neutralize the machine for mass stupefaction theorized by the psychologist of crowds, *What is to be Done?* appealed to the critical intelligence of vanguard workers, who were exhorted not to let themselves be swindled by the 'chocolate' dangled by the dominant class. And an initial demonstration of independent judgment consisted in the ability to resist the seductions of the 'insignia' of a 'Caesar'. Colonial expeditions, and the threat of war hanging over the capitalist metropolis itself, must be contested: 'the European states that have flung themselves upon China are already beginning to quarrel over the division of the booty, and no one can say how this quarrel will end'.[14]

The habitual criticism of Lenin for militarizing politics, thus, seems unjustified. The 'sword' of Caesar evoked by Le Bon aimed to impose 'authority' and arouse 'fear' inside the country as well. In rejecting an economistic view of class struggle, *What is to be Done?* stressed the importance of the political struggle for democracy. In the theorist of crowd psychology the theme, deeply rooted in the liberal tradition, of the 'childish multitude', now summoned to loyally follow its 'Caesar' in impending bellicose adventures, reached its apex. With his focus on colonial expeditions and the perils of war between the great powers, Lenin accused trade unionists (for whom the popular masses could be interested in nothing beyond economic demands) of treating workers 'with nursemaid concern'.[15]

Undoubtedly, the Bolshevik Party also succeeded in winning power because it was the only socialist party equal to the state of emergency which, having been peculiar to tsarist Russia, was diffused on a European and even global scale with the outbreak of the First World War. We are unquestionably dealing with a party organized in such a way as to be able to pass, if necessary, from the 'weapon of criticism' to 'criticism by weapons', in the young Marx's formulation.[16] Those who seek to write off the Leninist party as a machine exclusively committed to organizing violence would do well to reflect on the unwitting affidavit for it by an author with impeccable credentials. Ernst Nolte, the patriarch of historical revisionism, describes as follows how the crack troops of Lavr G. Kornilov, author in September 1917 of an attempted pro-tsarist coup d'état (supported by the liberal West), were confronted by the Bolsheviks:

They opposed an army of agitators to the supreme commander's advancing troops, to convince them that, in obeying their officers, they were acting against their true interests, prolonging the war and paving the way for the restoration of tsarism. And so, in the march on Petrograd, and already in various parts of the country, the troops yielded to the persuasive force of arguments that simply expressed their own deepest desires and anxieties, of which they were not fully conscious. None of the officers present will have been able to forget how their soldiers slipped away from them not under grenade fire, but under a hail of words.[17]

We have seen *What is to be Done?* contrast the trade-union leader, lacking genuine class consciousness, with the 'tribune of the people', protagonist of the revolutionary class struggle. Focusing exclusively on the 'concrete reality' of wage increases or better working conditions, the former closes his eyes to the oppression of colonial peoples—in fact, not infrequently winds up sharing the chauvinist arrogance of the bourgeoisie in the capitalist metropolis. He continues to demonstrate his subaltern character during the struggle for hegemony between the great powers and in imperialist war itself. Proclaimed 'concreteness' thus, turns out to be a frightening abstraction, which sometimes involves sacrificing the very life of popular masses on the altar of ruling-class interests and ambitions.

In criticizing trade unionism, Lenin was repeatedly accused by his opponents of 'depart[ing] from the class point of view, obscur[ing] class antagonisms, and put[ting] into the forefront the common nature of the discontent with the government'.[18] His insistence on the categories of 'nation' and 'people' (or 'population') was rejected as alien to Marxism and the standpoint of 'the class struggle'.[19] However, for the Russian revolutionary it was clear that progress could not be made towards achieving the proletariat's 'class goal' 'unless we ... uphold the equality of the various nations'.[20] What defined revolutionary class consciousness was precisely attention to the coercive relations that constitute the capitalist and imperialist system.

3 THE 'IMMENSE SIGNIFICANCE OF THE NATIONAL QUESTION'

Among them was national oppression. Accordingly, the struggle against it was an essential form of class struggle. Starting from this presupposition, Lenin was able to foresee the main contours of the twentieth century with amazing lucidity—and not only because he appreciated that a phase of comparatively peaceful development was set to come to an end. He was also able to anticipate the constitutive elements in the major historical crisis, the huge storm that was gathering. A text of December 1914 is illuminating. An unprecedented global war was raging and Lenin, appealing for the transformation of imperialist war into a revolution or a revolutionary civil war, expressed his utter contempt for the patriotic rhetoric also used by many socialists to justify the ongoing carnage. But this did not prevent him from stressing the 'immense significance of the national question' in the century that was in its early stages.[21] Even before the war, and then during it, Lenin identified the epicentres of the impending global clash over the national question with precision: Eastern Europe and Asia, on the one hand, and 'the semi-colonies and colonies', on the other.[22] As regards the first epicentre, one thinks of the dissolution of the tsarist Empire, Hitler's attempt to build 'German Indies' in the East and, finally, the disappearance of the Soviet Union. As to the second, national liberation movements in China, India, Vietnam and so forth come to mind.

Obviously, the two epicentres did not coincide with the crisis zone in its entirety. In October 1916, when Wilhelm II's army was at the gates of Paris, Lenin, on the one hand, reiterated the imperialist character of the world war underway, and on the other, drew attention to a possible reversal. Should the conflict end 'in victories like Napoleon's and in the subjugation of a number of viable national states …, then a great national war in Europe would be possible'.[23] Such is the scenario that materialized on much of the European continent between 1939 and 1945: the victory of a Napoleonic kind, won by Hitler, prompted a 'great national war' in France itself.

Finally, Lenin drew attention to the national oppression which, even in peacetime, could occur in the capitalist metropolis itself. As proof of 'the immense significance of the national question', he referred to 'the brutal oppressors of Negroes' in the North American democratic republic.[24] During the twentieth century, white supremacy was to be the target of fierce struggles in the USA, South Africa, and so on, as well as at a global level.

In the round, a revolutionary exit from the impending major historical crisis was inconceivable without taking account of the national question. In July 1916, Lenin mocked those who went in search of the class struggle and revolution in the pure state: '[t]o imagine that social revolution is *conceivable* without revolts by small nations in the colonies and in Europe

... is to *repudiate social revolution*. Whoever expects a "pure" social revolution will *never* live to see it. Such a person pays lip-service to revolution without understanding what revolution is'.[25] Naturally, not all national movements played a progressive role and merited support from the revolutionary party and 'tribune of the people'. In broaching this problem, Lenin had recourse to two theoretical models. In the early months of 1914, stressing the salience of the national question in a debate with Rosa Luxemburg, he added: 'Marx had no doubt as to the subordinate position of the national question as compared with the "labour question". But his theory is as far from ignoring national movements as heaven is from earth'. 'National demands' were prominent, but the politically conscious proletariat 'subordinates' them to the class struggle.[26] This formulation is not altogether satisfying. It seems to be based on a clear distinction between 'national question' and 'labour question', between national struggle and 'class struggle'. Here we are far removed from the viewpoint of Marx, for whom (in a colony like Ireland) the 'social question' could take the form of the 'national question' and the class struggle take the form, at least initially, of national struggle. On the other hand, we have seen Marx compare the role played by the 'Croats' in 1848–9 to that of the lumpenproletariat (see Chap. 6, Sect. 1). Like peoples in a subaltern position, subaltern classes can play a reactionary role; the problem of distinguishing between movements is general in kind.

Lenin's second formulation is more mature. Having recalled Marx and Engels' support for the Irish and Poles, but not the 'Czechs' and 'South Slavs' (and Croats), at the time 'serving as "Russian outposts" in Europe', he continued as follows in July 1916:

> The several demands of democracy, including self-determination, are not an absolute, but only a *small part* of the general-democratic (now: general-socialist) *world* movement. In individual concrete cases, the part may contradict the whole; if so, it must be rejected. It is possible that the republican movement in one country may be merely an instrument of the clerical or financial-monarchist intrigues of other countries; if so, we must *not* support this particular, concrete movement, but it would be ridiculous to delete the demand for a republic from the programme of international Social-Democracy on these grounds.[27]

Contrasted here are not 'national question' and 'labour question', but the 'small part' and the 'whole'. Insofar as they were instrumentalized and controlled by tsarism, the national aspirations of the Czechs (and

Croats) lacked legitimacy exclusively with reference to the 'national question'. They were a 'small part' that came into contradiction with the national liberation movement as a whole, whose main enemy was tsarist Russia. Whether the 'whole' is represented, in Lenin's terminology, by the bourgeois 'democratic movement' or the 'world socialist movement', the problem of subordination of the 'small part' to it cannot be avoided. And, naturally, the solution to the problem is not unequivocal and without its contradictions. This does not only apply to the revolutionary wave of 1848–9. We have seen Adam Smith invoking 'despotic government' against slave-owners. The representative bodies hegemonized by them were a 'small part' that came into contradiction with the 'whole'; and the same might be said of the self-government of the slaveholding South abolished by Lincoln and the Union army.

Lenin stressed that 'small-nation movements' could be manipulated by Bonapartism and tsarism—or (we might add) imperialism—'for their own benefit'.[28] The history of the twentieth century amply demonstrates the point. Columbia hesitated to concede or cede to the USA a strip of land for a canal intended to link the Atlantic and the Pacific, consecrating the imperial ascendancy of the North American republic. But the latter did not allow itself to be fettered by 'formal' law. A new country was created out of nothing. Having achieved 'independence', Panama promptly agreed to all of Washington's requests. In 1960, the independence of the Congo was followed by an attempt at secession by Katanga (a region rich in minerals), supported by the former colonial power (Belgium) and the West as a whole. Some years later, the USA combined terroristic bombing of Vietnam and Laos with encouragement and support to this or that separatist movement and 'small nationality'. And we could go on at length down to our own day.

While, between 1914 and 1918, he appealed for the transformation of imperialist war into revolutionary civil war, Lenin warned about the potential return of national war in the capitalist metropolis itself—a national war of which capitalist and colonialist France might be the protagonist. There is no doubt that intellectually too a tremendous effort is demanded of the 'tribune of the people'. In an intervention of June 1920, Lenin encapsulated the attitude that should inform the development of the revolutionary class struggle as follows: it should be guided by 'a concrete analysis of a concrete situation … the very gist, the living soul, of Marxism'.[29] The break with credence in the immediate self-evidence of exploitation and oppression could not be clearer! Awareness of the precise tangled skein of contradictions and class struggles, national and international, characteristic of a determinate historical situation, has erased any residue of immediacy.

In light of all this, the thesis that 'the lasting *theoretical* effect of Leninism has been an appalling impoverishment of the field of Marxian diversity',[30] is dubious, to say the least. Evasion of the great and terrible history of the twentieth century seems in search of a scapegoat here. Lenin's great theoretical merit is that he superseded the binary interpretation of class struggle for good and broke with the sensualist epistemology of Marx and Engels' early writings! That is why he was able to anticipate with amazing lucidity twentieth-century developments—a century unintelligible without the lesson, even more epistemological than political, of the great Russian revolutionary. Something else should be underscored: latent in the authors of the *Communist Manifesto*, the *tragic* vision of the historical process and class struggle now becomes clear. We have tragedy (in the philosophical sense of the term) when we are faced not with right and wrong, but two different rights, even if they are unequal and sometimes markedly so. The national demands of the Czechs or other nationalities can forfeit legitimacy, not because they are unjustified in themselves, but because they are absorbed by a more powerful reality, which represents a much more serious threat to the freedom and liberation of nations.

The 'tribune of the people' is called upon to appreciate all this and thereby become the protagonist of a class struggle that constantly changes its forms. Pursuit of the universal (the construction of a society finally free of any exploitation and domination) always materializes in a concrete engagement, which targets and contests war, fascism, colonial expansionism and national oppression.

4 THE BRIEF SEASON OF 'INTERNATIONAL CIVIL WAR'

The baptism of fire was the gigantic conflict that broke out in 1914, which was evoked and invoked implicitly by Le Bon and explicitly by Pareto (and the ruling classes of the time) as a tool that could set back the labour movement for decades (see Chap. 2, Sect. 13). Despite the fact that the chauvinist frenzy also infected parties of a socialist orientation, it was relatively easy for Lenin to issue the slogan of transforming the imperialist war (waged in the name of 'defence of the fatherland') into a revolutionary civil war (to overthrow in every country the capitalist bourgeoisie responsible, or jointly responsible, for the dreadful bloodbath). However, when, in the wake of the hopes aroused by the Bolshevik October, the revolution seemed set to spread rapidly in Europe and throughout the world, this slogan tended to lose any historical specificity and to be interpreted as if a new era had begun, marked by the irrelevance of state and national borders, as if the idea of the nation as such had become obsolete and even regressive.

The 'Platform' issued on 4 March 1919 by the First Congress of the Third (Communist) International called for the subordination of '*so-called* national interests to the interests of the international revolution'.[31] The word emphasized by me is revealing: there are no real national interests. The *Manifesto of the Communist International to the Proletariat of the Entire World* (6 March 1919), which not coincidentally was the work of Trotsky, painted a telling picture. Humanity ran the risk of becoming the slave of a single 'world clique' controlling the entire terrestrial globe through 'an "international" army and "international" navy'. Ranged against this was an equally monolithic international front, and hence, a 'proletarian revolution, which will liberate the productive forces of all countries from the constraint of the national state'. Indeed, the 'national state' was dead or in its death throes; having 'imparted a mighty impulse to capitalist development', it had 'become too narrow for the further development of the productive forces'. The 'small States hemmed in by the major powers of Europe and other continents' could survive thanks only to 'the uninterrupted antagonism between the two imperialist camps'. With the triumph of the Entente, this conflict had ended and the imperialist camp was unified. The proletarian camp was in the process of being formed against it.[32] Clearly, the binary interpretation of social conflict on a global scale, already encountered in certain pages of Marx and Engels, recurs here.

We can now understand the proposals which, on the eve of the Comintern's Second Congress, Tukhachevsky, commander of the Red Army, set out in a letter to Zinoviev. They should be prepared 'for the forthcoming civil war, for the moment of a world attack by all the armed forces of the proletariat on armed world capitalism'. Given 'the inevitability of world civil war in the near future', a general staff must be created and its composition and duties extend far beyond the Russian national framework. In the wake of this proposal, the Italian maximalist Giacinto Menotti Serrati imminently foresaw the day when 'the proletarian Red Army will consist not only of Russian proletarians, but of proletarians of the whole world'.[33] The ultimate objective was the creation of the international Soviet republic. One of the resolutions passed by the Congress reads: 'The Communist International proclaims the cause of Soviet Russia as its own cause. The international proletariat will not sheath the sword until Soviet Russia becomes a link in a federation of Soviet republics of the whole world'.[34]

At the time, all eyes were on the war with Poland. According to Zinoviev, '[i]n the congress hall hung a great map on which was marked every day the movement of our armies. And the delegates every morning stood with breathless interest before this map'.[35] They had the impression that they were witnessing promising developments in the global civil war—a trial of strength between opposed classes that knew no state and national boundaries. But they were very soon made aware of the persistence and power of such borders. The Red Army was advancing on Warsaw, in a war that was certainly provoked by the reactionary government of József Pilsudski, but which was in the process of being transformed on the Soviet side from a war of national defence into a revolutionary war to overthrow capitalism in Poland. The advance was blocked and, in fact, turned into a headlong retreat, thanks in part to the active engagement of Polish workers, who experienced the strong pull of patriotic appeals.

It is true that, defeated at Warsaw, the revolution had been victorious a year earlier in Budapest. But it is worth examining what happened in Hungary. In March 1919, Béla Kun arrived in power on the back of a broad national consensus, including the bourgeoisie, which regarded the communists as the only force capable of preserving the country's territorial integrity, threatened by the manoeuvres of the Entente. The latter was committed to creating a cordon sanitaire around Soviet Russia, while also giving free rein to the annexationist aims of Czechoslovakia and Romania.[36] It has rightly been observed that 'this bloodless revolution was a product of wounded national pride'.[37] On the eve of Béla Kun's arrival in power, Alexander Garbai, a Socialist Party leader, declared: 'i]n Paris they are bent on an imperialist peace ... From the West we can expect nothing but a dictated peace ... The Entente has driven us into adopting a new course which will secure for us from the East what the West has denied us'. Béla Kun himself saw a 'national phase' of the Hungarian Revolution preceding 'social revolution' proper.[38] In other words, the defeats and victories of the world revolution invoked by the Communist International cannot be understood in the absence of the role played by the national question in each instance.

In fact, on closer inspection, the national question had registered its presence in the October Revolution itself, which broke out amid the struggle against chauvinism and patriotic rhetoric, amid the transformation of imperialist war into a revolutionary civil war. Between February and October 1917, Stalin presented proletarian revolution as the vehicle required not only to build a new social order, but also to reassert the national independence of Russia.[39] The Entente sought to force it to fight on at any cost and bleed itself dry, with a view to turning it into 'a colony of Britain, America and France'. Russia was being treated as if it were 'Central Africa'. The Mensheviks, bowing to imperialist diktat, supported the 'gradual bartering away of Russia to foreign capitalists', were leading the country to ruin, and hence, revealed themselves to be the 'real betrayers' of the nation. Ranged against this, proletarian revolution would not only lead to the emancipation of the popular classes, but also 'pave the way for the real emancipation of Russia'.[40] Subsequently, the counter-revolution, unleashed by the Whites supported or egged on by the Entente, was defeated thanks to the Bolsheviks' appeal (Karl Radek distinguished himself in this respect) to the Russian people to engage in 'a national struggle of liberation against foreign invasion' and imperialist powers intent on turning Russia into a 'colony' of the West. This was the basis on which Alexei Brusilov gave his support to the new revolutionary government. The brilliant general of noble origin, one of the few to have proved his mettle during the First World War, justified his choice as follows: '[m]y sense of duty to the nation has often obliged me to disobey my natural social inclinations'.[41]

First making, and then defending the October Revolution, the Bolsheviks shielded the Russian nation from the disintegration and Balkanization that loomed as a result of defeat in war and destruction of the *ancien régime*. All this did not escape Gramsci, who on 7 June 1919 paid tribute to Lenin as 'the greatest statesman in contemporary Europe' and to the Bolsheviks as 'an aristocracy of statesmen which no other nation possesses'. They were to be credited with putting an end to the 'bottomless abyss of poverty, barbarism, anarchy and disintegration' created by a 'long and disastrous war', saving the nation, the 'immense Russian people'; and had thereby succeeded in 'soldering communist doctrine to the collective consciousness of the Russian people'. Placing themselves in a relationship of discontinuity, but also continuity, with the history of Russia, the Bolsheviks expressed 'class awareness', but were at the same time capable of 'winning to the new state the loyal majority of Russian people', of building 'the state of the whole Russian people'. Imperialism was not resigned to this and was continuing its policy of aggression. However, 'the Russian people were standing up to it … They were armed for their Valmy'. Inspired by 'class awareness', the Communist Party was in fact called upon to lead the struggle for national independence, in imitation of the Jacobins.[42]

5 'WORKERS OF ALL LANDS AND OPPRESSED PEOPLES OF THE WHOLE WORLD, UNITE!'

This confirms that class struggle never (or virtually never) presents itself in the pure state. Let us return for a moment to the nineteenth century. If in Britain the bourgeoisie and aristocracy could consolidate their rule thanks to the colonial subjugation of Ireland (where, as a result of the systematic expropriation of the island's inhabitants, the 'social question' ended up taking the form of the 'national question'), in the USA—as highlighted by the *Neue Rheinische Zeitung* in 1850—'every clash between the classes [was] concealed by the outflow of the surplus proletariat population to the West' (see Chap. 2, Sect. 1)—that is, by the expropriation and deportation of the 'redskins'. Later, during the American Civil War, Marx observed:

> Only by acquisition and the prospect of acquisition of new territories, as well as by filibustering expeditions [like that which saw William Walker conquer Nicaragua in the mid-nineteenth century and reintroduce slavery], is it possible to square the interests of ... 'poor whites' with those of the slaveholders, to give their restless thirst for action a harmless direction and tame them with the prospect of one day becoming slaveholders themselves.[43]

In this second case, rather than via the expropriation and deportation of the natives, class struggle within the white community was defused through the enslavement of African Americans (and other supposedly barbaric populations in Central America).

We have hitherto been dealing with processes that are in some sense 'spontaneous'. But with the exacerbation of social conflict in Europe, we witness the emergence of theories explicitly demanding the annexation of land, in the colonies to be assigned to the propertyless in the capitalist metropolis. In 1868, in France, not coincidentally the country where the long revolutionary cycle had issued in the emergence of a socialist movement, Ernest Renan attacked the French Revolution for having prevented 'the development of colonies ... thereby obstructing the only route by which modern states can escape the problems of socialism'. This was a thesis repeated three years later, in the months immediately following the Paris Commune: '[l]arge-scale colonization is a political necessity of the first order. A nation that does not colonize is irrevocably condemned to socialism, to war between rich and poor'. It was necessary to put 'inferior races' to work 'for the benefit of the conquering race'. It was clear: 'the Europeans are a race of masters and soldiers. Reduce this noble race to work for life like Negroes and Chinese, and it will revolt'.[44]

A couple of decades later, Theodor Herzl recommended the colonization of Palestine and Zionism also as an antidote to the ascendant revolutionary movement in the capitalist metropolis. A 'proletariat that instils fear' should be diverted towards a territory which 'requires men to cultivate it'. Freeing itself of 'a surplus of proletarians and desperate men', the European metropolis could at the same time export civilization to the colonial world:

> Hand in hand with this increase in civilization and order would go the emasculation of revolutionary parties. In this connection, it must be recalled that we are everywhere at grips with revolutionaries and will detach young Jewish intellectuals and workers from socialism and nihilism to the extent that we hold out a purer popular ideal.[45]

Indeed, abandoning their erstwhile revolutionary militancy, in Russia 'socialists and anarchists are converting to Zionism'. It is no accident if the leader of the Zionist movement sought, and established, contact with Cecil Rhodes, the champion of British imperialism.[46]

Lenin had Rhodes very much in mind, and cited him at length, in his essay on imperialism. How to solve the 'social problem' and prevent 'a bloody civil war'—that is, anti-capitalist revolution? It was necessary to 'acquire new lands'; '[i]f you want to avoid civil war, you must become imperialists'.[47] Rhodes arrived at this conclusion after having visited the East End, the working-class area of London which in 1889 Engels had enthusiastically seen converted from 'poverty-stricken stagnation' into an outpost of the workers' class struggle (see Chap. 4, Sect. 7). It was precisely this that worried the champion of imperialism: the revival of colonial expansion was the only effective response to the exacerbation of the social question and expansion of the socialist movement.

This political programme caught on far beyond Britain. Mention has just been made of Herzl. On the eve of the First World War, the nationalist leader Enrico Corradini called on Italian socialists to support their own country's colonial expansion, taking to heart what had been going on in Britain for a good while:

The British worker knows that in the massive British Empire, spread over five continents, an activity occurs on a daily basis of which he is part, and which has a far from negligible impact on his household budget: this is Britain's immense trade, which is strictly dependent on British imperialism. The London worker knows that Egypt and the Cape and India and Canada and Australia contribute and compete to increase his welfare and, above all, to disseminate it to an ever greater number of British workers and British citizens.[48]

Lenin referred to a 'wretched book' in connection with this statement.[49] In the preparatory materials for his essay on imperialism, he transcribed passages from a German historian on the colonial war against the Herero, who were annihilated after having had their land expropriated. Increasing numbers of the invaders settled on it, becoming 'farmers and cattle-breeders'. Lenin comments: 'rob the land and become landowners!'—this was how the imperialist powers proposed to resolve the social question.[50]

So the capitalist bourgeoisie sought to defuse conflict in the metropolis by systematically expropriating colonial peoples, so that in the colonies, as in Ireland according to Marx, the 'social question' was regularly posed as the 'national question'. At the same time, in the capitalist metropolis 'imperial socialism' spread in the ranks of the labour movement. In other words, while in the East (and, more generally, the South-East) colonial expansion sparked revolution, in the West it strengthened the dominant power, at least in the immediate present. Hence, according to Lenin's analysis, if in the West, appealing to Marx and Engels' teaching, the task was to counter 'social imperialism', in the East anti-colonial revolution must be unequivocally supported.

In summer 1920, the Congress of the Peoples of the East, which convened in Baku immediately after the Second Congress of the Comintern, felt obliged to complement the slogan with which both the *Communist Manifesto* and the *Inaugural Address* of the International Working Men's Association end. The new slogan read: 'Workers of All Lands and Oppressed Peoples of the Whole World, Unite!' 'Oppressed peoples' had now emerged alongside 'workers' as fully-fledged revolutionary subjects. This formulation, which undoubtedly represents an innovation vis-à-vis Marx and Engels, betokens not abandonment of the perspective of class struggle and internationalism, but an attempt to grasp the peculiar, determinate configuration assumed by each of them.

6 THE EAST AND THE DUAL STRUGGLE FOR RECOGNITION

We are now in a better position to understand why the revolution invoked by the *Communist Manifesto* occurred first in Russia, and then the colonial world, rather than the West. The reasons for the switch of class struggle and revolution to the South-East have long been subject to investigation. One thinks, in particular, of Lenin's theory of the weakest link in the chain: rather than the advanced industrial countries, socialist revolution breaks out where, as a result of an accumulation of multiple contradictions, the capitalist and imperialist system proves most fragile. This is a shrewd explanation, which breaks with the binary interpretation of the revolutionary process. Digging deeper, we can identify an even more basic datum: it was in the East that the need and demand for recognition were most strongly felt. We find a conjunction not only of political and social contradictions, but also of struggles for recognition.

Let us see what occurred in Russia with the February Revolution, immediately after the fall of tsarism. The oppression, exploitation, and humiliation of an enormous mass of peasants by a small aristocratic elite, which regarded itself as foreign to its own people (degraded to the status of a different, inferior race), were harbingers of an unparalleled catastrophe. On the theme of such non-recognition, Dostoevsky has left us memorable and terrible pages. Here is how, in the early nineteenth century, 'a general with high connections and a very wealthy landowner' punishes 'a house-serf, a little boy, only eight years old', who is guilty of having struck the paw of one of the master's hounds with a stone. Forced to strip naked and run, he is caught and torn to pieces by hunting dogs ordered to chase him: 'The house-serfs are gathered for their edification, the guilty boy's mother in front of them all'.[51] The First World War further dramatized such non-recognition, with noble officers *de facto* wielding a daily power of life and death over serf-soldiers. The fall of the *ancien régime* was the moment of revenge that had been dreamed of and desired for centuries. Prince G.E. Lvov acknowledged this in a significant self-criticism: 'the revenge of the serfs' was a settlement of accounts with those who had for centuries refused 'to treat the peasants as people rather than dogs',[52] or like game, as in the sequence of events described by Dostoevsky.

Moreover, this was not a problem confined to the countryside. In 1895, Lenin encouraged agitation in Russian factories thus: '[t]he workers must show that they consider themselves human beings just as much as the factory owners do, and that they have no intention of allowing themselves to be treated as dumb cattle'.⁵³ Eminent contemporary historians confirm the correctness of this formulation:

> [In tsarist Russia] workers demanded more respectful treatment by their employers. They wanted to be called by the polite 'you' (*vyi*) rather than the familiar one (*tyi*), which they associated with the old serf regime. They wanted to be treated as 'citizens'. It was often this issue of respectful treatment, rather than the bread-and-butter question of wages, which fuelled workers' strikes and demonstrations.⁵⁴

Another struggle for recognition was bound up with this one. The oppressed nations sought to shake off the yoke of autocracy and, in the case of Poland and Finland, constituted themselves as nation-states. But it was not only oppressed nations that mobilized and demanded recognition. We have seen the accusation levelled at the Entente by Stalin between February and October 1917—that it sought to force Russia to supply cannon fodder for the imperialist designs of London and Paris and treated it like a colony of 'Central Africa'. While it answered to a shrewd political calculation, this line of argument genuinely captured an aspect of what was happening: the crisis initiated with the catastrophe of the First World War, and the disintegration of the *ancien régime*, endangered the independence of Russia, which had in the interim been expelled from the zone of authentic civilization. The problem of recognition was further aggravated by this. Without the dual struggle for recognition, we cannot understand the October Revolution and the form it took:

> Mass popular pressure to enjoy what they had hitherto been deprived of—self-esteem, participation, culture—took the most disparate forms. Even if Lenin had wanted to, it would have been difficult for him to prevent the workers taking control of their factories and people referring with increasing frequency to *socialism*, which was to be achieved by nationalizing industry and immediately and triumphantly extended to the whole world. The impression rapidly spread that what was being realized in the revolution was a great revolt of all slaves against all masters.⁵⁵

As well as in Russia, revolutions of a socialist and Marxist persuasion occurred in countries in colonial or semi-colonial conditions, in situations where class differences tended to take the form of caste differences, rendering the problem of recognition acute domestically as well. When, subsequently, the upper classes or castes made common cause, or allied in a subaltern role, with the colonial masters, the internal dimension interlaced with the international dimension, which became a more pertinent one.

An essential role was played in the anti-colonialist movement as a whole by the demand for recognition. Lenin highlighted this. Among the various definitions of imperialism he offered, one of the most significant characterizes it as the claim of 'a few chosen nations' to base their own 'prosperity' and primacy on despoliation and domination of the rest of the humanity.[56] They regarded themselves as 'model nation[s]'and assigned themselves 'the exclusive privilege of forming a state'.[57] Regrettably, 'Europeans often forget that colonial peoples too are nations'.[58]

This discriminatory, and often openly racist, impulse manifested itself with particular clarity and virulence during colonial wars. These were conflicts in which 'hundreds of thousands of people belonging to the nations [the Europeans] were subjugating died', whereas 'few Europeans died'. And so, Lenin continued caustically, '[c]an you call them wars? Strictly speaking, they were not wars at all, and you could forget about them'. Colonial wars were not regarded as wars for a very simple reason: those on the receiving end were barbarians who 'could not be regarded as nations at all (you couldn't very well call those Asians and Africans nations!)', and who, in the final analysis, were excluded from the human community.[59] We can now understand the powerful impetus given to the anti-colonialist movement by the October Revolution. The inhabitants of Asia and Africa, 'hundreds of millions of people', rebelling against the yoke imposed by the capitalist metropolis, had 'recently reminded the world of [their] claim to *human* and not slavish existence'.[60]

We are dealing with a revolution that spread on a global scale and over a long period of time. It is interesting to see how, in the liberated zones of China, the soldiers of the Red Army responded to Edgar Snow, when he asked them about the reasons for their adhesion to the armed struggle undertaken by the Communist Party first against local lords and then against the Japanese invaders: '"the Red Army has taught me to read and write.... Here I have learned to operate a radio, and how to aim a rifle straight. The Red Army helps the poor." ... "Here everybody is the same. It's not like the White districts, where poor people are slaves of the landlords and the Kuomintang"'.[61] In the course of its struggle against the enemies impeding or preventing recognition, the Communist Party promoted social mobility and facilitated the achievement of recognition both in its own ranks and in the army led by it.

7 MAO AND THE 'IDENTITY BETWEEN THE NATIONAL STRUGGLE AND CLASS STRUGGLE'

The dual struggle for recognition had particular relevance in a country with an ancient civilization like China. From the Opium Wars onwards, it had been forced to endure one ignominy and humiliation after another, to the extent that in the late nineteenth century, in Shanghai, the French concession prominently displayed the sign: 'No Admittance for Dogs and Chinese'. But the most tragic period of national oppression occurred in the twentieth century, with a combination of civil war and open imperialist aggression.

The April 1927 *coup de force* whereby Chiang Kai-shek crushed the Chinese working class in Shanghai, and inflicted devastating losses on the Communist Party, was followed by a retreat to the countryside led by Mao Zedong, who engaged in building and defending 'soviet' power in areas that were under siege and constant attack from the Kuomintang. With the expansion of the Japanese invasion, a new phase began. Dogged by the fifth 'encirclement and extermination campaign' unleashed by Chiang Kai-shek, the Red Army embarked on the 'Long March' of thousands of miles in October 1934, both to escape its pursuers, who were determined to completely liquidate it, but also to reach the north-west region and encourage and organize resistance to the aggression of the Empire of the Rising Sun.

There is no doubt that this was an epic endeavour, but there is an aspect of its grandeur that has perhaps been insufficiently stressed. While they sought to evade their pursuers, the Red Army's leaders thought about how to integrate them, at least partially, into the requisite broad united front. It was now necessary to confront the new enemy, who (it became ever more apparent) was the principal enemy. Indeed, observed Mao on 27 December 1935, 'when the national crisis reaches a crucial point', and the nation risked being enslaved by Japanese imperialism, the main target must be invaders and collaborators, entailing a transition from the 'agrarian revolution' to the 'national revolution' and the conversion of a 'workers' and peasants' republic' into a 'people's republic'. The government of the zone controlled by the Chinese Communist Party represented 'not only the workers and peasants but other sections of the people too'; and the Party itself expressed 'the interests of the whole nation'.[62]

On the basis of this platform the Communist Party supported or promoted the 'December 9th Movement' of 1935, whose slogan was 'Stop the civil war, unite to resist foreign aggression!' But in so doing, did it not renounce class struggle and turn its back on the slogan ('transform the imperialist war into a revolutionary civil war') that had presided over the October Revolution and the foundation of the Third International? A radical change had occurred, and revolutionary class struggle now consisted in resistance to Japanese imperialism's attempts to enslave the Chinese nation as a whole. As a result, advocates of civil war had turned from champions of revolution, which is what they had been in Russia during the First World War, into champions of reaction and imperialism. Hence, 'our slogan is, "Fight to defend the motherland against the aggressors." For us defeatism is a crime'.[63]

The political platform outlined here is clear. But on a more strictly theoretical level things are more fluid. In an intervention of 5 November 1938, on the one hand an appeal was made 'to subordinate the class struggle to the present national struggle', while on the other it was asserted that '[i]n a struggle that is national in character, the class struggle takes the form of a national struggle, which demonstrates the identity between the two'.[64] The second formulation, which supplies the section of the text by Mao cited here, and this section of my book, with their title, is more rigorous: it is not only '[i]n the stage of democratic revolution' that 'there are limits to the struggle between labour and capital'.[65] Japanese imperialism knew no distinctions of class or even sex in its oppression. It aimed to subject the entire Chinese nation (not merely the proletariat) to a condition of slavery or semi-slavery. Women were not spared: forced to prostitute themselves to Japanese soldiers needing 'comfort', they become 'comfort women', subjected to sexual slavery. Given this, the struggle against the imperialism of the Rising Sun was the concrete way in which, in a very specific situation, the struggle between labour and capital manifested itself and erupted.

It takes us back to Marx's analysis of Ireland. The appropriation of the land by the British settlers and the consequent condemnation of the Irish people to deportation and starvation meant that the 'land question' (its possession), and hence, the 'national question', became 'the exclusive form of the social question'. Naturally, like the identity between 'social question' and 'national question', the 'identity between national struggle and class struggle' is partial—and not only because it is circumscribed in time. It was Mao himself who drew attention to the tensions between the different classes and parties making up the anti-Japanese united front. But it remains the case that, following the large-scale invasion by the Empire of the Rising Sun, class struggle and national resistance tended to merge in China.

Did concentrating on national tasks mean abandoning internationalism? Quite the reverse! Fighting and defeating Japanese imperialism was the concrete way in which Chinese revolutionaries could contribute to the cause of global revolution and emancipation: '[i]n wars of national liberation patriotism is applied internationalism. ... These are good patriotic actions and, far from running counter to internationalism, are its application in China. ... To separate internationalist content from national form is the practice of those who do not understand the first thing about internationalism'.[66]

This time we are taken back to the analysis developed by Engels in particular; subject to national oppression, the oppressed Irish and Poles were truly 'international' only when 'authentically national'.

8 'Racial Struggle' and Class Struggle at Stalingrad

The national and colonial question ended up erupting in Europe itself. In fact, it was precisely there (in the central-eastern part of the continent) that it assumed its most brutal form. We are familiar with the intellectual tradition which, as early as the nineteenth century, identified colonial expansion as the answer to the social question. Hitler drew on this tradition, proposing to build a colonial empire of a continental kind in Eastern Europe—in particular, in the immense Asian spaces of Russia. Here, in the almost unanimous view of Western elites, barbarism had returned and rampaged following the Bolshevik Revolution; and it was here that Germany was called upon to restore civilization with a vigorous or ruthless labour of colonization.

The continuity with Rhodes is obvious. Let us read *Mein Kampf*. The economic conquest of new markets simply could not replace colonial expansion. The latter alone made it possible to avoid 'an industrialisation as boundless as it [is] harmful', with its 'weakening of the peasant class', expansion of the 'mass of the big city proletariat' and irruption of 'political class division'. Without 'the acquisition of new soil', even the greatest 'economic prosperity' could not achieve the primary, imperative objective, which was to defuse social conflict and class struggle in the fatherland and capitalist metropolis. Indeed, '[i]n the country there could be no social question', given that the 'separation of worker and employer' had not as yet occurred.[67] This separation could only be abolished through colonial, territorial expansion facilitating the conversion of proletarians into farmers and landowners. It was a question of choosing between 'either a territorial policy, or a colonial and commercial policy'. To restore the social body to health, the role of 'industry and commerce' must be reduced. With the North American model in mind, it was necessary to implement 'a healthy territorial policy [through] the acquisition of new land in Europe itself'.[68]

Prior to seizing power, the Nazis, in particular, used the journal *Volk und Raum* to propagandize the thesis that Germany's expansion to the East also had the 'de-proletarianization' (*Entproletarisierung*) of the German people as its goal.[69] Later, after war had been unleashed on the Soviet Union, the Third Reich, in the person of Heinrich Himmler, theorized 'good blood socialism', which would ensure land and social security for German and Aryan settlers courtesy of the decimation and enslavement of the 'natives'.[70] The 'imperial socialism' advanced for the first time in Disraeli, and subsequently articulated very effectively by Rhodes, reached its acme.

We can now clearly understand the significance of the Third Reich. In 1935, the Communist International demonstrated that it had already grasped it. Fascism, whether that of the Third Reich or the Empire of the Rising Sun, was intent on 'enslaving the weak nations', on 'an imperialist war of plunder' against the Soviet Union and the 'enslavement and partition of China'.[71] In our day, it has rightly been observed that 'Hitler's war for *Lebensraum* was the greatest colonial war in history'.[72] It was a war that aimed at the reduction of entire peoples to a mass of slaves or semi-slaves in the service of the alleged master race. Addressing the industrialists of Düsseldorf (and Germany) on 27 January 1932, and winning their support for his rise to power, Hitler clarified his vision of history and politics. During the nineteenth century, 'white peoples' had wrested a position of unchallenged domination at the end of a process begun with the conquest of America and developed in the conviction of the 'absolute, innate master sense of the white race'. Challenging the colonial system, and causing or aggravating 'the confusion of white European thinking', Bolshevism represented a deadly threat to civilization. To confront it, the 'conviction of the superiority, and hence, the [superior] right of the white race' must be reasserted; 'the white race's position of domination of the rest of the world' had to be defended. Clearly formulated here was a programme of counter-revolution involving colonialism and slavery. To reassert the global domination of the white race, the lesson to be drawn from the history of the West's colonial expansion should be learnt: an 'utterly brutal lack of scruples' should be unhesitatingly shown; 'the exercise of an extremely brutal master right (*Herrenrecht*) was required'.[73] What was this, in substance, if not slavery? In July 1942, Hitler issued this order for the colonization of the Soviet Union and Eastern Europe: 'the Slavs must work for us. If we have no more need of them, let them die.... Education is dangerous. It is enough for them to know how to count up to one hundred. The only education allowed is that which procures useful manual labourers.... We are the masters'.[74]

In his confidential speeches, not addressed to the public, Himmler explicitly referred to slavery. There was an absolute need for 'alien race slaves' (*fremdvölkische Sklaven*) before whom the 'master race' (*Herrenrasse*) must never lose its 'lordly aura' (*Herrentum*), and with which it must never mix or mingle in any way. '[I]f we do not fill our camps with slaves—in this room I mean to say things very firmly and very clearly—with worker slaves who will build our cities, our villages, our factories, without regard to any losses', the programme of colonization and Germanization of the conquered territories in Eastern Europe could not be accomplished. The Third Reich, thus, became the artisan of a slave trade conducted posthaste, and hence, more brutally than the slave trade proper.[75]

This was the project, involving the reduction not only of the proletariat but of whole nations to slavery or semi-slavery, which the new Soviet power had to confront. Already impending was the 'Great Patriotic War' whose most crucial and epic moment was Stalingrad. The struggle of an entire people to avoid the fate of enslavement to which it had been condemned cannot but be characterized as a class struggle. But it was a class struggle that took the form of a national, anti-colonial war of resistance.

The same applies to Poland. As in the Soviet Union, the Third Reich proposed to liquidate the intelligentsia—social strata capable of organizing social and political existence, of preserving national consciousness and the historical continuity of the nation—en bloc. The subjugated countries, the new colonies, would thereby be able to supply servile labour-power in large quantities, without any impediment to the process. In the USSR, the constitutive element of the intelligentsia to be destroyed was communists, while an important role was played in Poland by the Catholic clergy. Common to both countries was the presence of Jews, who were incurably subversive intellectuals in Hitler's eyes, and for whom the only possible solution was the 'final' one. Such were the conditions for building German Indies in Central and Eastern Europe—an inexhaustible reserve of land, raw materials, and slaves in the service of the master race. The struggle against this empire, based on an international division of labour that involved a barely concealed return of slavery, the struggle against such a counter-revolution, was a class struggle *par excellence*.

A British historian whom we have already encountered argues differently and refutes Marx thus: the twentieth century was not 'all about class struggle'; the Third Reich embarked on the war in the East as a 'great racial war' (to use Hermann Göring's expression), and hence, 'ethnic divisions' proved 'more important than the supposed struggle between proletariat and bourgeoisie'.[76] There is no doubt about it. Himmler described and celebrated the campaign against the USSR as 'a primitive, original, natural racial struggle'.[77] In his turn, although he ended up allying with Japanese 'yellow men', Hitler claimed to be the champion of the white race—to the point that the Spain conquered by Franco was, in his view, a country returned 'to white hands',[78] even though Moroccan colonial troops made a significant contribution to the victory. But were this interpretative grid to be valid, we would have to interpret all international conflicts as exclusively ethnic or racial, from colonial wars to world wars, from the American War of Independence to Italy's Risorgimento wars. In 1883, publishing *The Racial Struggle*, Gumplowicz opposed Marx and the theory of class struggle. One of the most acclaimed historians of our time argues in a similar fashion.

9 A Ubiquitous and Elusive Class Struggle

It is true that, while the events treated here were unfolding, there were not a few even on the extreme Left who found it difficult to construe them in the light of the Marxian theory of class struggle. The unforeseen, shocking spread of 'global civil war' was bound to cause disorientation. The united front policy launched by the Communist International in 1935 sought to isolate the imperialist powers on the offensive. Having arrived late at their tryst with colonialism, Germany, Italy, and Japan aspired to catch up, resorting to an extra dose of brutality and subjugating and even enslaving peoples of ancient civilization. But the popular front policy, which did not appear to challenge capitalism as such, and not even imperialism as such, seemed like 'the strangulation of the class struggle' to Trotsky.[79] His followers in China argued in similar fashion, reproving Mao and the Chinese communists for having 'abandoned their class positions'. This denunciation is contained in a letter sent to the great and respected writer Lu Xun, who responded disdainfully that he wished to continue to stand shoulder to shoulder with those who 'were fighting and shedding their blood for the existence of today's Chinese'.⁸⁰ This was a vision that later met with consecration in Mao's formula about the identity in China of national struggle and class struggle.

This is a debate that continues down to the present. In their way, the words with which Trotsky's distinguished biographer describes and comments on the foundation of the Fourth International, the year before the outbreak of the Second World War, are illuminating:

> On 18 October 1938, in a speech recorded for American comrades, [Trotsky] stated:
> 'Permit me to finish with a prediction: During the next ten years the program of the Fourth International will become the guide of millions and these revolutionary millions will know how to storm earth and heaven.'
> It has to be acknowledged that this prediction was cruelly contradicted and, to say the very least, was guilty of excessive optimism.⁸¹

Did Trotsky's prediction prove completely unfounded? In reality, following Stalingrad and the defeat of the Third Reich's plan (and Japan's similar plan for Asia) to revive, radicalize and extend the territorial base of the colonial tradition, a massive wave of anti-colonial revolutions developed that radically altered the shape of the planet. However, Trotsky (as his biographer observes) conceived the Second World War 'by analogy with the first' and the upheavals that would follow the new conflagration by analogy with October 1917.⁸² This touches on, or at least brushes, the crucial point: the revolutionary upheavals foreseen by Trotsky did indeed occur, but not in the way he imagined; class struggle erupted, but not in the forms it had taken in previous decades.

In fact, what was involved was a veritable reversal. Deploying the slogan of turning imperialist war into revolutionary civil war, the Bolsheviks won power in Russia in 1917. But in subsequent decades they succeeded in retaining it first by undertaking industrial and military consolidation of the country, and then by promoting and leading the war of national resistance. In countries like Yugoslavia, Albania and China (and, later, Vietnam, Cuba, etc.), communist parties arrived in power by placing themselves at the head of national resistance and liberation. In a country like India, revolution from below was intertwined with revolution from above. There it was the colonial power itself, now weakened by the new international constellation, which abdicated, so as to avoid much a more radical revolution from below. These upheavals even ended up having an impact in the USA. The fall of the *ancien régime* based on racial hierarchy and white supremacy was inconceivable without the wave which, investing colonial peoples, included African Americans.

In some more or less developed capitalist countries, such as France and Greece, revolution took the form of a war of national liberation with the massive participation and, in the second case, leadership of the Communist Party, which seemed on the verge of winning power and initiating changes of a socialist kind.

In the Axis countries, the slogan of transforming imperialist war into revolutionary civil war remained valid, but in as much as the most advanced elements—for example, in Germany and Italy—allied with resistance and national liberation movements in the Soviet Union, Yugoslavia, Albania, Greece, and so forth. In other words, in a radical reversal compared with its predecessor, during the Second World War revolutionary commitment and revolutionary class struggle entailed support for resistance and national liberation movements, in one way or another.

The Italian case is of particular interest. Having entered the war with explicitly imperialist slogans (conquest of a place in the sun, return of the empire to the 'fatal hills of Rome', etc.), at the time of his fall Mussolini left the country not only prostrate and defeated, but also largely controlled by an occupying army, which tended to treat the ex-ally as a colonial people. A note in Goebbels' diary for 11 September is revealing: '[o]n account of their disloyalty and betrayal, the Italians have lost any right to a nation-state of a modern kind. They must be severely punished, as dictated by the law of history'.[83] In effect, in the eyes of some Nazi leaders, the Italians became 'negroids', with whom sexual contamination should be avoided and who, once the war was over, were to be used 'as labourers in the service of Germans'.[84]

In other words, the ex-ally ended up having to counter the danger of colonial subjugation by the Third Reich. Placing itself at the head of the national liberation struggle, the Communist Party succeeded in achieving significant political and social changes, and in winning such broad support that for a time it embodied the Gramscian lesson of the struggle to win hegemony in the eyes of much of international public opinion.

Hence, far from being contradicted, Trotsky's prediction of 1938 received striking historical confirmation. As regards revolutions and class struggle, the ensuing decades were among the richest in world history. But the unanticipated, unprecedented forms assumed by class struggles and revolutions resulted in this going unperceived by many. As sometimes happens, a particularly dense wood obscured sight of the long sought after trees.

10 FROM WORLD BOLSHEVIK PARTY TO THE DISSOLUTION OF THE INTERNATIONAL

In the course of the twentieth century, realization that the revolutionary process is always nationally specific in character was arrived at via a laborious, contradictory route. Following the October Revolution and the foundation of the Third International, a binary interpretation of conflict on a global scale prevailed. Significant in this regard are the Statutes approved by the Second Congress on 4 August 1920. Starting from the assumption that 'the emancipation of the workers is not a local, nor a national, but an international problem', and that the objective was 'an international Soviet republic', they stressed the 'strongly centralized' of the organization and concluded: 'the Communist International must, in fact and in deed, be a single communist party of the entire world. The parties working in the various countries are but its separate sections'.[85] This was a vision consummated four years later, during the Fifth Congress, which called for the creation of 'a homogeneous bolshevik world party permeated with the ideas of Bolshevism'. Subsequently, the Executive Committee reiterated that:

> The world party of Leninism must be strongly fused, not by mechanical discipline, but by unity of will and action.... Every party must give its best forces to the international leadership. It must be brought home to the broadest masses that in the present epoch serious economic and political battles of the working class can be won only if they are led from one centre and on an international scale.[86]

In the event, the concrete exigencies of political struggle resulted in a form of practice that was in marked contradiction with the theory. Initially, the Congresses of the International succeeded one another well-nigh annually: the First in 1919, the Second in 1920, the Third in 1921, the Fourth in 1922, and then the Fifth in 1924. But then things became more spaced out: the Sixth in 1928 and the Seventh and last in 1935. And it is easy to see why the Seventh Congress was also the last. At its heart was the national question, as clearly emerges from Dimitrov's report, which called for an end to an internationalism incapable of 'acclimatiz[ing] itself' and 'sink[ing] deep roots in its native land', which even issued in 'national nihilism', therewith proving utterly incapable of leading a struggle for the 'salvation of the nation'.[87] Not by chance, the Seventh Congress was held as the Communist Party in China called for suspension of the civil war and for national unity, while the advent of Hitler anticipated the accentuation of the national question in Europe as well.

It was now clear that in different national situations, social conflict could assume the most diverse configurations; and was on each occasion a peculiar tangle of multiple contradictions, involving the most diverse social subjects. The traditional organizational instrument (the International) long recognized by the labour movement as its own, thus, proved to be increasingly inadequate. Underlying it, to a greater or lesser extent, was a view we are already familiar with: the socialist revolution appears to derive from a single contradiction that sees two homogenous blocs, bourgeoisie and proletariat, arrayed against one another on a world scale. It found its most concentrated expression in the Third International, which projected itself as a 'world Bolshevik party' organized and centralized in iron fashion beyond national and state boundaries. Once this view had been superseded, the dissolution of the Third International was an imperative consequence. It did not simply answer to political calculation, though that was not lacking (the desire to consolidate the anti-fascist coalition, facilitating the formation of popular fronts in each country with the participation of communist parties, which it would now be more difficult to suspect of being mere Russian pawns); the role played by awareness of the concrete dialectic of the revolutionary process was more important.

The fact is that no International has ever made a revolution. This applies to the International Working Men's Association founded in 1864. Six years later, when the Franco-Prussian War was underway, it appealed to 'French workmen' not to succumb to revolutionary illusions, to take account of the real balance of power, and above all 'not allow themselves to be deluded by the national *souvenirs* of 1792'.[88] In the light of subsequent developments, the warning proved justified. However, the movement that resulted in the Paris Commune developed in accordance with an autonomous dialectic, starting from the conjunction of the bourgeoisie/proletariat contradiction and the national crisis caused by revelation of Prussia's expansionist plans and the French bourgeoisie's inability to counter them.

The October Revolution broke out in the wake of denunciation of the 'betrayal' by the Second International. Three years later, Lenin drew up a historical and theoretical balance-sheet that highlighted a crucial point: a revolutionary situation presupposes so many contradictions, of such severity, as to provoke 'a nation-wide crisis (affecting both the exploited and the exploiters)'.[89] In other words, the Bolsheviks ultimately prevailed because they proved to be the sole political force capable of offering an answer to the economic, political and social disintegration triggered by the war and the fall of the *ancien régime*.

Founded in 1919, with the explicit goal of spreading the Russian Revolution to the West, the Third International did not succeed in living up to its programme. A gigantic revolutionary wave did indeed develop after the defeat inflicted on Hitler's plan to build 'German Indies' in Eastern Europe and surged globally until the dissolution of the colonial system. But it occurred, only after the dissolution of the International decreed by Stalin 1943 and was fuelled by revolutions which, contrary to the expectations of 1919, saw social conflict and national conflict indissolubly fused.

Finally, it scarcely needs saying that the Fourth International turned out to be nothing but a farcical replica of the tragedy of the Third.

At this point, it is worth reflecting on a formulation by the mature Marx, according to which the exacerbation of the contradiction between the productive forces and the relations of production results not in a single revolution, but in 'an era of social revolution'.[90] In such an era, various particular revolutionary processes develop, each of which can be explained only on the basis of a specific national constellation and a tangle of contradictions that is different each time, and this applies to the bourgeois revolution. According to the *Manifesto*, it breaks out when 'feudal relations of property' come into contradiction with 'the already developed productive forces'.[91] If we apply this historical law country by country, we find that in no instance do we encounter a 'pure' bourgeois revolution. In France, where capitalism was under-developed, and where (as Marx himself acknowledged) agriculture remained predominant in 1850,[92] the revolt of the Third Estate in 1789 was preceded by the anti-absolutist and pro-feudal *fronde* of the Parlements (an institution typical of the *ancien régime*). It was followed by the massive entry onto the political stage of the popular masses, that achieved very advanced objectives (abolition of black slavery on Santo Domingo, introduction of compulsory education in the metropolis, etc.), clashing sharply with the bourgeoisie. In various countries, the overthrow of the *ancien régime* took the form of a national revolution. One thinks of the Italian Risorgimento or Germany, where (according to Engels' aforementioned analysis) the bourgeois revolution commenced in 1808–13—that is, with the struggle against Napoleon's occupation, imposed by a county which had the French Revolution behind it. The bourgeois revolution in the two classical countries of the liberal tradition turns out to be no less impure. It is not clear why the anti-capitalist revolution should be characterized by greater purity.

In conclusion, it might be said that the organizational model of the International proved inadequate because it frequently referred to a pure class struggle which very rarely existed; and was fuelled by expectations of a pure socialist revolution that never has occurred and never will. This does not mean that there is no longer any need for internationalist solidarity between those who, in one way or another, suffer from a system based on exploitation, oppression and the law of the strongest. Indeed, it remains to examine the forms that such solidarity might concretely take.

NOTES

1. Eduard Bernstein, 'Der Sozialismus und die Kolonialfrage', *Sozialistische Monatshefte*, 1900, p. 559.
2. Ludwig Gumplowicz, *Der Rassenkampf. Soziologische Untersuchungen*, Innsbruck: Wagner'sche Universitätsbuchhandlung, 1883, p. 249.
3. V.I. Lenin, *Collected Works*, London: Lawrence & Wishart, 1960–78, Vol. 4, pp. 372, 374.
4. Ibid., Vol. 4, p. 376.
5. Ibid., Vol. 4, p. 372.
6. Karl Marx and Frederick Engels, *Collected Works*, London: Lawrence & Wishart, 1975–2004, Vol. 47, p. 407.
7. Lenin, *Collected Works*, Vol. 39, p. 682.
8. Ibid., Vol. 5, pp. 412, 422.
9. Ibid., Vol. 5, p. 457.
10. Ibid., Vol. 5, p. 401.
11. Ibid., Vol. 5, pp. 422–3.
12. Ibid., Vol. 22, p. 283.
13. Gustave Le Bon, *The Crowd: A Study of the Popular Mind*, New York: Dover, 2002, pp. 78, 25.
14. Lenin, *Collected Works*, Vol. 4, p. 376.
15. Ibid., Vol. 5, p. 433.
16. Marx and Engels, *Collected Works*, Vol. 3, p. 182.
17. Ernst Nolte, *Der europäische Bürgerkrieg 1917–1945. Nationalsozialismus und Bolschewismus*, Frankfurt am Main and Berlin: Ullstein, 1987, p. 55.

18. Lenin, *Collected Works*, Vol. 5, p. 434.
19. Ibid., Vol. 20, p. 413 and n.
20. Ibid., Vol. 20, p. 413.
21. Ibid., Vol. 21, p. 102.
22. Ibid., Vol. 20, p. 434; Vol. 23, p. 40.
23. Ibid., Vol. 22, p. 310.
24. Ibid., Vol. 21, p. 102,
25. Ibid., Vol. 22, pp. 355–6.
26. Ibid., Vol. 20, pp. 436, 410.
27. Ibid., Vol. 22, p. 341.
28. Ibid., Vol. 22, p. 342 n.
29. Ibid., Vol. 31, p. 166.
30. Ernesto Laclau and Chantal Mouffe, *Hegemony and Socialist Strategy: Towards a Radical Democratic Politics*, London and New York: Verso, 2001, p. viii.
31. Jane Degras (ed.), *The Communist International 1919–1943: Documents*, London, New York and Toronto: Oxford University Press, 1956–65, Vol. I, p. 23.
32. Ibid., pp. 41–2.
33. Quoted in E.H. Carr, *The Bolshevik Revolution 1917–1923*, London: Macmillan, 1978, Vol. 3, pp. 210–11.
34. Quoted in ibid., Vol. 3, pp. 189–90.
35. Quoted in ibid., Vol. 3, p. 188.
36. See Gabriel Kolko, *Century of War: Politics, Conflict and Society since 1914*, New York: New Press, 1994, p. 159.
37. Arno J. Mayer, *Politics and Diplomacy of Peacemaking: Containment and Counter-Revolution at Versailles, 1918–1919*, London: Weidenfeld & Nicolson, 1968, p. 554.
38. Quoted in ibid., pp. 551–2, 540.
39. J. Stalin, *Works*, Moscow: Foreign Languages Publishing House, 1952–3, Vol. 3, pp. 143, 310.
40. Ibid., Vol. 3, pp. 227, 204–6.
41. Quoted in Orlando Figes, *A People's Tragedy: The Russian Revolution, 1891–1924*, London: Pimlico, 1997, pp. 699, 697.
42. Antonio Gramsci, *L'Ordine Nuovo 1919–1920*, ed. Valentino Gerratana and Antonio A. Sanctucci, Turin: Einaudi, 1987, pp. 56–8, 60.
43. Marx and Engels, *Collected Works*, Vol. 19, p. 41.
44. Ernest Renan, *Oeuvres complètes*, ed. Henriette Psichari, Paris: Calmann-Lévy, 1947–, Vol. 1, pp. 12, 390.
45. Theodor Herzl, 'Zionistisches Tagebuch', in *Briefe und Tagebücher*, ed. A. Bein et al., Berlin, Frankfurt am Main and Vienna: Propyläen, 1984–5, Vol. 2, 657, 713.

46. Ibid., Vol. 2, p. 605; Vol. 3, p. 327.
47. Lenin, *Collected Works*, Vol. 22, p. 257.
48. Enrico Corradini, *Scritti e discorsi 1901–1914*, ed. Lucia Strappini, Turin: Einaudi, 1980, p. 243.
49. Lenin, *Collected Works*, Vol. 39, p. 743.
50. Ibid., Vol. 39, p. 682.
51. Fyodor Dostoevsky, *The Brothers Karamazov*, trans. Richard Pevear and Larissa Volokhonsky, New York and London: Everyman's Library, 1997, pp. 242–3.
52. Quoted in Figes, *A People's Tragedy*, p. 365.
53. Lenin, *Collected Works*, Vol. 2, p. 52.
54. Figes, *A People's Tragedy*, p. 114.
55. Nolte, *Der europäische Bürgerkrieg*, p. 58.
56. Lenin, *Collected Works*, Vol. 26, p. 424.
57. Ibid., Vol. 20, p. 437.
58. Ibid., Vol. 23, p. 63.
59. Ibid., Vol. 24, p. 406.
60. Ibid., Vol. 33, pp. 349, 351.
61. Edgar Snow, *Red Star over China*, New York: Grove Press/Atlantic Monthly Press, 1994, p. 83.
62. Mao Tse-tung, *Selected Works*, Beijing: Foreign Languages Press, 1967, Vol. 1, pp. 157, 168.
63. Ibid., Vol. 2, p. 196.
64. Ibid., Vol. 2, p. 215.
65. Ibid., Vol. 1, p. 169.
66. Ibid., Vol. 2, pp. 196–7, 210.
67. Adolf Hitler, *Mein Kampf*, trans. Ralph Mannheim, London: Pimlico, 1992, pp. 213, 288.
68. Ibid., pp. 126–8.
69. Quoted in Klaus Hildebrand, *Vom Reich zum Weltreich. Hitler, NSDAP und koloniale Frage 1919–1945*, Munich: Fink, 1969, p. 164.
70. Quoted in Götz Aly, *Hitlers Volksstaat. Raub, Rassenkrieg und nationaler Sozialismus*, Frankfurt am Main: Fischer, 2005, pp. 28–9.
71. Georgi Dimitrov, 'The Fascist Offensive and the Tasks of the Communist International', in *Selected Speeches and Articles*, London: Lawrence & Wishart, 1951, pp. 39, 92.
72. David Olusoga and Casper W. Erichsen, *The Kaiser's Holocaust: Germany's Forgotten Genocide*, London: Faber & Faber, 2011, p. 327.
73. Adolf Hitler, *Reden und Proklamationen 1932–1945*, ed. M. Domarus, Munich: Süddeutscher Verlag, pp. 75–7.
74. Quoted in Ernst Piper, *Alfred Rosenberg Hitlers Chefideologe*, Munich: Blessing, 2005, p. 529.

75. See Mark Mazower, *Hitler's Empire: How the Nazis Ruled Europe*, London: Penguin, 2009, pp. 309, 299.
76. Niall Ferguson, *The War of the World*, London: Penguin, 2006, pp. xxxvii, xlii.
77. Heinrich Himmler, *Geheimreden 1933 bis 1945*, ed. B.F. Smith and A.F. Peterson, Berlin: Propyläen, 1974, p. 201.
78. Hitler, *Reden und Proklamationen 1932–1945*, p. 753.
79. Leon Trotsky, *The Revolution Betrayed: What is the Soviet Union and Where is it Going?*, trans. Max Eastman, New York: Pathfinder Press, 1980, p. 201.
80. Lu Xun, *Letteratura e sudore. Scritti dal 1925 al 1936*, ed. A. Bujatti, Isolola del Liri (Frosinone): Editrice Pisani, 2007, pp. 193, 196.
81. Pierre Broué, *La Rivoluzione perduta. Vita di Lev Trockij, 1879–1940*, Turin: Bollati Boringhieri, 1991, p. 726.
82. Ibid., p. 727.
83. Joseph Goebbels, *Tagebücher*, ed. R.G. Reuth, Munich and Zurich: Piper, 1992, pp. 1951-2.
84. See Gerhard Schreiber, *La vendetta tedesca 1943–1945: le rappresaglie naziste in Italia*, Milan: Mondadori, 2000, pp. 22-4.
85. Degras (ed.), *The Communist International*, Vol. 1, pp. 163-4.
86. Ibid., Vol. 2, pp. 154, 199.
87. Dimitrov, 'The Fascist Offensive and the Tasks of the Communist International', pp. 101-02.
88. Marx and Engels, *Collected Works*, Vol. 22, p. 269.
89. Lenin, *Collected Works*, Vol. 31, p. 85.
90. Marx and Engels, *Collected Works*, Vol. 29, p. 263.
91. Ibid., Vol. 6, p. 489.
92. Ibid., Vol. 10, p. 116.

CHAPTER 8

Lenin in 1919: 'The Class Struggle is Continuing—It has Merely Changed its Forms'

1 LENIN, THE BELGIAN WORKER AND THE FRENCH CATHOLIC

We have seen the revolution relocate in the course of the twentieth century from West to South-East. What happened in countries which, identifying with the *Communist Manifesto* and the theory of class struggle, overthrew the old capitalist regime or set out on the road to socialism? In the early 1920s, a symptomatic episode occurred in Soviet Russia. The crisis remained grave: what was to be done? Among the sympathizers with the Bolshevik Revolution in Moscow at the time was a French doctor, Madeleine Pelletier, who got to know the city very well, and was struck by workers' lack of commitment to work.[1] This is an impression confirmed by the testimony of an eminent philosopher, Walter Benjamin:

> A feeling for the value of time, notwithstanding all 'rationalization', is not met with even in the capital of Russia. 'Trud', the trade-union institute for the study of work … launched a poster campaign for punctuality. … 'Time is money'—for this astonishing statement posters claim the authority of Lenin, so alien is the idea to the Russians. They fritter everything away. …If on the street a scene is being shot for a film, they forget where they are going and why, and follow the camera for hours, arriving at the office distraught. In his use of time, therefore, the Russian will remain 'Asiatic' longest of all.[2]

In other words, the measures taken by the Soviet government to improve labour productivity had not yielded significant results. From the outset, however, they had been opposed by a Belgian worker who was likewise a sympathizer with the revolution—Nicolas Lazarevic—and found himself in the Russian capital. He denounced the speed-up of work without any increase in wages. In his view, this was synonymous with exploitation, and he called for class struggle and strikes, ending up being expelled from the country.[3]

For the Western worker who had come to Soviet Russia to help build a new society, the Bolsheviks' arrival in power (in which the influence of the working class was unquestionably strong) did not entail any change in the modalities of the class struggle. Lenin argued very differently. From October 1919, he frequently stressed that '[t]he class struggle is continuing; it has merely changed its forms'.[4] People should not lose sight of 'the essential difference between the class struggle of the proletariat in a [capitalist] state ... and the economic struggle of the proletariat in a state which does not recognise private ownership of the land and the majority of the large enterprises and where political power is in the hands of the proletariat'.[5]

Lazarevic was not an isolated case. He was an ideological ally and friend of a fervent French Catholic, Pierre Pascal, who interpreted and saluted the Bolshevik Revolution, which he witnessed, as follows:

> A unique and heady spectacle: the demolition of a society. This is the very realization of the fourth psalm of the Sunday vespers, and the Magnificat: the powerful cast from their throne and the poor man lifted from his hovel. ...There are no more rich people: only poor and poorer. Knowledge no longer confers either privilege or respect. The former worker promoted to director gives orders to engineers. Salaries, high and low, are getting closer to each other. The right to property is reduced to the rags on one's back. Judges are no longer obliged to apply the law if their sense of proletarian equity contradicts it.[6]

What immediately strikes us here is that generalized poverty is regarded as a condition of spiritual plenitude, not as a painful emergency. It is easy to see why Pascal felt no need for a revival of production. In fact, he looked with suspicion on attempts to restore order in the factories and condemned those who preached 'admiration for bosses, obedience, discipline—all of them virtues that are all too common in the people, and which are the greatest obstacles to the revolution'.[7] Lenin's position was quite different. In October 1920, he declared: '[w]e want to transform Russia from a poverty-stricken and wretched country into one that is wealthy'. To that end what was needed was 'organised' labour, 'conscious and disciplined labour', so as to assimilate and apply 'the latest achievements of technology'.[8] In its new forms, the class struggle required ending a situation of wretchedness and devastation in order to improve the people's living conditions, consolidate the social basis of support for Soviet power, and not leave it defenceless in the face of imperialism's economic and military pressure.

2 'Universal Asceticism' and 'Social Levelling'

How should we characterize the contrast between these two views? Is concern with production and material wealth contrary to the pursuit of more spiritual values and a community that is spiritually richer in that it is harmonious and unified? In the same intervention of October 1920, when he launched the appeal to transform Russia into a 'wealthy country', Lenin stressed the need to have done with a society so absorbed in its private egotisms that 'nobody cared a straw for the aged and the sick, or whether housework was the concern only of the women, who, in consequence, were in a condition of oppression and servitude'.[9] The imperative of introducing spiritually richer inter-subjective relations was also registered by the Soviet leader, who believed that the problem could not be solved without the development of the productive forces. Some fifteen years later, drawing on his memory of his experience in government, Trotsky wrote: 'the actual liberation of women is unrealizable on a basis of "generalized want"'.[10] The class struggle to restructure and revive the productive apparatus was also a struggle for women's liberation (and to guarantee the right to life for the 'old' and 'infirm'). In the words of *Capital*, the less developed the productive forces and social wealth, the more imperious and constraining was the 'realm of necessity', and the more it impacted negatively on the life (including the spiritual life) of men and women.[11]

Pascal's position was quite different. He was a fervent Christian, and in his view, the revolutionary class struggle was the revenge of the humiliated and rejected. This was also the view of the Belgian worker, Lazarevic, and not a few supporters of or sympathizers with Bolshevism who were far removed from Christianity, and yet found it difficult to identify with the measures with which the new government sought to reorganize and re-start the industrial apparatus. We are therefore dealing with a contrast not between devotees and enemies of the fetish of wealth, not between those who are deaf, and those who are attuned, to spiritual values, and not even with a contrast between atheists and Christians. Pitted against one another, ultimately, were Marxists and populists, the latter inclined to condemn wealth and 'luxury' as such, as the lifestyle peculiar to classes accustomed to extravagance and debauchery.

For this reason, populists concentrate exclusively on the problem of the distribution of wealth, completely ignoring the objective (key for Marx and Engels) of the development of the productive forces. Revolutionary class struggle signifies the realization of equality (levelling down) and little consideration for the pursuit of well-being. In this form, populism can exercise a power of attraction far beyond Christian circles. According to the *Communist Manifesto*, '[n]othing is easier than to give Christian asceticism a Socialist tinge'. Not by chance, the 'first movements of the proletariat' are often characterized by demands stamped by 'universal asceticism and social levelling in its crudest form'.[12]

In reality, this phenomenon has a spatial and temporal dimension far beyond that indicated by Marx and Engels. The great popular revolutions and the mass movements of subaltern classes tend to generate a spontaneous, naïve populism, which expects or celebrates the revenge of those occupying the bottom rung of the social hierarchy, the turn of the poor and the 'poor in spirit'. In France in 1789, even before the assault on the Bastille, the meeting of Estates General and the agitation of the Third Estate awakened 'in the popular spirit the old millenarianism, the impatient expectation of the revenge of the poor and the happiness of the humble: the revolutionary mentality was to be very profoundly impregnated by it'.[13] In Russia in February 1917, we find Christian circles greeting the fall of tsarism as the defeat of 'evil and sin', which had 'split the people into rich and poor'. The new society 'would be reorganized on the basis of more Christian attitudes' It would be 'a universal spiritual community … overriding class or party differences', a community witnessing the disappearance or suppression of any manifestation of the previous depraved, debauched opulence. There would, *inter alia*, be no place for alcohol.[14] Here we have 'social levelling in its crudest forms' intersecting with forced 'universal asceticism'. But the hopes reposed in the October Revolution by Pierre Pascal were not very different.

The Bolsheviks were not immune from this view of the world or state of mind. The disaster wreaked by the First World War and then the Civil War involved a crisis of terrible proportions financially as well. In practice, money ceased to exist as a factor in the Soviet economy. Housing, transport, education, and meals at work were free and wages were paid in kind, with everything at a very basic level—in the best case, a level of dignified poverty. Having elicited dismay and anguish, however, this situation ended up being transfigured: it was the desired disappearance of money (symbol of social polarization and debauched wealth); it was the end of the *auri sacra fames*, the advent of communism, albeit a 'war communism', with all the limits imposed by circumstances.[15]

In 1936–7, Trotsky critically recalled the 'ascetic tendencies of the epoch of the civil war', widespread among communists.[16] But it was a rank-and-file militant in the 1940s who more effectively described the spiritual climate that prevailed in the period immediately following the October Revolution—the climate which emerged from the horror aroused by the war caused by imperialist competition to plunder colonies, conquer markets and raw materials, by the capitalist hunt for profits and super-profits: '[w]e young Communists had all grown up in the belief that money was done away with once and for all. ...If money was reappearing, wouldn't rich people reappear too? Weren't we on the slippery slope that led back to capitalism?'[17]

Given these assumptions, the advent of barter represented an advance, at least spiritually. This was a climate that did not immediately disappear with war communism. An extraordinary text by Lenin dated 6–7 November attests to the fact:

> When we are victorious on a world scale, I think we shall use gold for the purpose of building public lavatories in the streets of some of the largest cities of the world. This would be the most 'just' and most educational way of utilising gold for the benefit of those generations which have not forgotten how, for the sake of gold, ten million men were killed and thirty million maimed in the 'great war for freedom', the war of 1914–18 ... and how, for the sake of this same gold, they certainly intend to kill twenty million men and to maim sixty million in a [coming] war....
> But however 'just', useful, or humane it would be to utilise gold for this purpose, ... we must save the gold in the R.S.F.S.R, sell it at the highest price, buy goods with it at the lowest price. When you live among wolves, you must howl like a wolf.[18]

In other words, the road of the New Economic Policy (NEP) had already been taken and yet the market economy, gold, and money continued to be regarded with suspicion as stained with the mud and blood of the Great War's trenches.

The self-critical reflection with which, on 17 October 1921, Lenin justified the need to renounce war communism also provides food for thought:

> Partly owing to the war problems that overwhelmed us and partly owing to the desperate position in which the Republic found itself when the imperialist war ended—owing to these circumstances, and a number of others, we made the mistake of deciding to go over directly to *communist production and distribution*. We thought that under the surplus-food appropriation system, the peasants would provide us with the required quantity of grain, which we could distribute among the factories and thus achieve *communist production and distribution*.[19]

I have emphasized the reiterated statement I propose to discuss here. On other occasions, Lenin had no hesitation in bluntly describing the real significance of the practice of appropriation or forced requisition of 'necessaries' regarded as 'surpluses', 'to meet the requirements of the army and sustain the workers', paid for with 'paper money' of dubious value.[20] This was a practice that met, and was bound to meet, with muffled, bitter or violent resistance from the peasants. Given the extremely serious crisis in exchange between city and countryside, long predating the Bolshevik conquest of power, with a decrease in agricultural production and the hoarding of the limited food available, the survival of the urban population and soldiers certainly dictated radical measures, widely accepted by the various contending parties, even those inspired by liberal economic ideology.[21] But how are generalized, desperate poverty, and requisitions directly or indirectly effected by force, communist? Personal self-interest and market calculation may well have disappeared. But is that enough to define a measure manifestly dictated by war, and which countries of a very different ideological and political persuasion tended to resort to, as communist? Or perhaps the populist transfiguration of 'universal asceticism' and 'social levelling' can be glimpsed even in Lenin's speeches.

3 A 'Collectivism of Poverty and Suffering'

We are dealing with an international debate in which Gramsci participated. His intervention was contained in an article that greeted the very recent Bolshevik Revolution as 'The Revolution against "Capital"'—against Marx's work construed in a positivist and determinist key, and hence, invoked to delegitimize socialist revolution in any country not among the more advanced capitalist states. The article has become famous for this anti-dogmatic stance. But it also warrants fame in connection with the problem we are discussing. Here is how in December 1917 Gramsci interpreted the turning point represented by Bolshevik victory in a country that was relatively backward and, what is more, exhausted by war:

> It will at first be a collectivism of poverty and suffering. But a bourgeois regime would have inherited the same conditions of poverty and suffering. Capitalism could do no more *immediately* than collectivism in Russia. In fact today it would do a lot less, since it would be faced *immediately* by a discontented and turbulent proletariat, a proletariat no longer able to support on behalf of others the suffering and privation that economic dislocation would bring in its wake. ...The hardships that await them after the peace will be bearable only if the proletarians feel they have things under their own control and know that by their efforts they can reduce these hardships in the shortest possible time.[22]

In this text, the war communism being imposed in Russia was legitimized tactically and delegitimized strategically, legitimized in the immediate present and delegitimized for the future. A 'collectivism of poverty and suffering' was justified in the concrete conditions in which Russia found itself: capitalism could not do any better. Far from being synonymous with spiritual plenitude and ethical rigour, however, the 'collectivism of poverty and suffering' must be overcome 'in the shortest possible time'. It is no cause for surprise if (as we shall see) Gramsci later justified the transition to the NEP, politically and theoretically.

Yet it was precisely as synonymous with spiritual plenitude and ethical rigour that 'war communism'—the 'collectivism of poverty and suffering' and 'socialized poverty' of which Gramsci and Trotsky, respectively, speak—was regarded by large sections of the communist movement in Russia and the West. The result was that the 'social levelling in its crudest forms' and 'universal asceticism' against which the *Manifesto* cautioned were transfigured into expressions of proletarian class struggle. It should not be supposed that this kind of spiritual climate remained confined to Soviet Russia. On the contrary, it seemed to find an even emphatic expression among Western intellectuals and militants. In 1921, disappointed by the introduction of the NEP, Pascal did not renew his Communist Party card, although continuing to live in Moscow and work at the Marx-Engels

Institute. In his turn, a French communist leader reconciled himself to the turn, but at the same time, writing in *L'Humanité*, added: 'the NEP brought with it something of the capitalist putrescence that had completely disappeared at the time of war communism'.[23]

Even figures far removed from the communist movement feared that the country born in the October Revolution was in the process of losing its idealistic charge. Thus, the great Austrian writer, Joseph Roth, who visited the land of the Soviets between September 1926 and January 1927, denounced the 'Americanization' underway: 'the America of soulless capitalism, the country where gold is king, is held in contempt. But the America of progress, the electric iron, hygiene and water mains, is admired'. In short, '[t]his is a modern, technologically advanced Russia with American ambitions. This is no longer Russia'. A 'spiritual vacuum' obtained there too.[24]

Having overcome his initial hesitations and fluctuations, Lenin began to harshly criticize the transfiguration of the 'collectivism of poverty and suffering'. The economy based on barter, characteristic of so-called war communism, was now synonymous with backwardness not only economically but also spiritually. Maintaining the lack of '*exchange* between agriculture and industry, the absence of connection and interaction between them', meant depriving the enormous Russian countryside of 'the material line with the big cities, large-scale industry, capitalism and culture'; it meant eternalizing 'patriarchalism, and semi- and downright barbarism' in these territories. It was true that '[c]apitalism is a bane compared with socialism'. But it was 'a boon compared with medievalism, small production, and the evils of bureaucracy which spring from the dispersal of the small producers'.[25] By comparison with a pre-modern, semi-feudal society, capitalism represented spiritual progress as well. Even if it was not made explicit, 'war communism', rather than being construed and criticized as an attempt, albeit rash, to construct a post-capitalist society, was presented as a regression to a pre-capitalist social state. Obviously, this relapse had primarily been caused by world war and civil war, as Lenin was repeatedly at pains to make clear. However, it had undergone a transfiguration—and not only at the hands of those who saluted the October Revolution from a position of Christian pauperism.

It was a process, and an optical illusion, not very different from what had occurred in the West. There the total mobilization of the population and economic resources, for the purposes of centralized conduct of the war, had prompted eminent intellectuals to celebrate the redemptive advent of 'war socialism' (or 'state and nation socialism', in Croce's words), which had supposedly answered the social question conclusively and done so in an orderly, organic fashion.[26] On closer inspection, this putatively new social regime was none other than the old capitalism, to which the regimentation and terroristic discipline of war had been added. Corresponding to the optical illusion of 'war communism' in Russia was the optical illusion (and ideological manipulation) of 'war socialism', or 'state and nation socialism', in the West.

Once the path of the NEP had been embarked on, Lenin proceeded to a settlement of accounts with populism: '[w]e must do everything possible to develop trade at all costs, without being afraid of capitalism ... [everything] must be brought into play in order to stimulate exchange between industry and agriculture at all costs'.[27] Just as 'war communism' had very little to do with the construction of a post-capitalist society, so disdain for the market economy pertained to 'the old Russian, semi-aristocratic, semi-muzhik and patriarchal mood, with their supreme contempt for trade', not to socialism and Marxism.[28]

Nevertheless, assuming a variety of forms over time, populism in Soviet Russia took a long time to die. In 1925, Bukharin criticized the bizarre conception of class struggle that involved deterring the development of the productive forces and viewing wealth—indeed, prosperity as such—with suspicion:

> Consider the fact that the well-to-do upper stratum of the peasantry, along with the middle peasant, who is also striving to join the well-to-do, are both *afraid at present to accumulate*. A situation has been created in which the peasant is afraid to buy an iron roof and apprehensive that he will be declared a *kulak*; if he buys a machine, he makes certain that the communists are not watching. Advanced technology has become a conspiracy.[29]

A line must be drawn under this: '[i]n general and on the whole, we must say to the entire peasantry, to all its different strata: enrich yourselves, accumulate, develop your farms. Only an idiot can say that the poor will *always* be with us. We must now implement a policy whose result will be the disappearance of the poor'.[30] As we can see, the exhortation to enrichment was addressed to 'the entire peasantry', but it was highly unlikely that everyone could attain prosperity at the same pace. Given the inequalities and contradictions which, at least for a time, would inevitably emerge from this process, only the 'idiots', or populists, referred to by the Soviet leader would have grounds to reaffirm the moral superiority of a social condition marked by an orderly, egalitarian distribution of poverty.

Some years later, they continued to make their voices heard: '[i]f everyone becomes prosperous ... and the poor cease to be with us, upon whom then are we Bolsheviks to rely in our work?' The date was 1930 and this, according to Stalin, was the anguished argument of 'Leftist blockheads, who idealise the poor as the eternal bulwark of Bolshevism'.[31] Once again, the influence of an ultimately religious tradition asserted itself. We are reminded of Hegel's critical remarks on the Gospel commandment to aid the poor. Losing sight of the fact that it is a 'conditional precept', and absolutizing it, Christians also wound up absolutizing poverty, which alone could confer meaning on the norm enjoining aid for the poor. The survival of poverty was a precondition for Christians, or at least some of them, enjoying a sense of moral nobility attendant upon their aid for the poor. The seriousness of help for the poor should instead be measured by its contribution to overcoming poverty as such.[32]

Even communists may be unaware of the 'conditional' character of the revolutionary precept that enjoins them to give a voice to the exploited and poor; they may be inclined to idealize poverty or, at any rate, scarcity as a prerequisite for revolutionary rigour. And Stalin felt obliged to underscore a key point: '[i]t would be absurd to think that socialism can be built on the basis of poverty and privation, on the basis of reducing personal requirements and lowering the standard of living to the level of the poor'. On the contrary, socialism 'can be built only on the basis of a vigorous growth of the productive forces of society' and 'on the basis of the prosperity of the working people'—in fact, 'a prosperous and cultured life for all members of society'.[33] On this point at any rate, he was in full agreement with Trotsky, who, invoking Marx, stressed even more emphatically the centrality of the task of increasing material wealth: '[o]n a basis of "generalized want," the struggle for the means of subsistence threatens to resurrect "all the old crap," and is partially resurrecting it at every step'.[34]

The appearance of populism in various forms, on different occasions, is not a phenomenon confined to Soviet Russia. Take China. In and through unprecedented mass mobilization, the Great Leap Forward of 1958–9 and the Cultural Revolution initiated in 1966 were intended to accelerate the development of the economy enormously, so as to enable China to forge ahead and catch up with the industrially most advanced countries in record time. This perspective was at the antipodes of populism. But the latter ended up emerging. Above all during the Great Leap Forward, the moral transfiguration of dignified, generalized poverty aimed to encourage the militaristic, 'egalitarian' mobilization of the population—indeed, of an army of labour called on to perform a miracle. Secondly, the failure of the extremely ambitious (in fact, amazing) attempt to catch up with the West in record time was faced down by (populist) propagandizing of socialism as a 'collectivism of poverty and suffering', and hence by repression of that major Marxian theme which has capitalist relations of production condemned by history because they have become an obstacle to further development of the productive forces.

Populism was to the fore during the international polemic conducted by the Chinese Communist Party in particular against the Soviet leader Khrushchev, who was allegedly guilty of pursuing 'goulash communism' under the sign of material prosperity and 'the bourgeois way of life', while neglecting the tasks and ideals of revolutionary transformation of the world.[35]

4 AN UNPRECEDENTED CLASS STRUGGLE FROM ABOVE

If, contrary to what populists seem to believe, revolutionary class struggle in the Russia and China that had just emerged from the overthrow of the *ancien régime* did not aim at a 'collectivism of poverty and suffering', what was its objective? The problem had already been broached by the *Manifesto*, according to which '[t]he proletariat will use its political supremacy' to initiate the socialist transformation of society, obviously, but also 'to increase the total of productive forces as rapidly as possible'.[36]

Let us now see how the debate unfolded in Soviet Russia. Lenin called for an end to the totality of intolerable social relations, starting with the domestic slavery of women, which persisted in the new society three years after the revolution. At this level, we might already note a basic novelty: action from below, which was imperative, could count on the support of the new political power; and in this sense class struggle from below intersected with class struggle from above. However, a key question remained to be answered: how did class struggle manifest itself in urban factories and workplaces, where the transformation of property relations in a socialist direction had already occurred?

When the Civil War and counter-revolutionary intervention erupted, there was a broad consensus that participation in revolutionary class struggle consisted in armed defence of Soviet Russia, on the one hand, and commitment to production in support of that armed defence, on the other. In Lenin's words, communists placed themselves at the head of the revolutionary class struggle, demonstrating 'heroism' and 'self-sacrifice' 'not only at the front, but also in the rear'.[37]

With the defeat of the counter-revolutionary armies supported by the Entente, people were called upon to prove their dedication in a protracted labour of economic construction no longer directly prompted by the dictates of war and military salvation of the revolution. What threatened the very existence of Soviet Russia now was not counter-revolutionary armies, but the difficulty of providing for the basic, daily needs of an exhausted population. In the Soviet leader's view, it should be obvious that commitment to satisfying these needs, so as to ensure the new regime a broad social base of support, was synonymous with concrete participation in revolutionary class struggle. In reality, the transition from poetry to prose, from defying death on the battlefield (and active solidarity with the heroes at the front) to meeting the challenge of the everyday exertion and monotony of workplaces and production sites—all this proved quite the reverse of easy and, in fact, generated unease and disenchantment.

Lenin had to engage in a struggle at once political and pedagogical to persuade his collaborators and comrades—especially youth—of the need to turn the page on revolutionary romanticism and embrace a less heady, but more concrete, view of the class struggle. October 1920: 'people are starving'—such was the situation that needed remedying.[38] 8 March 1921: it was necessary to focus on the problem of 'worsening equipment, lower crop yields, shortage of hands etc'.[39] End of October 1921: 'a revival of economic life ... and increased production' were imperative.[40]

To achieve these objectives, there should be no hesitation about learning from the most advanced countries of the capitalist West, in order to assimilate, along with science and technology, what would today be called management. Indeed, even Taylorism had to be critically assimilated. In the years immediately preceding the First World War, it had been branded 'a "scientific" system of sweating' wage-slaves.[41] Even then, however, Lenin had been concerned to make pertinent distinctions. Based as it was on 'competition', capitalism was led to 'convert all these devices into instruments for the further exploitation of the workers'.[42] But it was subsequently, starting from the exigencies of constructing the new society, that the distinction between science and the capitalist use of science also became clearer and sharper in connection with Taylorism:

> The Russian is a bad worker compared with people in advanced countries.
> ...The task that the Soviet government must set the people in all its scope

is—learn to work. The Taylor system, the last word of capitalism in this respect, like all capitalist progress, is a combination of the refined brutality of bourgeois exploitation and a number of the greatest scientific achievements in the field of analysing mechanical motions during work, the elimination of superfluous and awkward motions, the elaboration of correct methods of work, the introduction of the best system of accounting and control, etc. The Soviet Republic must at all costs adopt all that is valuable in the achievements of science and technology in this field. The possibility of building socialism depends exactly upon our success in combining the Soviet power and the Soviet organisation of administration with the up-to-date achievements of capitalism'.[43]

Obviously, among the Bolsheviks there were those who cried scandal, maintaining that this would recreate 'the enslavement of the working class' and lead back to capitalism. But Lenin's rejoinder was just as harsh. He regarded this attitude as 'an unheard-of reactionary thing'.[44] In fact, '[o]nly those are worthy of the name of Communists who understand that it is *impossible* to create or introduce socialism *without learning* from the organisers of the trusts', given that socialism presupposed 'the assimilation and application by the proletarian vanguard, which has seized power, of what has been created by the trusts'.[45]

With the introduction of the NEP, unease and disenchantment intensified. The Soviet leader redoubled his efforts to make it clear that the class struggle, in its new configuration, had acquired another dimension. It involved not only increasing productivity in general, but concretely demonstrating the superiority of the public sector of the economy to the private sector. On 27 March, he addressed supporters thus: '[s]how by your practical efforts that you can work no less efficiently than the capitalists. ...Look at things more soberly. Cast off the tinsel, the festive communist garments, learn a simple thing simply, and we shall beat the private capitalist'.[46]

This was a theme systematized and radicalized by Bukharin in 1925. Once power had been won, the proletariat had an interest in 'the unity of the social whole', 'civil peace', but this 'by no means spells the end of the class struggle ... [which] assumes a new form'.[47] Indeed, '[h]ow do we squeeze out our immediate opponents, the private capitalists? By means of competition and economic struggle. If they sell cheaply, we must reach a position where we can sell still more cheaply. This is the form taken by our *class struggle* under present circumstances'.[48] The objectives of the new class struggle (developing productivity generally and demonstrating the superiority of the state and public economy) could be achieved on one condition. Addressing the 'new generation', Lenin issued an appeal: '[y]ou are faced with the task of construction, and you can accomplish that task only by assimilating all modern knowledge'.[49]

With his customary lucidity and insight, in 1927 Benjamin observed: '[n]ow it is made clear to every Communist that the revolutionary work of this hour is not conflict, not civil war, but canal construction, electrification, and factory building. The revolutionary nature of true technology is emphasized ever more clearly'.[50]

Four years later—in the interim, the NEP had been abandoned for the collectivization of agriculture and hyper-industrialization—Stalin repeated: '[i]n the period of reconstruction, technique decides everything'; it was therefore necessary 'to study technique' and 'to master science'. All this might seem prosaic and banal. In reality, though, this new task was no less arduous than storming the Winter Palace: 'Bolsheviks must master technique' and become 'experts'. This was far from easy to achieve, but '[t]here are no fortresses that Bolsheviks cannot capture'.[51] Even the class struggle for the growth of the productive forces could be a rousing, memorable enterprise; it too could, or should, ignite revolutionary enthusiasm.

By contrast, Simone Weil in France argued very differently. In 1932, she reached the conclusion that Russia's model was now America, efficiency, productivism, Taylorism, the enslavement of the worker to production. Class struggle had been forgotten: 'the fact that, on a question which is at the heart of the conflict between capital and labour, Stalin has abandoned Marx's standpoint and allowed himself to be seduced by the capitalist system in its consummate form, shows that the USSR is still far from having a working-class culture'.[52]

The problem we have identified in connection with Soviet Russia also manifested itself in other revolutions. In summer 1933, Mao Zedong called for commitment to 'continued growth' of the economy in the zones governed by communists: '[t]his is a great task, a great class struggle'.[53] And in late 1964, referring to Algeria as well as Cuba, Ernesto Che Guevara addressed Algerian youth: 'this is a time for construction, something much more difficult, and seemingly less heroic, but demanding all the nation's forces ... It is necessary to work, because at times like these that is the best way of struggling ... Fatherland or death'.[54] Following a revolution's military victory, the key question became 'the work of combatants on the production front'. This involved striving to make 'the great mechanism of production' efficient. On the agenda was a solution to the problem of 'creating more wealth, creating more goods, so that our people have an ever greater quantity of things, so that we can call ourselves a socialist country'.[55]

5 Class Struggle and the Two Forms of Inequality

But what is the development of production and productivity geared towards? Once hopes for an extension of anti-capitalist revolution to the West had been dashed, the Bolsheviks in power soon realized that, on the basis both of their ideological and political programme and the international situation, they had to confront not one, but two different forms of inequality. There was not only the inequality dividing a single country. By dint of having won victory on the margins, or outside, of the more developed world, the October Revolution and other revolutions of a Marxist and communist inspiration had to face the problem of 'global inequities' at an international level.[56] In winning power, they all had to come to terms with the process whereby 'the inequality of nations was as profound as the inequality of classes', so that humanity was 'irrevocably divided'.[57] They had to come to terms with the 'great divergence' *par excellence*, which not only created a gulf between nations, but swept away 'a polycentric world with no dominant center' and ushered in 'a Europe-centred world system'.[58]

To facilitate things, I shall refer in this connection to the first type of inequality. In Soviet Russia, this was certainly experienced just as painfully as the second. In Lenin's words from January 1920, 'the working people must not forget that capitalism has divided nations into a small number of oppressor, Great-Power (imperialist), sovereign and privileged nations and an overwhelming majority of oppressed, dependent and semi-dependent, non-sovereign nations'.[59] Soviet Russia was located in or risked being ejected into this group of nations. Having suffered drastic territorial amputation at the hands of Wilhelm II's Germany, it had had to face intervention by the Entente. While the Bolsheviks managed to consolidate their power and stabilize the domestic situation, the international picture continued to be far from reassuring. The Versailles Treaty ended the First World War, but did not silence the wide range of voices evoking the danger of a new conflagration no less ruinous than the first. Lenin himself repeatedly warned of this danger. It was a further reason for boosting the struggle against the first type of inequality, which found Russia far behind the more advanced countries economically and technologically. Unfortunately, the revolution had not triumphed in those countries:

> We must remember that at present all their highly developed technology and their highly developed industry belong to the capitalists, who are fighting us.
> We must remember that we either strain every nerve in everyday effort, or we shall inevitably go under.
> Owing to the present circumstances, the whole world is developing faster than we are. While developing, the capitalist world is directing all its forces against us. That is how the matter stands. That is why we must devote special attention to this struggle.[60]

Hence, the first type of inequality was increasing and this could have catastrophic consequences for Soviet Russia, rendering any serious plan for countering the second type of inequality impossible. On this basis, Lenin never tired of stressing the need for scientific and technological development, assimilating the achievements of the West. A similar concern was expressed in 1925 by Bukharin, who, with the more advanced capitalist countries in mind, observed: 'we are growing, but *they* are growing as well'. The distance and the risks bound up with it, remained unaltered. In these conditions, 'the question of the *tempo* of development, or the speed of our development, assumes quite exceptional importance'; 'we must grow more rapidly'.[61] This theme subsequently became the guiding thread of Stalin's discourse.

Among the most urgent tasks was electrification of the great Eurasian country. Arendt may wax ironic about the 'curious formula' ('electrification plus soviets'), in which Lenin encapsulated 'the essence and aims of the October Revolution'. Silent on the subject of 'building socialism', it was a watchword that expressed 'an entirely un-Marxist separation of economics and politics'.[62] But no serious and responsible statesman could take this school lesson seriously. Certainly not Lenin and the Bolsheviks, who had to face invasion by counter-revolutionary powers and, even after having defeated it, knew full well that the danger had not been averted for good. Hence, electrification was a matter of life and death.

We are dealing with a problem which, in different ways, regularly arose in countries engaged in a revolutionary process while being located outside, or on the margins of, the more advanced West. In the 1960s, Che

Guevara observed in Cuba: '[s]ince monopoly capital took control of the world, it has kept the majority of humanity in poverty, dividing the spoils among the most powerful countries. The standard of living of these countries is based on the poverty of ours'.[63] Hence, 'a great technological leap is required to reduce the difference that exists today between our countries and the more developed ones', so as to acquire 'the technology of the advanced counties'. It was necessary to 'make a start on the new phase with a genuine international division of labour, based not on the history of what has been done so far, but on the future history of what should be done'.[64] A new international order was necessary, enabling the combined development of humanity and avoiding the subjugation of colonies and semi-colonies.

In one respect, the two class struggles against the two different types of inequality were interlinked: the electrification invoked in Soviet Russia would make it possible to overcome, or lessen, the isolation of the non-electrified countryside from the city and reduce the gap between urban and rural worlds.[65] At the same time, electrification and technological and scientific development as a whole would reduce the disparity in the military balance of power internationally and render colonial subjugation, and the veritable enslavement later pursued by the Third Reich, difficult or impossible. That is, they would make an extreme accentuation of inequality within the international division of labour difficult or impossible. As we can see, *pace* Arendt, the unity of economics and politics is clear on both fronts.

Up to here, the struggles against the two forms of inequality go hand in hand. In another respect, by contrast, a lag and contradiction inevitably occur: the limitation of one inequality can involve a temporary intensification of the other. If, as Lenin wrote between August and September 1922, Soviet Russia's main task was to 'adopt everything that is truly valuable in European and American science',[66] it is evident that such an operation was comparatively easier starting from the country's economic, intellectual, and technological commanding heights. In other words, it was an operation which, while it enabled Russia's more advanced regions to catch up (or reduce the gap) with the West, enhanced their advantage over the more backward regions of the Eurasian country.

That is not all. In October 1921, Lenin observed that the Soviet government was obliged to award 'specialists' 'exceptionally high' remuneration, 'in the bourgeois manner'.[67] Such was the price to be paid for the work of qualified technicians, required to accelerate Russia's development and thereby reduce the inequality between it and more advanced countries. The obverse of this tendentially egalitarian policy internationally was an aggravation of redistributive inequalities inside the country. The emphasis could be put on the struggle against the latter, foregoing the very costly contribution of 'specialists'. But the result would be to aggravate the economic and technological lag and inequality vis-à-vis technologically more developed (and potentially hostile) countries. For the purposes of reducing the first type of inequality, it was also necessary to attract foreign capital to Russia, thereby installing 'the most modern machinery' and progressively approximating to 'the modern, advanced trusts of other countries' and sooner or later catching up with them. However, foreign capital guaranteed the 'concession' of some natural resource, claimed or pursued 'fantastic profits'.[68] Albeit unavoidable, the acquisition of the most advanced technology involved significant political and social (as well as economic) costs.

Today, far from vanishing, the problem broached here has grown enormously. An authoritative US daily refers to the programme implemented by Washington since 2006. In the context of the policy of strangling Cuba, it aims to encourage the 'defection' of the rebel island's doctors, who distinguish themselves very positively by their work in Haiti and other parts of the world, but who might be attracted by the higher remuneration they could enjoy in the USA.[69] Or take China. Since 1978, and the open-door and reform policy introduced by Deng Xiaoping, around two million students and graduates have pursued their studies abroad; only one-third have returned home. In recent years, the percentage has increased markedly and is growing further, thanks to the authorities' policy of very strong material incentives. Repatriation is also encouraged by patriotic appeals. But they resonate more strongly with enhanced concrete possibilities of participating in building a country and nation that is catching up with the commanding heights of industrial and technological development in leaps and bounds and which, thanks to this, is reconquering self-esteem. The ineluctable character of the struggle against relations of inequality internationally emerges once again.

It is easy to see why this problem is posed with particular intensity in China—a country with an ancient civilization which, as a result of having missed its rendezvous with the industrial revolution, suffered the semi-colonial oppression imposed by the West. In a conversation of 10 October 1978, Deng drew attention to the fact that the technological 'gap' with the most advanced countries was growing larger; they were 'developing with tremendous speed' and China was not managing to keep pace with them.[70] And ten years later: 'high technology is advancing at a tremendous pace'; there was a risk that 'the gap between China and other countries will grow wider'.[71]

Had it missed its rendezvous with the new technological revolution, the great Asian country would have been condemned to permanent backwardness and found itself in a situation of weakness and inequality similar to that which rendered it defenceless in the Opium Wars and against the force majeure of Western capitalism and colonialism.

But have the policy of rapid economic and technological development, and chasing after the West, not wound up favouring (coastal) regions that enjoy a superior geographical location and at least possessed modest infrastructure, for good or ill bequeathed by colonial and semi-colonial domination? The more or less egalitarian distribution of poverty has given way to a process of development at an inevitably unequal pace. The problem we saw emerge immediately after the October Revolution has crystallized: is the objective of revolutionary class struggle the creation of a society where, the rich having 'disappeared', there is room only for the 'poor and very poor'? Or should it promote development of the productive forces and social wealth, so as to uproot poverty and penury and dramatically raise the living standards of the popular masses? Besides, how egalitarian can we consider a society where there is room only for the 'poor and very poor'?

6   QUANTITATIVE AND QUALITATIVE INEQUALITY

Two chapters in the history of the People's Republic of China have answered this question with tragic eloquence. The Great Leap Forward, whose author was Mao Zedong in the late 1950s, was an attempt to advance the struggles against the two forms of inequality in concert. On the one hand, the mass mobilization of men and women in work and economic construction dictated recourse to collectivist practices in production and service provision (laundries, canteens, etc.); and this created the impression or illusion of pronounced progress in the cause of equality at home. On the other hand, this intensely political mobilization on an exceptional scale was intended to accelerate China's economic development rapidly, therewith delivering decisive blows to international inequality. Similar considerations apply to the Cultural Revolution. Denouncing the 'bourgeoisie' or 'privileged layers' who had infiltrated the Communist

Party itself, it revived domestic egalitarianism. Criticizing the theory of 'socialism at a snail's pace' attributed to the deposed President of the Republic, Liu Shaoqi, it proposed to impart unprecedented acceleration to the growth of the productive forces, thus, taking the country with remarkable rapidity to the level of the most advanced capitalist countries, and thereby, also abolishing or radically eroding the first type of inequality.

All of this was based on the illusion that accelerated economic construction could be undertaken with the same methods as the political and military battles of the Chinese Revolution, relying on mass mobilization and enthusiasm and the illusion that such enthusiasm could manifest itself enduringly or indefinitely. The Great Leap Forward and the Cultural Revolution took no account of the process of secularization: appeals cannot constantly and eternally be made to the mobilization, self-abnegation, spirit of renunciation and self-sacrifice, the heroism of the masses. On account too of the unconducive, hostile international context (compounding the ruthless embargo implemented from the outset by the USA and the West was the rupture with the USSR and the other socialist countries), the outcome of the Great Leap Forward and the Cultural Revolution was disastrous and tragic. The upshot was a more or less drastic decline in economic development, which ended up aggravating both forms of inequality. Indeed, not only did it increase China's distance from more advanced countries, but domestically too egalitarianism, albeit sincerely proclaimed and passionately pursued, turned into its opposite. When poverty reaches a certain level, it entails the risk of death from starvation. In such an eventuality, the piece of bread that ensures the survival of the more fortunate, however modest, sanctions an absolute inequality—the absolute inequality that exists between life and death. While it dictates painful asceticism for everyone, the society yearned for by populism (not only the Christian variety), where 'there are no more rich people: only poor and poorer', is far from keeping the promise of equality, because diminished quantitative inequality ends up taking the form of, and manifesting itself as, absolute qualitative inequality.

Mao was compelled to realize this. In a conversation of May 1974 with the former British Prime Minister, Edward Heath, he drew up a bitter balance-sheet, full of self-critical accents. He responded as follows to the observation of his interlocutor, according to whom making mistakes is the fate of all great statesmen: '[m]y faults are more serious. Eight hundred million people want to eat and, moreover, China's industry is undeveloped. I can't boast much of China. Your country is a developed country and ours is an undeveloped one'.[72] International inequality had not been eroded and, as indicated by the reference to the problem of feeding people, domestic inequality had not been resolved—had even grown—given that, regardless of equity of distribution, starvation and death from starvation introduced an element of absolute inequality.

We can now understand Deng Xiaoping's turn: Marxists should finally realize 'that poverty is not socialism, that socialism means eliminating poverty. Unless you are developing the productive forces and raising people's living standards, you cannot say that you are building socialism'. Hence, 'to get rich is glorious!' Thus proclaimed Deng,[73] who, probably unwittingly, adopted the slogan with which, more than half a century earlier, Bukharin had sought to overcome the backwardness of Soviet agriculture, stimulating peasant commitment.

Almost 60 years later, the new Chinese leader found himself facing a similar problem, but on a larger scale. In 1986, he clarified the meaning of his slogan in an interview with a US TV journalist. It meant doing away with the view, attributed to the defeated Gang of Four, that 'poor communism was preferable to rich capitalism'. In reality, according to Marx's definition (*Critique of the Gotha Programme*), a communist society was one regulated by the principle: '[f]rom each according to his ability, to each according to his needs'. Hence, it presupposed an enormous growth of the productive forces and social wealth. It was, therefore, a contradiction in terms to speak of 'poor communism' or 'poor socialism' (given that socialism was the preparatory phase of communism).[74] At this point, as a follower of the 'principles of Marxism' and 'communism', Deng was concerned to distinguish the meaning of his slogan in different social orders. Unlike in capitalism, 'wealth in a socialist society belongs to the people'; 'prosperity' is something 'for the entire people': 'we permit some people and some regions to become prosperous first, for the purpose of achieving prosperity faster. That is why our policy will not lead to polarization, to a situation where the rich get richer while the poor get poorer'. This position was forcefully restated on several occasions: 'the welfare and happiness of the people' must be ensured; it was necessary to enable 'our people to lead a fairly comfortable life', to 'rais[e] people's living standards', to achieve 'common prosperity'. Obviously, especially for a continent-country like China, it was not possible for everyone to accede to 'common prosperity' at the same time. The first to attain the goal would be the coastal regions, which would then be in a position, and under an obligation, 'to give still more help to the interior'.[75]

From Deng Xiaoping's point of view, China's turn under his leadership was the 'second revolution', or a new stage in the revolution.[76] But for his domestic opponents, and a large number of Western Marxists, it is a bourgeois and capitalist counter-revolution. How are we to explain these opposed interpretations?

NOTES

1. See Marcello Flores, *L'immagine dell'URSS. L'Occidente e la Russia di Stalin (1927–1956)*, Milan: Il Saggiatore, 1990, p. 29.
2. Walter Benjamin, 'Moscow', in *One-Way Street and Other Writings*, trans. Edmund Jephcott and Kingsley Shorter, London: Verso, 1985, pp. 189–90.
3. Flores, *L'immagine dell'URSS*, p. 42.
4. V.I. Lenin, *Collected Works*, London: Lawrence & Wishart, 1960–78, Vol. 30, p. 60; Vol. 31, p. 293.
5. Ibid., Vol. 33, p. 186.
6. Quoted in François Furet, *The Passing of an Illusion: The Idea of Communism in the Twentieth Century*, trans. Deborah Furet, Chicago and London: University of Chicago Press, 1999, pp. 102–3.
7. Quoted in Flores, *L'immagine dell'URSS*, pp. 42–3.
8. Lenin, *Collected Works*, Vol. 31, pp. 298–9.
9. Ibid., Vol. 31, p. 298.
10. Leon Trotsky, *The Revolution Betrayed: What is the Soviet Union and Where is it Going?*, trans. Max Eastman, New York: Pathfinder Press, 1980, p. 145.
11. Karl Marx and Frederick Engels, *Collected Works*, London: Lawrence & Wishart, 1975–2004, Vol. 37, p. 807.
12. Ibid., Vol. 6, pp. 508, 514.
13. François Furet and Denis Richet, *La Révolution française*, Paris: Hachette, 1999, p. 85.
14. Orlando Figes, *A People's Tragedy: The Russian Revolution, 1891–1924*, London: Pimlico, 1997, p. 352.
15. E.H. Carr, *The Bolshevik Revolution 1917–1923*, London and Basingstoke: Macmillan, 1978, Vol. 2, pp. 260–3.
16. Trotsky, *The Revolution Betrayed*, p. 163.
17. Quoted in Figes, *A People's Tragedy*, p. 771.
18. Lenin, *Collected Works*, Vol. 33, pp. 113–14.
19. Ibid., Vol. 33, p. 62.
20. Ibid., Vol. 32, p. 342.
21. See Domenico Losurdo, *Stalin. Storia e critica di una leggenda nera*, Rome: Carocci, 2008, p. 98.

22. Antonio Gramsci, *Selections from the Political Writings 1910–1920*, ed. Quintin Hoare and trans. John Mathews, London: Lawrence & Wishart, 1977, pp. 36–7.
23. Quoted in Christian Gras, *Alfred Rosmer et le mouvement révolutionnaire international*, Paris: Maspero, 1971, p. 197.
24. Quoted in Flores, *L'immagine dell'URSS*, pp. 28–9, 53.
25. Lenin, *Collected Works*, Vol. 32, pp. 349–51.
26. See Domenico Losurdo, *Heidegger and the Ideology of War: Community, Death and the West*, trans. Marella and Jon Morris, Amherst, NY: Humanity Books, 2001, Chapter 1, §1.
27. Lenin, *Collected Works*, Vol. 32, pp. 352–4.
28. Ibid., Vol. 33, p. 115.
29. N.I. Bukharin, 'Concerning the New Economic Policy and Our Tasks', in *Selected Writings on the State and the Transition to Socialism*, ed. and trans. Richard B. Day, Nottingham: Spokesman, 1982, p. 196.
30. Ibid., p. 197.
31. J. Stalin, *Works*, Moscow: Foreign Languages Publishing House, 1952–5, Vol. 13, pp. 365–8.
32. See Domenico Losurdo, *Hegel and the Liberty of the Moderns*, trans. Marella and Jon Morris, Durham, NC and London: Duke University Press, 2004, Chapter 10, §2.
33. Stalin, *Works*, Vol. 13, pp. 367, 365.
34. Trotsky, *The Revolution Betrayed*, p. 120.
35. See Communist Party of China, *The Polemic on the General Line of the International Communist Movement*, Beijing: Foreign Languages Press, 1965, pp. 464–5.
36. Marx and Engels, *Collected Works*, Vol. 6, p. 504.
37. Lenin, *Collected Works*, Vol. 30, p. 202.
38. Ibid., Vol. 31, p. 297.
39. Ibid., Vol. 32, p. 176.
40. Ibid., Vol. 33, p. 95.
41. Ibid., Vol. 18, p. 593.
42. Ibid., Vol. 20, p. 152.
43. Ibid., Vol. 27, p. 259.
44. Ibid., Vol. 27, p. 299.
45. Ibid., Vol. 27, p. 350.
46. Ibid., Vol. 33, p. 285.
47. N.I. Bukharin, 'Towards a Critique of the Economic Platform of the Opposition', in *Selected Writings on the State and the Transition to Socialism*, ed. and trans. Richard B. Day, Nottingham: Spokesman, 1982, p. 112.
48. Bukharin, 'Concerning the New Economic Policy and Our Tasks', p. 189.
49. Lenin, *Collected Works*, Vol. 31, p. 290.
50. Benjamin, 'Moscow', p. 207.

51. Stalin, *Works*, Vol. 13, pp. 43–4.
52. Simone Weil, *Oeuvres complètes*, Vol. II, *Écrits historiques et politiques*,ed. André A. Deuvaux and Florence de Lussy, Paris: Gallimard, 1989–91, Pt. 1, pp. 106–7.
53. Mao Tse-tung, *Selected Works*, Vol. 1, p. 132.
54. Che Guevara, *Scritti, discorsi e diari di guerriglia 1959–1967*, ed. L. Gonsalez, Turin: Einaudi, 1969, pp. 1418–19.
55. Ibid., pp. 1345, 1375, 1373.
56. Giovanni Arrighi, *Adam Smith in Beijing: Lineages of the Twenty-First Century*, London and New York: Verso, 2007, p. xiii.
57. Mike Davis, *Late Victorian Holocausts: El Nino Famines and the Making of the Third World*, London and New York: Verso, 2001, p. 16.
58. Kenneth Pomeranz, *The Great Divergence: China, Europe, and the Making of the Modern World Economy*, Princeton and Woodstock: Princeton University Press, 2000, p. 4.
59. Lenin, *Collected Works*, Vol. 30, p. 293.
60. Lenin, *Collected Works*, Vol. 33, p. 72.
61. Bukharin, 'Concerning the New Economic Policy and Our Tasks', p. 184.
62. Hannah Arendt, *On Revolution*, London: Penguin, 2006, p. 55.
63. Guevara, *Scritti, discorsi e diari di guerriglia*, p. 1429.
64. Ibid., pp. 1425, 1424.
65. Lenin, *Collected Works*, Vol. 31, p. 289.
66. Ibid., Vol. 33, p. 368.
67. Ibid., Vol. 33, p. 88.
68. Ibid., Vol. 32, p. 183.
69. See Randal C. Archibold, 'Cuba's Imprint on Haiti', *International Herald Tribune*, 9 November 2011.
70. Deng Xiaoping, *Selected Works*, Beijing: Foreign Languages Press, 1992–5, Vol. 2, p. 143.
71. Ibid., Vol. 3, p. 273.
72. Mao Zedong, *On Diplomacy*, Beijing: Foreign Languages Press, 1998, p. 457.
73. Deng Xiaoping, *Selected Works*, Vol. 3, p. 122.
74. Ibid., Vol. 3, pp. 174–5.
75. Ibid., Vol. 3, pp. 33, 115, 12, 145, 271–2.
76. Ibid., Vol. 3, pp. 119, 175.

CHAPTER 9

After the Revolution: The Ambiguities of Class Struggle

1 THE SPECTRE OF THE NEW CLASS

Even before the Bolsheviks could really get down to implementing their programme, voices were raised in the West proclaiming the failure of the socialist programme. A few weeks after October 1917, without losing any time, Kautsky declared: '[w]hat is occurring in Russia is in fact the last of the bourgeois and not the first of the socialist revolutions'.[1] For the German socialist leader, no doubt was possible. It was not only that, in his view, the semi-Asian country was too backward to be capable of building a society beyond capitalism. Once socialism was cast as the end of any contradictions and conflict, and in any event, as totally different from the existing order—in fact, from any historically existing order—the affirmation of the non-socialist character of the revolution in Russia, or any other country, was in a sense tautological. Once socialism was defined in such a way as to entail the negation of any contamination by, or compromise with, the surrounding world, both at home and abroad, it was not difficult polemically to deploy the tautology of the failure to supersede bourgeois society.

Kautsky's 'demonstration' proceeds briskly. Brest-Litovsk, the peace treaty with Germany, by definition involved 'compromises with [German] capital'. Hence, the 'dictatorship of the proletariat' had destroyed 'Russian capital', but only to make room for capital from other countries. In the countryside, while small peasants had taken the place of the large-scale feudal property, overall, the putative socialist revolution had 'consolidated private property in the means of production and commodity production'. It might be said that small peasants were embarking on the path of cooperation, but it should not be forgotten that cooperative property was merely 'a new form of capitalism'. The new Soviet power might proceed to nationalize the whole economy, but it should be borne in mind that the 'state economy is not yet socialism'. The market and commodity production would continue to exist; and even were both of them to disappear, it remained to be seen whether the 'basis of [genuine] socialist production' had been realized. Hence, the liquidation of a determinate form of capitalism did not in and of itself signify the abolition of capitalism as such: the new government 'can abolish many forms of capitalist property', without really leaving behind the old social system. As we can see, the bar which the new regime was required to clear, in order to be defined as socialist, was set ever higher, so that this regime, whatever its efforts and results, by definition remained non-socialist.

The socialism referred to here is like the Kantian thing-in-itself. Contrasted with the phenomenal world (the only world accessible to human consciousness), it is so defined (according to Hegel's analysis) as to prove unattainable and unknowable. Analogously, the socialism of Kautsky (and so many other authors who argue like him), by dint of its ethereal, rarefied character, is unattainable and unrealizable. The countless propositions that eloquently demonstrate the unknowability of the thing-in-itself, or the failure to construct socialism, prove on closer inspection to be empty tautologies.

Although posing as a champion of orthodoxy, Kautsky did not challenge the 'universal asceticism' and 'social levelling in its crudest forms', harshly criticized by the *Communist Manifesto*, characteristic of Soviet Russia at the time. Instead, he denounced the emergence and self-assertion of a new exploiting class in the country ruled by the Bolsheviks: '[i]n place of those who were hitherto capitalists, and have now become proletarians, come intellectuals or proletarians who have now become capitalists'.[2] The October Revolution had only just occurred: the spectre of the advent of the power of a new exploiting class accompanied Soviet Russia from birth.

Grappling with such positions, Lenin responded. In an article published in *Pravda* on 7 November 1919, he stressed that the transition from capitalism to communism 'must combine the features and properties of both these forms of social economy' and encompassed 'a whole historical era'.[3]

In Kautsky's view, by contrast, the persistence of bourgeois social relations was proof that either an old or a new exploiting class held power in Russia. The Soviet leader argued the opposite: crying scandal because of the co-presence of heterogeneous social relations during the transition meant bemoaning the fact that the conquest of power did not betoken the cessation of class struggle. It was clear that '[p]etty-bourgeois democrats are distinguished by an aversion to class struggle, by their dreams of avoiding it, by their efforts to smooth over, to reconcile, to remove sharp corners. Such democrats ... avoid recognising any necessity for a whole historical period of transition from capitalism to communism'.[4]

But in this determinate situation how did class struggle manifest itself? As early as 1920, attempts by Soviet leaders to restore and revitalize the productive apparatus, reintroducing the principle of competence into factories, were met by recalcitrant circles with denunciations of the ascendancy of 'bourgeois specialists' or a 'new bourgeoisie'.[5] In Lenin's eyes, by contrast, measures to revive production and consolidate the social base of support for the revolutionary government, by recourse to 'bourgeois specialists' and the NEP and 'state capitalism' as well, were the concrete way that the proletariat waged class struggle in the new situation. For the inner-party opposition, the return to capitalism, albeit in limited form, was proof that the proletariat had lost, or was in the process of losing the class struggle and that the bourgeoisie, old and new, had reconquered power or was in the process of so doing. Dismayed, Lenin noted: it was 'assumed that [with the NEP] the change is from communism in general to the bourgeois system in general'.[6] Disappointed Bolsheviks felt confirmed in their bitter conviction because cries of triumph arose on the other side. For the Mensheviks, observed an indignant Lenin, the NEP betokened the 'collapse of communism'. Indeed, 'the leitmotif of the Mensheviks is: "The Bolsheviks have reverted to capitalism; that is where they will meet their end. The revolution, including the October Revolution, has turned out to be a bourgeois revolution after all!"'[7] A broad front of opinion argued thus. Astonishing reactions were not wanting. Amused, this time, Lenin referred to the fact that some of the 'Cadets' (Russian liberals), who had been defeated and were in exile, were calling for support for Soviet Russia, which had now set out on the path towards 'the ordinary bourgeois state'.[8]

Replicas of this debate occurred in the wake of other revolutions led by communist parties. In replying to cries of alarm or triumph at 'bourgeois restoration', the leaders of such parties were obliged to re-think the

Marxist theory of class struggle and class rule. The result was reflections that are sometimes of major interest, which not only help us to understand an extraordinarily important chapter in contemporary history, but also shed new light on the Marx and Engels' texts.

2 SOCIAL CLASSES AND POLITICAL CASTES

The Bolsheviks won power and proclaimed the 'dictatorship of the proletariat' precisely when that social class, as a result of the catastrophe of the war, civil war, and economic crisis, showed signs of passing away in Russia. In January 1919, a trade union leader sounded the alarm: '[w]e observe in a large number of industrial centres that the workers, thanks to a contraction of production in the factories, are being absorbed in the peasant mass, and instead of a population of workers we are getting a half-peasant or sometimes a purely peasant population'.[9] This is something to which Lenin first drew attention, as emerges in particular from an intervention of October 1921: the 'industrial proletariat' in Russia had been 'dislodged from its class groove, and has ceased to exist as a proletariat'. Given that 'large-scale capitalist industry has been destroyed, since the factories are at a standstill, the proletariat has disappeared'.[10]

In a country like Russia, the more the stress shifted from revolution from below to revolution from above, the more difficult and complex it became for the ordinary student of a Marxist persuasion to interpret the historical sequence initiated with the October Revolution; which class held power in the countries that used to identify with socialism or still do? To answer this question, we must first free ourselves from the mechanistic interpretation of the Marxian theory of the relationship between economics and politics, between social classes and government and state apparatus.

When he represented the government in a more or less democratic capitalist society as an executive committee of the bourgeoisie, Marx, rather than describing an empirical reality, delineated an ideal type. The two things tend to largely coincide as long as the subaltern classes are incapable of making their presence and pressure felt. In the early nineteenth century, in *The Liberty of the Ancients Compared with that of the Moderns*—a kind of liberal manifesto—Benjamin Constant observed: '[p]oor men look after their own business; rich men hire stewards'. And this is government: '[b]ut, unless they are idiots, rich men who employ stewards keep a close watch on whether these stewards are doing their duty'. Constant explicitly stated that wealth is, and must be, the arbiter of political power and that the very essence of modern liberty consisted in the uncontested and incontestable dependence of government on property-owners: '[c]redit did not have the same influence amongst the ancients; their governments were stronger than individuals, while in our time individuals are stronger than the political powers. Wealth is a power which is more readily available in all circumstances, more readily applicable to all interests, and consequently more real and better obeyed'.[11] Starting, in fact, with the *Communist Manifesto* and the proletariat's initial attempts to organize as a class, the picture changed. In 1864, the International Working Men's Association credited the British working class with having prevented the implementation of plans, entertained by the dominant social bloc in Britain, to intervene on the side of the secessionist, slave-holding American South. There was no longer an immediate identification between the dominant social class and the political line of the government.

What conclusively infirms the mechanical view of the relationship between economics and politics is the tendency to an autonomization of the political and governing caste that emerges in certain historical situations. Which social class exercised power during the period of absolutism? Not the feudal aristocracy, which in fact viewed the emergence and development of the bourgeoisie with dismay and increased anxiety. But it was not the bourgeoisie that held political power; at a certain stage of its development, it evinced ever greater impatience at the fetters imposed on it by the absolutist state and finally committed itself to overthrowing it. From his earliest writings, Marx stressed the social ambiguity of absolutist monarchy: it was characteristic of a situation of unstable equilibrium between (declining) feudal aristocracy and the (rising) bourgeoisie.[12] Later, Engels was to define 'absolute monarchy' as 'a natural compromise between aristocracy and bourgeoisie'.[13] Called upon to monitor the unstable equilibrium, and seal the labile compromise, was a regime which, for a whole historical epoch, was not identified with either of the two competing and then antagonistic classes.

A similar phenomenon occurs during more or less severe historical crises. Which social class exercised power in France during the most acute radicalization of the revolution? *The German Ideology* observes that only in and through a whole contradictory process did the bourgeoisie 'absorb the branches of labour directly belonging to the state and then all more or less ideological professions'.[14] On closer examination, it was not, strictly speaking, a social class that wielded political power in the years of Robespierre and the Jacobin Terror, but an ideological and political caste. On account of a set of circumstances (the general agitation prompted by the fall of the *ancien régime* and the state of emergency occasioned by the invasion of the counter-revolutionary powers and civil war), it acquired a certain degree of autonomy. We can now understand the irritation which, some decades later, Engels expressed at an essay on the French Revolution by Kautsky. In criticizing 'veiled allusions to new modes of production', he made this significant recommendation: 'I would say a great deal less about the modern mode of production. In every case a yawning gap divides it from the *facts* you adduce and, thus out of context, it appears as a *pure abstraction* which, far from throwing light on the subject, renders it still more obscure'. The discourse on the transition from the *ancien régime* to bourgeois society assumed an 'absolute' tone 'where the utmost relativity is called for'. Far from being the organic expression of the bourgeoisie and the bourgeois mode of production, the Jacobin Terror represented 'a military measure' and registered impetus from below to bend the 'equality and fraternity' proclaimed in 1789 in a plebeian direction. In conclusion, bourgeois rule and the 'bourgeois orgy' began only after Thermidor, which was facilitated by the victory of the French army and the disappearance of the need for the Terror at an international level.[15]

The German Ideology draws some general conclusions from its analysis of Jacobinism. There is a division of labour within the bourgeoisie between sections of it directly engaged in economic activity and ideological and political strata; and this division can become a 'cleavage'—a split which, in particular circumstances, 'can even develop into a certain opposition and hostility between the two parts'.[16]

The phenomenon being analysed here is not exhausted by the fall of Jacobinism. Thermidor was followed five years later by 18 Brumaire. But of which class was Napoleon I an expression? Let us read the answer given by *The Holy Family*:

> He fed the egoism of the French nation to complete satiety but demanded also the sacrifice of bourgeois business, enjoyments, wealth, etc., whenever this was required by the political aim of conquest. If he despotically suppressed the liberalism of bourgeois society ... he showed no more consideration for its essential material interests, trade and industry, whenever they conflicted with his political interests. His scorn of industrial *hommes*

d'affaires was the complement to his scorn of ideologists. In his home policy, too, he combated bourgeois society as the opponent of the state which in his own person he still held to be an absolute aim in itself.[17]

In conclusion, thanks to his domestic and foreign policy, Napoleon gave a strong impetus to the development of the French bourgeoisie. At the same time, however, in a situation marked by protracted revolutionary crisis and permanent war, he exercised a dictatorship over the very class benefited by him. This was a genuine conflict, which at a certain point saw 'Parisian speculators' and considerable sections of the 'liberal bourgeoisie' artificially create a famine, thereby sabotaging Napoleon's military operations and contributing to his fall.

In France, the process of autonomization of intellectual and political (and military) castes manifested itself again during the revolutionary crisis that resulted in the dictatorship of Napoleon III. According to Marx's analysis, the military apparatus developed by the bourgeoisie for anti-working class purposes ended up engulfing society as a whole and the dominant class itself. With the repression of the workers' revolt in June 1848, General Jean Baptiste Cavaignac (beloved by the liberal bourgeoisie) exercised 'the dictatorship of the bourgeoisie by the sabre', but this ended up being transformed into 'the dictatorship of the sabre over bourgeois society' and even over the bourgeoisie itself.[18]

Tocqueville may be regarded as the emblematic figure of this transition. As the clouds foreshadowing the tempest of June 1848 were gathering, he expressed the opinion that 'the National Guard and the army will be pitiless this time'. After the outbreak of the workers' rebellion, the French liberal was not only favourable to the granting of emergency powers to Cavaignac, but recommended shooting on sight any member of the populace caught 'in a posture of defence'. Sanguinary repression was not enough to assuage anxieties. Hence, the invocation of an 'energetic and definitive reaction on behalf of order', to put an end to the revolutionary and anarchical chaos. 'Palliatives' would not do. Not only the Mountain, but 'all the surrounding hills', must be swept away, without hesitation over a 'heroic ... remedy'. The option for the 'dictatorship of the bourgeoisie by the sabre' was clear and impassioned. But it was Tocqueville himself who added: 'France belongs to the one who will restore order' and terminate the 'lunacy of 1848'. Unwittingly, he evoked the figure of Napoleon III, who transformed 'the dictatorship of the bourgeoisie by the sabre' into the 'dictatorship of the sabre over bourgeois society', condemning Tocqueville and the liberal bourgeoisie as a whole to impotence and internal exile.[19]

The same dialectic seemed to be on the point of repeating itself following the ferocious repression of the Paris Commune in 1871. Marx wrote:

> After Whit-Sunday, 1871, there can be neither peace nor truce possible between the working men of France and the appropriators of their produce. The iron hand of a mercenary soldiery may keep for a time both classes tied down in common oppression. But the battle must break out again and again in ever growing dimensions....[20]

In this instance, for a variety of reasons (international détente and strong economic development), a new 'dictatorship of the sabre', or its prolongation, did not occur. But the reality of the phenomenon brilliantly analysed by Marx remains. In general, the duration of the historical crisis and revolutionary cycle in France explains the recurrent process of autonomization, or the recurrent tendency to autonomization, of ideological, political, and military strata.

Obviously, the autonomization we are referring to here can be more or less pronounced. In any event, however, it is far from being total. Taking the example of Napoleon III, the politico-military power wielded and jealously guarded by him, promoted, and developed, the social power of the bourgeoisie, which ended up being connected by multiple ties to the holder of politico-military power.

In a situation characterized by a permanent state of emergency, and a lack of clear ideas about the concrete shape of the new political and social order, communist parties in power and their leaders ended up establishing a relationship with the proletariat and popular masses that recalls the one established with the bourgeoisie by Louis Bonaparte. That is, paraphrasing Marx, 'the dictatorship of the proletariat by the sabre' turned into the 'dictatorship of the sabre over civil society' and over the proletariat itself. However, albeit slender and twisted, a thread continued to connect Louis Napoleon with the bourgeoisie behind the counter-revolution, just as a thread continues to connect communist leaders in power with the proletariat and popular masses who were the protagonists of the revolution. Bonapartism or Caesarism is one of the ways that the process of autonomiziation of ideological, political, and military castes occurs. Gramsci's distinction between regressive Caesarism and progressive Caesarism remains valid; and it also remains the case that in different historical situations the progressive or regressive character of Cesarism proves more or less pronounced.

3   Dominant Class and Delegated Class

The process of autonomization of ideological and political (and military) castes can undergo a significant variation. Here is how, in a letter sent from Manchester to Marx on 13 April 1866, Engels described the advent in Germany of 'Bonapartism' Bismarck-style:

> It would appear that, after some show of reluctance, the German bourgeois will go along with it, for Bonapartism really is the true religion of the modern bourgeoisie. It is becoming increasingly clear to me that the bourgeoisie does not possess the qualities required to rule directly itself, and that therefore, unless there is an oligarchy as here in England capable of taking over, for good, the management of state and society in the interest of the bourgeoisie, a Bonapartist semi-dictatorship is the normal form; it promotes the great material interests of the bourgeoisie even against the bourgeoisie, but allows it no share in the government itself. Conversely, this dictatorship itself is in turn compelled unwillingly to adopt these material interests of the bourgeoisie. So, now we have Monsieur Bismarck adopting the programme of the National Association [the quintessential organization of the liberal bourgeoisie].[21]

Germany and Britain are contrasted here. As regards the first, we see the reproduction of the phenomenon already analysed in connection with France: at work is a dictatorship or semi-dictatorship that 'promotes the great material interests of the bourgeoisie even against the bourgeoisie', which is excluded from political power. The British scenario is different. Ultimately, it is the aristocracy that retains 'the management of state and society', but now 'in the interest of the bourgeoisie'. Within the framework of a now fully capitalist society, the bourgeoisie, although the ruling class in the strict sense, has delegated the function of government to the aristocracy. In the case of Britain, we may speak of a variant of the process of autonomization of ideological, political, and military castes, in the sense that the latter, although pertaining to the aristocracy, render themselves autonomous vis-à-vis their class of origin and form the governing caste of a bourgeois state.

It is a practice to which, a few years later, the German bourgeoisie resorted. With the foundation of the Second Reich, and the ensuing powerful economic development, a division of labour was established which Gramsci summarized thus: 'the bourgeoisie obtained economic-industrial power, but the old feudal classes remained as the governing stratum of the political State, with wide corporative privileges in the army, the administration and on the land'. They thus 'became the "intellectuals" of the bourgeoisie, with a particular temperament conferred by their caste origin and by tradition'.[22] A celebrated contemporary historian has spoken in this connection of the 'persistence of the old regime' in Britain, Germany, and Europe as a whole until the First World War.[23] In my view, the explanation given by Engels and Gramsci seems more precise and persuasive: the *ancien régime* was over, but certain strata hailing from it continued to be entrusted with important functions by the dominant bourgeoisie, often with a new significance relative to the past. This is how, in a highly developed country like Britain, we can explain the existence even today of institutions like the House of Lords and the monarchy.

Recourse by a social class to ideological castes that are in a sense foreign to it can also occur in a progressive key. Marx's analysis of the period preceding the outbreak of the 1848 revolution in Prussia (the Rhineland province specifically) is significant:

> The middle class still too weak to venture upon active movements, felt themselves compelled to march in the rear of the theoretical army led by Hegel's disciples against the religion, the ideas and the politics of the old world. In no former period was philosophical criticism so bold, so powerful and so popular as in the first eight years of the rule of Frederick William IV ... The power of philosophy during that period was entirely owing to the practical weakness of the bourgeoisie; as they could not assault the antiquated institutions in fact, they must yield precedence to the bold idealists who assaulted them in the region of thought.[24]

In Engels' words, the bourgeoisie, 'being short ... of men able to represent them in the press', wound up in 'alliance with the extreme philosophical party'.[25] Marx himself belonged to the 'theoretical army' or 'philosophical party' referred to here. He now looked beyond the bourgeoisie, and yet the latter invited him for a time to edit its newspaper, the *Rheinische Zeitung*, retaining ownership and control, thereby enabling it, at an opportune moment, to get rid of the 'extremist' danger and pursue a more conciliatory policy towards the aristocracy.

Can the distinction between dominant class and class delegated to perform particular functions in a subaltern position also obtain in a society intent on building socialism? This is the thesis formulated by Lenin. He legitimized it by reference to a passage to be found in late Engels (1894) about the attitude to be adopted towards major landowners and industrialists after the anti-capitalist revolution: '[w]e by no means consider compensation as impermissible in any event. Marx told me (and how many times!) that in his opinion we would get off cheapest if we could buy out the whole lot of them'.[26] What is evoked here is a scenario where, in a society of socialist orientation, wealthy bourgeois, individual property-owners with major financial resources, survive to whom 'delegated' functions might be entrusted.

In truth, this scenario already emerges indirectly from an earlier text. While it calls for 'centralis[ing] all instruments of production in the hands of the State, i.e., of the proletariat organised as the ruling class', the *Communist Manifesto* also advances a more cautious line: an '[e]xtension of factories and instruments of production owned by the state' is tabled. The nationalization invoked here would appear not to be integral, especially since we encounter a qualification: at least 'in the beginning', the measures taken by the revolutionary government would 'appear economically insufficient and untenable'. What immediately stands out is a no less significant watchword: '[c]onfiscation of the property of all emigrants and rebels'.[27] More than a general measure of an economic kind, the expropriation of the bourgeoisie seems to be a partial action, dictated in part at least by political contingency. We once again find ourselves in the scenario which, even after the anti-capitalist revolution, envisages the partial persistence of major wealth that is bourgeois or bourgeois in origin.

However, it is likely that, referring to the passage by Engels just mentioned, Lenin forced its meaning. But let us take a look at the developments underlying the Soviet leader's stance.

4 'STATE', 'ADMINISTRATION' AND 'RANSOM' IN LENIN

After 1917, the first doubts about the feasibility and rationality of the original programme of rapid, complete expropriation of the property-owning classes soon emerged. Two years later, in an intervention of 7 November 1919, referring to 'exploiters', Lenin observed: '[t]hey still retain certain means of production in part, they still have money ... The "art" of state, military and economic administration gives them ... a very great superiority'.[28] The programme of expropriation seemed set to be comprehensively implemented, but a doubt emerged: was it possible to do without the 'art' on which the classes to be expropriated enjoyed a substantial monopoly? A few months later, on 29 March 1920, Lenin addressed the delegates at the Bolshevik Party's Ninth Congress:

> But do you think that when the bourgeoisie superseded the feudals they confused the state with the administration? No, they were no such fools. They declared that the work of administration required people who knew how to administer, and that they would adapt feudal administrators for that purpose. And that is what they did. Was it a mistake? No, comrades, the art of administration does not descend from heaven, it is not inspired by the Holy Ghost. And the fact that a class is the leading class does not make it at once capable of administering. We have an example of this: while the bourgeoisie were establishing their victory they took for the work of administration members of another class, the feudal class; there was nowhere else to get them from.[29]

It was right for the victorious proletariat to proceed in a similar fashion if it did not wish to lapse into 'sheer utopianism and meaningless phrase-mongering'. The need to control political power and the state apparatus remained, but 'for the work of administration, of organising the state, we need people who are versed in the art of administration, who have state and business experience, and ... there is nowhere we can turn to for such people except the old class'.[30]

Should the Bolsheviks confine themselves to this in drawing on the skills of the bourgeoisie or go further? In May 1921, Lenin went decisively further. Having affirmed that 'the question of power is the fundamental question of every revolution', he called upon the Bolshevik Party to register the 'discrepancy between our economic "forces" and our political strength'. And what then? In building the socialist system, they needed to know how to use members of the capitalist bourgeoisie. The latter would not agree to collaborate out of altruism. Hence, the 'need for a specific type of "buying out" operation which the workers must offer to the most cultured, the most talented, the most capable organisers among the capitalists who are ready to enter into the service of the Soviet power and to help honestly in organising "state" production on the largest possible scale'. It was necessary to 'use the method of compromise, or of buying out the cultured capitalists who agree to "state capitalism!', who could be 'useful to the proletariat as intelligent and experienced organisers of the largest types of enterprises, which actually supply products to tens of millions of people'.[31] It was for support for this line of argument that Lenin appealed to Marx and, more precisely, to the passage in Engels quoted above.

Here we have gone far beyond a distinction between 'state' or political power and 'administration'. It is no longer a question of hiring, and adequately remunerating, bourgeois specialists entrusted with more or less significant duties. What is involved is a compromise with capitalists who continue to be such—that is, do not surrender their property. 'Can the Soviet state and the dictatorship of the proletariat be combined with state capitalism? Are they compatible? Of course they are'.[32] It should be borne in mind that what is intended by 'state capitalism' here is not nationalized means of production in state hands. Instead, 'state capitalism' is synonymous with 'capitalism controlled and regulated by the proletarian state'.[33] That is, we are dealing with normal capitalist private property, which thrived once again under the NEP, albeit to a limited degree. However, it should be remembered that 'state capitalism in a society where power belongs to capital, and state capitalism in a proletarian state, are two different concepts'.[34] Granted this distinction, it was necessary to 'invite in' foreign capital, obviously 'without any power'.[35] If this line of renouncing nationalization and full state ownership of the means of production applied to industry, *a fortiori* it could and should apply to agriculture. In October 1921, Lenin summarized the path followed hitherto: '[w]e assumed that ... we would build up state production and distribution, and step by step win them away from the hostile system. We said that our task now was not so much to expropriate the expropriators as to introduce accounting and control, increase the productivity of labour and tighten up discipline'.[36] Clearly, economic expropriation of the dominant classes only corresponds in part to their political expropriation; and it is necessary and proper for it only to correspond in part for a determinate period.

Four years later, in 1925, in an article entitled 'Concerning the New Economic Policy and Our Tasks', Bukharin reached the same conclusions. Recourse to 'suppression' was required against 'insurgent strata and their remnants'. By contrast, 'there is a different relationship of the proletariat and its state power to the new bourgeoisie. With the existing balance of social forces the new bourgeoisie is a socially necessary stratum, fulfilling—to a *certain* extent, within *certain* limits, and for a *certain* period of time—a socially useful function'.[37] In Britain and Germany, the bourgeoisie in power availed itself of the collaboration of the aristocracy, whose political power proper had been expropriated. Similarly, in Soviet Russia the proletariat in power, or the new political power, availed itself of the bourgeoisie to an even greater extent, given that the ousted class was used not only in state 'administration', but also in the organization of economic life and promotion of the growth of the productive forces.

5 'Political Expropriation' and 'Economic Expropriation' in Mao

The NEP experiment only lasted a few years. While a role was also played in its demise by persistent ideological reservations about this experiment and political line, what mainly determined it was the deterioration in the international situation and serious threats of war.[38] But Soviet Russia of the NEP period is the starting-point for the People's Republic of China, for much of its history at least.

On the eve of the conquest of power, Mao Zedong clarified his programme for government thus: '[o]ur present policy is to regulate capitalism, not to destroy it'. To overcome backwardness, China 'must utilize all the factors of urban and rural capitalism that are beneficial and not harmful to the national economy and the people's livelihood'. An important role could be played in this by the 'national bourgeoisie', which 'should not have the chief role in state power'. Instead, it was enjoined to recognize 'the leadership of the working class (through the Communist Party)'. In their turn, Communists must acknowledge a key point. In taking power, they would be abandoning armed struggle and undertaking 'economic construction'. Hence, '[w]e shall soon put aside some of the things we know well and be compelled to do things we don't know well. ...We must learn to do economic work from all who know how, no matter who they are. We must esteem them as teachers, learning from them respectfully and conscientiously'.[39] The distinction between the political expropriation of the bourgeoisie and its economic expropriation, which had emerged in Marx and Engels and then during the Soviet NEP, came into sharp focus. While they exercised political power, communists must know how to learn economically from the class they had supplanted. Mao further clarified his view in a speech of 18 January 1957:

As for the charge that our urban policy has deviated to the Right, this seems to be the case, as we have undertaken to provide for the capitalists and to pay them a fixed rate of interest for seven years. What is to be done after seven years? That is to be decided according to the circumstances prevailing then. It is better to leave the matter open, that is, to go on giving them a certain amount in fixed interest. At this small cost we are buying over this class. ...By buying over this class, we have deprived them of their political capital and kept their mouths shut. ...We must deprive them of every bit of their political capital and continue to do so until not one jot is left to them. Therefore, neither can our urban policy be said to have deviated to the Right.[40]

What is articulated with especial clarity in this text is the distinction between the economic expropriation of the bourgeoisie and its political expropriation. The latter should be comprehensive, while the former, if not kept within strict limits, risked compromising the country's economic development and the new government's stability. In summer 1958, Mao reiterated his point of view to a rather wary Soviet ambassador: '[t]here are still capitalists in China, but the State is under the leadership of the Communist Party'.[41]

Having assumed the leadership of China after numerous vicissitudes, Deng Xiaoping reconnected with this political tradition, which he revived and radicalized. But this did not betoken a break. It needs to be remembered that, prior to winning power on a national scale, from 1928 onwards the Communist Party of China governed more or less extensive areas of the immense country, where 'a curious mixture of private capitalism, state capitalism, and primitive socialism', as well as co-operative property, co-existed.[42] In the decades since 1928, attempts at total nationalization of the economy have been limited to a fairly short period of time.

We know that the NEP was construed in the West as a camouflaged reversion to capitalism. Three exceptional witnesses argued differently, however. The first is Gramsci, who was in Moscow from May 1922 until December 1923, and who some years later drew up a balance-sheet. The USSR afforded an unprecedented spectacle: 'history has never seen a dominant class, in its entirety, experiencing conditions of living inferior to those of certain elements and strata of the dominated and subjected class'. The popular masses who continued to suffer a life of hardship were disorientated by the sight of 'the Nepman in his furs, with all the goods of the earth at his disposal'. But this should not be a cause for scandal or rejection, because the proletariat, just as it could not conquer power, could not retain it, if it was incapable of sacrificing particular, immediate interests to 'the general and permanent interests of the class'.[43]

The other two witnesses were less sympathetic to the country they were visiting. But on the key issue, they concurred with the Italian Communist leader. I am referring to the Austrian writer Joseph Roth, who visited Moscow between September 1926 and January 1927 and who, in correspondence for the *Frankfurter Zeitung*, wrote: '[i]f it is true that the proletariat is the dominant class, it is certain that the new bourgeoisie is the affluent class. The proletariat possesses all the institutions of the state. The bourgeoisie possesses all the institutions of an easy life'.[44] Finally, in 1927 Walter Benjamin summed up his impressions as follows:

> Under capitalism power and money have become commensurable qualities. Any given amount of money may be converted into a specific power, and the market value of all power can be calculated. ...The Soviet state has severed this communication between money and power. It reserves power for the Party, and leaves money to the NEP man.[45]

The latter was, in fact, subject to 'terrible social ostracism'. Economic wealth and political power in no wise coincided.

Hence, in the 1920s at least three very great intellectuals rejected any interpretation of the NEP as the expression of a bourgeois restoration. The People's Republic of China has not been as fortunate. Starting with Deng Xiaoping's turn, and despite the conspicuous exception of an eminent historian,[46] the view that China is a fully-fledged capitalist country goes virtually unchallenged.

6 Class Consciousness as 'Spirit of Cleavage' and 'Catharsis'

I have repeatedly spoken of the autonomization of the political and governing caste in connection with political regimes issuing from revolutions led by communist parties. It—let us be clear—is not a supersession of class struggle, but derives from its severity and endeavours to keep it under control. At first sight at least, the category I have employed recalls that of 'bureaucracy', of which Trotsky was fond. In fact, the latter, rather than deriving from political and social analysis, was primarily intended to register a negative value judgement and started from the presupposition that it is the working class at the point of production which expresses revolutionary consciousness in its purity. What thereby gets lost sight of are the ambiguities that characterize the class struggle, especially in the phase following the conquest of power by a party of communist persuasion. Immediately after the October Revolution, who represented the cause of proletarian emancipation? Was it Lenin (the 'bureaucrat'), who proposed to re-organize and re-start the productive apparatus, putting an end to absenteeism and anarchy in workplaces? Or was it the Belgian worker Lazarevic, determined to oppose the speed-up (and consequent 'exploitation') by striking? Was it the Soviet leader, who resorted to 'bourgeois specialists' (guaranteeing them high remuneration), and to capitalists disposed to collaborate with Soviet power in developing the productive forces and overcoming the first type of inequality? Or workers indignant at the persistence of the second type of inequality and the 'restoration of capitalism'? Even if we confine the contrast to workers, who furthers the cause of emancipation? Those who, stimulated by material and moral incentives, engage in the Stakhanovite movement to develop production (and social wealth)? Or those who oppose all this?

At a time when war communism had not yet come to an end—between March and April 1920—Lenin drew attention to the paradox that had been generated in Soviet Russia: the proletariat had 'become the governing class, and is being called upon to make great sacrifices, to starve and to perish'. It lived in worse economic conditions than the peasants, who had obtained major benefits from the new situation: 'for the first time [they] had more food than throughout the centuries of tsarist and capitalist Russia'.[47] The paradox deepened and added insult to injury with the introduction of the NEP. Now it was a class, or a section of a class, which had been ousted as an exploiting class that lived in far better economic circumstances than the politically dominant class.

The tolerance shown the nouveau riche, despite enduring proletarian poverty, prompted a widespread, intense feeling of 'betrayal' in Soviet Russia: '[i]n 1921–2 literally tens of thousands of Bolshevik workers tore up their party cards in disgust with the NEP: they dubbed it the New Exploitation of the Proletariat'.[48] Also abandoning the party was the 'Workers' Opposition'. This was not only a political crisis but a devastating existential crisis. In 1927, Benjamin observed: 'the halt the Party one day called to wartime Communism with the NEP had a terrible backlash, which felled many of the movement's fighters'.[49]

Far from being confined to Soviet Russia, this attitude possibly found its most impassioned or woeful followers among communist militants, even leaders, in the West. Lenin referred to them sarcastically: '[s]eeing that we were retreating, several of them burst into tears in a disgraceful and childish manner, as was the case at the last extended Plenary Meeting of the Executive Committee of the Communist International. Moved by the best communist sentiments, several of the comrades burst into tears'.[50]

But let us concentrate on Soviet Russia. Those who argued, felt, and suffered thus, were convinced that they were giving voice to the consciousness of the working class. How did Lenin react? He condemned the 'Workers' Opposition' as 'an expression of a syndicalist deviation'.[51] This category, which refers to *What is to be Done?*, is eloquent in itself. 'Trade-union' consciousness, or the 'syndicalist' deviation, manifests itself in an inability to subordinate economic demands to the struggle for the conquest and retention of political power. According to the Soviet leader, in a speech to the Third Congress of the Communist International on 5 July 1921, the fact was that 'dire suffering has fallen to the lot of the working class, precisely because it is exercising its dictatorship'. This was a paradox, but its underlying truth could be grasped by the politically most advanced elements of the working class.[52]

For Lenin, the terms of the situation were clear. Account must be taken of Marx's teaching: '[f]ollowing its seizure of political power, the principal and fundamental interest of the proletariat lies in securing an enormous increase in the productive forces of society'.[53] Secondly, it was clear that the Soviet government could not rule if it did not solve the problem of the desperate poverty and hunger afflicting the Russian people. To revive agricultural production, generous concessions had to be made to the peasantry and to cry scandal at this meant 'putting the craft interests of the workers above their class interests, and sacrificing the interests of the whole of the working class, its dictatorship ... for the sake of an immediate short-term and partial advantage for the workers'.[54] To revive industrial production, even, more generous concessions to bourgeois specialists, and the Russian and international capital prepared to collaborate with the NEP, were required. Opening up to foreign capital, whose advanced technology was an absolute imperative and which was guaranteed exceptional profits, induced disorientation. But it was this policy—not protests against it—which represented 'a form of struggle ... a continuation of the class struggle in another form'.[55]

Let us now glance at the situation in the factories. In the second half of the 1920s, Pierre Pascal, whom we have already encountered, lamented that 'from a material point of view, we are advancing towards Americanization' (in the sense of an idolatrous cult of economic and technological development). It was true that some economic progress had been made, but 'at the cost of tremendous exploitation of the working class'.[56] Lenin argued the converse between 1920 and 1921. He called upon trade unions to liberate themselves from 'craft prejudices'; they must 'act as mediators' and 'facilitate the speediest and smoothest settlement' of the disputes that inevitably arose,[57] but without ever losing sight of the objective of development of the productive forces—the only thing that could ensure a tangible improvement in the living conditions of the popular masses and, at the same time, strengthen Soviet power. To be clear, 'conditions primarily demand higher productivity of labour, greater labour discipline. At such a time improvements at home are the major achievements of the revolution: *a neither salient, striking, nor immediately perceptible* improvement in labour, in its organisation and results'.[58] I have italicized an assertion that further radicalizes the break with the sensualist epistemology to be found in Marx and Engels' early writings. The formation of revolutionary consciousness has still less to do with 'contemplation' of the proletariat's conditions of existence. While *What is to be Done?* stressed the need to analyse the totality of political and social relations, national and international, now the same result was reached starting from an assertion of the need to transcend the level of empirical perception. On the basis of observation of the high salaries and privileges enjoyed by bourgeois specialists and Nepmen, respectively, the overhasty conclusion might be reached that proletarian class struggle coincided with the struggle against those privileges and salaries. But this would mean losing sight of the wider national and international context and ignoring the complexity of the class struggle against the two forms of inequality.

Overall, the picture afforded by Soviet Russia could be summed up as follows: 'the proletariat, the revolutionary vanguard, possesse[s] sufficient political power', but permits 'state capitalism ... alongside it'—that is, the persistence of some zones of capitalism, albeit controlled by the state. This created an unprecedented historical situation, disorientating many. But only those who understood and supported this policy, which was imperative for the maintenance of Soviet power, displayed mature class consciousness.[59]

A situation that 'history has never seen': such were the words used by Gramsci, who clearly benefited from his stay in Soviet Russia. In his analysis of the paradox of the NEP and the USSR, he did not go beyond the picture drawn by Lenin. By contrast, the *Prison Notebooks* go much further, identifying 'the "cathartic" moment' as 'the starting-point for all the philosophy of praxis' and revolutionary theory.⁶⁰ How are we to interpret this sibylline, astonishing declaration? In European culture, revolution and revolutionary movements were long construed and discredited as expressions of envy, rancour, and resentment. It is enough to think of authors like Constant, Taine and, above all, Nietzsche. Gramsci's reflection refutes this commonplace. In NEP Russia, proletarians who could not rise above envy of the 'Nepman in his furs with all the goods of the earth at his disposal' were not in a position to help build the new society to which they aspired. General in character, Gramsci's thesis not coincidentally reached maturity while Nazism in Germany was intensifying the resentment and envy of more backward popular strata towards intellectuals, especially revolutionaries, and channelling the frustration of masses impoverished by war and economic crisis against Jews. Contrary to what Constant, Taine, and Nietzsche claimed, the revolutionary movement developed and matured only if it succeeded in expressing a 'cathartic moment'.

It is interesting to note that, thousands of miles away from Europe, another great communist leader was groping in the direction of the same theoretical result. In 1929, Mao Zedong engaged in a struggle against 'absolute egalitarianism'. With its pettiness, charge of envy and even *ressentiment* (when the Red Army quartered, '[e]quality was demanded in the allotment of billets, and Headquarters would be abused for occupying larger rooms'), it was the expression of mean-spirited social relations, 'the product of a handicraft and small peasant economy', and thereby frustrated or prevented the creation of the social bloc needed to reverse the *ancient régime*.⁶¹ Successful revolution required the consolidation of unity between the most immediate victims of exploitation and oppression, as well as a policy of alliances to isolate the power to be overthrown. All this was possible only on condition of banishing or containing individual pettiness as well as envy, rancour, and resentment towards the contiguous or immediately higher social strata who were the natural target of such mindsets.

In fact, the 'cathartic moment' played a key role in the process of forming class consciousness. In the same year that he developed his thinking on the NEP—1926—Gramsci wrote:

> The metal-worker, the joiner, the building-worker, etc., must not only think as proletarians, and no longer as metal-worker, joiner, building-worker, etc., they must also take a further step. They must think as workers who are members of a class which aims to lead the peasants and intellectuals. Of a

class which can win and build socialism only if it is aided and followed by the great majority of these social strata. If this is not achieved, the proletariat does not become the leading class....[62]

What is described here is a two-stage process. In the first, membership of a specific profession is transcended in membership of the proletariat as such (here we have not gone beyond the view of Marx and Engels). But it is the second stage that contains significant novel features: the proletariat exhibits mature class consciousness only when it rises to a view of the class it belongs to as the leading nucleus of a broader social bloc called upon to carry the revolution to victory. And catharsis proves even more necessary when it is a question of retaining and consolidating power, as demonstrated by the struggles, as well as the disappointments and even personal dramas, of the NEP years. The idea of catharsis was already stirring in Engels' thesis that communist consciousness presupposes transcending the immediate, narrow interests of the proletarian class (see Chap. 3, Sect. 4); and was operative in Lenin's polemic against trade unionism. But it was only now that it met with an organic, consistent formulation.

The acquisition of revolutionary consciousness involves a battle on two fronts. It is necessary to reject co-option into the dominant bloc, on the one hand, and to avoid retreat into corporatism, on the other. On the first front, it involves sharpening the proletariat's class antagonism, while on the second, it means increasing its capacity for mediation vis-à-vis classes or social strata that live in better material conditions than it does. Or, in Gramsci's terms, it might be said that class consciousness is expressed on the one hand as the 'spirit of cleavage', which enables a subaltern class to achieve 'integral autonomy'; and on the other as 'catharsis', thanks to which a class that was formerly subaltern, can make the transition 'from the purely economic (or egoistic-passional) to the ethico-political moment', thereby becoming a ruling class.[63]

7 BETWEEN RUSSIA AND CHINA: THE BOURGEOISIE AS A CLASS IN ITSELF AND A CLASS FOR ITSELF

'Catharsis' makes it possible to come to terms with the complexity of the class struggle in the society emerging from the Bolshevik October. Therein, especially after the introduction of the NEP, rich bourgeois continued to exist. But, not only were they not the ruling class politically; they were not even a class for itself.

The German Ideology stresses that 'separate individuals form a class only insofar as they have to carry on a common battle against another class; in other respects they are on hostile terms with each other as competitors'.[64] This is a discourse that does not refer to one specific class, but proposes to explain the process of formation of the proletariat and bourgeoisie alike and the class consciousness of both. Let us open *The Poverty of Philosophy*. By virtue of a 'common situation' and 'common interests', created by objective 'economic conditions', the proletariat is 'already a class as against capital, but not yet for itself'. It is in struggle that the mass of proletarians 'becomes united, and constitutes itself as a class for itself'; and the class struggle becomes a 'political struggle'. As regards the bourgeoisie, 'we have two phases to distinguish: that in which it constituted itself as a class under the regime of feudalism and absolute monarchy, and that in which, already constituted as a class, it overthrew feudalism and monarchy to make society into a bourgeois society'.[65] Hence, the bourgeoisie had long been a class in itself before also becoming a class for itself—that is, before acquiring a developed class consciousness and being capable of defining and practically pursuing its own class interests.

In the proletariat, the process of the formation of class consciousness is impeded, and can even be interrupted or set back, either by the competition that objectively occurs between individual workers, or as a result of the political and ideological initiative of the dominant class. Something similar applies to the bourgeoisie, following a revolution that has more or less radically abolished its political power and discredited it ideologically.

Let us see what occurred in the People's Republic of China. As emerges from the observation by Mao quoted above—it is important not to consummate the economic expropriation of the bourgeoisie—this class did not disappear following the Communist Party's arrival in power. In October 1978, initiating the policy of reforms and openness, Deng Xiaoping warned that '[w]e shall not allow a new bourgeoisie to come into being'. This objective is not contrary to tolerance of individual capitalists. As was clarified a few months later by the new Chinese leader, 'the struggle against these individuals is different from the struggle of one class against another, which occurred in the past (these individuals cannot form a cohesive and overt class)'. Naturally, residues of the old class struggle survive, but overall, with the consolidation of the revolution and the power of the Communist Party, a new situation had been created.[66] 'Is it possible that a new bourgeoisie will emerge? A handful of bourgeois elements may appear, but they will not form a class', especially given the existence of a 'powerful ... state apparatus' equipped to control them. The historical precedent invoked by the Chinese leader in August 1985 is significant: '[p]erhaps Lenin had a good idea when he adopted the New Economic Policy'.[67] We are directed back to a situation where the bourgeoisie, or individual bourgeois elements, continued to play—more precisely, resumed playing (after the phase of 'war communism')—a more or less pronounced economic role, even though they had been deprived of any possibility of playing a political role.

It is not only political power that counters the bourgeoisie's transition from class in itself to class for itself. We have seen Marx celebrate the nobility of the Polish aristocrats who allowed themselves be governed by the national interest as opposed to class interest. Particularly at times of more or less acute historical crisis, an individual can find him- or herself located not within a single contradiction, but within multiple contradictions. Marx's indictment of the French bourgeoisie, which in 1871 targeted the Paris Commune rather than the Prussian invader, is thought-provoking: '[i]n this conflict between national duty and class interest, the Government of National Defence did not hesitate one moment to turn into a Government of National Defection'.[68] As emerges from the indignation evinced by this text, that option was not self-evident. The Polish noble too was concerned by the agitation of the peasantry, which risked threatening his social position and privileges. But he could not ignore the fact that the dismemberment and subjection of his country stripped him of his national identity, thereby condemning him to political, cultural, and even (in some respects) social subalternity to the dominant power. We could summarize things by saying that, in this determinate situation, the Polish noble was compelled to choose between social identity and national identity. As we know, during the Russian Revolution, a general of noble origin—Brusilov—found himself faced with a similar choice. He rallied to the new Soviet government on the basis of his 'sense of patriotic duty', because the Bolsheviks were in the process of rescuing Russia from Balkanization and subjugation.

Such processes occurred on a much larger scale during the Chinese Revolution, led by a communist party that had placed itself at the head of the war of resistance against Japanese imperialism, at the head of a struggle to save the Chinese nation as a whole (including the dominant exploiting classes) from the enslavement for which the Empire of the Rising Sun intended it. It is likely that patriotism continues to play a role among the capitalists old and new who have no difficulty in realizing the support

Washington has extended to the most disparate separatist movements that can emerge, or be nurtured and encouraged, in the multi-ethnic, multicultural, continental country that is China.

Finally, we should not lose sight of the process lucidly described by the *Communist Manifesto*. Let us re-read a very famous passage: as and when the crisis is in full swing, and the existing order is set to collapse (or seems about to collapse), 'a small section of the ruling class cuts itself adrift, and joins the revolutionary class, the class that holds the future in its hands'. We are dealing with a switch of sides that is not motivated by national concerns, but explained mainly by intellectual and emotional adhesion to the party or movement in which the imminent, ineluctable future is embodied (or seemingly embodied). As protagonists of this change of camp, Marx and Engels point to intellectual strata, ideologists, 'who have raised themselves to the level of comprehending theoretically the historical movement as a whole'.[69] But it can involve very diverse social strata, even representatives and sections of the capitalist bourgeoisie, and historically has done. In the years immediately following the Second World War, out of gratitude and admiration for the role played by the USSR and communist parties in the resistance and the struggle against Nazi and fascist barbarism, Marxism and communism exercised a power of attraction extending far beyond the popular classes. The converse occurred before and after 1989 when the desire to repudiate what the USA and the West tirelessly branded as the wrong side of history—a political current destined to disappear or end up in the dustbin of history—was widespread and insistent. This process is still underway, but exhibits little vigour in a country that escaped a century of colonialist and imperialist humiliation in 1949 and which today, after decades of rapid economic development, seems destined to play a growing role on the international stage. These are circumstances that strengthen the patriotism of individual bourgeois and capitalists, who, for objective reasons, have very great difficulty in constituting themselves as a class for itself.

It is simplistic to make class consciousness and objective social situation correspond mechanically. The polemical exchange that occurred between Khrushchev and Chou En-lai during the Sino-Soviet conflict possesses an emblematic value. The former had proudly exhibited his humble origins, throwing the latter's aristocratic origins back in his face. Chou En-lai responded: 'we have both betrayed our class of origin'. Such 'betrayal', or switch of sides, is indeed to be taken into account; and during a historical crisis so grave as to represent a mortal danger to a nation, this 'betrayal', or change of sides, tends to be a more or less widespread and enduring phenomenon.

Obviously, a national crisis also influences the process of formation of the proletariat's class consciousness. It can be drawn into chauvinist positions supportive of colonialist and imperialist war. In this instance, it ceases to be a class for itself and becomes a mere appendix of the bourgeoisie. This is what, in the more mature phase of their development, Marx and Engels were compelled to register painfully in connection with Britain. But even in the case of a war of resistance and national liberation, while the proletariat is called on to participate actively, possibly assuming a leadership role, it must avoid losing its autonomy and merging with the bourgeoisie. In November 1938, having proclaimed 'the identity between the national and the class struggle', Mao went on to criticize the slogan 'Everything through the United Front'.[70] In waging a 'class struggle' that was at the same time a 'national struggle', the proletariat organized in the Communist Party must know how to safeguard class consciousness and identity along with national consciousness and identity. But it could genuinely do this only by eliminating any form of national nihilism.

Prior to the Bolshevik October, then, Lenin felt it necessary to underscore the inanity of setting off in search of class struggle and revolution in the pure state. After the victory of revolutions inspired by Marxism, the communist movement was impelled to clarify for its own purposes that it was no less inane to search for proletarian (or popular) power in the pure state. Important theoretical results ensued. Lenin distinguished between state and administration, between dominant class and delegated class. Gramsci further developed reflection on the historically unprecedented phenomenon whereby a politically ruling class might not be the economically privileged class, analysed Caesarism and the process of autonomiziation of the political and ideological caste in a post-capitalist society, and highlighted the role of 'catharsis' in a mature revolutionary class consciousness. Mao called for a clear distinction between the political expropriation of the exploiting classes and their economic expropriation. Finally, Deng Xiaoping also applied the distinction between class in itself and class for itself to the bourgeoisie whose political power has been expropriated.

In theory, such distinctions and reflections should have counselled caution in assessing post-revolutionary society. In reality, however, what happened? If we take the first fifteen years after the October Revolution, we find a succession of three social models that are patently different: the 'collectivism of poverty and suffering' (Gramsci), or 'socialized poverty' (Trotsky), peculiar to so-called 'war communism'; the NEP and recourse to a restricted zone of capitalism controlled from above, in order to reconstruct and re-start the productive system; and the juxtaposition of a collectivized agriculture and an even more heavily nationalized industry. None of these models really silences the thesis of the advent of a new exploiting class. How are we to explain the constant, widespread use of the category of betrayal? Or, formulating the question differently, how are we to explain the exhausting pursuit of a society undefiled by the slightest bourgeois contamination?

Notes

1. Karl Kautsky, *La dittatura del proletariato*, trans. Luciano Pellicani, 2nd ed., Milan: Sugarco, 1977, p. 100.
2. Ibid., pp. 113, 119–22.
3. V.I. Lenin, *Collected Works*, London: Lawrence & Wishart, 1960–78, Vol. 30, p. 107.
4. Ibid., Vol. 30, p. 108.
5. See Orlando Figes, *A People's Tragedy: The Russian Revolution 1890–1924*, London: Pimlico, 1997, pp. 730–1.
6. Lenin, *Collected Works*, Vol. 32, p. 342.
7. Ibid., Vol. 33, pp. 25, 21.
8. Ibid., Vol. 33, p. 286.
9. Quoted in E.H. Carr, *The Bolshevik Revolution 1917–1923*, London and Basingstoke: Macmillan, 1978, Vol. 2, pp. 193–4.
10. Lenin, *Collected Works*, Vol. 33, p. 65.
11. Benjamin Constant, 'The Liberty of the Ancients Compared with that of the Moderns', in *Political Writings*, ed. and trans. Biancamaria Fontana, Cambridge: Cambridge University Press, 1988, pp. 325–6.
12. Karl Marx and Frederick Engels, *Collected Works*, London: Lawrence & Wishart, 1975–2004, Vol. 6, p. 326.
13. Ibid., Vol. 48, p. 266.
14. Ibid., Vol. 5, p. 77 n.
15. Ibid., Vol. 48, pp. 267–8.
16. Ibid., Vol. 5, p. 60.
17. Ibid., Vol. 4, p. 123.
18. Ibid., Vol. 10, p. 76.
19. See Domenico Losurdo, *Liberalism: A Counter-History*, trans. Gregory Elliott, London and New York: Verso, 2011, Chapter 10, §1.
20. Marx and Engels, *Collected Works*, Vol. 22, p. 354.

21. Ibid., Vol. 42, p. 266.
22. Antonio Gramsci, *Selections from the Prison Notebooks*, ed. and trans. Quintin Hoare and Geoffrey Nowell Smith, London: Lawrence & Wishart, 1971, p. 83.
23. See Arno J. Mayer, *The Persistence of the Old Regime: Europe to the Great War*, London and New York: Verso, 2010.
24. Marx and Engels, *Collected Works*, Vol. 16, p. 159.
25. Ibid., Vol. 11, p. 17.
26. Ibid., Vol. 27, p. 500.
27. Ibid., Vol. 6, pp. 504–5.
28. Lenin, *Collected Works*, Vol. 30, p. 115.
29. Ibid., Vol. 30, p. 457.
30. Ibid., Vol. 30, p. 458.
31. Ibid., Vol. 32, pp. 338–9.
32. Ibid., Vol. 32, p. 345.
33. Ibid., Vol. 32, p. 458.
34. Ibid., Vol. 32, p. 491,
35. Ibid., Vol. 32, p. 182.
36. Ibid., Vol. 33, p. 88.
37. N.I. Bukharin, 'Concerning the New Economic Policy and Our Tasks', in *Selected Writings on the State and the Transition to Socialism*, ed. and trans. Richard B. Day, Nottingham: Spokesman, 1982, p. 112.
38. See Domenico Losurdo, *Stalin. Storia e critica di una leggenda nera*, Rome: Carocci, 2008, pp. 129–31.
39. Mao Zedong, *Selected Works*, Vol. 4, pp. 421–3.
40. Mao Zedong, *Selected Works*, Vol. 5, p. 357.
41. Mao Zedong, *On Diplomacy*, p. 251.
42. Edgar Snow, *Red Star over China*, New York: Grove Press/Atlantic Monthly Press, 1994, p. 227.
43. Antonio Gramsci, 'To the Central Committee of the Soviet Communist Party', in *Selections from Political Writings 1921-1926*, ed. and trans. Quintin Hoare, London: Lawrence & Wishart, 1978, p. 431.
44. Quoted in Marcello Flores, *L'immagine dell'URSS. L'Occidente e la Russia di Stalin (1927–1956)*, Milan: Il Saggiatore, 1990, p. 52.
45. Walter Benjamin, 'Moscow', in *One-Way Street and Other Writings*, trans. Edmund Jephcott and Kingsley Shorter, London: Verso, 1985, p. 193.
46. See Giovanni Arrighi, *Adam Smith in Beijing: Lineages of the Twenty-First Century*, London and New York: Verso, 2007.
47. Lenin, *Collected Works*, Vol. 30, p. 460
48. Figes, *A People's Tragedy*, p. 771.
49. Benjamin, 'Moscow', p. 207.
50. Lenin, *Collected Works*, Vol. 33, pp. 280–1.

51. Ibid., Vol. 32, p. 177.
52. Ibid., Vol. 32, pp. 489–90.
53. Ibid., Vol. 33, p. 188.
54. Ibid., Vol. 32, p. 342.
55. Ibid., Vol. 32, p. 346.
56. Quoted in Flores, *L'imaggine dell'URSS*, p. 53.
57. Lenin, *Collected Works*, Vol. 32, p. 246; Vol. 33, p. 187.
58. Ibid., Vol. 33, p. 39.
59. Ibid., Vol. 32, p. 279.
60. Antonio Gramsci, *Selections from the Prison Notebooks*, ed. and trans. Quintin Hoare and Geoffrey Nowell Smith, London: Lawrence & Wishart, 1971, p. 367.
61. Mao, *Selected Works*, Vol. 1, pp. 110–11.
62. Antonio Gramsci, *Selections from Political Writings 1921–1926*, pp. 448–9.
63. Gramsci, *Selections from the Prison Notebooks*, pp. 52, 366.
64. Marx and Engels, *Collected Works*, Vol. 5, p. 77.
65. Ibid., Vol. 6, p. 211.
66. Deng Xiaoping, *Selected Works*, Vol. 2, pp. 144, 178.
67. Ibid., Vol. 3, pp. 142–3.
68. Marx and Engels, *Collected Works*, Vol. 22, p. 311.
69. Ibid., Vol. 6, p. 494.
70. Mao Zedong, *Selected Works*, Vol. 2, pp. 215–16.

CHAPTER 10

After the Revolution: Discovering the Limits of Class Struggle

1　Revolutionary Hopes and the Idealism of Practice

Marx's position on the making of history oscillated somewhat. He criticized the racial mythology and naturalistic ideologies that affixed the stamp of eternity, to historically determinate social relations, insisting that the focus should be on history and the human beings who make history. But human action and the innovations that occur over the course of history have nothing to do with creation *ex nihilo*. Hence, at the start of his philosophical career, in a famous long letter to Pavel W. Annenkov of December 1846, Marx underscored the limits of human action and class struggle:

> Is man free to choose this or that form of society? By no means. If you assume a given state of development of man's productive faculties, you will have a corresponding form of commerce and consumption. If you assume given stages of development in production, commerce or consumption, you will have a corresponding form of social constitution, a corresponding organisation, whether of the family, of the estates or of the classes—in a word, a corresponding civil society. …Needless to say, man is not free to choose *his productive forces*—upon which his whole history is based—for every productive force is an acquired force, the product of previous activity.[1]

Against naturalistic ideologies, it is certainly necessary to refer to history and human activity, to history as a whole, to all activity, including the 'previous activity' of human beings—economic, social, political, and ideological. In the words of *The Eighteenth Brumaire of Louis Bonaparte*, '[m]en make their own history, but they do not make it just as they please; they do not make it under circumstances chosen by themselves'.[2]

On the other hand, it must be borne in mind that, with its stress on practice and changing the world, revolutionary thought is prey to what might be characterized as the idealism of practice. One thinks of Fichte, who established a parallel between his *Doctrine of Science* and the dynamic action of revolutionary France: '[j]ust as that nation vouchsafes man liberty from external chains, so my system liberates him from the shackles of things-in-themselves, external influences'.[3] The pathos with which Fichte refers to human action is well-known: a boundless field seems to open up before it. This was a viewpoint criticized by Hegel. His description of the French Revolution as a 'splendid dawn' after which, in an unprecedented development, 'man [stood] on his head, i.e. upon thought, and construct[ed] reality in accordance with it', is at once a supreme acknowledgement, but also a gesture of detachment. In the intervening years, the resistance encountered by endeavours to re-fashion social reality *ex novo*, thereby creating for the first and only time 'true reconciliation between the divine and the world', had become clear.[4]

It might be said that Fichte and Hegel co-exist, in an occasionally contradictory blend, in Marx and Engels (and the theory of class struggle formulated by them). They were formed at a time when echoes of the French Revolution were still strong and there were premonitory signs of the revolution that invested continental Europe in 1848, which, in the hopes of the two young revolutionaries, would end up challenging the bourgeois order as well as old feudal relations. Positioned as they were between these two gigantic historical upheavals, which seemed set to remodel the world from its foundations, and to open up boundless space for the revolutionary transformation furthered by the class struggle, it is easy to understand why Marx and Engels were inclined to slip into an idealism of practice. In the communist future evoked by them, along with class antagonism, the market, the nation, religion, the state, and perhaps even legal norms as such, seem to wither away, rendered increasingly superfluous by a development of the productive forces so prodigious as to enable satisfaction of any and every need gratis, thereby surmounting the difficult task of distributing resources. In other words, it is as if the 'shackles of things-in-themselves' had disappeared. It is no coincidence if the theme of the end of the state already emerges in Fichte.[5]

To the extent that he assimilated Hegel's lesson on the limits of revolutionary practice, Marx engaged in a less grandiloquent projection of the communist future, so that he sometimes referred to the 'withering away of the state' as such and sometimes to the 'withering away of the state in the present political sense'. The ideal of internationalism also assumed a more balanced shape, now signifying not the disappearance of nations, but a new kind of relationship between them based on equality and mutual respect.[6] However, these were occasional clarifications that do not really challenge the idealism of practice.

It is significant that, in drafting a balance-sheet of the communist movement, one of the greatest philosophers produced by it felt the need to construct an ontology of social being. Lukács rightly cautioned against a dual danger of historical idealism: 'either social being has not been distinguished from being in general, or it is regarded as something completely different, not in fact possessing the character of being'.[7] The first type of idealism is naturalism, against which the theory of class struggle was developed. Revolutionary thought is prey to the second type of historical idealism—the idealism of practice—wherein market, nation, religion, and state tend to lose 'the character of being'. They end up being readily and infinitely malleable by political action and class struggle.

2 WAR AND THE REVIVAL OF THE IDEALISM OF PRACTICE

What made the construction of an ontology of social being even more difficult was an event that played a decisive role in the history of the fortunes of Marx and Engels. During the First World War, the various contending states, even those with a solid liberal tradition, presented themselves as sanguinary Molochs, intent on sacrificing millions of human beings on the altar of defence of the fatherland—in reality, on the altar of imperialist rivalry for global hegemony. Such horror could not but revive and further radicalize the thesis—indeed, the more or less messianic expectation—of the end of state. Any political programme that fell short of demanding a social order without a state and military apparatus seemed wholly inadequate.

This was a spiritual climate which, along with major intellectuals, also swept up prominent political figures for a time. In publishing *State and*

Revolution amidst the carnage of the war, and on the eve of the revolution called upon to end to it, Lenin formulated the thesis that the victorious proletariat 'needs only a state which is withering away'.[8] Three years later, at a time when there were high hopes of revolution spreading to the West, a revolutionary leader generally distinguished by his uncommon realism and lucidity indulged in a prediction that belongs in the realms of political fiction: 'the generation of people who are now at the age of fifty cannot expect to see a communist society. This generation will be gone before then. But the generation of those who are now fifteen will see a communist society, and will itself build this society'.[9] The extinction of the state as such forms part of the communist future, which appears at hand.

Patriotic rhetoric and national hatreds, in part 'spontaneous' and in part fomented, had issued in unprecedented horror. The demand to have done with all this was urgent. What emerged in some sections of the communist movement was an unrealistic internationalism that tended to liquidate different national identities as mere prejudices.

What had caused the catastrophe was the race to conquer colonies, markets, and raw materials, the hunt for profit—ultimately, the *auri sacra fames*. In 1918, the young Bloch encapsulated the messianic expectations of the time. The Soviets had supposedly realized the 'transformation of power into love' and built a world forever free of 'any private economy', any 'economy of money' and, with it, of the 'market morality that consecrates everything most wicked in man'.[10] In short, the tragic experience of the First World War markedly strengthened the tendency towards an idealism of practice. Now it was moral conscience itself that dictated denial of the character of social being to state, nation, and market—the structures and relations regarded as responsible for the infamy that had been consummated between 1914 and 1918, and which threatened to be repeated (and would in fact be repeated) shortly.

In the light of all this, the late Lukács' warning not to lose sight of the objectivity of social being sounds a self-critical note. In 1922, in his youth, he too had failed to appreciate it when he wrote: '[o]nly when the core of existence stands revealed as a social process can existence be seen as the product, albeit the hitherto unconscious product, of human activity. This activity will be seen in its turn as the element crucial for the transformation of existence'.[11] The idealism of practice transpires here, even if the class struggle of the proletariat has taken on the task of abolishing the 'shackles of things-in-themselves'.

The idealism of practice dies hard. As late as 1936-7, Trotsky took up and reiterated Lenin's prediction: 'the generation which conquered power, the "Old Guard", will begin the work of liquidating the state; the next generation will complete it'. In fact, nothing visible on the horizon of Soviet Russia rendered such a prospect credible. As regards money, there was no trace of its 'gradual dying away'; in fact, it had in no wise lost its 'magic power'. Neither 'state compulsion' nor 'money compulsion' had been dented. Hence, the main characteristics of 'class society, which is incapable of defining the relations of man to man except in the form of fetishes, churchly or secular, after appointing to defend them the most alarming of all fetishes, the state', remained firmly in place.[12] The Fichtean 'shackles of things-in-themselves' persisted, heavy and resistant. It only remained to target the 'bureaucracy' that had insinuated its way into power, and prevented implementation of the original programme, with class struggle.

3 THE DIFFICULT TRANSITION FROM PRACTICE TO THEORY

The idealism of practice dies hard. Yet it was regularly belied by governmental practice, by practice in action. The new Soviet government raised the banner of the withering away of the state. However, in June 1919, Gramsci credited the 'aristocracy of statesmen' represented by the Bolsheviks with having saved the Russian state from the disintegration to which it seemed condemned by the catastrophe of world war, civil war, and the ambitions and manoeuvres of imperialism (see Chap. 8, Sect. 4). The Russian state saved by advocates of the end of the state! An anarchist reader of *L'Ordine Nuovo* was scandalized. He observed that the Soviet Constitution was committed to establishing an order in which 'there will no longer be class divisions *or state power*'.[13] In fact, the discrepancy between practice and theory in Bolshevism is manifest. It was practice that proved the more lucid of the two. Practice, revolutionary class struggle, averted an already prostrate country being plunged into a war of all against all, into an interminable cycle of Balkanization and anarchical fragmentation, violence, and private vendettas. Consequently, it averted the persistence of more or less feudal government in the regions of a country of continental dimensions and the retardation or failed construction of the new order.

In an important intervention ('Better Fewer, but Better') that confirms his greatness as a statesman, and which was published in *Pravda* on 4 March 1923, Lenin advanced extremely significant watchwords: 'improve our state apparatus', engage seriously in 'build[ing] up a state', 'create a republic that is really worthy of the name of Soviet [and] socialist'(a long-term task requiring 'many, many years'), improve administrative work, and do all this without hesitating to learn from 'the best West-European standards'.[14] The practice invoked here, and partially implemented, is in greater contradiction than ever with theory—and much more mature than it.

Perhaps the first vague elements of theoretical rethinking emerge here. Not only is the objective of the extinction of the state not mentioned, or deferred to a distant future, but there is an awareness that neglecting the task of constructing a new state ultimately means prolonging the survival of the old tsarist state apparatus: '[w]e must banish from it all traces of extravagance, of which so much has been left over from tsarist Russia, from its bureaucratic capitalist state machine'.[15] However, the theory of the end of the state as a distant objective of the revolutionary class struggle was not called into question.

Even so, in *The German Ideology* (and other texts by Marx and Engels) we read that the state is also the 'form of organization' via which individuals of the ruling class mutually safeguard one another.[16] And it is not clear why this function should become superfluous among a different 'ruling class', or in a different society, still comprising individuals between whom, obviously, the possibility and reality exist of disagreements, tensions, and conflicts. Initial doubts about the withering away of the state were formulated when the civil war between the Bolsheviks and the Great Terror were dramatizing the absence of a 'form of organization' through which members of the party and society could safeguard one another. Expressing himself cautiously, aware that he was moving in a minefield, Stalin, in listing the functions of the socialist state, along with the traditional one of defence against the class enemy at home and abroad, theorized a 'third function: ...economic and organizational work and cultural and educational work performed by our state bodies', work geared to 'developing the young shoots of the new, socialist economic system and re-educating the people in the spirit of socialism'.[17] The great jurist Hans Kelsen immediately highlighted the 'radical alteration to the doctrine developed by Marx and Engels'.[18] However, this mutation was in a sense concealed from itself, and hence, did not yield a real shift. With the thesis of the withering away of the state not being explicitly called into question, the issue of the legal and institutional mechanisms required to ensure mutual security between individuals continued to be avoided. In the history of 'real socialism', the problem of the rule of law began to emerge only much later, with the advent of Deng Xiaoping at the head of China,[19] following a Cultural Revolution likewise motivated by the conviction of the purely 'formal', and largely meaningless, character of legal norms destined to wither away along with the state.

Secondly, the October Revolution and class struggle of the Russian proletariat were supposed to set in train a process at the end of which there would no longer be room for national identity and borders. Here the contradiction between theory and practice predated the conquest of power by the Bolsheviks. 'The working men have no country', asserted the *Communist Manifesto*.[20] But it was its authors who identified with the national struggles of oppressed peoples and placed them at the heart of the agitation of the International Working Men's Association. In more strictly theoretical terms, it was Marx who emphasized that, in a country like Ireland, the 'social question' took the form of the 'national question'. After October 1917, when the revolutionary wave seemed on the point of spreading in Europe (and throughout the world), assuming the office of People's Commissar for Foreign Affairs, Trotsky graphically summed up the seemingly imminent prospect: 'I will issue a few revolutionary proclamations to the peoples of the world and then shut up shop'.[21] With the advent of a globally unified humanity, the first ministry to become superfluous would be the one that normally presided over inter-state relations. Lenin's stance was no different. In concluding the First Congress of the Communist International, he declared: 'the victory of the proletarian revolution on a world scale is assured. The founding of an international Soviet republic is on the way'.[22] Some months later, on 4 January 1920, Lenin stressed that the 'question of the demarcation of frontiers now' had to be tackled, but only 'for the time being—for we are striving towards the complete abolition of frontiers'. Waged comprehensively, revolutionary class struggle would result in the foundation of a 'world federal Soviet republic'.[23]

However, Lenin was soon impelled by the concrete requirements of the class struggle to defend Russia and build the new society to sound patriotic notes. Indirectly rejecting accusations of national betrayal directed at the Bolsheviks by advocates of continuation of the war to the bitter end, he observed in October 1921 that with Brest-Litovsk, 'Russia emerged from the imperialist war, mutilated, it is true, but not so mutilated as she would have been had she continued'.[24] A few months later (March 1922), the Soviet leader called on his collaborators and supporters to demonstrate realism in these terms: 'the peasants will say: "You are splendid fellows; you defended our country. That is why we obeyed you. But if you cannot run the show, get out!"'[25] As for Stalin, he led the struggle for an immediate peace and for the Bolshevik Revolution advancing national slogans—that is, denouncing the Entente's attempt to force Russia to continue the war as an expression of imperial and neo-colonial arrogance. But it was with a certain astonishment on his part too that Stalin called in 1929 for acknowledgement of a phenomenon largely unsuspected by the protagonists of the October Revolution: 'nations ... possess an extraordinary stability'.[26]

More important than such indirect theoretical acknowledgement of the idea of nation and fatherland were the actual results of government activity. In 1927, Benjamin highlighted 'the strong national feeling that Bolshevism has given all Russians without distinction'.[27] Even more eloquent was the conclusion arrived at by Trotsky ten years later. In the USSR, a new 'Soviet patriotism' was spreading, a sentiment that was 'undoubtedly very deep, sincere, and dynamic'—all the more profound, sincere, and dynamic in that it involved not the oppression of non-Russian 'backward nationalities', but respect for them and their participation in the 'benefits' of overall economic and cultural development.[28]

Soviet—and, in reality, especially Russian—'patriotism' subsequently played a decisive role in the defeat inflicted by the USSR on Hitler's plan to colonize and enslave the peoples of Eastern Europe. To summarize, the revolutionary class struggle which, following the conquest of power, should have inaugurated a process destined to result in the withering away of state and nation, actually witnessed the emergence of an 'aristocracy of statesmen' and a patriotism that saved state and nation from a horrific catastrophe.

And that is not all. Along with national identities, linguistic identities were set to vanish, in the wake of the creation of a linguistically unified world community following the supersession of the old cultures and languages, which were branded with the stigma of class-divided society, and hence, incapable of long surviving the collapse of capitalism. Not a few argued thus in Soviet Russia. In this case, the opposition between theory and practice was particularly striking. No sooner had they conquered power than the Bolsheviks engaged in a massive literacy campaign, which involved the diffusion of Russian among broad masses hitherto incapable of reading and writing. Of particular importance was what happened in connection with national minorities. In 1936–7, Trotsky painted a telling picture:

> In the schools of the Union, lessons are taught at present in no less than eighty languages. For a majority of them, it was necessary to compose new alphabets, or to replace the extremely aristocratic Asiatic alphabets with the more democratic Latin. Newspapers are published in the same number of languages—papers which for the first time acquaint the peasants and nomad shepherds with the elementary ideas of human culture.[29]

However, so tenacious was the miraculous view of a class struggle capable of generating a totally new world that three years before his death, in 1950, Stalin felt compelled to intervene critically. The limits of class struggle had to be recognized. Language 'was created not by some one class, but by the entire society, by all the classes of the society'. To claim that language was not above social conflict might appear more of a 'class' position and revolutionary. In reality, to lose sight of the fact that language was 'the product of a whole number of epochs', and to claim to invent a proletarian language from scratch, once again forgetting Marx's 'previous activity' of preceding generations, was fanciful. Above all, the 'class' view of language ignored the fact that it was 'a means of intercourse between people'.[30] Undue dilation of the framework of class struggle compromises inter-subjective communication and eliminates the dimension of universality constitutive of Marxian class struggle as the struggle for recognition.

Practice managed to achieve lucidity soon enough. But the operation required to adapt theory to practice proved extremely difficult and full of contradictions and often tragic lacerations.

4 THE EXACTING DISCOVERY OF THE MARKET

In connection with the market too, we may note the habitual discrepancy between theory and practice. In this case, however, the picture is more complicated. On the one hand, the dialectic we have already analysed made its appearance. Reviving the economic and productive apparatus of a disintegrating country, where sometimes the only form of exchange was barter, the Soviet government actually expanded the market, and further expanded it when it embarked on a large-scale campaign of industrialization and urbanization. We may venture a general observation: in the mostly backward and semi-feudal countries where communist parties arrived in power, the development of the economy and the productive forces also entailed the extension of market relations, and hence, the advent of a genuine national market. But what accompanied this in theoretical terms was demonization of the market, which was particularly intense in countries where the shock of the First World War continued to be felt. On the eve of his death, Stalin had to engage in a difficult ideological battle: '[c]ommodity production must not be identified with capitalist production. They are two different things'.[31] More than 30 years later, Deng Xiaoping stressed: '[t]here is no fundamental contradiction between socialism and a market economy. The problem is how to develop the productive forces more effectively'.[32] What distinguishes socialism is not planning as such, which is a tool sometimes used by capitalist countries; the market is an instrument that can be utilized by a country of socialist orientation.

We have hitherto been dealing with the familiar problem of adapting theory to practice. But the converse problem also presents itself. Marx had too profound a knowledge of the economic universe to be unaware that, without competition, it is impossible to promote the development of the productive forces. The *Critique of the Gotha Programme* makes it clear that socialism is based on remuneration according to labour performed, which by definition is 'unequal'.[33] But in Soviet Russia practice failed, or struggled, to conform to theory: the horror of the First World War and the disintegration of the economy, aggravated by the Civil War, created propitious conditions for the diffusion of a populist vision of socialism (criticized by the *Communist Manifesto*), stamped by crude 'social levelling' based on coercive 'universal asceticism'.

Lenin soon perceived the need for a practical switch, but did not proceed to a settlement of theoretical accounts. The self-critical reflection contained in an intervention entitled 'Fourth Anniversary of the October Revolution' is certainly significant:

> Borne along on the crest of the wave of enthusiasm, rousing first the political enthusiasm and then the military enthusiasm of the people, we expected to accomplish economic tasks just as great as the political and military tasks we have accomplished by relying directly on this enthusiasm. ...Not directly relying on enthusiasm, but aided by the enthusiasm engendered by the great revolution, and on the basis of personal interest, personal incentive and business principles, we must first set to work in this small-peasant country to build solid gangways to socialism by way of state capitalism.[34]

At all events, in the economic field, one could not look to militarily organized mass enthusiasm for long; 'personal interest' would have to be relied on sooner or later. Unfortunately, this important theoretical acquisition was neutralized by the persistent employment of military terminology: it was necessary to abandon any 'direct assault' or 'offensive' and 'retreat'; and it sounds as if this retreat was to be a short-lived tactical expedient.[35]

For a long time—too long—countries of a socialist orientation entrusted their economic development to revolutionary enthusiasm and patriotic fervour. But these are moods that involve a particular emotional intensity, which by definition cannot be permanent. Appeals to the spirit of self-sacrifice, and even heroism, can form the exception, not the rule. It might be said with Bertolt Brecht: '[b]lessed is the people that needs no heroes'. Heroes are required for the transition from the state of emergency to normality and are heroes only in so far as they succeed in ensuring the transition to normality. That is, heroes are such only to the extent that they are capable of rendering themselves superfluous. A communism that presupposed pursuit of the spirit of self-sacrifice and renunciation *ad infinitum* (or almost) would be decidedly bizarre.

Historically, with the fading of revolutionary enthusiasm or patriotic fervour over time, the problems that emerged on the morrow of the October Revolution presented themselves in ever graver form. There was persistent anarchy in the workplace, calmly deserted by its employees who, even when physically present, seemed engaged in a kind of go-slow, which, moreover, was tolerated. This was the somewhat perplexed and rather admiring impression gained by labour and trade-union delegations visiting the USSR in its last years.

It is a problem that invests the history of the 'socialist camp' as a whole. In China, which was beginning to leave Maoism behind it, customs and practices prevailed in the public sector that have been described as follows by a Western journalist: '[e]ven the lowliest attendant ... can, should he wish, stay at home for one or two years and continue to receive his pay at the end of each month'.[36] Let us now turn to Cuba. In October 1964, Che Guevara felt compelled to say: '[w]e further witnessed the problem of absenteeism'.[37] This formulation is erroneous or illusory, because it suggests the problem was in the process of being solved. In fact, with the passage of time, appeals to revolutionary consciousness met with an increasingly feeble echo. Cuba obstinately strove to avoid recourse to the market and material incentives, on account of the element of inequality involved in remuneration according to labour. In the end, however, it had to take cognizance of reality. So now we have Raúl Castro exhorting his compatriots to 'abolish once and for all the idea that Cuba is the only country in the world where one can live without working'.[38]

The real turning-point occurred with Deng's assumption of the leadership of China. He drew up a judicious balance-sheet: '[i]nitiative cannot be aroused without economic means. A small number of advanced people might respond to moral appeal, but such an approach can only be used for a short time'.[39] In the history of socialism, the appreciation of the market (and competition) as the motor of development of the productive forces expressed in *The German Ideology* was henceforth registered: via 'universal competition' and the market, large-scale industry 'forced all individuals to strain their energy to the utmost'.[40]

In philosophical terms, the discovery of the objectivity of social being proved especially difficult in the economic field. For too long entrenched in an idealist position, the communist movement resisted before facing the fact that, however triumphant the revolutionary class struggle, it has nothing to do with the creation *ex nihilo* of a 'new man' motivated solely by noble ideals and utterly deaf to material self-interest.

5   The 'Socialist Camp' and 'Class Struggle'

Expansion of the framework of class struggle played an especially pernicious role in the regulation, or non-regulation, of relations between socialist countries or countries inspired by socialism. In 1916, having drawn attention to Engels' warning against the tendency that can arise in the 'victorious proletariat' to foist 'blessings' on other peoples, Lenin commented: '[j]ust because the proletariat has carried out a social revolution it will not become holy and immune from errors and weaknesses. But it will be inevitably led to realise this truth by possible errors (and selfish interest—attempts to saddle others)'. However, as long as this lesson had not been fully assimilated, as long as the victorious proletariat continued to express chauvinist or hegemonic tendencies, 'revolutions—against the socialist state—and wars are possible'.[41] In other words, even when victorious, the class struggle of the proletariat does not entail the immediate disappearance of rivalry, tensions and conflicts between nations.

The communist movement proved capable of learning this lesson only at highpoints in its history. Of particular significance is a position adopted in 1956 by the Communist Party of the China (and Mao Zedong) on the breach eight years earlier between the Soviet Union and Yugoslavia. It was stressed that within the socialist camp, 'systematic efforts are needed to overcome great-nation chauvinist tendencies'—tendencies which, far from vanishing with the defeated bourgeois or semi-feudal regime, might be fuelled in the 'sense of superiority' created by the victory of the revolution. This was a phenomenon 'not peculiar to any one country. For instance, country B may be small and backward compared to country A, but big and advanced compared to country C. Thus country B, while complaining of great-nation chauvinism on the part of country A, may often assume the airs of a great nation in relation to country C'.[42] Although this passage is confined to generalities, it is clear that country B refers to Yugoslavia which, while legitimately complaining of the chauvinism and highhandedness of the Soviet Union (A), exhibited hegemonic ambitions towards Albania (C). This analysis confronts us with bitter conflicts that are irreducible to a struggle between opposing classes in power in the different countries.

By contrast, we witness a radical change of perspective in subsequent years, once the split in the international communist movement had been consummated. Let us see what the Communist Party of China had to say on the subject of Yugoslavia in 1963: operative there were 'ruthless exploitation' and 'the dictatorship of the bureaucrat-comprador bourgeoisie'. The following year, the polemic directly involved the Soviet Union: after Khrushchev had set about 'restoring and extending the system of exploitation', a 'new bourgeoisie' was on the rampage.[43]

In these positions, the crucial aspect is not the extreme bitterness of the polemic, but the new philosophical approach. Persistent conflicts between countries identifying with socialism are now explained by the fact that some of them have, in fact, already undergone a capitalist restoration. The confrontation between the USSR and China was represented as a class struggle on an international scale, pitting a country dominated by the bourgeoisie against one ruled by the proletariat. Such an approach seems more in accord with historical materialism, in as much as it involves social classes in analysing the international situation. In reality, however, it represents a lapse into an idealism of practice—the view that, as a result of revolutionary class struggle, the material objectivity of different national interests would disappear. This view committed the error of once again repressing national contradictions, with a consequent relapse into a utopian and idealistic vision of socialism.

6   Class Contradictions and 'Non-Class' Contradictions

On closer examination, Marxist reflection on the general problem of the persistence of contradictions in a post-capitalist society has been episodic and occasional. And to the extent that it has occurred, it has referred much more to the East than the West.

A few years after the October Revolution, Lenin deemed strikes against 'bureaucratic distortions of the Soviet apparatus, safeguarding the working people's material and spiritual interests', wholly legitimate; they were an expression of 'the *non-class* economic struggle'. In this respect, trade unions were called on 'to act as mediators' and 'facilitate the speediest and smoothest settlement' of the disputes that inevitably arose even in a society engaged in building socialism.[44] In contrast, agitation and mobilization that challenged the conquests of the revolution were to be regarded as (counter-revolutionary) class struggles.

The first developed theoretical position on such issues derives from China, and not by chance. Here the First World War did not have the same traumatic impact as in Europe and did not create messianic expectations. Furthermore, called on to put an end to the 'humiliations' that began with the Opium Wars, from the outset the Chinese Revolution not only had an explicitly national dimension, but was also situated in an extended temporal perspective, which saw the process of political and social transformation unfolding in successive phases. Finally, it should not be forgotten that in China the communists arrived in power nationally with two decades of experience of government behind them in 'liberated' areas—areas under siege not only militarily, but also economically, which therefore also had to be defended with the development of production and trade. Generally speaking, the conditions conducive in Europe to branding state, nation, and market (as such) as expressions of class domination and exploitation were absent.

Publishing *On Practice* in 1937, Mao saw truth emerging 'in the course of social practice (material production, class struggle or scientific experiment)'.[45] Manifestly, the ambit of class struggle is not unlimited. External to it is science, about which a note is sounded that is reminiscent of Marx: '[k]nowledge is a matter of science, and no dishonesty or conceit whatsoever is permissible. What is required is definitely the reverse—honest and modesty'.[46] Material production itself is not determined in class struggle: material production and 'scientific experiment' are two forms of social practice beside class struggle, even if the latter has a strong influence on them.

For Mao this afforded an opportunity to define the scope of the class struggle: 'the development of the movement of human knowledge ... is full of contradictions and struggles'. These contradictions and struggles obviously impact on the class struggle and can be influenced by it, but there is no identity between them. Like socialists of a Marxist persuasion, supporters of Luddism were an expression of the proletariat—only, engaging in 'machine-smashing', they remained at the stage of perception, had not progressed in the process of knowledge of the social system responsible for their sufferings. Unlike Marxists, they had not understood the difference between machinery and the capitalist use of machinery. And likewise arrested at the stage of perception were national movements in China that struggled against invasion by triggering 'indiscriminate anti-foreign struggles', rather than against imperialism.[47]

In themselves the contradictions inherent in the knowledge process are not class contradictions, so much so—the famous text *On the Correct Handling of Contradictions among the People* observed in 1956—that they would continue to exist under communism, even after the disappearance of classes and class struggle: struggles between the true and the false 'will never end'; nor would those between the old and the new, which could be hindered only by 'lack of discernment'.[48]

Knowledge of the new international situation created by the victory of anti-capitalist and anti-imperialist revolutions in several countries was a process rich in contradictions, which were not class contradictions, at least judging from a text of 1956:

> The international solidarity of the communist parties is a type of relationship entirely new to human history. It is natural that its development cannot be free from difficulties. ...If the communist parties maintain relations of equality among themselves and reach common understanding and take concerted action through genuine, and not nominal, exchange of views, their unity will be strengthened. Conversely, if, in their mutual relations, one party imposes its views upon others, or if the parties use the method of interference in each other's internal affairs instead of comradely suggestions and criticism, their unity will be impaired.
>
> In the socialist countries, the communist parties have assumed the responsibility of leadership in the affairs of the state, and relations between them often involve directly the relations between their respective countries and peoples, so the proper handling of such relations has become a problem demanding even greater care.[49]

In subsequent years, this approach was unfortunately abandoned and an accentuation and absolutization of 'class struggle' prevailed. An analogous process occurred domestically, with the outbreak of the Cultural Revolution.

7 AN UNFINISHED LEARNING PROCESS

The transition from theoretical patching up to theoretical rethinking began to emerge only on either side of the collapse of socialism in Eastern Europe. Breaking with the Cultural Revolution (sometime greeted by the Western Far Left as the start, or potential start, of the withering away of the state), from the late 1970s Deng Xiaoping called for extension and improvement of the 'legal system' and for the introduction of the 'rule of law' in the party and 'society at large', as a precondition for the real development of 'democracy'.[50] Just as it does not betoken the end of the state, so socialism does not entail either the disappearance of the market, or the fusion of the countries engaged in constructing a new social order into a community free of tensions and conflicts.

In interviews given shortly before his death in 1980, Tito acknowledged that what provoked the split with Stalin's Soviet Union in 1948 was the national question, while the opposition of Yugoslav socialist self-management to Soviet state planning had merely served to justify and dignify Belgrade's defiant stance.[51] Later, meeting Gorbachev on 16 May 1989 in Beijing, Deng pondered the reasons for the split that had occurred between the two countries and parties. What cast a shadow of suspicion was the attitude adopted by the USSR along with the other great powers at Yalta, the 'secret agreement dividing up spheres of influence among them, greatly to the detriment of China's interests'. The influence of the national question had been decisive: 'I don't mean it was because of the ideological disputes; we no longer think that everything we said at that time was right. The basic problem was that the Chinese were not treated as equals and felt humiliated. However, we have never forgotten that in the period of our First Five-Year Plan the Soviet Union helped us lay an industrial foundation'. Thanks to the awareness that had been painfully acquired, it was now possible to turn the page.[52] But for the Soviet Union, at least, it was too late; and for China too, the situation was not free of dangers, as demonstrated by the Tiananmen Square 'incident'.

Let us jump ahead three years. In drawing up a critical and self-critical balance-sheet, Fidel Castro arrived at the conclusion that '[w]e socialists made a mistake in underestimating the strength of nationalism and religion'.[53] When we remember that religion can be a key moment in the construction of national identity, this is another reason for casting doubt on the thesis of the inevitable disappearance of religion after the victory of proletarian class struggle.

The instances I have mentioned are shoots of belated, incomplete theoretical rethinking. The idealism of practice, and the attribution to class struggle of a sovereign power to remould (and even erase) the social being of the state, nation, religion, market and so forth, made a decisive contribution to the defeat suffered by the socialist project between 1989 and 1991. In difficult or dramatic situations, this view acts like a kind of drug, burdening the struggle for social change with excessive expectations. Intoxication gave way to exhaustion. And on the eve of its collapse the condition of real socialism in Eastern Europe was one of exhaustion.

Notes

1. Karl Marx and Frederick Engels, *Collected Works*, London: Lawrence & Wishart, 1975-2004, Vol. 38, p. 96.
2. Ibid., Vol. 11, p. 103.
3. See Domenico Losurdo, *Hegel e la Germania. Filosofia e questione nazionale tra rivoluzione e reazione*, Milan: Guerini/Istituto Italiano per gli Studi Filosofici, 1997, Chapter 4, §1.
4. G.W.F. Hegel, *Vorlesungen über die Philosophie der Weltgeschichte*, ed. Georg Lasson, Hamburg: Meiner, 1919-20, p. 926.
5. See Losurdo, *Hegel e la Germania*, Chapter 3, §2.
6. See Domenico Losurdo, *Antonio Gramsci dal liberalismo al 'comunismo critico'*, Rome: Gamberetti, 1997, Chapter 5, §§ 2 & 7.
7. György Lukács, *Ontologia dell'essere sociale*, trans. Alberto Scarponi, Rome: Editori Riuniti, 1976-81, p. 3.
8. V.I. Lenin, *Collected Works*, London: Lawrence & Wishart, 1960-78, Vol. 25, p. 402.
9. Ibid., Vol. 31.
10. Ernst Bloch, *Geist der Utopie*, Frankfurt am Main: Suhrkamp, 1971, p. 298.
11. Georg Lukács, *History and Class Consciousness*, trans. Rodney Livingstone, London: Merlin Press, 1971, p. 19.
12. Leon Trotsky, *The Revolution Betrayed: What is the Soviet Union and Where is it Going?*, trans. Max Eastman, New York: Pathfinder Press, 1980, pp. 161, 65.

13. Antonio Gramsci, *L'Ordine Nuovo 1919–1920*, ed. Valentino Gerratana and Antonio A. Santucci, Turin: Einaudi, 1987, pp. 56–7. The letter from the anarchist can be found in no. 8 of *L'Ordine Nuovo*.
14. Lenin, *Collected Works*, Vol. 33, pp. 487–502.
15. Ibid., Vol. 33, p 501.
16. Marx and Engels, *Collected Works*, Vol. 5, p. 90.
17. J. Stalin, *Problems of Leninism*, Moscow: Foreign Languages Publishing House, 1953, p. 796.
18. Quoted in Domenico Losurdo, *Stalin. Storia e critica di una leggenda negra*, Rome: Carocci, 2008, p. 122.
19. Deng Xiaoping, *Selected Works*, Beijing: Foreign Languages Press, 1992–5, Vol. 3, pp. 166–7.
20. Marx and Engels, *Collected Works*, Vol. 6, p. 502.
21. Quoted in E.H. Carr, *The Bolshevik Revolution 1917–1923*, London and Basingstoke: Macmillan, 1978, Vol. 3, p. 16.
22. Lenin, *Collected Works*, Vol. 28, pp. 476–7.
23. Ibid., Vol. 30, pp. 292, 297.
24. Ibid., Vol. 33, p. 61.
25. Ibid., Vol. 33, p. 290.
26. J. Stalin, *Works*, Moscow: Foreign Languages Publishing House, 1952–2, Vol. 11, p. 363.
27. Walter Benjamin, 'Moscow', in *One-Way Street and Other Writings*, trans. Edmund Jephcott and Kingsley Shorter, London: Verso, 1985, p. 196.
28. Trotsky, *The Revolution Betrayed*, pp. 164–5, 171.
29. Trotsky, *The Revolution Betrayed*, p. 171.
30. J. Stalin, *Marxism and Problems of Linguistics*, Peking: Foreign Languages Press, 1972, pp. 5, 7.
31. J. Stalin, *Economic Problems of Socialism in the USSR*, Peking: Foreign Languages Press, 1972, p. 13.
32. Deng Xiaoping, *Selected Works*, Vol. 3, pp. 151, 203.
33. Marx and Engels, *Collected Works*, Vol. 24, pp. 86–7.
34. Lenin, *Collected Works*, Vol. 33, p. 58.
35. Ibid., Vol. 33, pp. 93, 280–1.
36. Francesco Sisci, *La Differenza tra la Cina e il mondo. La rivoluzione degli anni ottanta*, Milan: Feltrinelli, 1994, p. 102.
37. Ernesto Che Guevara, *Scritti, discorsi e diari di guerriglia 1959–1967*, ed. Laura Gonsalez, Turin: Einaudi, 1969.
38. Roberto Livi, 'La riforma di Raúl', *Il Manifesto*, 3 August 2010.
39. Quoted in Ezra Vogel, *Deng Xiaoping and the Transformation of China*, Cambridge, MA and London: Harvard University Press, 2011, p. 243.
40. Marx and Engels, *Collected Works*, Vol. 5, p. 73.
41. Lenin, *Collected Works*, Vol. 22, pp. 353, 352.

42. *Renmin Ribao, More on the Historical Experience of the Dictatorship of the Proletariat*, Beijing: Foreign Languages Press, 1957, pp. 37–8.
43. Communist Party of China, *The Polemic on the General Line of the International Communist Movement*, Beijing: Foreign Languages Press, 1965, pp. 154–5, 460.
44. Lenin, *Collected Works*, Vol. 32, p. 100; Vol. 33, p. 187.
45. Mao Zedong, *Selected Works*, Vol. 1, p. 296.
46. Ibid., Vol. 1, p. 300.
47. Ibid., Vol. 1, pp. 307, 301.
48. Mao Zedong, *Selected Readings from the Works of Mao Tse-tung*, Beijing: Foreign Languages Press, 1967, pp. 375, 374.
49. *Renmin Ribao, More on the Historical Experience of the Dictatorship of the Proletariat*, p. 36.
50. Deng Xiaoping, *Selected Works*, Vol. 2, pp. 196, 166–7.
51. Slavoj Zizek, *Living in the End Times*, London and New York: Verso, 2011, p. 459.
52. Deng Xiaoping, *Selected Works*, Vol. 3, pp. 286–7.
53. Quoted Arthur Schlesinger, Jr., 'Four Days with Fidel: A Havana Diary', *New York Review of Books*, 26 March 1992, p. 25.

CHAPTER 11

Class Struggle at the 'End of History'

1 'COLONIALISM'S BACK—AND NOT A MOMENT TOO SOON'

The collapse of the 'socialist camp' and 'real socialism' represents the nadir in the history of Marx's fortunes to date. At the time, a cartoon circulated that portrayed the revolutionary militant and philosopher exclaiming: 'Workers of the world, forgive me!' Theoretically, the summons to class struggle with which the *Communist Manifesto* ends was supposedly incapable of explaining anything, while in practice, it had resulted in disasters. The disappearance of regimes inspired by Marx from Eastern Europe was construed by the most intoxicated representatives of the dominant ideology as the definitive 'triumph of the West, of the Western idea', even as the 'end of history'. Thus argued Francis Fukuyama,[1] the intellectual and US State Department functionary, according to whom the West had completed the final stage of the historical process, represented by liberal capitalist society. It was now only a matter of adding a sort of appendix to a book that was essentially already finished, raising the rest of the world to the level of the most advanced countries. However, this might involve the need to teach some harsh lessons to those who still resisted bowing before the 'triumph of the West, the Western idea' and the 'end of history'.

Three years later, referring to the former colonies, the more or less official philosopher of the 'open society' and the liberal West proclaimed: '[w]e freed these states too quickly and too simplistically'; it was like 'abandoning a playschool to its own devices'. Such flippancy should be rectified: '[w]e must not be afraid of waging wars for peace. In current circumstances, it is inevitable. It's sad, but we must do it if we want to save the world'. But who is this 'we' invoked by Popper? The crusade was proclaimed in the name of 'civilized states' or the 'states of the civilized world'. Which were these? Clearly, the reference-point is the 'West', whose geographical and political confines are not specified, but which decides in sovereign fashion which is 'civilized' and which is not. In and through a series of wars, the capitalist and liberal West was called upon to realize a '*pax civilitatis*'.[2] The rehabilitation of colonialism and colonial wars was explicit.

What dispels any possible doubt is the *New York Times Magazine* dated 18 April 1993, containing the headline: 'Colonialism's Back—and Not a Moment Too Soon!' This encapsulated the thinking of the British historian Paul Johnson, who enjoyed considerable media success and was an acclaimed exponent of the dominant ideology. He saluted the 'altruistic revival of colonialism', to which there was no alternative in 'a great many third-world countries': 'there is a moral issue here; the civilized world has a mission to go out to these desperate places and govern'. In fact, it was not merely a question of intervening in countries deemed incapable of self-government by Washington, but also in those which, in governing themselves, displayed 'extremist' tendencies. For example, Reagan had been right in 1983 to invade the small, defenceless Caribbean island of Grenada and overthrow its government.[3]

What is striking about such discourse is the rehabilitation of categories which, following the tragic experience of Nazism and fascism, seemed to have generally been discredited. Another well-known British historian, a passionate celebrant of the British and American empires, was right to observe a few years later that the 'real historic turning point' was represented not by the terrorist attacks of 11 September 2001, but the 'fall of the Berlin Wall' in 1989, which created the conditions for the revival of colonial and imperial projects.[4]

The start of the collapse of the 'socialist camp' in Eastern Europe coincided with an event that has been largely repressed by the dominant culture. In late 1989, the invasion of Panama occurred. Preceded by intensive bombardment, it was carried out without any declaration of war, without any warning, and without any authorization by the UN Security Council. Densely populated districts were struck by bombs and conflagrations during the night. Hundreds—more likely, thousands—died, the vast majority of them 'civilian and poor and dark-skinned'; at least 15,000 were made homeless. As a US scholar notes, this was the 'bloodiest episode' in the history of the small country.[5] Thanks to it, however, the USA rid itself of the dictator and drug trafficker it had installed, but who had now run out of control.

Three years later, the first Gulf War occurred. In Italy, the editor of a daily regarded as 'centre-left' explained the reasons for it. 'All the industrial powers' had decided to 'severely punish Saddam Hussein', intent as they were on keeping the price of oil low, and therefore, on 'suppress[ing] the possibility of another oil crisis that would have checked the expansionist momentum of Western capitalism'.[6] And, as another journalist made clear in the same newspaper, the punishment had been administered without undue subtlety, since the USA had not hesitated to 'wipe out fleeing, unarmed Iraqis'.[7]

Undermined in its time by the Cuban Revolution, a classical doctrine of the age of colonialism and imperialism—the Monroe Doctrine—came back into vogue. 'In Moscow I'll Ask for Castro's Head', read a headline in summer 1991 in an Italian daily, heralding the meeting between a triumphant Bush Sr. and Gorbachev, who was politically in his death throes. The article made it clear that 'the President has been very explicit on Castro: ... "His presence eighty miles from our coast is intolerable"'.[8]

In this political and ideological climate, even the category of imperialism enjoyed a new and charming lease on life: '[o]nly Western imperialism—though few will like calling it that—can now unite the European continent and save the Balkans from chaos'.[9] A couple of years later, the discourse became more precise. Formerly 'western', imperialism now became unequivocally American. And so we have *Foreign Affairs*, a journal close to the State Department, proclaiming in the title of the page introducing one of its numbers, and then in the opening article, that 'the logic of imperialism [or] neo-imperialism is too compelling for the Bush administration to resist'.[10] These were not isolated voices, but a chorus that admiringly compared the US Empire to the Roman Empire, which even invoked the establishment of a 'Colonial Office' following the distinguished precedent of the British Empire and which, with reference to Washington, extolled 'the most magnanimous imperial power ever'.[11]

This was the power called on to enforce respect for human rights throughout the world. The twentieth century thus ended as it had begun. Having won its independence from Spain, Cuba had been forced, by Washington, to include the so-called Platt Amendment in its Constitution, whereby the USA was granted the right to intervene in the island militarily whenever, in its judgement, peaceful enjoyment of property, liberty, and ultimately, human rights was imperilled. It was as if at the height of the 'unipolar moment' God's 'chosen nation', tasked with leading the world, claimed to apply the Platt Amendment on a global scale.

The United Nations was neutralized. It had been created and progressively enlarged while an international anti-colonial revolution was underway; and, notwithstanding its limitations, paid homage to the principle of equality among nations in its Charter. The UN was neutralized not only because the USA arrogated to itself the sovereign right to mount punitive expeditions without Security Council authorization (as in 1999 against Yugoslavia and in 2003 against Iraq). More important was the fact that this alleged sovereign right could be applied, in utterly devastating fashion, without resorting to war in the strict sense.

In June 1996, the director of the Center for Economic and Social Rights highlighted what the 'collective punishment' inflicted by an embargo had meant for the Iraqi people. Already 'more than 500,000 Iraqi children have died from hunger and disease'; more were set to suffer the same fate. What had been assaulted in devastating fashion were the 'human rights of 21 million Iraqis'. Three years later, an article in *Foreign Affairs* drew up a disturbing balance-sheet. Following the collapse of 'real socialism', in a unified world under US hegemony, embargos represented the quintessential weapon of mass destruction. Officially imposed to prevent Saddam accessing non-existent weapons of mass destruction, the embargo in Iraq 'may have contributed to more deaths during the post-Cold War era than all weapons of mass destruction throughout history' put together. Hence, it was if the Arab country, criminalized on the grounds of a charge that turned out to be completely unfounded, had simultaneously suffered the atomic bombing of Hiroshima and Nagasaki, the mustard gas attacks perpetrated by the armies of Wilhelm II and Benito Mussolini, and more besides.[12] The threat of this weapon of mass destruction did not only loom over small countries. In the early 1990s, an Italian daily referred as follows to a debate that occurred on the UN Security Council: 'China opposed sanctions against Libya and the three Western powers threatened trade reprisals'.[13] And such reprisals could be so devastating, a well-known US political scientist stressed at the end of the decade, as to represent the commercial equivalent of recourse to 'nuclear weapons' (see Chap. 12, Sect. 6).

The highly successful, quasi-official historian of the West is unimpressed by such details. Having composed a eulogy to 'liberal' empire and imperialism, he called upon the rulers in Washington to pursue the imperial course the USA had embarked on at the time of its foundation uninhibitedly and with greater urgency: 'there were no more self-confident imperialists than the Founding Fathers themselves'.[14] Once again, the celebration of colonialism and imperialism was explicit and brazen, as if the 'imperialism' of the Founding Fathers, and their attitude towards colonial peoples, had not betokened the expropriation, deportation, and annihilation of Native Americans, as well as the enduring enslavement of blacks.

In international relations, there is no doubt about the reactionary significance of the turn that occurred between 1989 and 1991. Precisely in 1991, the year of the collapse of the Soviet Union and the first Gulf War, a prestigious British review (*International Affairs*) published in its July number an article by Barry Buzan, which concluded with an enthusiastic announcement of the good news: 'the West has triumphed over both communism and *tiers-mondisme*'. The second victory was no less important than the first: 'the center is now more dominant, and the periphery more subordinate, than at any time since decolonization began'. The chapter of history containing the anti-colonial revolutions could be regarded as safely filed.[15] Some years later, from the converse position, an eminent historian observed with concern that the collapse of classical colonialism was accompanied by 'the establishment of the most extensive and potentially destructive apparatus of Western force the world had ever seen'.[16]

No country, however large, was safe from this unprecedented 'destructive apparatus'. Recently, a former adviser to Vice-President Dick Cheney has revealed that in the early 1990s, being 'invulnerable', US naval and air forces violated China's 'airspace and territorial waters' without scruple and 'with impunity'.[17] The law of the strongest was manifestly operative. But it was (and is) transfigured by the dominant ideology into a redemptive phenomenon. The petty, provincial principle of the inviolability of state sovereignty (and the equal right of countries, large and small, to have such inviolability recognized) had finally lapsed. On closer examination, the arguments with which the putative redemptive phenomenon was celebrated ended up resurrecting the commonplaces of an ominous tradition.

Does the universality of human rights override national borders and render the principle of respect for state sovereignty obsolete? In *Foreign Affairs*, we read: '[i]t is a vision in which sovereignty becomes more conditional for countries that challenge Washington's standards of internal and external behavior'.[18] It is clear that, arrogating to itself the right to declare the sovereignty of other states superseded, the great Western powers grant themselves expanded sovereignty, to be exercised far beyond their own national territory. To all intents and purposes, this reproduces the dichotomy that marked colonial and imperial expansion, whose protagonists constantly refused to recognize the countries they subjugated, or converted into protectorates, as sovereign states.

Are we not assured that contemporary colonialism is 'altruistic' and humanitarian in a cast? Such assurances are far from new. It is enough to think of Kipling's theme: the 'white man's burden'. Voluntary assumption of such a heavy, demanding burden can be accepted, only if motivated by an altruistic and humanitarian spirit. The imperial universalism of 'civilization', to be diffused throughout the world, has today assumed the garb of an imperial humanism of human rights to be enforced the world over. Arrogating the right to define the boundary between civilization and barbarism, or between respect for universal norms and violation of them, *de facto* means granting oneself universal sovereignty.

In the same year as the *New York Times Magazine* celebrated the 'altruistic' character of the colonialist revival desired by it, an Italian general (who was at the same time a teacher and scholar of geopolitics) expressed himself more bluntly. Having emphasized that the tendencies towards 'recolonization' were a constitutive feature of the 'new international order', he added: '[i]n fact, this trend comes up against its limits only in the inconvenience to the West of getting involved in crises whose management would be costly, without deriving any concrete benefit from them'.[19]

The 'concrete benefit' is immediately obvious. There is no need to posit a strict one-to-one relationship between individual military operations and profits. Instead, we need to keep the big picture in mind. To arrogate to oneself the right of military intervention in certain countries, which for the most part are not lacking in energy resources and are often located in areas of great geopolitical significance, means conditioning their international relations to the advantage of the great powers that *de facto* exercise sovereignty.

If the reaction that followed 1989 did not achieve all its objectives, it was down to economic and political processes outside the West's control. One thinks, in the first instance, of China's extraordinary economic and technological development or one thinks of Russia. In 1994, a prestigious intellectual, who until 1989 had been a dauntless dissident, observed that his country was in effect experiencing 'colonial democracy'.[20] Only later did Russia manage to regain control of its enormous energy assets—and this following the advent of political forces and figures hated in Washington and Brussels. Also worthy of attention is the failure of the attempt to instil in Cuba, an obedience and submission to the Monroe Doctrine—a doctrine challenged by a growing number of Latin American states. Nor should we lose sight of the resistance to military occupation in Iraq and Afghanistan. These processes and movements, unanticipated by the triumphant bourgeoisie of the years of the turn, all directly or indirectly pertained to the enduring anti-colonialist and anti-imperialist impulse deriving from the October Revolution. The power of the USA and the West to blackmail is thus diminishing—all the more so in that they are now invested by an extremely serious economic crisis. However, neo-colonial ambitions have not disappeared. Against the latter, as against classical colonialism, a national struggle has developed that is, at the same time, a class struggle. I shall focus on its modalities in the next chapter.

2 The Return of 'Primitive Accumulation'

Let us go back to the turning point. From 1989 onwards, Russia was invested by a wave of privatizations that enabled a privileged few, to literally rape state assets, and which was summarized by the *Financial Times* as follows: 'the majority of the public has been given an object lesson in Proudhon's maxim that "property is theft"'.[21] While this plumped-up bourgeoisie was being formed, a dreadful tragedy was being consummated elsewhere. A well-known French political scientist referred to a 'collapse in average life expectancy', even 'a veritable genocide of the elderly', whose culprits were the privileged few who had succeeded in 'accumulating enormous wealth' that was speculative and parasitic in origin, were not patently illegal.[22]

The picture is completed by testimony all the more striking for being published in journals engaged at the time in celebrating the turn. In the weeks immediately preceding its official dissolution, when the neo-liberal reforms proposed or imposed by the West were already ravaging the Soviet Union, the International Red Cross announced that the survival of 1.5 million people was at stake because of a 'shortage of food and medicine'.[23] In subsequent months, the situation deteriorated further: 'more than half the population [is now] below the poverty threshold';[24] 'in the first six months of 1993, GDP was 14 per cent below the first months of 1992'.[25] In some respects, memories harked back to the tragic years of Hitler's invasion: 'in 1992, for the first time in the post-war period, there were fewer births in Russia than deaths'.[26] A sharp drop (six years for males) occurred in average life expectancy.[27]

The weakest groups were the most heavily hit. This emerges from dramatic testimony concerning not the elderly, but *besprizòrniki*, or abandoned babies. There were

> at least 200,000 in the whole country, according to experts. As many as in Russia in 1925, after the Civil War.... They are the primary victims of a country that is sacrificing everything to the God of money, which has abandoned the old scale of values without replacing it, which has set in train a process of degradation that is perhaps unstoppable. Ten years ago, in the totalitarian, Brezhnevite USSR *besprizòrniki* were practically non-existent. Orphanages were terrible places, often scandalous from a logistical point of view, and even more often bereft of human warmth. But they guaranteed a roof, a dining hall, a school and, later, a job. In ten years, everything has changed. The funds to maintain young internees and prisoners are ever fewer, and institutions that basically lived at state expense are now closing one after the other.

While the abandoned boys took to crime, 'for the girls there is only one profession: prostitution'.[28]

These were social relations that seemed to have disappeared from Europe long ago. And in 1992, a US author, who in his book's dedication celebrated the Western creators of 'the most productive economy the world has ever seen', had no hesitation in forecasting that some of the former socialist countries would end up swelling the ranks of the Third World.[29] In fact, something worse happened: in *Foreign Affairs*, we read that a country like Bulgaria is to be regarded as a 'mafia state'.[30]

There is no doubt that the turn of 1989 swept away the economic and social rights hitherto enjoyed by the population in Eastern Europe. In practice, they were travestied. One thinks, for example, of the 'right to rest and leisure' itemized (article 24) by the Universal Declaration of Human Rights, issued by the United Nations in 1948. In Russia, the 'new rich', who emerged with 'privatization', exhibited 'aggressive wealth' in tourist sites from which workers who had previously had a right to a free or semi-free holiday were now excluded.[31]

This extreme social polarization was the result of such an aggressive and unscrupulous class struggle by the new privileged that it recalls the 'primitive accumulation' discussed by *Capital* in connection with England after the Glorious Revolution: 'state lands ... were given away, sold at a ridiculous figure, or even annexed to private estates by direct seizure. All this happened without the slightest observation of legal etiquette'. From this derived the 'princely domains of the English oligarchy'[32]—or its Russian equivalent... With his theory of class struggle, Marx demonstrated his incisive contemporary relevance even as he was being written off as a dead dog.

3 EMANCIPATION AND DIS-EMANCIPATION

Obviously, we must not lose sight of the big picture. Notwithstanding major social achievements, what weighed negatively on Eastern Europe before 1989 was a problem of democracy, which was glaring and present at two levels. Having emerged victorious but devastated from the struggle against Hitler's aggression, the USSR had sought to strengthen its security by interposing a kind of Soviet Monroe between itself and potential enemies. But this was bound to create resentment in the countries that saw their sovereignty curtailed and democracy in international relations violated. The turn was unavoidable and its significance was clarified as follows by the Latvian ambassador to Oslo, in a letter to the *International Herald Tribune*. His country was determined to join NATO and the EU in order to reaffirm 'our European roots and Nordic cultural connections';[33] all links with Asia and barbarism must be severed for good. In other words, democracy in international relations posted a success in Eastern Europe, but in the context of an alteration of converse significance in the global picture. The West proclaimed its primacy, challenged the results of the anti-colonial revolutions, and exercised its sovereign right of military intervention throughout the world, in wars involving the participation of countries liberated from the Monroe Doctrine imposed on Eastern Europe by the USSR, but resolved to help impose an American and European Monro globally.

The picture is more complex when it comes to political and civil rights. A preliminary remark is indicated. In the USSR and Eastern Europe, improvements in the situation regarding these rights had begun well before 1989, and even before Gorbachev's arrival in power. It started with the end of the most acute phase of the Cold War, which had involved the resort to severely repressive measures by the West as well (McCarthyism in the USA, the banning of the Communist Party in West Germany, etc., not to mention the imposition, often promoted and blessed by Washington, of ferocious military dictatorships, especially in the Third World). The waning of the Cold War created a new, more favourable situation. But it would be absurd to give the credit for this exclusively to those who, bearing at least equal responsibility for the outbreak of the Cold War, had contributed (directly in the area controlled by them and indirectly in enemy territory) to the drastic restriction or abolition of political and civil rights. That said, there can be no doubt that for millions of people in Eastern Europe the turn of 1989–91 meant access to fundamental political rights previously denied them. However, it occurred at a time when the influence of money in elections became so strong that in the USA, it ended up 'limit[ing] politics to candidates who have money of their own or who take money from political action committees'—in the final analysis, lobbies.[34] In other words, as regards political rights, the process of emancipation in Eastern Europe formed part of a converse global process wherein, as a result of the triumph of the bourgeoisie internationally, traditional censitary discrimination, expelled by the front door, climbed back in through the rear window.

When it comes to civil rights too, still bearing in mind the general preliminary remark, the balance-sheet is positive. But it must be added that, in the wake of the upheavals in Eastern Europe, the trade union movement was weakened and the power of the bourgeoisie in workplaces strengthened in the West. And we cannot adequately assess the state of civil rights if we confine ourselves to the sphere of circulation and ignore production. Marx drew attention to this point, in a famous passage in *The Poverty of Philosophy*:

> While inside the modern workshop the division of labour is meticulously regulated by the authority of the employer, modern society has no other rule, no other authority for the distribution of labour than free competition. …It can even be laid down as a general rule that the less authority presides over the division of labour inside society, the more the division of labour develops inside the workshop, and the more it is subjected there to the authority of a single person. Thus authority in the workshop and authority in society, in relation to the division of labour, are in *inverse ratio* to each other.[35]

It might be said that under 'real socialism' an inversion of the dialectic of capitalist society, as described by Marx, sometimes occurred. Considerable anarchy in factory and workplace (with the disappearance of traditional, more or less pronounced employer despotism) was flanked by the terror exercised by the state over civil society. All this came to an end with the turn of 1989–91.

By contrast, China sought to put an end to anarchy in the workplace with 'market socialism' and the reforms introduced from 1980. But it was not a straightforward operation. As late as 1994, the journalist we have already cited referred to the difficulties in disposing of the legacy of the Maoist era when a dependent labourer could 'decide to do absolutely nothing', although continuing 'to receive his wage at the end of each month'. But here is how a respected Italian daily described the situation in Turin's motor industry in the same year:

> The employee approaches cautiously, careful not to draw attention to himself. He hesitates, then suddenly turns and says it all in one go.... After that he flees and mingles with the Fiat cadres and workers who, having set off from Corso Marconi, walk with him.... They are terrified of the future: 'How will I live without a job?' ... But they are also terrified of Fiat: 'I'm begging you, don't put down my name. The two colleagues that came out in the papers with their name and surname were destroyed by the company. They don't come to meetings any more. And then look there. That man in plain clothes is the superintendent of my gate at Mirafiori.[36]

In the West, what corresponded to the workplace anarchy of Maoist China was the dictatorship in the factory, but also projected beyond it.

Dis-emancipation was most marked in the area of the welfare state. Its dismantlement in the East also had consequences in the West and was sanctioned theoretically. Some decades earlier, Hayek had already waged a campaign to demonstrate that the 'freedom from want' proclaimed by Roosevelt, and the 'social and economic rights' promulgated by the UN, were the result of the influence—deemed ruinous by Hayek—of the 'Marxist Russian Revolution'.[37] In truth, for the patriarch of neo-liberalism it was a question of erasing the legacy not only of October 1917, but also of June 1848. It was necessary to sweep away '"social" or totalitarian democracy' for good, everywhere.[38] But this programme enjoyed definitive consecration in the years 1989–91, when neo-liberalism arrived in triumph in Moscow in its most radical version. On the eve of the Soviet Union's collapse, O.T. Bogomolov, well-known leader of the Russian 'reformist' economists, invoked the capitalist West, which he regarded as a model society and in fact identified with '*normal* society' as such, to express his contempt for those who persisted in speaking, for example, of the right to health or education: '[i]n a normal society, this sphere [the market] includes everything.... Among us, by contrast, health services and education are not *market* categories'. And, by way of reinforcement, another exponent of the new course argued: '[w]e need *normal* medicine based on [individual] insurance. Free medicine is a scam'.[39] To escape barbarism, and be admitted into the circle of genuinely civilized countries, internationally it was necessary to join NATO and take part in its neo-colonial wars, while domestically one had to proceed to abolition of the welfare state.

4 OLD ORDER AND NEW ORDER

The turning-point in Eastern Europe coincided with the bicentenary of the French Revolution. On the basis of this coincidence, it was easy to play the game of analogies, with the order overthrown in Eastern Europe becoming the 'old regime' or the 'old order'.[40] But are there any good grounds for this?

As is well known, in Russia the *ancien régime* (aristocratic and tsarist) was overthrown in February 1917. While the liberals and Mensheviks were still in power, a period of extreme violence and chaos commenced. Partial, fragile stability arrived only with the consolidation of the Bolshevik government. Obviously, we can express our horror at this historical and political cycle. Regardless of value judgements, however, it is the case that what felled the *ancien régime* (in the strict sense of the term) in Russia was the 1917 revolution. This revolution also helped eliminate the remnants of the *ancien régime* in the West, where censitary discrimination (in Britain itself the upper chamber was the preserve of the aristocracy and the haute bourgeoisie), and discrimination against women (who were excluded from political rights), persisted.

The innovations ensuing from the October Revolution, in particular, are even more apparent if we introduce colonial peoples and peoples of colonial origin into the picture. Relying on the reconstruction by an eminent historian, let us see how George V, having been crowned in London in 1910, took part the following year in the ceremony that raised him to the rank of emperor in India:

> Dressed in coronation robes, their trains held by richly vested pages of princely Indian blood, Their Imperial Majesties mounted the steps to an extravagantly elevated dais isolated in the center of the amphitheatre. Seated in two resplendent throne chairs surrounded by maces and emblems, they accepted the homage of their servants and subjects. Lord Hardinge, the

governor general, in his political uniform and the flowing robes of the Order of the Star of India, ascended to the raised platform in a bowing posture to kneel and kiss the king-emperor's hand. Once the members of the viceroy's council had made their reverence from the foot of the throne dais, it was the turn of the proud and striking but compliant ruling maharajas of India and their tribal chiefs of the frontier areas to make obeisance to their overlord.[41]

Britain's residual *ancien régime* was intimately bound up with the *ancien régime* maintained and nurtured in the colonies by the London government.

If such was the picture in the capitalist world's leading country in decline, let us glance at the picture in its leading country in the ascendant. In these years, the institution of slavery had disappeared from the USA, but the 'old lords in the South' or 'barons' referred to by Engels[42] continued to exercise power over the blacks. The latter were deprived not only of political rights, but also of civil rights. They were prey to a regime of terroristic white supremacy, which sometimes condemned them to lynching, slow torture and agony, providing a mass spectacle for a festive, jubilant crowd (of men, women, and children from the white community).

Such was the universe, challenged by the October Revolution. What collapsed between 1989 and 1991 was therefore, not the 'old regime' or 'old order'; overthrown were the inheritors or epigones of the revolutionary new regime or new order, which was never able to go beyond the stage of insecurity. A revolution may be regarded as stably victorious only when the class that is its protagonist, after having gone through a more or less protracted period of conflicts and contradictions, trial and error, succeeds in expressing the enduring political form of its rule. This is a learning process that extended from 1789 until 1871 in the case of the French bourgeoisie, which (as Gramsci correctly stressed) only discovered the political form of its rule thereafter, creating a parliamentary republic on the basis of universal (male) suffrage. That rule proves enduring in a modern society on condition that it can combine hegemony and coercion and can activate coercion and dictatorship only at times of acute crisis.

As a result of objective circumstances and subjective responsibilities, the revolution initiated in 1917 was incapable of yielding this outcome. In Russia, breaking the chains of the *ancien régime*, the new order achieved a massive diffusion of education and culture, and created extraordinary social mobility, laying the foundations for a civil society that became progressively more mature and exacting, to the point of being unable to identify with a fossilized order. In this sense, what occurred between 1989 and 1991 was the result at once of the success and the defeat of the communist project.

To understand this complex, paradoxical dialectic, we should bear in mind a famous page written by Hegel in Jena in the early nineteenth century. On the one hand, memories of Thermidor was still fresh; on the other, its political and historical implications had become ever clearer. Already consul for life, in 1804, Napoleon was on the point of becoming French emperor, in a substantial normalization of the French regime on the model of hostile countries and the very universe of the *ancien régime*. What attitude should be adopted towards this turn? It could either be condemned as a 'betrayal' of revolutionary ideals or celebrated as a liberation from the Jacobin Terror. If the latter, the period that began in 1789 (with the storming of the Bastille), or 1792 (with the Jacobins' assumption of power), could be branded as a manifestation of sanguinary madness. Hegel took a different route. On the one hand, he regarded the Jacobin terror as legitimate and necessary: '[i]n the French Revolution, a terrible force took hold of the state, and indeed everything. This force is not despotism, but *tyranny*, pure, terrifying dominance. But it is *necessary* and *just* to the extent to which it *constitutes* and *maintains* the state as a real individual entity'. On the other hand, the philosopher recognized the legitimacy and necessity of Thermidor as well. With the supersession of the state of emergency, 'tyranny' became 'superfluous' and had to make way for the 'dominance of laws'. Robespierre was oblivious of this and was overthrown: '[h]is power abandoned him, because *necessity had abandoned him*, and so he was violently overthrown'. The antagonists in this struggle became the embodiment of two different moments 'of necessity'.[43]

With this major theoretical precedent behind it, the bourgeoisie of the West (and Eastern Europe) could have extolled 1989 without demonizing the Bolshevik Revolution, and hence without transfiguring the world challenged by the latter. But this was too sophisticated an operation for the habitual binary logic, which remained precious and, in fact, indispensable for the purposes of delegitimizing the Chinese Revolution and anti-colonial revolutions. So starting from the depiction of 1989 as an *annus mirabilis* (Dahrendorf) or, ultimately, as the *plenitudo temporum* (Fukuyama), the dominant ideology proceeded to the liquidation not only of 1917, but of a much longer historical cycle. According to Dahrendorf, it was necessary to have done not only with Marx, whose teaching 'has come to grief in 1989, if not long before', but also Hegel and Rousseau. It was necessary to go back to Burke, drawing inspiration from the theoretician of the 'open society' and unbending enemy of the French Revolution.[44] Thus, having characterized the world that collapsed in Eastern Europe in 1989 as the 'old regime', Dahrendorf ends up casting himself as a follower of the champion of nothing less than the *ancien régime*.

5   THE IMPASSE OF THE NEW ORDER AND RESTORATION: 1660, 1814, 1989–91

It emerges from the general picture we have drawn that, although containing contradictory tendencies, the principal aspect of the political change which occurred in Eastern Europe and the world consisted in restoration. But does not employing this category mean legitimizing discredited regimes, whose fall was greeted with virtual unanimity in world public opinion? A kind of political blackmail has, it seems, paralyzed many of those who, though not identifying with the existing order, nevertheless refuse—and rightly so—to be branded as nostalgic for Brezhnev and the gulag. In fact, the historical process is more complex than the crude alternative implicit in this question and objection suggests. Think of the historical sequence initiated with the French Revolution. At the point when what any history textbook characterizes as the Restoration occurred, it seemed difficult to question the failure of the project or hopes of 1789, which was followed by the Terror, the unbridled corruption of the post-Thermidor years, military dictatorship and then empire, with an emperor-warlord who conquered vast territories and distributed them to relatives and friends, in accordance with a patrimonial conception of the state that not only contravened any principle of democracy, but also seemed to reproduce worst aspects of the *ancien régime*. There is more. In overthrowing absolutism and feudalism, the French revolutionaries insisted that they aimed to eradicate war so as to establish perpetual peace. Instead, in Engels' words, with 'Napoleonic despotism', 'the promised eternal peace was turned into an endless war of conquest'.[45] In 1814, then, the plans and hopes of 1789 were completely unrecognizable. At the end of the initial phase of a major historical crisis, the return of the Bourbons installed a regime that was unquestionably more liberal than the Terror, the military dictatorship and the bellicose, expansionist empire that had succeeded revolutionary enthusiasms. Similar remarks could be made, for example, of the first English revolution, which issued in Cromwell's military dictatorship, bound up with the exceptional character of its founder and incapable of surviving his disappearance.

Despite all this, it is correct to apply the category of restoration to the return of the Bourbons or Stuarts, who sought to smother the novelties that were emerging laboriously from trial and error, blind alleys, contradictions, regressions, and deformations of every kind. There is no reason to proceed differently in the case of the changes in Eastern Europe, notwithstanding the pitiless interpretation we can and must give of the history of the regimes that collapsed between 1989 and 1991. Use of the category of restoration is all the more convincing if we bear in mind the fact that in the capitalist West itself the crisis, and then collapse, of 'real socialism' paved the way for the deletion of economic and social rights from the catalogue of rights.

We reach the same conclusion if we focus on the international context. The planet was a kind of private property owned by a handful of capitalist great powers on the eve of the October Revolution, which instigated a massive wave of anti-colonial revolutions. Here too, however, the eclipse of the *ancien régime* ended up being followed by a situation of deadlock. In fact, the national question played a decisive role in the dissolution of the 'socialist camp' and the country created by the October Revolution. Its protagonists were convinced that national conflicts, tensions and even identities would disappear along with capitalism. But let us glance at the gravest moments of the crisis and discrediting of the 'socialist camp': in 1948, the split between the Soviet Union and Yugoslavia; in 1956, the invasion of Hungary; in 1968, the invasion of Czechoslovakia; and in 1969, bloody incidents on the Sino-Soviet border. Barely evident then, war between countries claiming to be socialist became a tragic reality a decade later, with the trial of strength between Vietnam and Cambodia and then China and Vietnam. In 1981, martial law in Poland to prevent a possible 'fraternal' intervention by the USSR and to check an opposition movement that had gained a large following by appealing to a national identity trampled over by Big Brother. Albeit very different, what these crises have in common is the centrality of the national question. Not by chance, the dissolution of the socialist camp began on the periphery of the 'empire', in countries long restive at the limited sovereignty imposed on them. Within the USSR too, even before the obscure 'coup' of August 1991, the decisive spur to the final collapse came from the agitation of the Baltic countries, where socialism had been 'exported' in 1939–40. In a sense, the national question, which facilitated the victory of the October

Revolution, also sealed the end of the historical cycle initiated with it. And in this instance too, the element of restoration is obvious, as is confirmed by the occasionally explicit rehabilitation of colonialism (and even imperialism).

We may venture a comparison with the other great revolutions that have punctuated modern and contemporary history. In England, following Cromwell's death and the ephemeral succession of his son Richard to the post of Lord Protector of the Republic, the commander of the Scottish army George Monk marched on London and a new Convention Parliament was summoned, which sanctioned the return of the Stuarts. In 1814, Napoleon, back from the disastrous venture in Russia and defeat at Leipzig, and confronted by a formidable enemy coalition and the growing disaffection of the French people, was forced to abdicate and accept the return of the Bourbons. Between 1989 and 1991, the dissolution of the USSR and the order derived from the October Revolution occurred. Granted the radical differences between the three revolutions, the crises in which they resulted share some common features. Firstly, having exhausted their hegemonic phases, all three had to face serious international political problems (respectively, Irish and Scottish insurrections and national rebellions that undermined first the *Grande nation* and then the doctrine and/or practice of limited sovereignty). Secondly, domestically, they had to confront opposition both from supporters of the overthrown *ancien régime* and from the growing number of people disillusioned and disappointed with the new regime, who withdrew in disgust from political life and engagementor, worse, proclaimed that the original plans and ideals had been abandoned and betrayed. The upshot was the impossibility of stabilizing the new order, which ended up lacking a principle of legitimation and being, as it were, suspended in a vacuum. Thirdly, and finally, the impasse in the search for stabilization, and a principle of legitimation that could ground it, issued in a reversion (albeit only partial) to the *ancien régime*. To a certain extent, moreover, this reversion was promoted or, at any rate, accepted by a more or less significant fraction of the ruling group hailing from the revolution. One thinks of the role played by Monk and the Parliament summoned in England in 1660, by the conservative Senate, minister Talleyrand and Marshall Marmont in France in 1814, and by Gorbachev and Yeltsin in the Soviet Union in 1989–91.

In all three cases, the impasse of the new order made the return of the old dominant classes to power possible.

Notes

1. Francis Fukuyama, 'The End of History?', *The National Interest*, Summer 1989, p. 3.
2. Karl Popper, 'Kriege führen für den Frieden', interview in *Der Spiegel*, 23 March 1992, p. 208 'Io, il Papa e Gorbaciov', interview in *La Stampa*, 9 April 1992, p. 217.
3. Paul Johnson, 'Colonialism's Back—and Not a Moment Too Soon!', *New York Times Magazine*, 18 April 1993, pp. 22, 43–4.
4. Niall Ferguson, *Colossus: The Rise and Fall of the American Empire*, London: Penguin, 2005, p. 27.
5. Kevin Buckley, *Panama: The Whole Story*, New York: Simon & Schuster, 1991, pp. 240, 264.
6. Eugenio Scalfari, 'Al pettine i nodi di Reagan e Thatcher', *La Repubblica*, 26–27 January 1992.
7. Giorgio Bocca, 'Dimenticare Hitler…', *La Repubblica*, 6 February 1992.
8. Ennio Caretto, '"A Mosca chiederò la testa di Castro". Bush annuncia sue richieste per aiutare le riforme in URSS', *La Repubblica*, 19 July 1991.
9. R.D. Kaplan, 'A NATO Victory Can Bridge Europe's Growing Divide', *International Herald Tribune*, 8 April 1999.
10. Sebastian Mallaby, 'The Reluctant Imperialist', *Foreign Affairs*, March–April 2002.
11. See Ferguson, *Colossus*, pp. 4–6.
12. See Domenico Losurdo, *Il linguaggio dell'Impero. Lessico dell'ideologia americana*, Rome and Bari: Laterza, 2007, Chapter 1, §5.
13. Caretto, 'L'ONU vuol punire la Libia', *La Repubblica*, 29–30 March 1992.
14. Ferguson, *Colossus*, p. 34.
15. Barry Buzan, 'The New Pattern of Global Security in the Twenty-first Century', *International Affairs*, no. 6, July 1991, p. 451.
16. Giovanni Arrighi, *The Long Twentieth Century: Money, Power, and the Origins of Our Times*, London and New York: Verso, 1994, p. 20.
17. A.L. Friedberg, 'Menace: Here Be Dragons—Is China a Military Threat?', *The National Interest*, September–October 2009, pp. 20–1.
18. Gilford John Ikenberry, 'America's Imperial Ambition', *Foreign Affairs*, September–October 2002, p. 44.
19. Carlo Jean, '"Guerre giuste" e "guerre ingiuste", ovvero i rischi del moralismo', *Limes. Rivista italiana di geopolitica*, no. 3, June–August 1993, p. 264.
20. Aleksandr Zinoviev, *La caduta dell' "impero del male". Saggio sulla tragedia della Russia*, Turin: Bollati Boringhieri, 1994, p. 11.
21. Quoted in Giuseppe Boffa, *L'ultima illusion. L'Occidente e la vittoria sul comunismo*, Rome and Bari: Laterza, 1997, p. 71.
22. See Maurice Duverger, 'Mafia e inflazione uccidono la Russia', *Corriere della Sera*, 18 October 1993.

23. Enrico Franceschini, 'Emergenza in Russia. Un milione alla fame, Eltsin corre ai ripari', *La Repubblica*, 17 October 1991.
24. Andrea Bonanni, 'Si apre la sfida al Congresso. Eltsin è pronto a ricorrere alle urne per contrastare l'opposizione', *Corriere della Sera*, 1 December 1992.
25. Cesare Martinetti, 'Il Parlamento riabilita il vecchio rublo', *La Stampa*, 29 July 1993.
26. Fiammetta Cucurnia, 'Mosca, tra furti e racket dilaga la baby-delinquenza', *La Repubblica*, 5 May 1993.
27. See Andrea Goldstein, *BRIC. Brasile, Russia, India, Cina alla guida dell'economia globale*, Bologna: Il Mulino, 2011, p. 25.
28. Cucurnia, 'Mosca, tra furti e racket dilaga la baby-delinquenza'.
29. Lester Thurow, *Head to Head: The Coming Economic Battle among Japan, Europe and America*, New York: Morrow, 1992, pp. 14–15.
30. Moisés Naím, 'Mafia States: Organized Crime Takes Office', *Foreign Affairs*, May–June 2012, p. 104.
31. Enrico Franceschini, 'Mafia e donne in topless sulle rive del mar Nero', *La Repubblica*, 18–19 August, 1991.
32. Karl Marx and Frederick Engels, *Collected Works*, London: Lawrence & Wishart, 1975–2004, Vol. 35, p. 714.
33. Valdis Krastins, 'Latvia's Past and Present', *International Herald Tribune*, 7 April, 2000.
34. Arthur Schlesinger, Jr., *The Cycles of American History*, Boston and New York: Houghton Mifflin, 1986, p. 270.
35. Marx and Engels, *Collected Works*, Vol. 6, pp. 184–5.
36. Ricardo De Gennaro, 'Paura a Torino E gli impiegati vanno in corteo', *La Repubblica*, 16 January 1994.
37. F.A. von Hayek, *Law, Legislation and Liberty*, Abingdon: Routledge, 2013, p. 264.
38. F.A. von Hayek, *The Constitution of Liberty*, ed. Ronald Hamowy, Chicago and London: University of Chicago Press, 2011, p. 109.
39. Quoted in A. Berelowitch, 'L'Occidente, o l'utopia di un mondo normale', *Europa/Europe*, no. 1, 1993.
40. Ralf Dahrendorf, *Reflections on the Revolution in Europe*, New Brunswick, NJ: Transaction, 2005, p. 10; Tony Judt, *Postwar: A History of Europe since 1945*, London: Penguin, 2005, p. 585ff.
41. Arno Mayer, *The Persistence of the Old Regime: Europe to the Great War*, London and New York: Verso, 2010, p. 139.
42. Marx and Engels, *Collected Works*, Vol. 42, p. 167.
43. G.W.F. Hegel, *Jenaer Realphilosophie*, ed. Johannes Hoffmeister, Hamburg: Meiner, 1969, pp. 246–8.
44. Ralf Dahrendorf, *Reflections on the Revolution in Europe*, London: Chatto & Windus, 1990, pp. 5, 25, 70, 26.
45. Marx and Engels, *Collected Works*, Vol. 25, p. 244.

CHAPTER 12

Class Struggle between Exorcism and Fragmentation

1 ARENDT AND THE 'INCUBUS' OF CLASS STRUGGLE

If the 'end of history' was lacking incredibility, or even sense, when it was proclaimed, more ambitious attempts to exorcize class struggle are in crisis today. We may start with a thinker of undoubted intellectual courage. The years are the 1960s and 1970s. Widespread agitation by workers in the capitalist metropolis coincided with the revolution of colonial peoples, both determined to challenge 'exploitation' and wage the 'class struggle' which (according to Marx) developed—and justifiably so— against 'exploitation'. In these circumstances, which challenged the reigning social and political order globally, Hannah Arendt had no hesitation in radically de-legitimizing both categories and the movements inspired by them. 'Exploitation'? 'The value of this hypothesis for the historical sciences is small indeed'. If it had 'survived more than a century of historical research', it was certainly not because of its 'scientific content'. Class struggle? Marx's grave mistake consisted in having persuaded the masses that 'poverty ... is a political, not a natural phenomenon'; in having identified the alleged victims of exploitation as the agents of a major emancipatory process, when it should be plain to all that 'the condition of misery ... by definition can never produce "free-minded people" because it is the condition of being bound to necessity'.[1] 'The emancipation of the working class must be the work of the working class itself', accomplished in and through class struggle: thus argued Marx and the International Working Men's Association. Arendt's answer was clear: 'it was never the oppressed and degraded themselves who led the way, but those who were not oppressed and not degraded and could not bear it that others were'.[2] Emancipating themselves through class struggle, the exploited are supposed to achieve an outcome that is positive for society as a whole. Once again, Arendt is sharply opposed to Marx: 'the rarity of slave rebellion and of uprisings among the disinherited and downtrodden is notorious'; as and when they did occur, they were 'nightmares for everybody'.[3] The great black slave revolution led by Toussaint L'Ouverture, which set off a chain reaction of abolitions of slavery, is ignored.

Arendt's radicalism is unquestionable. With her attempt to delegitimize the category of 'exploitation', she unwittingly comes into contradiction with a long intellectual tradition. In Marx, 'exploitation' is synonymous with the appropriation of 'surplus-value' by the class that has ownership of the means of production. Well, in *The Spirit of the Laws*, Montesquieu identifies the source of the luxury enjoyed by the upper classes in 'the work of others' (*travail d'autrui*).[4] This was a far from isolated instance. In the great critic of the French Revolution, Hippolyte Taine, we find this striking summary of the *ancien régime*: at work in it was a 'class, bound to the land, which suffered hunger for sixty generations to feed other classes', the upper classes.[5] As we know, the category of 'surplus-value' is also present in authors like Calhoun and Nietzsche, the second of whom had no difficulty acknowledging the reality and (to his mind) the necessity of 'exploitation' (see Chap. 3, Sect. 3).

Concerned as she is to expel the spectre of any suspicion of 'exploitation' from a sociopolitical system that seemed, at the time, to be in difficulties even on the American continent, Arendt does not really measure up to Marx. To demonstrate that 'surplus-labour' and 'exploitation' can also be immediately empirically self-evident, he cited the *corvée*. After having worked his own land, the peasant was compelled to perform labour on the feudal lord's land. In this instance, the spatial distance between the plots of land indicates the difference between 'necessary labour' and 'surplus-labour'.[6] Forced labour in the colonies would afford another example of the immediate empirical self-evidence of the reality of surplus-labour (performed by natives in the service of their colonial masters, not feudal lords). In addition, the fact that Britain, a state 'ruled by capitalists and landowners', felt the need to set legal limits to the working day, so as to save 'the living force of the nation' (manifestly threatened by the unrestrained drive for surplus-labour and surplus-value, and hence, unbounded exploitation), should give us pause for thought.[7]

Arendt pursues a very different line of argument. There was something lethal about Marx's interpretation of 'the compelling needs of mass poverty in political terms', and 'transformation of the social question into a political force' in his theory of exploitation and class struggles. In reality, 'it is only the rise of technology, and not the rise of political ideas as such, which has refuted the old and terrible truth that only violence and rule over others could make some men free'.[8]

Until the 'rise of technology' at any rate, responsibility for mass poverty is to be laid exclusively at the door of Mother Nature. This thesis ignores the fact that, in the recurrent crises of over-production which invest capitalism, 'a great part not only of the existing products, but also of the previously created productive forces, are periodically destroyed'.[9] This thesis is more relevant than ever in the light of the crisis that erupted in 2008; it was already contained in a text (the *Communist Manifesto*) published 160 years earlier. In other words, we are dealing with a social system that involves not only unjust relations of distribution, but also recurrent destruction of social wealth. And the development of technology is powerless in the face of such destruction.

In any event, if technology is the solution to the social problem, how are we to explain the fact that when Arendt formulated her thesis, according to a journal with impeccable credentials, in Washington (in the world's most technologically advanced country), '70 per cent of patients in the paediatric hospital suffer from malnutrition' (see Introduction). In this instance, at any rate, the reality of 'exploitation', and the necessary and positive character of class struggle, should be recognized. But that is not what Arendt argues. She never frees herself from the 'incubus' of class struggle and assigns technology a positive, decisive role independently of politics and political action. It is here that the contrast with Marx is sharpest.

Marx insisted even more forcefully on the prodigious emancipatory potential of the progress of technology, the 'objectified power of knowledge'. But such an outcome was far from taken for granted. As long as 'science' continued to be 'presse[d] ... into the service of capital',[10] technological development was not synonymous with social wealth. *Capital*, a 'critique of political economy' (as indicated by its sub-title), is also a critique of the one-sided, miraculous view of technological development held by bourgeois political economists (and accepted and radicalized by Arendt). History demonstrates that in the context of capitalist society, technology can have disastrous consequences for the subaltern classes: 'the rise of the English woollen factories, together with the gradual conversion of arable land into sheep pasture, brought about the superfluity of agricultural labourers that led to their being driven in masses into the towns'.[11] This was the tragic moment when, in Thomas More's words taken up by Marx, thanks to the mechanical processing of wool, 'the sheep eat the men' (see Chap. 4, Sect. 3). More than two centuries later, during the Industrial Revolution, 'insofar as machinery dispenses with muscular power', we have the introduction of the 'labour of women and children'.[12]

Two examples adduced by *Capital* are especially striking. Let us see what happened in the USA in the late eighteenth century, following the introduction of the cotton gin: '[p]rior to this invention, a day of a Negro's most intensive labour barely sufficed to separate a pound of cotton fibre from the cotton seed. After the invention of the cotton gin, an old Negro woman could comfortably supply a fifty pounds of cotton daily, and gradual improvements have subsequently doubled the efficiency of the machine'.[13] The emancipatory potential of this technological development is obvious. But what actually happened?

> The rapid strides of cotton spinning not only pushed on with tropical luxuriance the growth of cotton in the United States, and with it the African slave trade, but also made the breeding of slaves the chief business of the border slave-states. When, in 1790, the first census of slaves was taken in the United States, their number was 697,000; in 1861 it had nearly reached four millions.[14]

Far from abolishing or reducing the work of slaves, technology, which greatly facilitated cotton ginning, increased it terribly. This state of affairs was challenged by class struggle and the abolitionist revolution, in the particular forms they took during the American Civil War.

Given the relations of exploitation extant at home and abroad, technological progress could represent a disaster not only for the working class in a particular country, but also for entire populations:

> History discloses no tragedy more horrible than the gradual extinction of the English hand-loom wavers, an extinction that was spread over several decades ... On the other hand, English cotton machinery produced an acute effect in India. The Governor General reported in 1834–35: 'The misery hardly finds a parallel in the history of commerce. The bones of the cotton-weavers are bleaching the plains of India'.[15]

Once again, such processes are countered by class struggle. Arendt counter-poses the material reality of technological progress to class struggle and its ruinous results. However, stresses *The Poverty of Philosophy*, technological development is itself strongly influenced by the class struggle: '[i]n England, strikes have regularly given rise to the invention and application of new machines. ... If combinations and strikes had no other effect than that of making the efforts of mechanical genius react against them, they would still exercise an immense influence on the development of industry'. Indeed, '[a]fter each new strike of any importance, there appeared a new machine'.[16] *Capital* further clarifies this dialectic of strikes by workers and reactions by owners. In Britain, class struggle in the factories imposed the legal limitation of the working day, with a consequent reduction in absolute surplus-value, which depends on the length of the working day: 'capital threw itself with all its might into the production of relative surplus value, by hastening on the further improvement of machinery' and increasing the pace of work.[17]

The approach recommended by Arendt risks being devastating intellectually and ethically: it becomes impossible to appreciate the motives of the victims of technological progress (and, in fact, of the capitalist system). Supporters of Luddism, who set fire to modern factories and smashed the machines whose introduction caused unemployment and poverty, appear plain mad, even criminal. In reality, the latter also protested for another reason, already highlighted by 'utopian' socialism. Here is what Robert Owen, as reported by Marx, had to say: '[s]ince the general introduction of inanimate mechanism into British manufactories, man, with few exceptions, has been treated as a secondary and inferior machine, and far more attention has been given to perfect the raw materials of wood and metals than those of body and mind'.[18] *The Poverty of Philosophy* graphically describes the consequences of the 'introduction of machinery' and the related simplification and parcellization of work: 'capital has been concentrated, the human being has been further dismembered'.[19] The *Communist Manifesto* seeks to understand the reasons for Luddism and to direct the anger of its supporters at the real target ('bourgeois relations of production'), rather than machinery *per se*, thereby bringing maturity to a class struggle which, in its spontaneity, risks being blind.[20]

While Luddism was to be rejected, it was necessary (observed *Capital*) to criticize the 'optimism' beloved of a bourgeois political economy (and Arendt). A distinction must be drawn between machines, which are potentially capable of reducing the hardship of work, and 'the capitalist use of machinery', which can afflict workers as 'a most frightful scourge', increasing 'the sufferings of the workmen displaced by machinery' or, when not made redundant, further 'crippled by the division of labour'.[21]

Above all, we must reflect on one aspect of Marx's analysis. As becomes particularly clear during recurrent 'commercial crises', the 'increased speed of machinery', and its 'unceasing improvement', bring about an 'increase of the work exacted in a given time' and 'make the wages of the workers ever fluctuating' and 'their livelihood more and more precarious'.[22] This brings us to the immediate present. Prodigious technological development is far from performing the miracles attributed to it. Quite the reverse: it may very well occur in tandem with increasing job insecurity and casualization, with a reduction in living standards and the re-emergence of the figure of the working poor, with an intensification in the polarization between wealth and poverty, with the concentration of economic and political power in the hands of a shameless oligarchy. If it makes it impossible to pay the victims of the past their due, recommendation of technology as the only solution to the social problem sounds like a joke to today's victims.

Two further considerations. Let us note the date of the text in which Arendt positively opposes technology to political and social struggle, to class struggle. It is 1963. About twenty years later, on the night of 2–3 December 1984, possibly the most appalling ecological disaster in human history (with thousands of deaths) occurred. Its protagonist was Union Carbide, an agricultural fertilizer and insecticide transnational that was highly advanced technologically, and whose headquarters were in the USA. But the tragedy unfolded in Bhopal, in India. In the light of the ecological question (which is clearly bound up with the social question nationally and internationally), the distinction between machines and 'capitalist use' of them is more imperative than ever.

Finally, at an international level technological development, and the related Revolution in Military Affairs (RMA), reinforces the USA's and the West's temptation to apply the law of the strongest at the expense of countries incapable of putting up real resistance to overwhelming military power. The only thing that can counter all this is political struggle, class struggle. It is striking to see Arendt, passionate theoretician of Aristotelian praxis and inter-subjective action, call for praxis and action to step aside at key moments, so that technology can unfold its beneficent effects in tranquillity!

2 THE REPRESSION OF CONFLICT IN HABERMAS

Unlike Arendt, at least until the mid-1970s, Jürgen Habermas continued to employ the concepts of 'exploitation', 'class society' and class 'struggle', although stressing the need to differentiate between different evolutionary circumstances.[23] About a decade later, he stated his conviction that, following the advent of the welfare state and the ensuing 'pacification' in the West, everything had changed by comparison with Marx's time. Unlike in Arendt, the class struggle was not ruinous; it had quite simply become obsolete and superfluous. Where Arendt had been disquieted by the 'incubus' of the class struggle, in Habermas' view, people could sleep soundly (at least in the West).

It might be said that the German philosopher was rather unfortunate. He formulated his reassuring thesis in the years when Dahrendorf drew attention to the figure of the working poor, who staged an ominous return even in the most developed capitalist countries while the financial aristocracy enriched itself yet further. In the USA, the prisons were increasingly crowded with the poor, old and new, on account of ever more inflexible laws (on minor crimes committed by members of the subaltern classes). In 1991, in France, a caustic observer proceeded to a comparison between the North American republic and the South African republic, which at the time was still segregationist and dominated by the white minority. In the space of a decade, 'the American prison population doubled to reach an overall proportion of 0.426 per cent (beating the previous world record-holder, South Africa's 0.333 per cent, by nearly a third). Our language as yet lacks a word for this kind of "Gulag" and the question resurfaces: What on earth is happening to America?'[24]

Subsequent historical and political developments were inclement to Habermas' thesis. He demonstrated the occurrence of 'pacification' by reference to the welfare state, whose construction (in Europe) proceeded 'under social-democratic or conservative governments'. But today it is obvious to everyone that it is being dismantled 'under conservative or social-democratic governments'! There is more. In the prestigious weekly (*Die Zeit*) to which the German philosopher has frequently confided his reflections, we find this explanation of the advent (or return) of a liberal 'social Darwinism': '[r]etrospectively, it might be said that the eclipse of socialism disinhibited capitalism and led its ideologues from fine words to the rhetoric of rigour. The competition between systems has disappeared, and capitalism has concluded that it need no longer be concerned with its acceptability'.[25] We may pass over the indirect tribute to the defunct socialism of Eastern Europe. Let us focus on the theoretical aspect. A product of class struggle (waged by popular masses emboldened by the challenge represented by socialism), the welfare state prompted a reaction from the privileged classes—a new and different class struggle which, in the decidedly propitious global conditions for the big capitalist and financial bourgeoisie created after 1989, is inflicting fatal blows on welfare. What, in Habermas' view, is an elementary fact refuting the theory of class struggle proves to be the unstable outcome of a process witnessing bitter class struggles, which are wrongly ignored and repressed.

Further examples of this singular way of proceeding can be adduced. In an essay from the 1970s, Habermas noted that the world over, 'only 17 states possess a balance sheet greater than that of General Motors'.[26] This is a datum that prompts a variety of reflections. How to explain the enormous gap between the developed capitalist countries of the West (those to which the major transnationals primarily pertain) and the countries of the Third World (with a colonial past behind them)? Is the gap referred to here, which has been called the 'great divergence', a natural, eternal datum? Or is it the result of historical processes and conflicts that need to be examined and clarified? And what new conflicts are sparked by this 'great divergence', with the possibility it affords the most opulent transnationals and the wealthiest, most powerful countries to restrict and even neutralize the independence of the most backward, weakest countries (via economic pressure or direct military force)? And are the latter resigned to their fate or are they struggling to achieve both economic development and genuine political independence? There is no trace of any of this in Habermas, who draws a single, unequivocal conclusion from the datum he reports: the gradual erosion of state sovereignty and the emergence of a post-national constellation. Thus, once again, the conflicts inherent in a determinate sociopolitical situation vanish. The proclamation of the advent of the post-national constellation is the obverse (the international one) of the putative 'pacification'.

Drawing attention to the 'pacification' in Western Europe, Habermas believed he was refuting Marx's theory of class struggle. But let us glance at the climate prevailing at the time of the foundation of the International Working Men's Association in 1864. In his *Inaugural Address*, Marx drew a bleak picture:

The discoveries of new goldlands [in the USA] led to an immense exodus, leaving an irreparable void in the ranks of the British proletariat. Others of its formerly active members were caught by the temporary bribe of greater work and wages, and turned into 'political blacks'. All the efforts made at keeping up, or remodelling, the Chartist Movement, failed signally; the press organs of the working class died one by one of the apathy of the masses, and, in point of fact, never before seemed the English working class so thoroughly reconciled to a state of political nullity.[27]

Engels wrote in similar terms in a letter sent to Marx the previous year, bemoaning the disappearance of 'revolutionary energy' in a proletariat now reconciled with the 'bourgeoisie' (see Chap. 6, Sect. 5). What the two revolutionary philosophers denounced as the 'political nullity' of the working class, and as capitulation to the dominant class, is celebrated by Habermas as 'pacification'. The reversal of the value judgement is patent, but the most important difference lies elsewhere. Marx and Engels did not repress the conflicts that proceeded and succeeded the so-called 'pacification'. What explains it, and the discouragement of the English proletariat, which ended up accepting its 'political nullity', is the 'defeat of the continental working classes', the 'iron hand of force' they were subjected to as a result of the failure of the 1848 revolution, compelling the vanguard elements, 'the most advanced sons of labour', to seek refuge across the Atlantic.[28] And, naturally, we must bear in mind the colonial expansion that muffled social conflict in the metropolis, in fact accentuating national (and social) conflict in the colonies, as demonstrated by the Sepoys' rebellion in India some years before the foundation of the First International.

Habermas proceeds very differently. He dates the start of the 'pacification' from 1945. One of the greatest class struggles in world history was scarcely over. The Third Reich's attempt to revive the colonial tradition, and radicalize it to the point of imposing a new form of slavery on Slavs in Eastern Europe, had suffered a resounding defeat. On the other side, the prestige and influence of the Soviet Union and international communist movement were at their height. In these conditions, anti-colonial revolutions exploded in the East and South of the globe; in Western Europe (but not the USA, where the labour movement has always played a lesser role), the struggle for a welfare state posted important successes. These processes were inter-connected, as is confirmed by the support extended to the national liberation movements by the movements engaged in Western

Europe in building the welfare state. It is very difficult to describe all this as the onset of the disappearance of class struggle!

Although lacking a genuine social state, and despite the explosion of the economic crisis, the USA is experiencing the phenomenon of 'pacification' today. Rather than blaming the dominant class, workers suffering from unemployment or job insecurity tend to blame the unfair competition of which China and other emerging or Third World countries are supposedly guilty. 'Pacification' is thus ensured, but in this instance as well it is far from being a new phenomenon! We have seen Engels observe that in Britain, the mass of 'genuine working men' tended to target, not their own bourgeoisie, but competitors in international markets, whom they accused of unfair competition and contraventions of fair trade, and against whom they called for protectionism (see Chap. 7, Sect. 1). Some decades later, Oswald Spengler called on German and Western workers to consider 'class struggle' at an end because 'race struggle' had supervened. According to the German theoretician troubled by the 'decline of the West', the Soviet Union, imposing starvation wages on its workers and keeping the price of its goods artificially low, threatened 'the existence of the white working class'.[29] Here too 'pacification' within the West and the white race was a function of a remorseless 'race struggle' that aimed to preserve an international division of labour favouring the colonial and imperial powers, which thus in reality represented a class struggle of a conservative or reactionary stamp. In our day, fair trade is the slogan advanced by Washington and often echoed by American workers, who are wholly 'pacified' within the USA, but extremely pugnacious towards China primarily, invoking trade war against it. But is it legitimate to separate 'pacification' from conflict, or are they two sides of the same coin? The *Communist Manifesto* stresses that the acquisition of class consciousness by the proletariat is impeded by 'competition' within it, which the bourgeoisie has an interest in stoking.

3 A Change of Paradigm?

Today, notwithstanding Arendt's warning and Habermas' reassurance, the theory of class struggle once again enjoys a large and sometimes sympathetic audience. But what are its objectives? And what are we to make of Fraser's thesis that, since the 'death of communism' at any rate, emancipatory movements have made their objective not the redistribution of resources, but recognition (see Chap. 4, Sect. 1)? In reality, we have seen that on three fronts (the emancipation of the working class, oppressed nations, and women), Marxian class struggle rejected any such distinction.

The moment of the struggle for recognition is never absent. This applies even to the denunciation of the militarism for which the socialist movement criticized the capitalist (and imperialist) system. Gramsci's line of argument is significant. The country is Italy, dragged by its rulers into the First World War over the opposition of broad masses of Catholic or socialist persuasion—and this, at a time when the enormous price to be paid in human lives was apparent. We can now understand Gramsci's conclusion. Invariably treated as a childlike multitude, and hence, incapable of political intentions and volition, the popular masses were calmly sacrificed by the dominant class on the altar of its imperialist projects. Hence, the struggle for recognition was more than ever on the agenda: it was necessary to act so that the 'labouring population' did not remain 'prey to everyone', mere 'human material' at the disposal of the elite, 'raw material for the history of the privileged classes'.[30] Communist engagement must avoid any repetition of the enormous tragedy played out between 1914 and 1918.

In the wake of the October Revolution emerged the global struggle for recognition represented by the anti-colonial revolution. Do we want to focus on the 30 years from the end of the Second World War to the mid-1970s—the three decades that witnessed the expansion of the welfare state, which have been construed as the epoch *par excellence* of the struggle for redistribution? But a mere glance beyond the West indicates that this was when some of the most memorable struggles for recognition in world history occurred.

In 1949, Mao Zedong solemnized the conquest of power, proclaiming: '[o]urs will no longer be a nation subject to insult and humiliation. We have stood up. ... The era in which the Chinese were regarded as uncivilized is now ended'.[31] The Chinese Revolution was consummated even as the Algerian Revolution was beginning. Frantz Fanon observed of it: 'the colonized ... took up arms not only because they were dying of hunger and witnessing the disintegration of their society, but also because the colonist treated them like animals'. To free themselves from their 'inferiority complex', the colonized embarked on a struggle that 'rehabilitate[d]' them in their own eyes.[32] The date is 1961. The Vietnamese Revolution was entering its hardest phase; not long after defeating France, it was at grips with the world's greatest power. The leader and artisan of this liberation struggle remained Ho Chi Minh, who in 1960, on the occasion of his 70th birthday, recalled his intellectual and political path: '[i]nitially it was patriotism, not Communism, which had prompted me to believe in Lenin and the Third International'. What primarily attracted him were the appeals and documents supporting and promoting the liberation struggle of colonial peoples, asserting their right to constitute themselves as independent nation-states: 'Lenin's theses [on the national and colonial question] roused me to great emotion, great enthusiasm, great faith, and helped me to see the problems clearly. My joy was so great that at times I was reduced to tears'.[33]

There is no doubt that we are dealing with three epic national liberation struggles, which at the same time were conscious of being three epic struggles for recognition. All this certainly occurred outside the West, but it is not unconnected with it. The anti-colonial revolution exercised influence even inside the USA, impelling African Americans into a struggle against segregation, discrimination, and the persistence of the regime of white supremacy. Secondly, in a country like France, oppressed, rebellious colonial peoples made their presence—including their physical presence—felt on the territory of the colonial power that oppressed and humiliated them in the metropolitan territory itself. In the North American republic, as Palmiro Togliatti observed in 1948, along with blacks, racial discrimination also affected 'other peoples, including Italians, regarded as an inferior species'.[34] In any event, having for decades carried the banner of the struggle for recognition, in order to further their emancipation, the subaltern classes of the capitalist metropolis could scarcely remain deaf to the demand for recognition advanced by peoples in colonial conditions or of colonial origin. In 1954, debating with Norberto Bobbio, Togliatti counter-posed the universalistic charge of the communist movement to the persistent exclusion clauses of the bourgeois universe: '[w]hen, and how far, have the liberal principles on which the nineteenth-century British state claimed to be based—the model, I think, of a perfect liberal regime for those who argue like Bobbio—been applied to colonial peoples?'. The truth was that 'liberal doctrine ... is based on barbaric discrimination between human creatures'.[35]

Nor is the paradigm of the struggle for recognition operative only when it is a question of expressing solidarity with colonial peoples or peoples of colonial origin. It is interesting to see how in 1940 the Labour Minister Ernest Bevin, a leader of the Labour Party with long experience as a trade unionist, justified the need for the construction of a welfare state in Britain: 'there will have to be a great recasting of values. The conception that those who produce or manipulate are inferior and must accept a lower status than the speculator must go'.[36] The welfare state was not demanded solely in the name of redistribution!

Persistent adherence (direct or indirect) to the paradigm of the struggle for recognition facilitates support for the women's liberation movement and construal of it precisely as a struggle for recognition. The following significant statement by a communist leader enjoying great international prestige was made at the start of the 1945–75 period: 'the emancipation of women should be one of the central problems of the renovation of the Italian state and Italian society'; 'legislation sanctioning the inferiority of women' should be repealed. The 'rights of man' were insufficient; it was necessary to go further and have 'the ability and the courage to arrive at the proclamation of the rights of woman'. This not only involved improving women's material living conditions, but also dictated respect for their 'dignity'.[37] The date is 1945. In subsequent years, the feminist movement underwent significant developments and radicalization. But the misleading character of the opposition between the paradigms of recognition and redistribution remains.

While the struggle for recognition certainly did not disappear in the decades when construction of the welfare state was on the agenda in the West, the struggle for redistribution is more relevant than ever following the explosion of the economic crisis in 2008. In reality, the two paradigms are closely connected. The unemployed and the working poor protest or feel resentment not only at the heavy sacrifices imposed on them but also because their difficult living conditions are experienced as an insult and humiliation in such a wealthy and opulent society. The sense of non-recognition is reinforced by the growing influence of wealth in the selection of those called on to occupy the highest political offices. Both paradigms are likewise present in women's struggle for liberation—a struggle which, while it has posted important results in the West (albeit threatened by the crisis, which impacts on female employment in the first instance), is less advanced or only just beginning in other cultures.

Finally, prominent in the struggle against the neo-colonialism practiced by self-styled 'chosen nations', which control the centres of international economic power and claim to be the only ones entitled to genuine sovereignty, the link between the struggle for the distribution of resources and the struggle for recognition is immediately self-evident in a phenomenon like the Palestinian situation. The 'natives' have their land expropriated and are condemned to poverty and marginalization. At the same time, they suffer dual non-recognition: they are not regarded as worthy either of constructing an independent nation-state or of becoming citizens of the state which, annexing their territory, prevents them from constituting themselves as an independent nation-state.

4 The Fragmentation of 'Class Struggles'

The situation since the crisis, and then collapse, of the 'socialist camp' is not characterized by a paradigm switch. But the opposition between the paradigm of redistribution (represented by the labour movement) and the paradigm of recognition (which supposedly found its principal embodiment in the feminist movement) is a sign of the real change that has intervened. To understand it, we must not lose sight of a point to which I have frequently drawn attention. The subjects of class struggle are diverse, and struggles for recognition and emancipation are multiple. There is no preordained harmony between them. For objective and subjective reasons, misunderstandings and divisions can occur. The high points in the history that started with the *Communist Manifesto* are those where fragmentation was avoided, so that that the various struggles merged in a single powerful wave of emancipation.

This is the exception rather than the rule. However, progressive in itself, there is no class struggle that cannot be instrumentalized by the dominant power and integrated into a general project of a conservative or reactionary stamp. This not a new phenomenon. But it has been accentuated and acquired a new qualitative potency in the wake of disenchantment at the results of twentieth-century revolutions and subsequent theoretical disorientation.

Disraeli extended the suffrage to the popular classes, thereby promoting their political emancipation, but in exchange for support for the policy of British colonial expansion. It was a successful policy. Marx and Engels were obliged to note that even the quintessential revolutionary class—the proletariat—could succumb to the siren of colonialism. This syndrome is much more pronounced today given that, with the advent of neo-colonialism and what an American political scientist highly attentive to geopolitical themes has defined as 'human rights imperialism',[38] the oppressor and aggressor can easily envelop violence against an oppressed country in a fog of mystification.

It is not the only factor fragmenting class struggle. Let us glance at the third front of the class struggle—the women's liberation movement. The extension of political rights to women was long demanded by the labour movement as an integral part of the project of overthrowing or superseding the old capitalist regime. In 1887, Eleanor Marx, tackling the 'woman question' along with her husband Edward Aveling, and demanding political rights for women, not only compared the 'oppressed condition' and 'merciless degradation' of women to that endured by workers, but added that 'the relation between men and women' was the clearest, most repugnant expression of the 'gruesome moral bankruptcy' of capitalist society as such.[39] However, in this same period representatives or ideologues of the dominant classes regarded female suffrage from a completely different, even opposed, political and social perspective: it might (suggested a French author) represent 'conservatism's largest reserve'. In Europe, as in the USA, votes for women were often invoked as a counter-weight to the dreaded growing political influence of the popular masses consequent upon the relaxation of censitary discrimination.[40] In other words, we find the dominant power utilizing women's class struggle and struggle for recognition in order to neutralize or counter the class struggle and struggle for recognition waged by the popular classes. A different scenario can obtain. In the early twentieth century, in a country like Britain, there was no shortage of women distinguishing themselves in celebration of colonial expansion and the role of 'Crusader for Empire'. Nor were feminists lacking who demanded women's emancipation in the name of the role they played in building the empire.[41] In this case, the women's liberation movement came into contradiction with the colonial peoples' liberation movement.

Rather than simply being the result of manoeuvres by the powers that be, such multiple contradictions reflect a complex objective situation. Only in special circumstances, in the presence of compelling theoretical syntheses, or under the influence of major revolutions or mature revolutionary projects, can they be resolved or unified—and even then not without oscillations and difficulties of various kinds. While the First World War was raging, Lenin, on the one hand, called on the proletariat in the West to rise up against the bourgeoisie and transform the imperialist war into a revolutionary civil war, and on the other saluted the national liberation struggles and wars waged by 'colonial nations' and 'oppressed nations', and drew attention to the permanent condition of 'domestic slavery' imposed on women,[42] who not by chance were excluded from political rights along with the 'poor' and the 'lower stratum of the proletariat proper'.[43] The three fronts of the class struggle converge here.

Almost a decade later, starting out from rural zones, Mao promoted a revolution which, in the context of the radical national and social revival of China, also sought to challenge 'the authority of the husband', the additional 'thick rope' that women carried round their neck along with the others strangling the whole Chinese people.[44]

On other occasions, unification of the different fronts of the class struggle proves more difficult. Certainly, for Fanon too, 'the liberation of the Algerian people ... became identified with woman's liberation, with her entry into history'. This was not only a statement of principle. Active involvement in the partisan war meant that woman was no longer a 'minor', especially since it challenged sexual segregation and the 'demand of virginity'. In any event, 'the old fear of dishonor had become altogether absurd in the light of the immense tragedy being experienced by the people'.[45] However, another aspect of the question should not be ignored:

> The officials of the French administration in Algeria, committed to destroying the people's originality, and under instructions to bring about the disintegration, at whatever cost, of forms of existence likely to evoke a national reality directly or indirectly, were to concentrate their efforts on the wearing of the veil, which was looked upon at this juncture as a symbol of the status of the Algerian woman. ... The occupier's aggressiveness, and hence his hopes, multiplied ten-fold each time a new face was uncovered. ... Algerian society with every abandoned veil seemed to express its willingness to attend the master's school and to decide to change its habits under the occupier's direction and patronage.[46]

In a very specific objective context, national liberation can come into conflict with women's liberation, at least in the immediate present. This risk has greatly increased today because, following the crisis of communism and Marxism, parties of a religious persuasion find themselves at the head of national liberation and resistance movements. In the past, colonial powers (including Mussolini's Italy) promoted their expansion in the name of emancipation from the slavery still extant in Africa, only to proceed to impose forced labour in even more odious forms—and not merely on a specific class, but on the whole indigenous population. In our day, the neo-colonialist project sometimes hoists the banner of woman's emancipation, not without success. But it targets not countries such as Saudi Arabia, where female segregation and domestic slavery persist in their strictest, most benighted form, but countries recalcitrant to the West like Iran, where forms of discrimination against women remain onerous and odious, but have been considerably dented (young women form a majority of the university population and enjoy greater social mobility).

5 BETWEEN TRADE UNIONISM AND POPULISM

What exacerbates the fragmentation of class struggles is the split that has occurred between the anti-capitalist struggle in the metropolis, in the most industrially developed countries, and the struggle which the former colonies are compelled to wage against neo-colonialism and the gunboat diplomacy or outright aggression practiced by great powers unwilling to renounce their domination or hegemony. This is a split explicitly theorized by a celebrated philosopher, who is unsparing in his irony about a trend he regards as utterly erroneous. According to it, the class struggle no longer has 'capitalists and the proletariat in each country' as its protagonists, but unfolds in an international context, pitting states rather than social classes against one another. Marx's 'critique of capitalism as such' is thereby reduced and distorted into a 'critique of "imperialism"', which loses sight of the main thing: capitalist relations of production.[47] Is this irony and argument justified? It should have targeted Marx in the first instance. His attention to the national question was constant and his analysis of the way that, in a country like Ireland, the 'social question' took the form of the 'national question' is especially thought-provoking.

In Zizek's view, in the twentieth century, the quintessential rebel is Mao, whom we have seen asserting more clearly and sharply than anyone else 'the identity between national struggle and class struggle'. Of course, this was at a time when China faced attempted enslavement by Japanese imperialism (while in Europe Slavs in general, and the Soviet Union in particular, were confronting German imperialism). But the assertion is quite the reverse of a tactical expedient, motivated by patriotic fervour. In 1963, with reference to the struggle of African Americans for their civil and political rights, the Chinese leader stressed: '[n]ational struggle, in the final analysis, is a question of class struggle'. This was a point of view reiterated five years later: '[r]acial discrimination in the United States is a product of the colonialist-imperialist system. The contradiction between the broad masses of black people and the U.S. ruling clique is a class contradiction'.[48] When we refer to African Americans, we are obviously dealing with a particular country. But would the conclusion be different if we were analysing the oppression suffered not by a people of colonial origin, but a colonial people in the strict sense?

In order to clarify this problem, we may reflect on a chapter of history that attracts Zizek's passionate interest. I am referring to the great revolution (the great class struggle) of the black slaves of Santo Domingo.

In his view, it regressed to 'a new form of hierarchical rule' after the death of Jean-Jacques Dessalines in 1806.[49] So let us focus on the preceding period. Santo Doming's black slaves rebelled not against capitalism as such, but against the slave system reserved for colonial peoples by the capitalist metropolis. That is, from the outset, the black revolution included a national liberation component: the insurrection led by Toussaint L'Ouverture freed not a specific subaltern class, but black people as a whole from the shackles of slavery.

The national liberation component became even more explicit in the second stage of the revolution. The powerful army dispatched by Napoleon, under the command of Charles Leclerc (his brother-in-law), was intended to restore both French colonial rule and black slavery. It was defeated by revolutionaries who cast themselves as the 'Army of the Incas' or the 'Indigenous Army', yelling: 'Anathema to the French name! Eternal hatred of France!'[50] *De facto* independence now also demanded *de jure* recognition and Santo Domingo was renamed Haiti, significantly employing a name that derived from the pre-Columbian epoch. In other words, the black revolutionaries identified with the original victims of the West's colonial expansion, 'seeking to connect their struggle for freedom from slavery with the earlier battles of indigenous peoples against Spanish invaders'.[51]

In short, the anti-slavery revolution was simultaneously an anti-colonialist revolution and wound up taking the form of a war of national resistance and liberation. It would manifestly be absurd to define the first stage of this process as a revolutionary class struggle, but consider such a characterization invalid when it comes to the second stage. It would be bizarre to regard the insurrection to abolish slavery and colonial rule as a revolutionary class struggle, but not the armed resistance to prevent the restoration of both. In both stages, the national question played a key role and both are viewed favourably by Zizek, who nevertheless ironizes about the tendency to reduce anti-capitalist class struggle to anti-colonialist and anti-imperialist struggle.

In the twentieth century, a sequence of events occurred that might well be compared to what we have just seen in the case of Santo Domingo-Haiti. Its symbol is Stalingrad—the battle that inflicted defeat on Hitler's plan to colonize and enslave entire peoples in Eastern Europe. Not by chance, the two sequences generated similar ideological processes. The colonialist and pro-slavery counter-revolution attempted by Napoleon felt obliged to liquidate the universal concept of man inherent in the interpretation of the 1789 Declaration of the Rights of Man by Santo Domingo's slaves. Toussaint L'Ouverture, whom we have seen proclaim the unconditional principle whereby, whatever their skin colour, no human being 'can be the property of his fellow' (Chap. 4, Sect. 3), seems to be answered by Napoleon: 'I am for the whites because I am white; I have no other reason, and that one is good'.[52] Responding to the even more marked universalistic ethos of the October Revolution, with its appeal to colonial slaves to break their chains, was theorization of the *Under Man/Untermensch*. This is a category which, having been coined by the American author Lothrop Stoddard for predominantly anti-Negro purposes, presided over Hitler's campaign to colonize Eastern Europe and enslave the Slavs, and also presided over the extermination of the Jews, branded along with the Bolsheviks as ideologues and instigators of the deplorable revolt of the 'inferior races'.[53]

It is a kind of commonplace to compare Napoleon's invasion of Russia with Hitler's invasion of the Soviet Union. But it would be much more apt to stage a comparison between the latter and Napoleon's expedition against Santo Domingo. In both cases, what was at stake was the fate of the colonial system and the institution of slavery. In both cases, there was a class struggle that was simultaneously a war of resistance and national liberation.

Should we view the co-presence of the national struggle as a contaminating factor in the class struggle? On closer inspection, this is a problem and debate that runs throughout the history of the socialist and communist movement. Marx and Engels bemoaned the fact that British workers were committed to improving their living conditions and winning political rights, but ignored the independence struggle of Ireland, Poland or India. Later, in criticizing trade-unionism and elevating support for national liberation movements into a key component of revolutionary class consciousness, Lenin, in turn, was accused of abandoning a class standpoint, of drowning the cause of proletarian emancipation in an undifferentiated, insipid mess (see Chap. 5, Sect. 2) Let us jump ahead some decades. In 1963, invoking Lenin, the Communist Party of China repeated: 'the national question in the contemporary world is one of class struggle'. To demand 'a clear line of demarcation' between 'oppressed nations' and imperialism was 'the Marxist-Leninist class stand'.[54] This was an argument against the Soviet Communists, who in their turn accused the Chinese of forgetting the proletarian class struggle in the capitalist metropolis.

The danger of a fragmentation of class struggles is ever present. In 1963, it was certainly difficult to adopt the attitude branded by Lenin as trade-unionism and to regard the anti-colonial revolutions exploding in Vietnam, Algeria, and Latin America, which were countered with genocidal practices by imperialism, as foreign to the class struggle. The contemporary global picture seems more favourable to the resumption of trade-unionism. Should we locate Zizek's position in this context? In reality, in a situation of the theoretical crisis of Marxism, a tendency to evade the challenge involved in interpreting the tangle of contradictions—what might be characterized as the populist tendency to fall back on the binary interpretation of conflict—asserts itself.

6 Liberation Struggles Poised between Military Victory and Economic Defeat

To examine the problem in depth, we must pose a preliminary question: how do things stand today with the massive anti-colonial revolution stimulated by the October Revolution and accelerated by Stalingrad? In Palestine, colonialism and anti-colonialism continue to confront one another in classic form. And in the rest of the world? Let us set down a premise: not only have the decisive class struggles of modern history wound up taking the form of national struggles, but they have been (and are) conducted economically as well as militarily.

Once again, the most striking case is the revolution of Santo Domingo's black slaves. It managed to defeat the strongest army of the day—namely, Napoleon's. The independent country that emerged—Haiti—played a revolutionary role far beyond its borders. It impelled Simón Bolívar to abolish slavery in Spanish Latin America and aided him in his struggle for independence; it inspired the revolt of the black slaves in Demerara (today's Guyana) and Jamaica and cultivated relations with British abolitionists. The first country on the American continent to abolish the institution of slavery, proudly presented itself as the land of freedom; and the slaves of Cuba or the American Deep South looked to it with hope.

For this very reason, the efforts of the colonialist slave-holding state, whose global power was intact, and which aimed to neutralize and eliminate the potentially incendiary example of a country governed by former slaves, did not end with the defeat of the army sent by Napoleon. Only now the crusade to restore uncontested white supremacy resorted to new methods. According to Thomas Jefferson, having isolated them diplomatically, it was necessary to condemn those who dared to defy the international order and turn it upside down to 'starvation'. In likewise refusing to recognize Haitian independence, France brandished the threat of a resumption of military intervention and it led the rulers of the Caribbean country in 1825 to accept an agreement that proved disastrous. In exchange for recognition by Paris, they committed themselves to compensating the colonists who had been divested of their human livestock (the black slaves). Haiti ended up getting ever more heavily into debt: in 1898, half of state expenditure went to repay the creditor country and in 1914, the percentage had risen as high as 80 %.[55] The spiral of growing economic dependence increasingly neutralized formal political independence. Victorious militarily, the Haitian Revolution was unquestionably defeated economically. The people and country that had overcome Napoleon's army could not challenge the international division of labour imposed by the colonialist system. The consequences were grave—and not only because the living conditions of the popular masses inside the country deteriorated. Internationally, the decline in the prestige of the country emerging from the black slave revolution meant the regime of white supremacy obtaining in the American South and, in the final analysis, globally could carry on undisturbed.

A re-run of this sequence occurred in the twentieth century in two stages. Let us glance at the first. Immediately after October 1917, Herbert Hoover, at the time, a senior representative of the Wilson administration and later US President, explicitly brandished the threat of 'absolute famine' and 'starvation' not only against Soviet Russia but also against peoples inclined to allow themselves to be infected by the Bolshevik Revolution. They were all confronted with a crude alternative encapsulated by Gramsci in the title of an article in *Avanti!* on 16 December 1918: *O la borsa o la vita, o l'ordine borghese o la fame* ('Your money or your life, the bourgeois order or hunger'). And now let us turn to the second stage. Having emerged from the Second World War bled white, in May 1947 an erstwhile ally of the USA was confronted by the Marshall Plan with a choice summarized as follows by a US scholar. If they did not wish to renounce the credits and trade they urgently needed, 'the Soviets [must] open their economy to Western investment, their markets to Western products, their account books to Western administrator' and 'accept economic and media penetration' by the countries about to form NATO.[56] This is a familiar piece of blackmail: 'your money or your life, the bourgeois order or hunger'. The economic struggle manifestly played a far from negligible role in the ultimate defeat of the October Revolution in Eastern Europe.

Having faced albeit limited military intervention by the USA in the civil war, the Chinese Revolution likewise had to come to terms with an offensive conducted predominantly on the economic front. Representatives of the Truman administration were explicit at times: China must be 'plagued' with 'a general standard of life around and below the subsistence level', 'economic backwardness', and a 'cultural lag'. There must be 'a heavy and long protracted cost to the whole social structure'. A 'state of chaos' and a 'catastrophic economic situation' must ultimately be created, leading China 'towards disaster', 'collapse'. In the White House, Presidents came and went, but the embargo persisted and included medicine, tractors, and fertilizers. In the early 1960s, a collaborator in the Kennedy administration—Walt W. Rostow—observed that, thanks to this policy, China's economic development had been set back by decades at least. The threat of economic war did not even cease on the eve of China's entry into the World Trade Organization. Not without satisfaction, a well-known American political scientist, Edward Lutwak, observed: '[m]etaphorically speaking, it might be said that a ban on Chinese imports is the nuclear weapon that America keeps pointed at China'.[57]

7 'POLITICAL ANNEXATION' AND 'ECONOMIC ANNEXATION'

Marx was well aware of the economic component of any major class struggle and national struggle. We have seen him denounce British colonialism for having reduced Ireland to 'simple pastureland', to a mere supplier of 'meat and wool at the cheapest possible price' (Chap. 2, Sect. 3). In a letter to Engels of 30 November 1867, Marx hypothesized a popular revolution in Ireland terminating colonial rule and formalizing independence. The new revolutionary government would have to halt the de-industrialization implemented by the colonizers and pursue a protectionist policy, imposing 'protective tariffs against England' in the first instance.[58] Marx repeatedly stressed how free trade promoted the development of the productive forces, but this did not prevent him from recommending protectionism, for a limited period, in the case of a country that had to extricate itself from under-development and colonial dependency, and which had to advance the process of emancipation from the politico-military to the economic stage.

The problem is prominent in Lenin, who with customary clarity distinguishes between 'political annexation' and the 'economic' variety. Abolishing the first is insufficient for liberation from the second. Formally independent, Argentina was 'in reality a "trade colony" of Britain' and Portugal was 'in reality a "vassal" of Britain'.[59] In analysing the forms of power and rule in an individual country, Marx observed that a (feudal) situation characterized by '[r]elationships of personal dependence' was replaced by a situation of '[p]ersonal independence based upon dependence mediated by things', characteristic of capitalist society.[60] We can now understand the transition in the sphere of international relations from colonialism to neo-colonialism; 'political annexation' corresponds to 'personal dependence', while 'economic' annexation with formal national independence corresponds to material 'dependence' with 'personal independence'.

The phenomenon we are discussing certainly cannot be regarded as obsolete in a historical period when, thanks to their economic and technological power, the capitalist great powers, resorting to economic warfare or warfare proper, are in a position to destroy Third World countries, in practice without suffering any loss, as in the classical epoch of colonialism, and in fact even more starkly! Hence, today, once again, the 'social question' can, to a certain extent, take the form of a 'national question' and a partial 'identity between national and class struggle' (to employ the terminology of Marx and Mao, respectively) can exist.

The anti-colonial movement has shown itself fully aware of the economic dimension of its struggle for emancipation in its moments of greatest strength and maturity. On 16 September 1949, on the eve of conquering power, Mao Zedong drew attention to Washington's desire that China be compelled 'to live on U.S. flour', thereby winding up 'a U.S. colony'.[61] The struggle to develop production was cast as a continuation of the struggle against colonial or semi-colonial domination. Four decades later, Deng Xiaoping repeated that '[t]o achieve genuine political independence a country must lift itself out of poverty'.[62]

Thousands of miles away, in Cuba, Che Guevara adopted a similar stance. In the 1960s, he called for vigilance against 'economic aggression' as well and enjoined newly independent countries to 'free themselves not only from the political yoke but also the imperialist economic yoke'.[63]

In the same years, on the eve of the Algerian Revolution's triumph, Fanon posed the problem of a national liberation movement's transition from the politico-military to the politico-economic phase of the struggle. To impart material reality and solidity to the independence won via armed struggle, the newly independent country must escape under-development. Application in work and production thus took over from courage in battle; the figure of the more or less skilled worker replaced that of the guerrilla.

When compelled to capitulate, the colonial power seemed to say to the revolutionaries: '[i]f you want independence, take it and suffer the consequences'. In this way, 'the apotheosis of independence becomes the curse of independence'. This was the new challenge, non-military in kind, which had to be met: the country 'requires capital, technicians, engineers and mechanics, etc'.[64]

The deadlock of so many African countries, which failed to make the transition from the military phase of the revolution to the economic, is in a way anticipated here. But so is the turn that occurred in such anti-colonial revolutions as the Chinese or Vietnamese. The date is 1961. That year, another eminent theoretician of the ongoing anti-colonial revolution devoted a book to Toussaint L'Ouverture, which was at the same time a balance-sheet of the revolution whose main protagonist was the black Jacobin. After the military victory, he had had the merit of posing the problem of economic construction. To that end, he had promoted a culture of work and productivity and also sought to employ white technicians and experts from the ranks of the defeated enemy. This is what Lenin exactly did in the years of the NEP, introducing 'the strictest discipline' into the workplace and employing 'bourgeois specialists'.[65]

Comparative history is always problematic, and the same author draws attention to the limitations of the militaristic approach adopted by the black slave leader once in power. But the essential fact remains: the comparison was born out of an awareness of the transition that needs to be made at a certain point in any anti-colonial revolution, in any revolution that challenges the international division of labour imposed by capitalism and imperialism. We must then register the tragedy that unfolded during the revolution led by Toussaint L'Ouverture. Having resorted to white specialists and technicians, he was suspected and accused of betrayal; and his political line suffered a severe defeat. The consequences were grave. Santo Domingo was a very wealthy island, thanks to the sugar, mainly for export, produced on large, highly efficient plantations. Obviously, the wealth created by the slaves was pocketed by their masters. Could the ex-slaves operate the advanced economic structure they had inherited from the revolution to their own advantage? In the event, the system of slavery and colonial rule was replaced by a backward subsistence agriculture. The island thus experienced generalized poverty and to this day is one of the poorest countries in the world. After the agreement made with France by Haiti, a French author exulted: the former colonial power had restored its domination without recourse to war, but employing, much more effectively, the economic tool.[66] Later, Haiti largely escaped French control, but only because the European country was supplanted by the closer, more powerful North American republic.

At this point, it might be interesting to reflect on the history of the Third World as a whole. At the 1955 conference which met in Bandung, the Indonesian leader Ahmed Sukarno, having enthusiastically greeted the initial results of the anti-colonial revolution then in full swing, called for the newly independent countries to also liberate themselves from the 'economic control' exercised by the old colonial powers. The following year, the Ghanaian Kwame Nkrumah published a book intended to demonstrate that 'a State in the grip of neo-colonialism is not master of its own destiny'.[67]

We witness the global irruption of the dialectic that had already manifested itself in various countries, and with particular clarity in the USA. There, following the abolition of slavery, the blacks sought to consolidate or give effect to their emancipation by acceding to land ownership. The failure of this endeavour, obstructed by the white elite by any and every means, condemned African Americans to segregation on the bottom rungs of the labour market, and economic and social subalternity down to the present. The Union's victory, achieved in part thanks to an influx of slaves into the ranks of its army, was followed by the economic and social defeat of the former slaves. It should be clear that the class struggle manifests itself in both the military and economic phases of liberation struggles.

Today, in the advanced capitalist countries even the intellectual culture influenced by Marx finds it hard to include the struggle to shake off 'political annexation' (Lenin) or the 'political yoke' (Guevara), to repel military aggression, in the category of emancipatory class struggles. The refusal to interpret endeavours to end 'economic' annexation (Lenin) or the 'imperialist economic yoke', and to foil 'economic aggression' (Guevara), in terms of class struggle, is prejudicial. Happily, this attitude is not without its fluctuations and inconsistencies. Zizek expresses disdain for the alleged degeneration of class struggle into a struggle against imperialism. But in his better political moments, he ends up problematizing his own theoretical presuppositions. With patent reference to Israeli policy in Palestine, Zizek draws attention to 'colonial land-grabbing'.[68] Here 'political annexation' effected by military force is subject to criticism. But things do not end there. In connection with Salvador Allende's Chile, the philosopher reports the instruction sent by Henry Kissinger to the CIA—'make the economy scream'—and stresses that a similar policy is being implemented against Chávez's Venezuela.[69] The tone is one of bitter condemnation—a condemnation that clearly invests imperialism, which is excoriated even more for its policy of economic aggression than its military aggression. The national question can be negated, but the conduct towards Palestine, Chile, and Venezuela highlighted by Zizek, although it impacts on subaltern classes, in particular, affects the nation as such, so that a class struggle which ignores this question lacks credibility and effectiveness.

However, given the ever-present danger of chauvinism, is it legitimate to refer to the national question and, in specific circumstances, connect and even identify it with the class struggle? In 1916, while an imperialist bloodbath was underway in the name of 'defence of the fatherland', Lenin had no hesitation in affirming that '[i]n a *genuinely* national war, the words "defence of the fatherland" are *not* a deception and *we are not opposed to it*'.[70] This was a valuable hint, destined to play a key role in the resistance and national liberation struggles against the Third Reich and colonial rule generally. On the other hand, those who, by analogy with the First World War, ridiculed 'defence of the fatherland' and enjoined defeatism, actually ended up playing the game of the Third Reich or the Empire of the Rising Sun. This confirms that substituting the easy game of analogies for the 'concrete analysis of a concrete situation' is a source of nothing but disasters.

Besides, there is no category or slogan that does not suffer from contamination by political and social struggles. Has the term 'democracy' remained immaculate? 'Democratic Party' is the name of the US party that long fought to defend first the institution of slavery and then white supremacy. The fate of words which, at first blush, would seem to be the unchallenged property of the Left—revolution, socialism, working class—is similar. In 1933, we had the 'revolution' of the 'National Socialist Party of German Workers' led by Adolf Hitler! Linguistic affinities are not necessarily synonymous with politico-ideological affinities, as a superficial view would have it. They can also denote antagonism—intense struggle to construe in one sense or another watchword which, in a determinate historical situation, impose themselves on common consciousness or public attention.

8 China and the End of the 'Columbian Epoch'

In the case of China, the (partial) identity of class struggle and national struggle did not end with the close of the 'century of humiliation'. 1949 saw the birth of the People's Republic, which has not in fact completed the process of national reunification and restoration of its territorial integrity—indeed, must beware plans for dismemberment entertained by the West, which supports and fuels secessionist movements (in Tibet, Xinjiang, Inner Mongolia, and elsewhere). The target of a ruthless economic war, the PRC remained exposed to the danger of military aggression. It would have been no accident if it was long excluded from the United Nations. Above all, it was among the poorest countries in the world, and hence, according to Mao's statement of 16 September 1949, risked dependency on 'U.S. flour' and becoming a 'U.S. colony'. Until the late 1950s, the leader of the Chinese Revolution did not call into question his own thesis of the identity or, at any rate, substantial convergence between class struggle and national struggle in China. The picture certainly changed with the launch of the Great Leap Forward and then, in particular, the Cultural Revolution, when the slogan 'one divides into two' reverberated. The anti-imperialist united front was split, and the principal target of the class struggle was identified as domestic. As we know, however, in May 1974, Mao himself expressed profound disappointment at the results. Acknowledging, in the course of his conversation with Heath, that he had not succeeded in solving the problem of food supplies, he must have had in mind the danger, evoked almost a quarter of a century earlier, of China become a colony of the country equipped to supply it with the 'flour' required for its survival.

The thesis of a substantial convergence between class struggle and national struggle came back into vogue with Deng Xiaoping's assumption of power. The policy of reform and opening up initiated by him has often been construed as China conforming to the West and the advent of a kind of dead calm on the world scene. But this is a rather superficial interpretation. In some respects, the policy was an attempt to evade the most devastating forms of the economic war, which did not come to an end. While the threat of a 'nuclear' attack in commercial guise remained, an intricate game became apparent. The USA hoped to have at its disposal an enormous country supplying a low-cost labour force and products with low technological content at knock-down prices. China sought to access the advanced technology on which the West, in the aftermath of the crisis and collapse of the Soviet Union and the socialist camp, had a monopoly. In this way, the gap between it and the most advanced capitalist countries could be bridged and the first form of inequality eliminated. However, this was far from easy to accomplish, given that the USA, in particular, sought to subject the PRC to a kind of technological embargo. Where are we in the development of this duel?

In the late twentieth century, Huntington observed that, were the industrialization and modernization of China to succeed, its attainment of the status of 'major power will dwarf any comparable phenomena during the last half of the second millennium'.[71] A decade and a half later, there was no doubt about it. In the interim, China had been admitted to the World Trade Organization, and the USA was no longer able to brandish the threat of a 'nuclear' attack in a commercial guise. As a result, Ferguson today concludes as follows on the subject of the epochal changes in Asia: '[w]hat we are living through now is the end of 500 years of Western predominance'.[72] The two authors cited here use the same pointed dating. If we work our way back approximately five centuries, we come to the discovery-conquest of America and the beginning of what Halford J. Mackinder, one of the fathers of geopolitics, defined as the 'Columbian epoch' of the discovery and 'political appropriation' of the world by the West, which expanded triumphantly in the face of 'almost negligible resistance'.[73]

The end of the 'Columbian epoch' is, at the same time, the beginning of the end of the 'great divergence' that created a profound gulf between the West and the rest of the world, primed the overwhelming military might of the former, and prompted (or facilitated) the cultural, and often racial, arrogance displayed by the restricted area of more advanced economic and technological development. The prospect of a radical mutation in the international division labour has now emerged. And, once again, the political, diplomatic, and economic contest to alter or conserve the international division of labour imposed by capitalism and imperialism is itself a class struggle—a class struggle seeking to further or obstruct an emancipatory process of global dimensions. From Marx and Engels' standpoint, engagement in overcoming the patriarchal division of labour in the family was to be regarded as an integral part of the process of emancipation (and class struggle). It would be very strange if engagement to end the division of labour imposed internationally by force of arms in the 'Columbian epoch' were to be regarded as foreign to the process of emancipation (and class struggle)!

In any event, the shrinking of 'global inequality' has an enormous historical significance, which manifests itself on a world scale. All the more so in that 'global inequality' facilitated a terrible and tenacious relationship of compulsion. Adam Smith had already observed that at the time of the discovery-conquest of America (hence, at the start of the 'Columbian era'), 'the superiority of force happened to be so great on the side of the

Europeans, that they were enabled to commit with impunity every sort of injustice in those remote countries'.[74] Many years later, Hitler addressed the industrialists who were investing him with power:

> The white race can genuinely maintain its position only if the difference in living standards in the world persists. If our so-called export markets are accorded the same standard of living as us, you will find that the dominant position of the white race will become unsustainable as regards both the political power of the nation and the economic situation of individuals.[75]

The Soviet Union should be first in the firing line. '[W]ith the crutches of the capitalist economy', it was on the point of becoming 'the most threatening economic competitor' of the white race countries. In defence of what would today be called global inequality, Hitler was prepared to unleash one of the most ferocious reactionary class struggles in world history. Marxism or post-Marxism of the trade-unionist/populist variety seems indifferent to all this. It proclaims a desire to struggle against inequality, provided it is not global inequality—the form of inequality most pregnant with violence, which creates the profoundest rift between human beings.

9   THE WEST, CHINA AND THE TWO 'GREAT DIVERGENCES'

If the global 'great divergence' is shrinking, within the more developed capitalist world another 'great divergence' is expanding.[76] Already underway for some time, this second 'great divergence' was accentuated in the wake of the crisis of 2008. The financial editor of the *Wall Street Journal* has observed that in the USA 'one per cent of the population owns more than one-fifth of the country's wealth, and fifteen per cent of people live below the poverty line'.[77] Thus, we are dealing with power relations that void the freedom of the popular classes: '[o]nly 27 percent of the unemployed are covered by unemployment insurance ... [This] allowed companies to bust unions and threaten employees who tried to organize'.[78]

A question is indicated: does the second 'great divergence' also affect the country which, more than any other, is challenging the first 'great divergence'? While the qualitative absolute inequality (the difference between life and death) ever present in a situation of penury has disappeared in China, the distribution of social wealth has become markedly more unequal. This is not a new dialectic in the history of the movement that emerged from the October Revolution. In the case of Soviet Russia, it was well described by Trotsky in 1936–7:

> In its first period, the Soviet regime was undoubtedly far more equalitarian and less bureaucratic than now. But that was an equality of general poverty. The resources of the country were so scant that there was no opportunity to separate out from the masses of the population any broad privileged strata. At the same time the 'equalizing' character of wages, destroying personal interestedness, became a brake upon the development of the productive forces. Soviet economy had to lift itself from its poverty to a somewhat higher level before fat deposits of privilege became possible.[79]

Notwithstanding its polemical tone—the book we are quoting from denounces the 'betrayal' of the revolution in its very title—this is an illuminating passage: (a) one cannot remain at the stage of 'general poverty'; (b) that stage is marked by 'the "equalizing" character of wages'. But we should note the quotation marks around the adjective. What obtains is equality in poverty, in the forced 'universal asceticism' from which the *Communist Manifesto* clearly distances itself, and which (I add) can involve slippage into absolute qualitative inequality; (c) to escape this condition, it is necessary to promote the 'development of the productive forces', banking on 'personal interestedness'. The result is inequalities that are justified by the differential quantity and quality of the labour performed, but which can turn into intolerable 'privileges'.

Here we have an analysis and warning that can also be applied to China. The changes that have occurred over recent decades might be illustrated with a metaphor. Two trains are leaving the station named 'Underdevelopment' and proceeding in the direction of the station named 'Development'. One of the trains is high-speed, the other slower. As a result, the distance between them progressively increases. Such a gap is readily explained if we bear in mind China's continental dimensions and tormented history. The coastal regions, which already possess albeit basic infrastructure and benefit from the vicinity to and the possibility of trade with, developed countries, are more favourably situated than traditionally more backward regions, which lack an outlet to the sea and border on countries and areas that are economic backwaters. The picture presented by the West is very different. Observers note a return of the poverty that seemed to have been eradicated, in a society where opulence is concentrated in an ever narrower circle. In the case of China, by contrast, we must speak of a restoration of welfare or a dignified condition of existence, in a process admittedly replete with contradictions. Albeit at different speeds, the two trains of our metaphor are advancing towards the same goal.

In the USA and Western Europe, the emergence or exacerbation of the second 'great divergence', and the dismantling of the welfare state, were preceded by an ideological campaign which, at Hayek's hands, deleted economic and social rights from the schedule of rights regardless of any economic considerations. In China, a completely different ideological and political process has occurred. In making the turn of 1979, far from challenging economic and social rights, Deng Xiaoping underscored their centrality. He criticized the old model on the grounds that, incapable as it was of developing the productive forces and overcoming the state of penury, it could not genuinely satisfy the right to life and a dignified existence—the economic and social rights of the citizens of the world's most populous country. A change of direction was required. There was a need to recognize 'that poverty is not socialism, that socialism means eliminating poverty' and realizing 'common prosperity', 'welfare' and 'happiness' for the 'people' as a whole (see Chap. 8, Sect. 6). On this basis, opposition to 'capitalism', which 'can only enrich less than 10 per cent of the Chinese population; it can never enrich the remaining more than 90 per cent', remained firm. The choice made in 1949 must be abided by, putting a stop to lapses into populism, which identified wealth as a potential source of contamination of revolutionary purity and which, abolishing any material incentives, in fact rewarded lack of commitment to work: 'if we adhere to socialism and apply the principle of distribution to each according to his work, there will not be excessive disparities in wealth'. As in the Soviet NEP (explicitly referred to), public property was flanked by private property, but assigned a leading role.[80]

The ideological and political struggle that dictated the new course in China is now becoming clear: on one side, advocates of an egalitarian distribution of penury, inclined to a populist transfiguration of this condition into a synonym for political and moral excellence; on the other, advocates of a 'prosperity' that is 'common', to be achieved through competition between individuals and enterprises, the market, a mix of public and private industry, with the leading role of the state and the public sector of the economy (and public power) taken as read. As demonstrated by Deng's reference to the experience of the Soviet NEP, this is not a new debate in the history of countries of a socialist orientation. Albeit with unprecedented radicalism, a very familiar dilemma is being recreated: staking everything on 'universal asceticism' and crude 'social levelling' (mocked by the *Communist Manifesto*); or taking seriously the task which, according to the *Manifesto*, a communist party in power should acquit—namely, 'increas[ing] the total of productive forces as rapidly as possible'?

After at least three decades of prodigious economic development, which amid contradictions and conflicts of every kind has made it possible to liberate hundreds of millions of people from poverty, from absolute qualitative inequality or the danger of succumbing to it, in today's China we also witness efforts to tackle the various manifestations of quantitative inequality. In recent years, Tibet, Inner Mongolia, and other regions have posted a growth rate superior—and sometimes markedly so—to the national average. The same can be said of an enormous megalopolis like Chongqing and a large metropolis like Chengdu, which are nearly a thousand miles from the eastern and coastal regions—the most developed—and which seem to have embarked on a furious chase. Hence, in the country-continent of China regional disparities are diminishing and are doing so in an accelerated process of economic development. By contrast, such differences are growing in Europe (and within individual countries like Italy), and are doing so during a process of stagnation (at best) or recession.

Certainly, the gap between the cities (which attract the youngest, most enterprising elements) and the countryside is continuing to grow in China. But this trend is in a way contained by the rapid process of urbanization. The passengers on the express (urban) train are becoming ever more numerous, but there is no lack of endeavour to increase the speed of the slower (rural) train. In urban areas themselves, access to welfare, and sometimes wealth and even opulence, is far from uniform. But such inequalities and distortions are in a sense contained or defused by the rapid rise in wage levels and the introduction of the first elements of a welfare state.

Overall, the different speeds at which poverty has been left behind and the comforts of modern civilization attained, cannot be accurately described with the category of 'great divergence'. Especially given that the remaining obstacles on the road to 'common prosperity' are major hurdles that prevent full enjoyment of economic and social rights, and which society is enjoined to clear as soon as possible. Ideologically, too, there is a patent antithesis with neo-liberalism, which furthers and justifies both of the 'great divergences'.

10 CHINA AND CLASS STRUGGLE

What form, then, do class relations and class struggle take in China? Any answer that ignores the international context would be superficial. It is appropriate to recall the criticisms which the US TV journalist Mike Wallace conveyed to Deng Xiaoping on 2 September 1986: 'Western investors complain that China is making it difficult to do business here: exorbitant rent for offices, too much bickering about contracts, too many special taxes, labour that is too expensive'.[81] Such complaints are renewed whenever the Beijing government enacts laws favourable to the working class or seeking to restrict its exploitation. Today, in the face of a rapid increase in wages and the introduction of stricter environmental and ecological norms, transnationals react by relocating their plants to more backward, more accommodating countries, sometimes even returning home—especially to the USA, where labour costs have declined significantly in the interim. We can understand why initially, to overcome penury and the absolute qualitative inequality bound up with it, the rulers in Beijing were mainly concerned to consolidate the industrial and technological base.

The international conditioning of China's economic policy—something regularly ignored by adherents of the idealism of practice—does not end there. Let us look at the situation in the second half of the 1990s. We are already familiar with Washington's recurrent threat to close the US market to Chinese goods, resorting to a measure that had for some time represented the commercial equivalent of using 'nuclear weapons'. China was able to seek shelter by joining the World Trade Organization. However, the latter, and the other international economic organizations hegemonized by the USA and the West, pressed for rapid, massive dismantling of state industry, regardless of the social costs—growth in unemployment and the loss of social benefits (child care, health provision, etc.), which have traditionally been linked to employment in a state factory in China.[82] On other occasions, Washington's interventions have been more direct. The US press has referred to the warnings issued by the American ambassador in Beijing about the 'adverse consequences' of the retention of an extensive state and collective economic sector and 'not making a stronger commitment to the market'. A policy which, rather than closing loss-making state enterprises, 'tr[ied] to make them more competitive', was deemed worrying and unacceptable. Frank indignation was provoked by the emergence of a 'strategy' based on the 'proposition' that 'foreign investors' would collaborate 'with Communist Party bosses to bring modern technology and management techniques to China's state industries'.[83]

In the meantime, China has been admitted to the World Trade Organization. Thanks to this, and the Asian country's prodigious economic development, the commercial 'nuclear weapon' has been neutralized. But this does not mean that the arsenal of commercial weapons at Washington's disposal is empty. If China wishes to be recognized as a country with a market economy (and thereby in one way guaranteed against the threat of protectionism), especially if it wishes to have the technological embargo it remains subject to, relaxed, it is exhorted to make further concessions of the kind we have already noted. We know that, like other countries with an anti-capitalist and anti-colonial revolution behind them, China finds itself having to confront two different inequalities: global inequality and domestic inequality. Hence, it is as if Washington addressed Beijing as follows: if you wish to clear the obstacles that impede overcoming the first type of inequality (with the abolition of the rules that prevent or impede access to the most advanced technology), you must make concessions that actually aggravate the second type of inequality (dismantling the state sector would entail reduced capacity to intervene on behalf of less developed regions and thereby make the struggle against regional inequalities more difficult).

In theory, China could avoid such pressures and conditions by embarking on a more or less autarkic road of development. In reality, as the *Communist Manifesto* had already explained, the economic and technological lag cannot be overcome in isolation from an ongoing process at a global level, which sees 'old-established national industries' replaced by 'new industries, whose introduction becomes a life and death question for all civilised nations, by industries that no longer work up indigenous raw material, but raw material drawn from the remotest zones; industries whose products are consumed, not only at home, but in every quarter of the globe'.[84] In other words, the development of a country that has made an anti-capitalist or anti-colonial revolution is inconceivable if it does not hook up with a world market still largely controlled by the bourgeoisie. There is no real alternative to the option of dancing with wolves.

We may draw a conclusion. If we wish to understand the terms of the class struggle in China correctly, we must bear in mind the role of the Western, and especially the US bourgeoisie. Its offensive is not restricted to the state sector of the economy and, more generally, the leadership role of political power in the economy. It is a politico-ideological offensive that seeks to demonize Mao on the basis of an absolutization and decontexualization of his unhappiest years in power. In the case of a leader who died in 1976, and who governed the whole of China from 1948 and more or less extensive areas of it from 1928 onwards, only the years of the Great Leap Forward and the Cultural Revolution are taken into account. What gets repressed is the essential thing. Taken as a whole, the 'social achievements of the Mao era' were 'extraordinary'; they involved a marked improvement in economic, social, and cultural conditions and a significant increase in the Chinese people's 'life expectancy'. Without these premises, we cannot understand the prodigious economic development that subsequently freed hundreds of millions of people from hunger and even from death by starvation.[85]

Secondly, Western ideologues are silent about the fact that the Great Leap was, in many respects, a desperate attempt to deal with a devastating embargo. It also applies in part to the Cultural Revolution, which was characterized by the illusion that it was possible to promote extremely rapid economic growth by appealing to mass mobilization and methods successfully adopted in the military struggle. All of this was undertaken in the hopes of putting an end to the devastation of the 'economic war' behind which could be glimpsed the threat of an even more total war. By virtue of these two distortions, those jointly—or perhaps mainly—responsible for a tragedy pose as judges and pronounce sentence: Mao, the protagonist of an epic national liberation struggle that defeated the plans for colonization and enslavement pursued by the Third Reich's Asian imitators, is put on a par with Hitler! This operation aims to undermine the self-respect of members of the Communist Party and citizens of the People's Republic, in the context of a crusade seeking to wield the power of wealth over Beijing, in order to suppress what is regarded as an intolerable anomaly. The combination of economic and politico-ideological pressures represents the principal class struggle in and over China.

An elementary consideration suffices to appreciate this: major industrial and technological development, and the escape from 'poverty' of 'more than 600 million people',[86] or (according to other calculations) '660 million people',[87] would not have been possible had China not defeated US plans for regime change. And the success of any such project now would block the road to the further advances required in the struggle against the two inequalities and would, in fact, imperil what has already been achieved.

Naturally, the domestic bourgeoisie, which is growing rapidly, cannot be ignored. Workers struggling for higher wages and better living and working conditions, who have achieved (and are achieving) significant results, often clash with it. But such struggles are not aimed at overthrowing or challenging the government, and in fact often call on its support to face down the arrogance and resistance of particular local employers or bosses.

It is an attitude that often amazes Western Marxists. They call on Chinese workers to reject any compromise with state power in their industrial struggles and regard themselves as radical and even revolutionary in so doing. In reality, they recall to mind the Belgian worker Lazarevic, who in a Soviet Russia devastated by world war and civil war was ready to denounce any attempt by the Soviet government to reorganize the industrial and economic apparatus as synonymous with exploitation (Chap. 8, Sect. 1). Obviously, the situation in today's China is very different. Yet, Chinese workers, who are often members of the Communist Party, and in that capacity are also concerned with promoting the technological development of the firms they work in and the nation they belong to, have possibly learnt something, directly or indirectly, from *What is to be Done?*. Lenin criticized the corporatist trade-union secretary for losing sight of the struggle for emancipation in its different national and international aspects, thereby sometimes becoming the prop of 'a nation which exploits the whole world' (at the time, Britain). The revolutionary who is a 'tribune of the people' adopts a very different attitude. He or she must be able to take account of the totality of political and social relations, nationally and internationally. Chinese workers, although only vaguely aware of the fact that their country's technological development frustrates 'economic annexation' (Lenin), or 'economic aggression' and the 'economic yoke' (Guevara) imposed by imperialism on rebellious countries, are much closer to the 'tribune of the people' (agent of revolutionary class struggle) than Western Marxists, preoccupied exclusively with wages. Unlike their putative defenders, these workers intuit that the main antagonists in the class struggle in and around China are the American and Western bourgeoisie and a revolutionary political stratum which has become autonomous but which, in contrast to Eastern Europe, still enjoys great prestige because it consistently embodies the cause of national emancipation.

Nobody can foresee the outcome of this struggle. Not Chinese capitalists, who are obliged to come to terms with the policy described by Mao as the 'political expropriation' of the bourgeoisie, but its only partial 'economic expropriation'. This political expropriation does not simply entail the impossibility of converting economic power into political power. In reality, it is the bourgeoisie's economic power itself that is subject to powerful political conditioning. It is enough to enter a privately owned Chinese firm to realize the influence wielded in it by the Communist Party and organized Communist workers. They encourage the owners to either reinvest a significant share of the profits in the enterprise's technological development, so as to further the growth of the productive forces and the country's modernization, and to reduce or eliminate the first type of inequality; or to use part of the profits for social initiatives. Given that private firms largely depend on the credit supplied by the state-controlled banking system, a conclusion dictates itself: in private firms the power of private ownership is balanced and limited by a kind of counter-power. Chinese capitalists who cannot adapt to this situation leave the country but find it difficult to transfer their wealth.

The outcome of the struggle cannot be foreseen by the Communist Party either. It is conscious of the need to advance along the road of democratization, despite the persistence and, in some respects, exacerbation of military encirclement and threat. But even in the vagueness of its features, the democracy pursued in Beijing is not that invoked by the West, which by democracy ultimately means the possibility of the Chinese bourgeoisie ultimately converting economic power into political power. At the same time, we must bear in mind that within the Communist Party of China there seems to be a clash between a purely national current, which regards the revolutionary process as concluded with the achievement of national objectives (modernization, restoration of territorial integrity, and the renaissance of China), and a current with much more ambitious objectives pertaining to the history and ideals of the communist movement.

One thing is certain. With its development, which continues to be largely directed by the political power, and even now seeks to subordinate the hunt for profit by private sectors of the economy to general ends, China is the country that more than any other is challenging the international division of labour imposed by colonialism and imperialism, and furthering the end of the Columbian epoch—a fact of enormous, progressive historical significance.

Notes

1. Hannah Arendt, *On Revolution*, London: Penguin, 2006, pp. 52–3.
2. Hannah Arendt, *Crises of the Republic*, San Diego, New York and London: Harcourt Brace Jovanovich, 1972, p. 204.
3. Ibid., p. 123.
4. See Charles-Louis Montesquieu, *The Spirit of the Laws*, ed. and trans. Anne M. Cohler, Basia C. Miller and Harold S. Stone, Cambridge: Cambridge University Press, 1989, Book 7, Chapter 1, p. 96.
5. Hippolyte Taine, *Le origini della Francia contemporanea. L'antico regime*, Milan: Adelphi, 1986, p. 430.
6. Karl Marx and Frederick Engels, *Collected Works*, London: Lawrence & Wishart, 1975–2004, Vol. 35, p. 245.
7. Ibid., Vol. 35, p. 247.
8. Arendt, *On Revolution*, pp. 52, 104.
9. Marx and Engels, *Collected Works*, Vol. 6, p. 489.
10. Marx and Engels, *Collected Works*, Vol. 29, p. 92; Vol. 35, p. 366.
11. Ibid., Vol. 35, p. 447.
12. Ibid., Vol. 35, p. 398.
13. Ibid., Vol. 19, p. 54.
14. Ibid., Vol. 35, p. 447.
15. Ibid., Vol. 35, pp. 432–3.
16. Ibid., Vol. 6, pp. 207.
17. Ibid., Vol. 35, p. 416.
18. Quoted in ibid., Vol. 29, p. 97.
19. Ibid., Vol. 6, p. 188.
20. Ibid., Vol. 6, p. 492.
21. Ibid., Vol. 35, pp. 443–5.
22. Ibid., Vol. 6, pp. 491–2.
23. Jürgen Habermas, *Communication and the Evolution of Society*, trans. Thomas A. McCarthy, Cambridge: Polity Press, 1991, pp. 151–2.
24. Michel Albert, *Capitalism against Capitalism*, trans. Paul Haviland, Oxford: Blackwell, 1993, pp. 22, 40.
25. Jens Jessen, 'Unterwegs zur Plutokratie', *Die Zeit*, 1 September 2011.
26. Jürgen Habermas, *Per la riconstruzione del materialismo storico*, Milan: Etas, 1979, p. 89.
27. Marx and Engels, *Collected Works*, Vol. 20, p. 10.
28. Ibid., Vol. 20, p. 10.
29. Oswald Spengler, *Jahre der Entscheidung*, Munich: Beck, 1933, pp. 120–1.
30. Antonio Gramsci, *Cronache Torinesi 1913–1917*, ed. Sergio Caprioglio, Turin: Einaudi, 1980, p. 175 and *L'Ordine Nuovo 1919–1920*, ed. Valentino Gerratana and Antonio A. Santucci, Turin: Einaudi, 1987, p. 520.

31. Mao Zedong, *On Diplomacy*, Beijing: Foreign Languages Press, 1998, pp. 87–8.
32. Frantz Fanon, *The Wretched of the Earth*, trans. Richard Philcox, New York: Grove Press, 2004, pp. 89–90, 61.
33. Quoted in Jean Lacouture, *Ho Chi Minh*, trans. Peter Wiles, London: Allen Lane, 1968, pp. 22–3.
34. Palmiro Togliatti, *Opere*, Vol. 5, ed. Luciano Gruppi, Rome: Editori Riuniti, 1984, p. 382.
35. Ibid., p. 866.
36. Quoted in Peter Hennessy, *Never Again: Britain 1945–1951*, New York: Pantheon, 1993, p. 69.
37. Togliatti, *Opere*, Vol. 5, pp. 146, 151.
38. Samuel Huntington, *The Clash of Civilizations and the Remaking of World Order*, New York: Simon & Schuster, 1996, p. 195.
39. Eleanor Marx-Aveling and Edward Aveling, 'The Woman Question', *Marxism Today*, March 1972, pp. 82, 81.
40. See Domenico Losurdo, *Democrazia o bonapartismo. Trionfo e decadenza del suffragio universale*, Turin: Bollati Boringhieri, 1993, Chapter 6, §3.
41. See Helen Callaway and D.O. Helly, 'Crusader for Empire: Flora Shaw/Lady Lugard', and Antoinette M. Burton, 'The White Woman's Burden: British Feminists and "The Indian Woman", 1865–1915', in *Western Women and Imperialism: Complicity and Resistance*, ed. N. Chaudhuri and M. Strobel, Bloomington and Indianapolis: Indiana University Press, 1992.
42. See V.I. Lenin, *Collected Works*, London: Lawrence & Wishart, 1960–78, Vol. 23, pp. 34, 72.
43. Ibid., Vol. 25, p. 461; Vol. 22, p. 282.
44. Mao Zedong, *Selected Works*, Beijing: Foreign Languages Press, 1969–75, Vol. 1, pp. 43–6.
45. Frantz Fanon, *A Dying Colonialism*, trans. Haakon Chevalier, New York: Grove Press, 1965, pp. 107–09.
46. Ibid., pp. 37, 42–3.
47. Slavoj Zizek, 'Mao Tse-tung, the Marxist Lord of Misrule', introduction to Mao Zedong, *On Practice and Contradiction*, London and New York: Verso, 2007, pp. 2, 5.
48. Mao Zedong, *On Diplomacy*, pp. 379, 439.
49. Slavoj Zizek, *First as Tragedy, then as Farce*, London and New York: Verso, 2009, p. 125.
50. See Laurent Dubois, *Avengers of the New World: The Story of the Haitian Revolution*, Cambridge, MA and London: Belknap Press of Harvard University Press, 2004, p. 299.
51. Ibid., p. 299; Laurent Dubois, *Haiti: The Aftershocks of History*, New York: Metropolitan Books, 2012, p. 18.

52. Quoted in Dubois, *Avengers of the New World*, p. 261.
53. For the history of the category of *Under Man/Untermensch*, see Domenico Losurdo, *Nietzsche, il ribelle aristocratico. Biografia intellettuale e bilancio critico*, Turin: Bollati Borringhieri, 2002, Chapter 27, §7 and *Il linguaggio dell'Impero. Lessico dell'ideologia americana*, Rome and Bari: Laterza, 2007, Chapter 3, §5.
54. Communist Party of China, *The Polemic on the General Line of the International Communist Movement*, Beijing: Foreign Languages Press, 1965, p. 213.
55. See Dubois, *Haiti*, pp. 7–8.
56. Stephen F. Ambrose, 'When the Americans Came Back to Europe', *International Herald Tribune*, 20 May 1997, p. 10.
57. For Bolívar and Jefferson, see Domenico Losurdo, *Liberalism: A Counter-History*, trans. Gregory Elliott, London and New York: Verso, 2011, Chapter 5, §8; for the economic war against the USSR and the PRC, see Domenico Losurdo, *Stalin. Storia e critica di una leggenda nera*, Rome: Carocci, 2008, pp. 196–7, 288–9.
58. Marx and Engels, *Collected Works*, Vol. 42, p. 487.
59. Lenin, *Collected Works*, Vol. 23, p. 44.
60. Marx and Engels, *Collected Works*, Vol. 28, p. 95.
61. Mao Tse-tung, *Selected Works*, Vol. 4, p. 453.
62. Deng Xiaoping, *Selected Works*, Vol. 3, p. 202.
63. Ernesto Che Guevara, *Scritti, discorsi e diari di guerriglia 1959–1967*, ed. Laura Gonsalez, Turin: Einaudi, 1969, pp. 883, 1429.
64. Fanon, *The Wretched of the Earth*, pp. 53–4, 57.
65. Aimé Césaire, *Toussaint Louverture. La Révolution française et le problème colonial*, Paris: Présence Africaine, 1961, p. 242.
66. See Dubois, *Haiti*, p. 102.
67. Quoted in Vijay Prashad, *The Darker Nations: A People's History of the Third World*, New York: The New Press, 2007, pp. 33–4, 110.
68. Slavoj Zizek, *Living in End Times*, London and New York: Verso, 2011, p. 461.
69. Ibid., p. 453.
70. Lenin, *Collected Works*, Vol. 23, p. 31.
71. Huntington, *The Clash of Civilizations and the Remaking of World Order*, p. 231.
72. Niall Ferguson, *Civilization: The West and the Rest*, London: Penguin, 2011, p. 322.
73. H.J. Mackinder, 'The Geographical Pivot of History', *Geographical Journal*, vol. 23, no. 4, 1904, pp. 421–2.
74. Adam Smith, *An Inquiry into the Nature and Causes of the Wealth of Nations*, Indianapolis: Liberty Classics, 1981, Vol. II, Book IV, Chapter 7,

p. 626. Cf. Giovani Arrighi, *Adam Smith in Beijing: Lineages of the Twenty-First Century*, London and New York: Verso, 2007, pp. 3, 5.
75. Adolf Hitler, *Reden und Proklamationem 1932–1945*, ed. Max Domarus, Munich: Süddeutscher Verlag, 1965, pp. 75, 77.
76. See Timothy Noah, *The Great Divergence: America's Growing Inequality and What We Can Do about It*, New York: Bloomsbury Press, 2012.
77. Francesco Guerrera, 'Ascoltiamo quell'urlo in Piazza', *La Stampa*, 2 October 2011.
78. Robert B. Reich, 'When America's Rich Get Too Rich', *International Herald Tribune*, 5 September 2011.
79. Leon Trotsky, *The Revolution Betrayed: What is the Soviet Union and Where is it Going?*, trans. Max Eastman, New York: Pathfinder Press, 1980, p. 112.
80. Deng Xiaoping, *Selected Works*, Vol. 3, pp. 73, 143, 145.
81. Quoted in Deng Xiaoping, *Selected Works*, Vol. 3, p. 173.
82. See E. Stern, 'The Way Ahead for China: More Change, Sustainably', *International Herald Tribune*, 19 May 1994 and Robert A. Manning, 'Getting China to Play by the World Trade Rules', *International Herald Tribune*, 9 January 1996.
83. See Philip Bowring, 'Toward More Efficient State Capitalism, if Beijing Has its Way', *International Herald Tribune*, 9 November 1995 and P.E. Tyler, 'Industrial Reform is under Assault in China', *International Herald Tribune*, 19 June 1995.
84. Marx and Engels, *Collected Works*, Vol. 6, p. 488.
85. See Arrighi, *Adam Smith in Beijing*, p. 370.
86. Andrea Goldstein, *BRIC: Brasile, Russia, India, Cina alla guida dell'economia globale*, Bologna: il Mulino, 2011, p. 31.
87. Stephen S. Roach, 'Transforming Economic Structure Risky but Vital Task of Nation's Future', *Global Times*, 15 November 2012.

CHAPTER 13

The Class Struggle Poised between Marxism and Populism

1 Weil and the 'Struggle of Those who Obey against Those who Command'

Especially since the crisis that erupted in 2008, which has often been compared to the Great Depression, edifying discourse à la Arendt and Habermas, who oppose the miracles of technological development or 'pacification' to class struggle, have lost credibility. Internationally, too, the picture is becoming clearer. The grand bourgeoisie, promoter and beneficiary of the second 'great divergence', creating ever more extreme polarization in the West, follows the reduction in the first 'great divergence'—global inequality—with increasing alarm and seems determined to counter it with extra-economic means as well. This dangerous situation should facilitate a revival and unification of class struggles. Why is this not happening or happening only on an utterly insufficient scale? We must come to grips with a way of thinking and feeling (populism) I have frequently referred to, but which we must now examine more closely.

We may start with a philosopher who turns out to be particularly significant in this context. With a Marxist formation behind her, and inspired by a strongly sympathetic interest in the condition of the working class, she collaborated on journals of a socialist or communist, even revolutionary, stamp (*La Révolution prolétarienne*), was actively engaged in trade-unionism (and working-class struggles), had experience of factory work, and ended up breaking first with the USSR and then with Marx. In 1937, Simon Weil—the philosopher in question—having stated that

© The Editor(s) (if applicable) and The Author(s) 2016
D. Losurdo, *Class Struggle*, Marx, Engels, and Marxisms,
DOI 10.1057/978-1-349-70660-0_13

'class struggle' was 'an expression in need of quite some clarification', summarized her interpretation of it thus:

> The struggle of those who obey against those who command, when the type of domination involves the destruction of human dignity by the latter, is the most legitimate, the most justified, the most authentic thing in the world. This struggle exists from the moment those who command tend, without necessarily being conscious of it, to crush the human dignity of those in their power.[1]

By dint of its clarity, this formulation serves to bring Marx and Engels' contrasting view into sharper focus. For Weil, one can speak of class struggle only when there is a clash between the rich and powerful, on the one hand, and the weak and poor, on the other. The cause of justice and emancipation is invariably and exclusively represented by those devoid of power and material goods: class struggle exists only starting from that opposition. While it is the ordinary state of the historical and social process in Marx and Engels, in Weil, class struggle is a morally privileged moment in the history and existence of human beings.

The French philosopher construes class struggle as a moral imperative: social relations involving 'the destruction of human dignity' must be done away with. This sense is also to the fore in the authors of the *Communist Manifesto*: the 'workers of the world' exhorted to unite in struggle are the interpreters of 'the categorical imperative to overthrow all relations' that degrade and humiliate man (see Chap. 4, Sect. 3). However, we must not forget that the struggle to perpetuate exploitation and oppression is also class struggle—for example, the massacre with which the French ruling class repressed the workers' revolt of June 1848. Class struggle understood as 'more or less veiled civil war', and (according to the *Manifesto*) destined sooner or later to become 'open revolution',[2] erupted but ended, provisionally, in the triumph of the bourgeoisies. Unlike in Weil, class struggle in Marx and Engels does not necessarily involve a positive value judgement.

Even if we attend exclusively to emancipatory class struggles, the latter by no means exactly correspond to 'the struggle of those who obey against those who command' referred to Weil. It is not only members of subaltern classes who are victims of national oppression and the 'domestic slavery' imposed on women; and hence, the subjects of struggles for national liberation or women's liberation are not exclusively 'those who obey'.

Let us focus on the conflict between capital and labour. Weil's schema does not even work here. Take the bitterest class struggles experienced by Marx and Engels. In June 1848, what ensured the victory of the bourgeoisie was the support of lumpen-proletarian elements, lacking wealth and power, but inclined to place themselves in the service of those who possessed both. As regards the agitation that issued in the legal regulation of working hours in Britain, it was 'the result of centuries of struggle between capitalist and labourer', a 'civil war', 'a protracted civil war, more or less dissembled, between the capitalist class and the working class'.[3] The conflict had sometimes approached breaking point: there were moments when 'the antagonism of classes had arrived at an incredible tension'.[4] However, whereas in France the class struggle led to the revolution of June 1848, in Britain the danger of proletarian revolution from below was countered by reform from above. But this did not involve a clash exclusively between proletarians and capitalists. Among those pressing for change were also more far-sighted sectors of the dominant classes and a government which, not coincidentally, was accused of Jacobinism by its opponents.[5]

Even the Paris Commune did not witness a clash exclusively between 'those who obey' and 'those who command'. In Marx's words, an important role was played in it by 'national *souvenirs* of 1792'—indignation that the Prussia advance was not adequately resisted by the French government, which was challenged for its weakness and impotence. These memories and this sentiment tended to widen the social basis of the revolt beyond the popular classes (see Chap. 7, Sect. 10).

The inadequacy of Weil's schema is revealed with especial clarity by a historical crisis that developed across the Atlantic. I am referring to the American Civil War. Pitted against one another on the battle field were not the powerful and the weak, the rich and poor, but two regular armies. That is also why significant figures and sections of the labour movement and (more or less) socialist movement viewed the gigantic clash with detachment and condescension, especially given Lincoln's initial pronouncement that his aim was to suppress not slavery, but merely secession. From the outset, however, Marx identified the South as the self-declared champion of the cause of slave labour and the North as the more or less conscious champion of the cause of 'free' labour. In utterly unanticipated fashion, the class struggle for the emancipation of labour was embodied in a regular, disciplined, and powerfully equipped army. In 1867, publishing Volume One of *Capital*, Marx pointed to the Civil

War as 'the one great event of contemporary history', in a formulation that recalls the definition of the workers' insurrection of 1848 as 'the most colossal event in the history of European civil wars' (see Chap. 2, Sect. 7). Here, then, we have two crucial phases in the history of class struggle in the nineteenth century: class struggle could assume such 'different forms' that the protagonist of the emancipatory process might be the famished workers in rags of June 1848 or the formidable army commanded by Lincoln.

It is true that in the course of its march on the South, the Union army saw its ranks swollen by an influx of slaves or ex-slaves, who abandoned their masters or former masters to help defeat the pro-slavery secession. It was an army supported outside the USA by the sympathy of the workers most aware of what was at stake: the freedom or manifest slavery of labour. Nevertheless, it was a regular army, which for the first time in history, systematically applied industrial technology to military operations; an army which, far from lacking power, wielded it imperiously. When Lincoln, determined to defeat the South, introduced conscription, the poor immigrants—especially Irish—of New York rebelled. An army corps marched on the city to suppress the uprising with an iron fist.[6] Invariably committed to the national liberation struggle of the Irish people, in this instance, Marx had no hesitation in branding the 'Irish rabble'.[7] The European working class was enjoined to identify with the Union army, not with immigrants from the island oppressed by British imperialism. In this case, at least, the weak and poor were arrayed with reaction; actually furthering the cause emancipation were not those who obeyed (to employ Weil's language), but those who commanded.

Given Weil's theoretical presuppositions, it is easy to understand her uncertainties and oscillations in the face of the major political struggles and class struggles of the twentieth century. A text that probably followed Hitler's arrival to power by a few months expressed concern at what it might mean internationally: '[t]o defend the conquests of October against foreign capitalism would represent an aspect not of the struggle between nations but of the struggle between classes'.[8] As we can see, the conflict between Soviet Russia and Nazi Germany is subsumed under the category of class struggle (between proletariat and bourgeoisie) here. However, a contemporaneous text reached the opposite conclusion. In formulating the hypothesis of an attack on the USSR mounted by 'a fraction of the German bourgeoisie', the French philosopher was immediately concerned to make it clear that the most aggressive fraction of the German bourgeoisie was pursuing plans for an attack 'to satisfy its imperialist appetites, not—as Stalinists and even Trotskyists believe—in order to destroy a class enemy'.[9] The category of class struggle made sense in the phase immediately following October 1917, when the Bolsheviks, on the verge of losing power in Russia, were threatened by the 'so-called anti-Soviet bloc of all the capitalist states'. The schema of the opposition between the weak and the powerful, those who obey and those who command, the rich and the poor, still in some sense applied then. Now, however, as demonstrated by the 'Franco-Russian rapprochement', Soviet power had been consolidated, was a state like any other, 'a power like the rest';[10] and it made no sense to speak of class struggle in connection with a clash between constituted powers. The Third Reich certainly intended to subjugate Russia, but where was the conflict between proletariat and bourgeoisie? Where was the class struggle?

A few years later, civil war broke out in Spain. Overcoming her perplexity and hesitation, the philosopher decided to set off for the front and fight in defence of the republic. The class struggle seemed to have staged a return: the legitimate government embodied the cause of the workers and peasants and was facing a revolt by the property-owning classes, who enjoyed the support of the powerful Nazi and fascist military apparatus. Disenchantment soon set in and Weil decided to return to France. This is scarcely surprising. Ranged against one another were two armies and power apparatuses. Furthermore, the same horrible 'smell of civil war, blood and terror', even sadistic violence, emanated from both sides.[11] Above all, an international trial of strength was now bound up with the civil war. Italy and Germany had intervened in support of Franco, while Madrid's republican government enjoyed the support of the Soviet Union. And if it was difficult to distinguish between the opposed fractions of the Spanish Civil War, it proved impossible to perform this operation in the case of the alignment of the great powers. 'Given the international circulation of capital', 'antagonisms between nations' were incomprehensible. Even more so was 'the opposition between fascism and communism': 'no two such structurally similar nations as Germany and Russia, which are mutually threatening one another, exist'.[12] It was not possible to speak of class struggle because the weak—'those who do not command'—were not to be found on either side.

In reality, here is how a captain in Franco's army, Gonzalo di Aguilera, put things:

> The masses in this country ... are slave stock. They are good for nothing but slaves and only when they are used as slaves are they happy. ...When the war is over, we should destroy the sewers. The perfect birth control for Spain is the birth control God intended us to have. Sewers are a luxury to be reserved for those who deserve them, the leaders of Spain, not the slave stock.[13]

As we know, the leaders of the Third Reich intended to reduce the Slavs to conditions of slavery. Whether as regards Spain or the international conflict, we can ask what sense it makes to put aspirant slave-holders and potential slaves on a par. To speak of class struggle, Weil seeks the weak—'those who do not command'—and does not notice the overwhelming mass of slaves or potential slaves on the horizon.

2 WEIL AND 'MENDICANCY' AS THE SOLE REPOSITORY OF TRUTH

Yet, Weil immediately understood the change in the international picture that occurred with Hitler's rise to power: '[o]n the one hand, war is simply the continuation of the other war that is called competition, which makes production itself a mere form of the struggle for mastery; on the other, the whole of economic life is currently geared towards a future war'.[14] Great power rivalry for hegemony had not come to an end in 1918 and was played out economically before exploding on the battle field. This situation impacted severely on the popular masses:

> Not only the firm, but any kind of working collective, needs to limit the consumption of its own members to the maximum, so as to devote as much time as possible to forging weapons against rival collectives. So that as long as there is a struggle for power on the Earth's surface, and as long as the decisive factor in victory is industrial production, the workers will be exploited.[15]

As for Soviet Russia, it risked being reduced to a colony: '[t]o defend itself, it must constantly expand its productive apparatus and armaments, and this at the cost of complete enslavement of the labouring masses'.[16]

Were it not for the conclusions, which seem utterly incompatible with the premises, reading this analysis we might be browsing through some of the most developed resolutions of the Communist International. Even before war and massacres, imperialism entailed a decline in living standards and an intensification of the speed of work, posing an even more serious threat to Soviet Russia. An acute class struggle was underway; and for a people seeking to avoid colonial enslavement, it could only be waged by strengthening the productive and military apparatus. In Weil's view, by contrast, the general reinforcement of the productive and military apparatus proved that the exploitation of workers and the strictest factory discipline were being enforced in all countries. The proletarian was everywhere 'work fodder before being cannon fodder'. The same bleak picture everywhere presented itself of 'the despised masses, without any control over the diplomacy that threatens their life without them realizing it'.[17] Even if countries were distinguished by their greater or lesser readiness and alacrity in transforming their inhabitants into 'cannon fodder', in Weil's eyes, they were largely indistinguishable when it came to employing 'labour fodder'. The Soviet Union was no exception. In fact,

> As Marx himself recognized, the revolution cannot be made at the same time everywhere; and when it is made in a country, this does not abolish, but actually increases, that country's need to exploit and oppress the working masses, because it is afraid of being weaker than other nations. The history of the Russian Revolution affords a painful example of this.[18]

Weil was referring to a country that had emerged from a revolution which issued appeals for a dual class struggle: of Western workers against the capitalist bourgeoisie and of 'colonial slaves' (as they were characterized) against the colonialist and slave-holding great powers. The Soviet Union's commitment to developing its productive and military apparatus in order to avert colonialist enslavement can be interpreted as perfectly consistent with the second appeal. Instead, Weil interpreted it as a betrayal of the first appeal by a country which, to develop its productive and military apparatus, had no hesitation in 'exploiting and oppressing the working masses'. On closer examination, what Weil condemns is the race against time to escape the danger of colonial enslavement. However paradoxical, such is the obligatory conclusion of the (populist) view for which the only class struggle worthy of the name is the 'struggle of those who obey against those who command'.

With the outbreak of the world war, there seemed to be a shift. The horror of the war unleashed in the East by Hitler clarified the nature of Nazism. Reflecting on the history of colonialism, in 1943 Weil arrived at a significant conclusion: '[c]olonization has the same legitimacy as Hitler's analogous claim on Central Europe.... Hitlerism precisely consists in Germany's application of the methods of colonial conquest and rule to the European continent and, more generally, to white race countries'.[19] This time it was the Western colonial powers that were compared to the Third Reich, not Soviet Russia: '[f]or the English living in India, for the French living in Indochina, the human environment is composed of whites. The natives form part of the landscape'.[20] The very logic of colonialism reduced subject peoples 'to the status of human material'. Indeed, 'the populations of occupied countries are nothing else in the eyes of the Germans' and the Japanese, who were 'imitators' of Nazi Germany.[21] Colonial rule—in particular, that imposed by Hitler and his 'imitators'—entailed patent de-humanization of its victims. On the basis of Weil's own definition—class struggle combats 'the destruction of human dignity'– we must unquestionably speak of class struggle in connection with the Great Patriotic War and other liberation struggles against German and Japanese imperialism. But the French philosopher did not use this category: the possibility, in specific circumstances, of class struggle taking the form of national struggle lay beyond her intellectual horizons.

In other words, Weil's position shifted politically, rather than theoretically. She did not place the various participants in the war on par. On the contrary, she sought to make a contribution to the defeat of the Third Reich, organizing a nursing corps for the front and being ready to die herself. But now let us read a letter that is sometimes celebrated, but which seems to me to be morally questionable: '[i]n this world, only beings who have succumbed to the lowest level of humiliation, well beneath mendicancy, who not only lack any social consideration but are regarded by everyone as if they were devoid of the first element of human dignity, reason—only such beings are actually capable of speaking the truth'.[22] The date was 4 August 1943. Despite Stalingrad, Hitler was not yet conclusively beaten and had not in fact given up on building his continental empire. More than ever, he resorted to genocidal practices to reduce the peoples of Eastern Europe to the condition of redskins (whose land was to be expropriated) and blacks (fated to work like slaves in the service of the master race). But what Weil seems to be concerned about is a single contradiction that divides all countries from top to bottom, pitting mendicants against non-mendicants. This represents the triumph of populism: independently of any concrete historical and political analysis—there is no room for Marx's distinction between proletariat and lumpen-proletariat— the locus of moral excellence resides in those bereft of power and wealth, the weak—in fact, the humiliated and the most humiliated of all. In this instance, populism functioned as a way of evading the class struggles that were raging all around.

3 WEIL AND 'MODERN PRODUCTION' AS THE SITE OF SLAVERY

Having asserted that war and threats of war invariably result in enhanced productive efforts, a reinforcement of hierarchical and authority structures in factory and society alike, and an intensification of labour exploitation, Weil took a further step. Regardless of the international situation, even in the absence of conflicts and tensions between different countries, 'the very regime of modern production, that is, large-scale industry' should be challenged. The reason was simple: '[w]ith the industrial prisons that are large factories, only slaves can be made, not free workers'.[23] The overthrow of capitalism and nationalization of firms would not bring any real change: 'the total subordination of the worker to the firm and those who manage it rests on the factory structure, not the property regime'; 'the abolition of private property would not be enough to prevent toil in mines and factories weighing like slavery on those subject to it'.[24]

At this point, a break with Marx is inevitable. He was accused of having cultivated a 'religion of the productive forces' not dissimilar from the bourgeois cult, not dissimilar from the religion 'in whose name generations of entrepreneurs have crushed the labouring masses without any remorse'. For Marx, 'the task of revolutions essentially consists in the emancipation not of men, but of the productive forces'.[25]

In reality, we have seen Marx cast the class struggle as a struggle for recognition, waged against a socio-political system that dehumanizes and reifies a huge mass of concrete individuals; and denounce capitalist production for 'sqander[ing] human lives', for a 'Timur-Tamerlanish prodigality of human life', indeed for 'incessant human sacrifices from among the working class' (see Chap. 4, Sect. 3 and Chap. 2, Sect. 12). As long as capitalism exists, 'all methods for raising the social productiveness of labour are brought about at the cost of the individual labourer; all means for the development of production transform themselves into means of dominion over, and exploitation of, the producers'.[26] What escaped Weil is the fact that, as a result of the unity between humanity and nature and the decisive role of consciousness in the development of the productive forces, the squandering and prodigality of human lives is, at the same time, a squandering and prodigality of material wealth. Capitalist destruction of the productive forces and capitalist destruction of human resources are intimately related—in fact, go hand in hand. The 'greatest productive power is the revolutionary class itself', the proletariat.[27] Driving workers into an early grave through an excessive work load and life of hardship also means eroding social wealth. To have at its disposal 'a mass of human material always ready for exploitation', capitalism condemns 'one part of the working class to enforced idleness'. In and through its competition, the industrial reserve army makes it possible to saddle the employed section of the working class with an excessive work load.[28] Once again, 'enforced idleness' and overwork alike involve the humiliation and degradation of concrete individuals, flesh-and-blood human beings, while they also represent the squandering and destruction of material resources. This is a process that occurs on an even larger scale during recurrent crises of over-production.

In a sense, the French philosopher recognized the incongruity of her critique when she observed that 'in Marx vigorous formulations abound about the enslavement of living labour to dead labour', of concrete individuals to the exigencies of capitalist accumulation.[29] In fact, the bone of contention is different. Marx was historically right to condemn Luddism's rage against the modern factory as such. In the first place, it can employ free workers or slaves, as occurred in Hitler's Germany and empire. The defeat of the Third Reich certainly did not betoken the end of the modern factory, but it did save a huge mass of human beings from the enslavement for which they were destined. Secondly, it is clear that within capitalism itself, in addition to foiling the reintroduction of slavery, class struggle and political action can improve the working environment and reduce working hours, and can contain and limit the 'despotism' invoked by the *Communist Manifesto*. Thirdly, however hard modern factory work might be, it becomes even more unbearable if, outside the factory gates, what awaits the worker is a condition of poverty and degradation—if, that is, productivity increases, peculiar to the modern factory, serve only to enrich a handful of exploiters. For these three reasons class struggle and political action are decisive and can produce radical changes. We may conclude with Marx: 'the present use of machinery is one of the relations of our present economic system, but the way in which machinery is exploited is quite distinct from the machinery itself. Powder is still powder, whether you use it to wound a man or to dress his wounds'.[30] Acquisition of a mature class consciousness presupposes overcoming Luddism: it is a question of fighting not machines and modern industry, but capitalist utilization of them.

For Weil, by contrast, the target of genuine class struggle was modern industry, which entailed 'the total subordination of the worker'. The struggle for freedom had to target 'large factories', which 'can make nothing but slaves'. If supporters of Luddism seem mad and criminal from Arendt's standpoint, in that they are guilty of preventing the only possible solution of the social question and poverty, they become saints and martyrs in the calendar of struggles for freedom and emancipation notionally compiled by Weil. While Arendt flees class struggle as an 'incubus', Weil warmly embraces it, but interprets it in a Luddite key and deflects it towards a Quixotic objective.

Criticizing Sismondi, Marx observed that it was inane to seek to 'proscribe science from industry, as Plato expelled poets from his Republic'. In truth, '[s]ociety is undergoing a silent revolution, which must be submitted to'.[31] In a world where knowledge has become the productive force *par excellence*,[32] the development of science, technology and methods of production that increasingly incorporate both is a destiny which can be escaped only by an inconceivable, disastrous mutilation of human intellectual capacities.

It should be added that, in a far from a unified world where international conflicts are often the order of the day, for a poorly developed country to renounce modern industry is to expose itself to extremely grave dangers. It is a point underscored by Weil herself, when she analysed the international situation in the inter-war period. Populists can obviously skip over all this and regard as morally relevant only the contradiction, internal to each country, between 'those who obey' and 'those who command'. But it is the case that, in abdicating from the task of promoting modern industry and science and technology, and *de facto* consigning itself to the laws and rule of the strongest, an undeveloped country adopts a stance that is also problematic morally.

In the inter-war years, while Weil recognized the risk Russia ran of becoming a colony, she criticized the cult of productivism prevalent in a country that sought to free itself from backwardness and penury and, at the same time, defend and consolidate its independence. Even today, there is no affinity between populism and the class struggle that less advanced countries are committed to waging against penury and neo-colonial dependence. In 2006, the Vice-President of Bolivia (Garcia Linera) expressed sentiments that are very widespread in Latin America (and the Third World generally), when he stressed the need to achieve a 'progressive dismantling of colonial economic dependence', and launched the slogan of 'industrialization or death'.[33] The motto 'Fatherland or death', with which Fidel Castro's speeches and Che Guevara's speeches and letters sometimes conclude,[34] now reverberates as 'industrialization or death'. The second formulation is simply a clarification of the first. While the first expresses the identity, in specific circumstances, of the 'social question' and the 'national question' (Marx), or 'class struggle' and 'national struggle' (Mao), the second expresses an awareness that political independence proves fragile and even illusory if not sustained by economic (and technological) independence—an awareness that termination of 'political annexation' is not in and of itself the overcoming of 'economic' annexation (Lenin). And without that, the recognition that makes self-constitution as a nation-state possible is not really achieved. This is proved today by wars whose victims are countries unable to mount any real resistance to the Western great powers.

4   Populism as Nostalgia for 'Original Fullness'

In Weil, the remorseless critique of modernity and industry is the obverse of a vision of the past full of *pietas*. This is a feature of populism that we can analyse with Marx's help. He offered a dazzling summary of the tragedy of India colonized by Britain. This was a society deprived of its 'old world' without being compensated by the 'conquest of a new world' (see Chap. 6, Sect. 3). Such a situation generates a 'particular kind of melancholy', inclined to transfigure the past. Hence, the widespread tendency in India at the time to regret a society 'contaminated by distinctions of caste and by slavery', where the individual was subject to inviolable 'traditional rules', imprisoned in a narrow circle (which seemed like 'never changing natural destiny') and, especially in the case of the poor, forced to lead an 'undignified, stagnatory, and vegetative life'.[35] However, in the absence of a 'new world', the 'old world', idealized and transfigured in the light of the sufferings of the present and vague memories of the past, continued to be an object of heart-rending nostalgia.

This was not something exclusive to the colonial world. It also manifested itself in Europe in the midst of the industrial revolution, which (in the words of the *Communist Manifesto*) 'has put an end to all feudal, patriarchal, idyllic relations … and has left remaining no other nexus between man and man than naked self-interest, than callous "cash payment". ...It has resolved personal worth into exchange value'.[36] What ensued (observes the *Grundrisse*) was 'complete emptiness', inspiring regret for a mythical 'original fullness' and 'the illusion of the "purely personal relationships" of feudal times' and the pre-modern, pre-industrial world in general.[37]

This is the context in which to situate a mass movement like Luddism, on the one hand, and an eminent contemporary of Marx's, on the other, criticized by him for 'retreat[ing] into the past, becom[ing] a *laudator temporis acti*'.[38] I am referring to Sismondi. Escaping with his family from revolutionary France, sceptical about its plans for radical socio-political transformation, and yet sympathizing with popular suffering, in order to avoid or alleviate it he seemed to propose putting a brake on industrial development. In his view, the introduction of new, more powerful machinery brought about an 'increase in productivity', but ended up destroying the preceding balance, without yielding any real, enduring advantage. The picture was a bleak one: the 'old looms will be lost' and, with them, the world of the weak, which was certainly marked by modest living conditions and even penury, but nevertheless rich in its serenity and dignity.[39]

Here we encounter the first form of populism, subjected by Marx to caustic criticism: 'original fullness' was a figment of the imagination and of the repression of travails and suffering even more grievous than those from which an escape was being sought. Turning to the past, we find not a more vibrant spirituality, but a world where the daily struggle for survival can render it impossible. We find not richer personal and inter-subjective relations, but much greater poverty. In fact, on closer inspection, the figure of the subject, of the individual, has not yet really emerged.

In as much as it evinces genuine sympathy for the sufferings of the weak in the grips of the Industrial Revolution, this first form of populism expresses, albeit immaturely, a legitimate, indisputable protest. But it can take a very different, rather instrumental form. It is employed by those who wish to neutralize, blunt or deflect the protest of the subaltern classes. As regards this second aspect, Marx is perhaps the harshest critic of the topos wherein, for example, Mandeville has it that the 'greatest King' would envy the 'peace of mind' met with in the 'meanest and most uncivilised Peasant', the 'calmness and tranquillity of his soul'.[40] The peasant constantly on the verge of starvation is enjoined to be content with his situation and, indeed, cling to it as though it were an asset and privilege. The 'charming' world over which Mandeville goes into ecstasies becomes the 'idiocy of rural life' referred to by the *Communist Manifesto*,[41] which does not bode well. Later, Marx explained the broad support enjoyed by Louis Bonaparte in the peasant world thus: there was 'no wealth of social relationships' and 'intercourse with society' was extremely limited. This served to disarm peasants in the face of manoeuvring by the Bonapartist adventurer and dictator.[42]

Arguably, no one is further removed from Marx than Tocqueville, who described the condition of the poor man in the *ancien régime* as follows. Characterized by 'limited' desires and serene indifference towards 'a future that did not belong to him', his fate was 'less to be lamented than that of men of the people today'. Habituated to their condition, the poor of the *ancien régime* 'enjoyed the kind of *vegetative* happiness whose appeal is as difficult for the civilized man to understand as it is to deny its existence'. The word I have emphasized is thought-provoking: it is the term we have seen Marx use to stigmatize the 'undignified, stagnatory, and vegetative life' peculiar to Indian caste society, which is ultimately unworthy of a human being.

The view we find in Mandeville and Tocqueville—that economic and material penury goes hand in hand with spiritual wealth or, at all events, with 'serenity' or some form of 'happiness'—is nothing but a mystificatory consolation. In addition to a different, more just distribution of income, the class struggle must aim to overcome material poverty, which is also synonymous with poverty of social relations, and hence, spiritual poverty—primarily, thanks to a different mode production and more intensive development of the productive forces.

Marx also contradicted another commonplace of the rhetoric peculiar to this first form of populism. It is fond of contrasting the cocoon-like serenity of a small village community with the upheavals of the political world and global history. Such rhetoric was already widespread in Germany at the time of the French Revolution and the reaction to it. In the *Aesthetics*, Hegel had observed that, while it could encourage an attitude of 'blinkered philistinism', the narrow social circle peculiar to a small strip of the countryside did not afford protection against the 'greatest world events', the major historical upheavals.[43] Marx went further, as emerges from his observation that it was precisely the 'idiocy of rural life' which furnished the base for the disaster of the advent of Bonapartism in France, with its sequel of ruthless military dictatorship at home and sanguinary military adventures abroad.

Populism simply does not fulfil its promise. Yet historical situations emerge that are conducive to its re-emergence. One thinks of the years between the two world wars, both of which were marked by the large-scale application of science and technology to colossal bloodbaths. This was when the Great Depression succeeded the expectation of uninterrupted growth in social wealth. If a solution seemed to emerge, it was represented by military 'Keynesianism', as demonstrated in particular by the case of Hitler's Germany. The development of the productive forces, thus, corresponded to novel, enormous destruction of material resources and human lives. In this spiritual climate, which found its highest expression in Simone Weil, regret for a mythical 'original fullness' was bound to make its reappearance.

Let us turn to our day, to the world in the aftermath of the defeat of the revolutionary project or, at least, the end of hopes for total regeneration. The more large-scale industry subjects agricultural sectors to its control and destroys artisanal manufacture and traditional domestic industry, and the greater the impact of the upheavals of globalization, the more space there is for regret for, and transfiguration of, past social relations. At least in the past—so it is argued and often fantasized—community bonds and shared values existed, in a world that was not yet invested by division and crisis, and hence, meaningful. One thinks of an author like Pasolini and his denunciation of the 'genocide' for which, despite its significant extension of life expectancy, industrial and neo-capitalist development was responsible, with its 'suppression of broad swathes of society'—that is, widely diffused cultures and life forms.[44] And the populist temptation becomes even stronger following the advent or exacerbation of the ecological crisis.

5 THE POPULISM OF TRANSFIGURATION OF THE OPPRESSED

A second form of populism is, or can be, related to this first form. It is characterized by a transfiguration not of the past, but of the victims of the present, who are represented and idealized as the embodiment of moral excellence. This is the context in which to situate Weil's celebration of 'beings who have fallen to the lowest level of humiliation, well below mendicancy', as the only ones in a position to state the truth. They are strangers to the luxury, artifice, inauthenticity and, ultimately, dishonesty peculiar to the affluent and dominant classes. Far removed from power and rule, mendicants and the weak also represent clemency. This is the first variant of the second form of populism.

There is a second variant, which identifies not the subaltern classes or any particular one of them, but some oppressed people, as the locus of moral excellence. During the twentieth century, Gandhi conjoined denunciation of British and Western colonial rule with celebration of 'Hinduness' as proximate to nature, foreign to luxury, and inclined to modesty and frugality, as a well as a guardian of moral values (starting with a rejection of violence and the logic of subjugation) unattainable by the oppressors. In his turn, the African politician and intellectual Leopold Senghor intoned a hymn to 'negritude', contrasting it with the lethal culture of the frigid white man, supposedly bereft of sympathetic impulses and interested only in calculation and calculating rationality, and who not by accident had imprinted domination, destruction and death on the history of the world.[45]

Finally, the populism of transfiguration of the oppressed presents itself in a third variant, which identifies the locus of moral excellence not in the 'mendicancy' celebrated by Weil, and not in the 'Hinduness' or 'negritude' of Gandhi or Senghor, but in 'gender difference' and a different social figure who is the victim of oppression. Qua creator of life, it is now woman who is closer to nature and further removed from artifice and inauthenticity, and who represents the antithesis to the culture of violence and domination, now embodied in male humanity.

In the struggle to free themselves from the self-hatred and the denigration they have traditionally been subjected to, the protagonists of social, national, and sexual liberation movements often adopt stereotypes from conservative and reactionary culture, while reversing their value judgements and turning them against their oppressors. For centuries, discrimination against subaltern classes, colonial peoples, and women was justified by their alleged inability to genuinely raise themselves above the state of nature and argue in rigorously and abstractly logical terms, by their lack of courage and martial spirit, by their tendency to let themselves be governed by their feelings and emotional reactions. The reversal of the value judgement does not make the traditional stereotypes credible. Such an operation is obviously an understandable and legitimate form of protest, a moment in the struggle for emancipation. But use is being made of an ideology that is also liable to be employed in a conservative sense.

We can see this at once in connection with the third variant of populism. In May 1846, Marx and Engels felt compelled to polemicize against Hermann Kriege. The latter preached a form of 'communism' understood as overcoming the existing 'kingdom of hatred' based on the religion of profit, on cold insensitivity to the needs and griefs of neighbours, and on subjugation. In its stead, the 'kingdom of love' that 'flees before the rattle of money' was to be realized, and a community animated by the warmth of sentiment and love of one's neighbour founded. In the event, women alone could be the protagonists of this transformation. They were exhorted 'to turn their backs on the politics of old' and 'pronounce the first consecration of the long-promised kingdom of bliss'. Marx and Engels mocked this sentimental effusion, whose only content was '[w]oman's hypocritical and ignorant *captatio benevolentiae*'.[46] The ideology vigorously countered here was represented in a slightly different form two years later by an author—Daumer—whom we have seen commending the tranquillity and felicity of nature against the tumult and destruction of the 1848 revolution (see Chap. 2, Sect. 11). In Daumer, the place of nature was sometimes taken by woman: 'nature and woman are the really divine ... The sacrifice of the human to the natural, of the male to the female, is the genuine, the only true meekness and self-externalisation, the highest, nay, the only virtue and piety'. Having criticized Daumer's tendency to 'flee before ... historical tragedy ... to alleged nature, i.e. to a stupid rustic idyll', Marx and Engels also ridiculed his conjunction of the 'cult of nature' and 'cult of woman'. By virtue of her intimate connection with the reproduction of life, and hence, nature, woman supposedly represented an escape from the violence rampant in the historical and political universe. In reality, nature was synonymous not with peace and reconciliation, but with catastrophic violence and, as regards the animal world, a war of all against all. Just as the 'rustic idyll' has nothing to do with the struggle against environmental degradation, so the conjunction of a 'cult of nature' and a 'cult of woman' can be tantamount to an evasion of the struggle for female emancipation. In effect, Daumer was not only silent about 'the present social position of women', but utilized his 'cult' to enjoin them to put up with the familial and civil subalternity imposed on them.[47] It might be said that Marx and Engels counter-posed feminism as class struggle for emancipation to feminism as edifying populism.

About a century after Kriege and Daumer, in 1938 Virginia Wolf wrote: 'to fight has always been the man's habit, not the woman's ... Scarcely a human being in the course of history has fallen to a woman's rifle; the vast majority of birds and beasts have been killed by you [men], not us'.[48] The factual datum foregrounded here is indisputable. The issue is whether it pertains to the nature of man and woman, or rather to a historically determinate social division of labour. To take an example, in the time of Muhammad women converted to the cause of the prophet may not have fought, but they were not external to the war machine. They urged on the combatants with their exhortations and songs: 'If you advance, we will embrace you,/We will spread cushions for you;/If you retreat, we will leave you/And in no way that is loving'.[49]

Albeit in less pronounced form, a similar division of labour has been operative in the West, even in the most tragic and bloody periods of its history. When we read that in Great Britain, even before 1914, women engaged in 'shaming boyfriends, husbands, and sons into volunteering for wartime service',[50] we are led to think of the women or the Graces and Muses who encouraged and spurred on Muhammad's warriors. The role of women in this division of labour, marked by total mobilization and generalized militaristic fervour, did not escape Kurt Tucholsky, who in 1927 levelled a serious accusation: '[a]long with the evangelical clergy, in the war there was another human species that never tired of sucking blood: this was a particular stratum, a specific type of German woman'. As the massacre assumed ever more terrible forms, she sacrificed 'sons and husbands' and bemoaned not 'having enough of them to sacrifice'.[51]

While he did not explicitly pronounce on this subject, Marx underscored the key role of the division of labour on several occasions. *The Poverty of Philosophy* identifies completely with Adam Smith's thesis:

> The difference of natural talents in different men is, in reality, much less than we are aware of; and the very different genius which appears to distinguish men of different professions, when grown up to maturity, is not upon many occasions so much the cause, as the effect of the division of labour. The difference between the most dissimilar characters, between a philosopher and a common street porter, for example, seems to arise not so much from nature, as from habit, custom, and education.[52]

Having quoted this passage, *The Poverty of Philosophy* appears to go even further: '[i]n principle, a porter differs less from a philosopher than a mastiff from a greyhound. It is the division of labour which has set a gulf between them'.[53]

Those sections of the women's movement that regard woman as such as incarnating a rejection of the culture of death, refer in support of their thesis to women's role in reproducing life. However, historically, this role has sometimes assumed the converse significance to that attributed to it. In Sparta, it was precisely the mother who exhorted the son born of her to learn to face death in battle: 'return with this shield or on top of it'—that is, victorious and with arms in hand or dead as a courageous, honoured warrior. Historically, it has also been the case that, in desperate situations, it is precisely mothers who inflicted death on their new-born children to save them from a horrible or intolerable future. Such was the conduct of Indian women afflicted by the infamies of the *conquistadores*, or of black slaves or, even earlier, in the Middle Ages of Jewish women at grips with persecution by Christian crusaders, who were determined to convert them along with their children at any cost.[54] Once again, those who extinguished a life were those who had brought it into the world.

In any event, the traditional division of labour is now coming to an end, as indicated, *inter alia*, by the growing presence of women in the armed forces (sometimes even in elite corps). As regards world views, it is likely that the distance separating a female from a male soldier is less than that separating both from someone practicing a liberal profession, for example. It is further confirmation of Smith's and Marx's thesis of the centrality of the division of labour, and hence, in Marx's eyes, of the centrality of class division and class struggle.

Each of the three variants of the second form of populism prevents or impedes the unification of class struggles. With a discourse that celebrates the weak as the exclusive embodiment of moral excellence, it is very difficult to construct the broad social bloc required to advance the struggle for the emancipation of oppressed nations and women and, in reality, to effect the anti-capitalist revolution itself. Identifying oppressed peoples, and them alone, as the repository of moral excellence, makes it difficult to appeal to the solidarity of the subaltern classes in oppressor nations. If what is hallowed is a single oppressed people, then solidarity between peoples also become difficult. Similarly, the transfiguration of women into the eternal incarnation of moral excellence risks creating a fundamental, permanent contradiction with the male sex, which would undermine all three forms of class struggle. It should be added that all three variants of the second form of populism distract attention from the real cause of exploitation, oppression, and war.

6   Populism and the Binary Interpretation of Conflict

Regarded as the exclusive repository of authentic values, the weak are the sole agents of morally relevant, significant social change in all circumstances and situations. Populism intersects with the binary interpretation of social conflict.

We can analyse the dialectic governing this nexus starting with Proudhon. While he stressed the devastating consequences for the poor of the theft of property by the narrow circle of the wealthy, he branded the women's movement, which was in its early stages, as 'pornocracy'. It was prompted not by sexual phobia, and not even primarily by the cult of patriarchal power in the family, though the latter was certainly not absent. The real explanatory key lies elsewhere. In the emergent women's movement, a far from negligible role was played by women who were not of popular extraction. It is far from surprising. We know from Adam Smith that, forced into the strictest economy and a rigid division of labour within the family, 'common people' generally express a 'strict or austere' morality in sexual matters, while 'liberal' morality, for the most part, finds expression in more or less affluent classes.[55] The critique of 'austere morality', which entails consecration of the patriarchal power of the male, tends to find more fertile ground where 'liberal morality' takes root. Western European countries, thus, witnessed the development of two different social contradictions at the time. In addition to that, pitting proletariat against bourgeoisie, the contradiction highlighted by the feminist movement was operative. The subjects of these conflicts are different. From Marx's standpoint, they are two different manifestations of 'class struggles', which is difficult to unify and merge in a single social and political bloc. A bourgeois woman can be committed to the cause of women's liberation, so that in the ambit of the male/female contradiction she pertains to the oppressed, while within the bourgeoisie/proletariat contradiction, she pertains (by dint of her social location) to the oppressor. Denunciation of the feminist movement as pornocracy allowed Proudhon to dispense with such problems and adhere to the populist schema involving the opposition exclusively of the weak and the powerful, oppressor and oppressed.

If by switching our attention from more developed countries of Western Europe, we now look east to Poland, we see a third contradiction emerge in force: the national one. We know that Marx saluted participation by the nobility, or its most advanced elements, in the national liberation struggle (itself a manifestation of class struggle, in this instance mainly targeting the Russian aristocracy, the bulwark of the *ancien régime* and imperial expansion). But this was not how Proudhon argued. He derided and condemned the national aspirations of oppressed peoples as an expression of obscurantist attachment to outdated prejudices. In Poland, an extremely broad social alliance, extending far beyond the ranks of the powerless, participated in the struggle for independence and national renaissance.

It is not surprising, given that the nation as a whole suffered oppression. But it is a scandal for the populist, inclined to believe that the only genuine contradiction is the one between rich and poor, between the weak, uncorrupted 'people' and the great and powerful (bourgeoisie and nobility). Hence, Proudhon's mocking, sarcastic attitude towards national movements. Property is theft: such is the guiding thread of the French author's most famous book. A single line of demarcation divides the whole of humanity into property-owners and non-property-owners, robbers and robbed, the wealthy and the destitute. For the populist this is the only genuinely relevant contradiction. And thus, populism betrays another of its aspects: it is also a flight from complexity.

7 THE 'TOTALITY OF BOSSES AGAINST THE TOTALITY OF WORKERS'

As we know, to implement his projects for aiding the poor and weak, Proudhon appealed to the government. The binary interpretation of conflict had not yet yielded a rigorous, consistent populism. It also applies to the expectations of 'global civil war' widespread in the ranks of the Third International for a time. Here too the binary interpretation of conflict is patent, with a state—in fact, a great power (Soviet Russia)—and highly organized hierarchical parties as protagonists on the side of the oppressed. When the state and party factor vanishes, we have populism in the pure state, as it were: the protagonists of the impending struggle are those bereft not only of wealth but also of any form of power.

In the twentieth century, with the advent of the Third Reich, Weil displayed an awareness of what was impending: not only a large-scale expansionist war but one that aimed to transform Soviet Russia into a colony. Hence, the accumulating contradictions were multiple and explosive. But the French philosopher considered only one of them to be morally and politically significant:

> Marx powerfully demonstrated that the modern mode of production is characterized by the subordination of labourers to the instruments of labour, instruments possessed by those who do not labour; and he also demonstrated that competition, knowing no weapon but exploitation of the workers, turns into a struggle of each boss against his own workers and, ultimately, *of the totality of bosses against the totality of workers*.
>
> In the same way, war is characterized today by the subordination of the combatants to the instruments of combat; and the weapons—the real heroes

of modern warfare—like the men destined to serve them, are directed by those who do not fight. Given that this apparatus of direction has no way of beating the enemy except sending its soldiers under duress to their death, the war of one state against another immediately turns into a war of the state and military apparatus against its own army; and war finally appears as a *war waged by the totality of state apparatuses and general staffs against the totality of eligible men of an age to shoulder arms.*[56]

I have italicized the passages that clearly, and even naively, express Weil's viewpoint on class struggle, or the only class struggle which may be regarded as authentic: it sees the universal embrace of the weak pitted against the universal embrace of the powerful.

A few decades later, here is how a highly prestigious Marxist intellectual commented on what occurred in Hungary in 1956: 'not with theoretical discussion, but with the explosion of armed insurrection, the Hungarian Revolution demolishes the biggest fraud in history: presentation of the bureaucratic regime as "socialist"—a fraud in which bourgeois and Stalinists, "right-wing" and "left-wing" intellectuals alike, have collaborated, because all of them found it to their personal advantage'.[57] The insurgents were obviously supported by the West. This factor, which problematizes the binary schema, is repressed: 'bourgeois and Stalinists' appear united in their attitude of repression, or barely concealed hostility, towards an insurrection from below that represents a challenge to power in the East and the West. These were the years when the Cold War, which sometimes seemed about to turn into a nuclear holocaust, reached its peak. But all this is reduced to a mere semblance, and hence, utter insignificance. No attention is paid to the Monroe Doctrine with which the Soviet Union sought to strengthen its security, but which created resentment and protest in the 'fraternal countries'. Specifically in the Hungarian case, we have seen that, in the absence of the national question, Béla Kun's brief communist experiment is inexplicable. But without it, we cannot explain the events of 1956 either.

All this is absent from Castoriadis. In his view, a single conflict was relevant: 'behind all history for a century' (i.e., since the *Communist Manifesto*) 'the struggle of the working class against exploitation, the struggle of the working class for a new form of organization of society', had been at work.[58] Not included in the category of class struggle are the gigantic struggles that prevented the Third Reich and the Empire of the Rising Sun from reducing whole populations to conditions of slavery or the anti-colonial movements that were still very much alive in the mid-twentieth century, like colonial rule in Asia, Africa, and the Middle East.

In the last, the Anglo-French-Israeli military intervention against the Egyptian (and Algerian) national revolution unfolded at the same time as the Hungarian insurrection. For Castoriadis the world picture was homogeneous: 'workers suffer the same exploitation, the same oppression to similar degrees and in similar forms'. All of them could and should draw inspiration from the Hungarian Revolution: '[i]ts lessons are also valid for Russian, Czech or Yugoslav workers, and they will be valid for Chinese workers tomorrow. And in the same way they are valid for French, British or American workers'.[59] Particularly interesting here is the reference to 'Chinese workers', invited to rise up against the directors of nationalized factories at a time when a devastating economic embargo and military threat, not excluding resort to nuclear weapons, hung over the country.

Approximately half a century later, two jointly-authored books met with an extraordinary success on the left. In them, we find the thesis that, in today's world a largely globally unified bourgeoisie is pitted against the 'multitude', which is itself unified by the disappearance of state and national boundaries.[60] Fleetingly evoking the question of Palestine, the authors write: '[f]rom India to Algeria and Cuba to Vietnam, *the state is the poisoned gift of national liberation*'. The Palestinians can count on the sympathy of the two authors. But once they are 'institutionalized', Hardt and Negri will 'no longer be at their side'. The fact is that '[a]s soon as the nation begins to form as a sovereign state, its progressive functions all but vanish'.[61] Working backwards, on the basis of this approach the epic class struggle whereby the former slaves of Santo Domingo-Haiti, having constituted themselves as a nation-state, prevented Napoleon's army from restoring colonial rule and the institution of slavery, is de-legitimized. Above all, the contemporary class struggles whereby ex-colonies seek to impart economic reality to hard-won political independence are delegitimized. In Hardt and Negri's view, one can sympathize with the Vietnamese, Palestinians, or others only as long as they are oppressed and humiliated; one can support a national liberation struggle only so long as it continues to be defeated!

This is a further expression of populism: moral excellence lies with the oppressed who rebel and those who offer help to the oppressed and rebels. But once they have won power, the latter cease to be oppressed and rebels and forfeit their moral excellence. And the one who, by virtue of aiding them, basks in their moral excellence also finds himself in serious difficulties. This is a dialectic already analysed by Hegel in connection with the Christian commandment to aid the poor, which manifestly assumes the permanence of poverty.

An author who invokes Marx, professes a revolutionary ethos, and explicitly recommends renouncing power and endeavouring to change the world 'without taking power', can be situated in the same context.[62] In this way, the weak and oppressed no longer run the risk of changing their nature and forfeiting their moral excellence. The cult of the rebel is configured as a celebration of her or his powerlessness to create and govern a new socio-political order.

Finally, in the light of these considerations we can understand the warmth with which Zizek refers to Weil's 'simple and poignant formulation' that only mendicants and outcasts are in a position to tell the truth, while everyone else lies and cannot but lie.[63] We are prompted to ask: who will tell the truth once the situation for which every critic of capitalism and neo-liberalism struggles obtains—once, that is, there is no longer mendicancy? And as to the present, who authorizes those who are not mendicants to speak in their name?

Hardt and Negri's approach throws no light on the twentieth century, which saw colonialism undermined, and Hitler's attempt to revive the colonial (and slave) system defeated, in the wake of memorable struggles waged by *national* liberation movements. Does their approach at least illuminate the present? In reality, if the dominant classes are globally unified, how are we to explain the interminable tragedy that strikes not the 'multitude', but a whole people, in Palestine? And how to explain the recurrent wars waged by the West and its premier state, which, targeting small, defenceless countries, sometimes arouse the irritation of great powers like Russia and China? During the war against Yugoslavia, one of the two authors cited above wrote: '[w]e must realize that this is not the deed of American imperialism. In fact, it is an international (or, rather, supranational) operation. And its aims are not informed by the narrow national interests of the United States. It is actually intended to safeguard human rights (or, in truth, human life)'.[64] On the one hand, we have a tautology: if Empire is without boundaries, the conflicts that occur inside it are not wars between sovereign states, but policing operations conducted against refractory, rebellious and primitive provinces. On the other, we come upon a contradiction ignored and repressed by the theoreticians of the advent of global Empire: there is not only the conflict between the dominant classes and the multitude, which knows no national and state boundaries; there is also the conflict ranging countries and states guilty of violating 'human rights' against countries and states upon whom the task of enforcing respect for them devolves; and the latter tend to coincide with the traditional protagonists of colonial domination. This convergence with the champions of what, by analogy with erstwhile white supremacy, might be called Western supremacy, is curious. But even more curious is the lack of requisite reflection: the countries tasked, independently of the UN, with intervening militarily, wherever they regard human rights as having been violated, are accorded a massively enhanced sovereignty. The obsolescence of state sovereignty, on which *Empire* lays so much stress, has turned into its opposite. Populism, which regards the constitution of a national liberation movement as a state as contamination, winds up being heavily contaminated by support for the military interventions of the most powerful state in the world.

8 'IT IS FORBIDDEN TO FORBID!' AND 'IT IS RIGHT TO REBEL!'

Failing to explain actual historical developments, (left-wing) populism encourages a vision of class struggle that leaves decisive events in world history outside of its field of vision. Let us take a deservedly famous British intellectual: David Harvey. In a chapter devoted by him to the prospects for class struggle in the world, whose title refers to Lenin (*What is to be Done?*), we read:

> Many of the revolutionary movements in capitalism's history have been broadly urban rather than narrowly factory based (the revolutions of 1848 throughout Europe, the Paris Commune of 1871, Leningrad in 1917, the Seattle general strike of 1918, the Tucuman uprising of 1969, as well as Paris, Mexico City and Bangkok in 1968, the Shanghai Commune of 1967, Prague in 1989, Buenos Aires in 2001–2 ... the list goes on and on). Even when there were key movements in the factories (the Flint strike in Michigan of the 1930s or the Turin Workers Councils of the 1920s), the organised support in the neighbourhoods played a critical but usually uncelebrated role in the political action (the women's and unemployed support groups in Flint and the communal 'houses of the people' in Turin).
>
> The conventional left has been plain wrong to ignore the social movements occurring outside of the factories and mines.[65]

It is a list that correctly argues against a narrow view of class struggle, but which immediately prompts a series of questions about omissions and inclusions alike. Let us start with the former. In the nineteenth century, we pass from the European revolutions of 1848 to the Paris Commune.

But did not the American Civil War have something to do with class struggles, by dint of being a war to end or impede what Marx characterized as a 'crusade of property against labour', saluting it in 1867 as 'the one great event of contemporary history'? Did not that massive clash, which in its final phase saw black slaves, emulators in a sense of Toussaint L'Ouverture, take up arms to fell a regime that reduced them to the condition of human livestock, have something to do with class struggle?

And in a list which (with its references to Bangkok and Shanghai) seems intent on encompassing the whole world, how are we to explain the silence on the Taiping Rebellion (1851–64), 'the bloodiest civil war in world history with an estimated 20 to 30 million dead'? The fact is that this conflict possessed a national dimension as well: the rebels took up arms in the name of social justice, but also to put an end to a dynasty that had capitulated to the aggression of 'British *narcotraficantes*' and rulers,[66] to terminate 'the Ching regime, the running dog of imperialism'.[67] It is no accident if, in the areas controlled by them, the Taiping hastened to prohibit the consumption of opium—a *de facto* challenge to the London government, which lined up behind the tottering dynasty. Once again evincing both prophetic foresight and revolutionary impatience, Marx observed in 1853 that 'the chronic rebellions subsisting in China for about ten years past ... [have] now gathered together in one formidable revolution', which was destined to make its influence felt well beyond Asia. This revolution certainly had internal 'social causes', but was motivated by a national impulse as well. It was also a consequence of the humiliation, financial drain and general breakdown devastating a whole nation from the first Opium War onwards.[68] A question is indicated: is all this foreign to class struggle or is it one of the most important chapters in nineteenth-century class struggle?

No less significant is the absence from Harvey's list of the Sepoys' revolt in India in 1857, which has been characterized by a contemporary Indian historian as a 'gigantic class struggle' and, at the same time, a major anti-colonial revolution. This 'patriotic and ... class, civil war' was waged primarily by peasants, targeted colonial rule and 'pro-British big princes and big merchants', and lasted far beyond 1857. At times, it developed along the lines of the model later theorized by Mao of the countryside encircling the city and cost more than ten million Indian lives.[69] Is the silence explained by the 'identity between national struggle and class struggle' which, according to Mao, tended to obtain in anti-colonial revolutions?

Even more radically selective, in the list reproduced above, is the interpretation of class struggles and revolutionary movements in the twentieth century. From 1917 and the October Revolution, we jump half a century to arrive at 1967–9. And Stalingrad? What occurred in Seattle between 1918 and 1919 was certainly a major class struggle, in which 100,000 workers went on strike against starvation wages, the abolition of trade-union rights in the wake of imperialist war and, ultimately, capitalism. But it would be very strange not to refer to class struggle when it comes to the epic resistance mounted by tens of millions of people, a whole people who, arms in hand, repulsed the most powerful army in the world and its attempt to enslave them. And how are we to assess the uprisings against the Nazi occupation that occurred in successive European countries, and the revolutions in the colonial or semi-colonial world which continued to develop even later, effecting unprecedentedly radical changes in the global set-up? To judge from the British scholar's silence, one would say that wars of resistance and national liberation, and anti-colonial insurrections and revolutions, have little or nothing to do with class struggle.

The upshot is paradoxical. It might be said that class struggle occurs exclusively on the occasion of isolated events—when, neatly separated by a clear line of demarcation, exploited and exploiter, oppressed and oppressor, clash directly. That is to say, Marx and Engels' theory is applied, and considered applicable, only in connection with a restricted micro-history—the only history that is truly significant from the standpoint of the emancipation of the exploited and oppressed—while everything else is demoted to the status of a profane macro-history, which is extraneous and irrelevant to the sacred history of salvation or the cause of emancipation.

In reality, when Marx refers to history as the history of class struggle, his intention is to construe thus, not only the strikes and social conflicts that occur on a daily basis but also and above all major crises, the great historical turning-points which occur in full view of everyone. Class struggle is an exoteric macro-history, not the esoteric micro-history to which it is often reduced. We are clearly dealing with a dilemma. Either the theory of 'class struggles' formulated in the *Communist Manifesto* is valid—and then we must know how to interpret history as a whole in this key, starting with the decisive events of the nineteenth, twentieth and early twenty-first centuries. Or, if such events have nothing to do with class struggles, we must take our leave of this theory.

Now let us glance at some surprising inclusions in the list of 'revolutionary movements' and revolutionary class struggles compiled by Harvey. Along with 'Leningrad in 1917' we find 'Prague in 1989'. Harvey writes of the 'centuries' during which 'the principle of equality has animated political action and revolutionary movements, from the Bastille to Tiananmen Square'. From 1789 at least, 'radical egalitarianism' has not ceased to fuel hopes, agitation, revolts, and revolutions.[70] And so, directly or indirectly, we have events like Petrograd or 'Leningrad in 1917', 'Prague in 1989' and 'Tiananmen Square' juxtaposed under the sign of 'radical egalitarianism'! Should we, therefore, situate Václav Havel and the Chinese student leaders, exiles who have found their new home in the USA, in a direct line with the protagonists of the October Revolution? Both would regard, or would have regarded, the comparison as an insult. But let us pass over this. Are we to consider these figures as exponents of 'egalitarianism'—'radical egalitarianism', even? In international relations, they champion the supremacy of the West, to which they assign the right (and sometimes the duty) of military intervention anywhere in the world, in absence of any UN Security Council resolution. If we focus on social relations in a particular country, there is no doubt that Havel and the majority of the exiles from China identify with neo-liberalism. If victorious, the events in Tiananmen Square in 1989 would, in all probability, have meant the rise to power of a Chinese Yeltsin. It is hard to conceive of an egalitarian revolution in China at the very moment when the capitalist and neo-liberal West was triumphing in Eastern Europe, as well as Latin America (one thinks of the defeat of the Sandinistas in Nicaragua), when communist parties the world over were rushing to change their name, and when the power of the USA and the influence and prestige of the Washington Consensus were so uncontested and incontestable as to seed the idea of the 'end of history'! Only a populist can believe in such miracles—on condition, that is, of abandoning secular analysis of classes and class struggle (domestic and international), and replacing it by mythological credence in the redemptive value of the 'people' and the 'masses'.

It might be said that late twentieth-century and early twenty-first century Marxism is occasionally the heir of the culture of 1968, which coined the slogan 'It is forbidden to forbid!' and also sought to bend the slogan with which Mao unleashed the Cultural Revolution—'It is right to rebel!'—in the same direction. In reality, 'rightful' rebellion had very precise limits, and could certainly not be pushed to the point of challenging the revolution that gave birth to the People's Republic of China. It would be no accident if Mao had the army intervene to put an end to a situation that seemed about to issue in a war of all against all and destructive anarchy. But the culture of '68 was not unduly concerned about that. From its standpoint, progressive or revolutionary class struggle coincided with rebellion from below against constituted government, which was inherently synonymous with oppression.

Starting from that presupposition, it is not difficult to juxtapose Tiananmen Square with the storming of the Bastille and the events of 1989–91 in Eastern Europe—the 'second Restoration' referred to by Badiou[71]—with the October Revolution. We would then have to include in the list of popular revolutions and rebellions the Vendée and, in the twentieth century, the Kronstadt insurrection against the Bolsheviks, as well as the endemic peasant uprisings against the new central government in Moscow. In fact, if we wish to be wholly consistent, not even the agitation and revolts that occurred when the Soviet Union had to face the aggression of Hitler's Germany should be missing from the list. In absolutizing the contradiction between masses and power, and condemning power as such, populism proves incapable of drawing a line of demarcation between revolution and counter-revolution.

Perhaps it would be better to learn the lesson of old Hegel, who, with the Sanfedista and anti-Semitic agitation of his time in mind, observed that sometimes 'courage consists not in attacking rulers, but in defending them'.[72] The populist rebel who would be bound to consider Hegel insufficiently revolutionary could always heed Gramsci's warning against the phraseology of 'primitive, elementary "rebellionism," "subversionism" and "anti-statism," which are ultimately an expression of de facto "a-politicism"'.[73]

9 Beyond Populism

When we find scholars who are major readers and prestigious interpreters of Marx and Engels lapsing into populism, we are bound to pose a question: are such outlooks and sentiments wholly foreign to the authors of the *Communist Manifesto*? As regards the first form of populism, there is no doubt that we are indebted to Marx for the most incisive critique of nostalgia for a mythical 'original fullness'. When we come to the second form, more nuanced conclusions are indicated. In this instance, we must distinguish between the different variants of the populism involving transfiguration of the oppressed. Let us start with the second. Although denouncing the martyrdom of the Irish people at the hands of British colonialism, far from indulging in celebration of some essential Irish soul, Marx and Engels concurrently highlighted the reactionary, anti-abolitionist role played by immigrants of Irish origin in the USA during the Civil War.

Similar considerations can be ventured in connection with the third variant of the populism of transfiguration of the oppressed. Denouncing the condition of women as the 'first class oppression', Marx and Engels unquestionably gave strong impetus to the feminist movement. The *Communist Manifesto* vigorously condemns not only the oppression of women, but also the process of reification to which they are subject. At the same time, however, it has no difficulty referring to 'the exploitation of children by their parents', not excluding mothers.[74] There is no room for essentialism. As in the case of oppressed peoples, so with women it makes no sense to explain their condition by reference to some alleged nature that has long been despised, but whose moral superiority must now, in an inversion of the traditional value judgement, be recognized and celebrated. Instead, it is a question of analysing and challenging a historically determinate division of labour, which entails colonial or semi-colonial subjugation and domestic slavery or segregation.

Some further observations are in order regarding the first variant of the populism of transfiguration of the oppressed: the variant that tends to transfigure subaltern classes. In their early writings, opposing those who sounded the alarm over the new barbarian invasion, Marx and Engels tended to assign the proletariat a ready capacity to acquire a mature revolutionary consciousness, a kind of immunity from 'national prejudices', insularity and chauvinistic hatred, as well as a nobility of soul altogether lacking in the property-owning classes. From the outset, however, attention to concrete historical and social analysis clearly had the upper hand. 'Nobility of soul' was also predicated of the Polish nobility, which sacrificed its class or caste interests to the cause of national liberation. Similarly, on the other side, no attempt was made to mask the depravity of the sub-proletariat—a class into which the capitalist system continually threatens to cast individuals and strata from the working class.

However, we find a residue of populism in the view that the state is destined to wither away in communist society. I have already underscored the utterly unrealistic character of this expectation. We can now add a further consideration: it is not clear why the absorption of the state by civil society should represent progress. Historically, such diverse measures as the introduction of compulsory schooling in the West, the proscription of *sati* (the 'voluntary' suicide of widows) in India, and the desegregation of schools in the American Deep South have all been the result of the state imposing on civil society. Today, in some Islamic countries the emancipation of women is easier when undertaken by the state than civil society. It is true that, when Marx and Engels looked to the absorption of the state into civil society, they had in mind a civil society liberated from class antagonism. However, in their discourse a certain idealization of civil society (conceived in opposition to power) is present and, with it in this sense, a residue of populism.

This residue of populism explains the slippage into the binary interpretation of conflict we sometimes encounter in Marx and Engels. When they analyse a concrete historical event (e.g., the struggle to reduce working hours or the American Civil War), they repeatedly draw attention to multiple contradictions and the occasionally progressive role played by the state, even the bourgeois state. In other words, we are at the antipodes of populism. However, during the Paris Commune, Marx saw the 'international counter-organisation of labour' arrayed against the 'cosmopolitan conspiracy of capital'. Above all, 'in a word', the *Manifesto* reduces class struggle to the struggle between 'oppressor and oppressed'. If we take this agitprop formula literally, we are not far removed from Weil's (populist) view of history as the 'struggle of those who obey against those who command'. In reality, given Marx and Engels' basic view and overall development, a different interpretation is more persuasive. It can indeed be said that the epic class struggles waged at Valmy, Port-au-Prince, Paris (June 1848), Gettysburg, and Stalingrad witnessed the clash of oppressor and oppressed. But this is true only in the last analysis. That is, given the absolute centrality and urgency of what was at stake on each occasion (the respective fates of the *ancien régime*, black slavery on Santo Domingo, wage slavery in France, black slavery in the USA, and the new colonial slavery that the Third Reich was resolved to impose on Slavs), all the other contradictions, all the other relations of coercion, became (in that determinate historical moment) altogether secondary.

10 'Wall Street' and 'War Street'

Today, even the magnates of capital and finance sometimes feel obliged to re-read Marx, first-hand or second-hand. Does anyone offer a better explanation of the economic crisis that erupted in 2008? From the windows of their offices, these magnates cast a glance at the unprecedented, disturbing demonstrations staged now and again. These call for the occupation of Wall Street and target the privileged 1 %, who wield power and enrich themselves at the expense of the remaining 99 % of the population. How the ideological and political climate has changed compared with the triumphant proclamation of the 'end of history' twenty years ago! Along with history, class struggle seems to have returned. But if the demonstrators confine themselves to denouncing the grave consequences of the economic crisis, we are witnessing not so much the return of Marxian class struggle as its permanent and effective mutilation by the dominant class and ideology.

Proceeding with their reading, the magnates possibly experience a shudder when they come to the analysis of crises of relative over-production. These offer confirmation of the destined end of a social system that recurrently destroys an enormous quantity of social wealth and plunges masses of people into unemployment, insecurity, workplace 'despotism' (referred to by the *Communist Manifesto*), and poverty. They feel repulsed in their struggle for recognition and experience their condition ever more painfully, because, under a different set of social and political relations, contemporary science and technology could powerfully accelerate the growth of the productive forces and social wealth. However, in the West parties capable of giving organized expression to the burgeoning mass discontent do not exist. There is no reason for the magnates to be particularly anxious.

A potential reason for particular concern is the placards waved by the demonstrators that express their fury not only at Wall Street, but also War Street. The district of high finance is identified as the district of war and the military-industrial complex. An awareness of the link between capitalism and imperialism is emerging or starting to emerge. Targeting areas of major geo-political and geo-economic significance, and ending with the installation of new, formidable military bases and further stimulus to the arms trade, the wars unleashed by the USA and the West are presented as humanitarian operations. But here is the balance sheet of the humanitarian operation in Libya drawn up by an irreproachable author: '[t]oday we know that the war led to at least 30,000 deaths, as opposed to the 300 victims of the initial repression', perpetrated by Gaddafi.[75] The overwhelming superiority of the West's multimedia apparatus makes it possible, albeit with decreasing effectiveness, to manipulate public opinion. But awareness that both truth and its repression refer to the class struggle, its multiple forms and their inter-connexion, is emerging.

These multiple forms and their inter-connexion end up emerging even when we focus exclusively on social conflict in the capitalist metropolis.

We immediately encounter a growing mass of migrants. Hailing from the poorest countries in the world, they are a product of the first 'great divergence' imposed by Western capitalism and colonialism on the rest of the world: global inequality. And they are arriving in the capitalist metropolis even as the second 'great divergence'—increasing social polarization between an ever narrower privileged circle and the rest of the population—is growing. In these circumstances, it is perfectly understandable if migrants are often regarded and treated like 'niggers' in the USA of the white supremacy. They often leave behind countries (or regions) where they have been condemned to expropriation and marginalization by classical colonialism (such is the case with Palestine); countries that have recently been the target of wars unleashed by the West or which, not having succeeded in making the transition from the politico-military phase to the politico-economic phase of the anti-colonial revolution, are still prey to under-development, penury and the civil wars that sometimes result. Arriving in the West, these migrants bring with them their history and culture, which often (one thinks, in particular, of the condition of women) generates serious conflicts. How is this utterly heterogeneous mass to be organized into a single bloc of women and men capable of conducting an effective class struggle against capitalism and its various manifestations (from social polarization to militarism)?

Compounding the objective difficulties is the political and ideological initiative of the dominant class. In the USA, especially, following an established tradition and tried-and-tested technique, it seeks to externalize social conflict, diverting growing popular anger to emerging countries—particularly China, which, having left behind the 'century of humiliation' and desperate mass poverty that followed the Opium Wars, is now challenging the 'Columbian epoch' and 500 years of uncontested Western supremacy.

Hence, the organization of dependent workers into a coherent class struggle in the capitalist metropolis requires a capacity for orientation amid the multiple contradictions and class struggles traversing the contemporary world. What is needed more than ever is a re-reading of Marx's theory of 'class struggles' (plural). Only thus, can we re-appropriate an indispensable tool for understanding the historical process and undertaking struggles for emancipation.

Notes

1. Simone Weil, *Oeuvres complètes*, ed. André A. Devaux and Florence de Lussy, Paris: Gallimard, 1989–91, Vol. II, *Écrits historiques et politiques*, pt. 2, p. 124.
2. Karl Marx and Frederick Engels, *Collected Works*, London: Lawrence & Wishart, 1975–2004, Vol. 6, p. 495.
3. Ibid., Vol. 35, pp. 276, 300, 303.
4. Ibid., Vol. 35, p. 296.
5. Ibid., Vol. 35, pp. 247, 289.
6. See Domenico Losurdo, *War and Revolution: Rethinking the 20th Century*, trans. Gregory Elliott, London and New York: Verso, 2015, Chapter 2, §5.
7. Marx and Engels, *Collected Works*, Vol. 19, p. 263.
8. Weil, *Oeuvres complètes*, Vol. II, pt. 1, p. 237.
9. Ibid., Vol. II, pt. 1, p. 258.
10. Ibid., Vol. II, pt. 1, pp. 312–13, 258.
11. Simon Weil, *Écrits historiques*, Paris: Gallimard, 1960, p. 221.
12. Weil, *Oeuvres complètes*, Vol. II, pt. 3, pp. 52–5.
13. Quoted in Paul Preston, *The Spanish Civil War, 1936–39*, London: Harper Perennial, 2006, p. 219.
14. Weil, *Oeuvres complètes*, Vol. II, pt. 1, p. 292.
15. Ibid., Vol. II, pt. 2, p. 32.
16. Ibid., Vol. II, pt. 1, p. 312.
17. Ibid., Vol. II, pt. 1, p. 238.
18. Ibid., Vol. II, pt. 2, p. 32.
19. Weil, *Écrits historiques et politiques*, pp. 367–8.
20. Ibid., pp. 373–4.
21. Ibid., pp. 369–70, 375.
22. Simone Weil, *Écrits de Londres et dernières lettres*, Paris: Gallimard, 1957, p. 255.
23. Weil, *Oeuvres complètes*, Vol. II, pt. 2, pp. 32, 104.
24. Ibid., Vol. II, pt. 2, p. 33, 38.
25. Ibid., Vol. II, pt. 2, pp. 36, 34.
26. Marx and Engels, *Collected Works*, Vol. 35, p. 639.
27. Ibid., Vol. 6, p. 211.
28. Ibid., Vol. 35, p. 626, 630.
29. Weil, *Oeuvres complètes*, Vol. II, pt. 2, pp. 32–3.
30. Marx and Engels, *Collected Works*, Vol. 38, p. 99.
31. Ibid., Vol. 11, p. 531.
32. Ibid., Vol. 29, p. 92.

33. Quoted in Pablo Stefanoni, 'Bolivia a due dimensioni', *Il Manifesto*, 22 July 2006.
34. Fidel Castro, *Socialismo e comunismo: un processo unico*, Milan: Feltrinelli, 1969, p. 145; Ernesto Che Guevara, *Scritti, discorsi e diari di guerriglia 1959–1967*, ed. Laura Gonsalez, Turin: Einaudi, 1969, pp. 1418–19, 1448–54.
35. Marx and Engels, *Collected Works*, Vol. 12, pp. 126, 132.
36. Ibid., Vol. 6, pp. 486–7.
37. Ibid., Vol. 28, pp. 99–101.
38. Ibid., Vol. 32, p. 248.
39. J.C.L. de Sismondi, *Nuovi principi di economia politica o della ricchezza nei suoi rapporti con la popolazione*, ed. Piero Barucci, Milan: ISEDI, 1975, pp. 208–9.
40. Bernard de Mandeville, *The Fable of the Bees*, ed. F.B. Kaye, Indianapolis: Liberty Classics, 1988, Vol. 1, pp. 311–16.
41. Marx and Engels, *Collected Works*, Vol. 6, p. 488.
42. Ibid., Vol. 11, pp. 187–8.
43. G.W.F. Hegel, *Werke in zwanzig Bänden*, ed. E. Moldenhauer and K.M. Michel, Frankfurt am Main: Suhrkamp, 1969–79, Vol. 13, p. 340.
44. Pier Paolo Pasolini, 'Il genocidio', in *Scritti corsari*, Milan: Garzanti, 1981, p. 277.
45. See Domenico Losurdo, *Non-Violence: A History beyond the Myth*, trans. Gregory Elliott, Lanham, MD: Lexington, 2015, Chapter 2, §7 and Chapter 4, §8.
46. Marx and Engels, *Collected Works*, Vol. 6, pp. 36, 39–41.
47. Ibid., Vol. 10, pp. 244–5.
48. Virginia Wolf, *A Room of One's Own and Three Guineas*, ed. Morag Schiach, Oxford and New York: Oxford University Press, 2008, pp. 158, 148.
49. Maxime Rodinson, *Muhammad*, trans. Anne Carter, London: Allen Lane, 1971, pp. 177, 180.
50. Geoffrey Best, 'The Militarization of Western Society, 1870–1914', in *The Militarization of the Western World*, ed. J.R. Gillis, New Brunswick and London: Rutgers, 1989, p. 20.
51. Kurt Tucholsky, 'Der Krieg und die deutsche Frau', in *Gesammelte Werke*, ed. M. Gerold-Tucholsky and F.J. Raddatz, Hamburg: Rowohlt, 1985, Vol. 5, p. 267.
52. Adam Smith, *An Inquiry into the Nature and Causes of the Wealth of Nations*, Indianapolis: Liberty Classics, 1981, Vol. 1, Book I, Chapter 2, pp. 28–9.
53. Marx and Engels, *Collected Works*, Vol. 6, p. 180.

54. See Domenico Losurdo, *Il linguaggio dell'Impero. Lessico dell'ideologia americana*, Rome and Bari: Laterza, 2007, Chapter 1, §10.
55. Smith, *An Inquiry into the Nature and Causes of the Wealth of Nations*, Vol. II, Book V, Chapter 1, part III, art. 3, p. 794.
56. Weil, *Oeuvres complètes*, Vol. II, pt. 1, pp. 292–3.
57. Cornelius Castoriadis, 'La rivoluzione proletaria contro la burocrazia', *MicroMega*, no. 9, 2006, p. 119.
58. Ibid., p. 121.
59. Ibid., p. 118.
60. See Michael Hardt and Toni Negri, *Empire*, Cambridge, MA and London: Princeton University Press, 2000 and *Multitude: War and Democracy in the Age of Empire*, London: Hamish Hamilton, 2005.
61. Hardt and Negri, *Empire*, pp. 134, 109.
62. See John Holloway, *Change the World without Taking Power: The Meaning of Revolution Today*, London: Pluto Press, 2002.
63. Zizek, *Living in End Times*, p. 456.
64. Michael Hardt, 'La nuda vita sotto l'Impero', *Il Manifesto*, 15 May 1999, p. 8.
65. David Harvey, *The Enigma of Capital and the Crises of Capitalism*, London: Profile Books, 2010, pp. 243–4.
66. Mike Davis, *Late Victorian Holocausts: El Nino Famines and the Making of the Third World*, London and New York: Verso, 2011, pp. 6, 12.
67. Mao Zedong, *Selected Works*, Beijing: Foreign Languages Press, 1967, Vol. 4, p. 455.
68. Marx and Engels, *Collected Works*, Vol. 12, pp. 92–3.
69. Amaresh Misra, *War of Civilisations: India AD 1857*, New Delhi: Rupa, 2008, pp. 1866, 1874–5, 1897.
70. Harvey, *The Enigma of Capital and the Crises of Capitalism*, p. 231.
71. Alain Badiou, *The Century*, trans. Alberto Toscano, Cambridge: Polity Press, 2007, p. 26.
72. G.W.F. Hegel, *Berliner Schriften*, ed. Johannes Hoffmeister, Hamburg: Meiner, 1956, p. 699; cf. Domenico Losurdo, *Hegel e la Germania. Filosofia e questione nazionale tra rivoluzione e reazione*, Milan: Guerini/Istituto Italiano per gli Studi Filosofici, 1997, Chapter 7, §11.
73. Antonio Gramsci, *Quaderni del carcere*, ed. Valentino Gerratana, Turin: Einaudi, 1975, pp. 2108–9, 326–7.
74. Marx and Engels, *Collected Works*, Vol. 6, p. 500.
75. Tzvetan Todorov, 'La guerra impossibile', *La Repubblica*, 26 June 2012.

BIBLIOGRAPHY

Adler, Georg. *Die imperialistische Sozialpolitik. Disraeli, Napoleon III, Bismarck. Eine Skizze.* Tübingen: Laupp'sche Buchhandlung, 1897.
Albert, Michel. *Capitalism Against Capitalism.* Trans. Paul Haviland. Oxford: Blackwell, 1993.
Albertini, Mario. Nota biografica. In Pierre-Joseph Proudhon, *La Giustizia nella rivoluzione e nella chiesa*, ed. Pierre-Joseph Proudhon. Turin: UTET, 1968.
Althusser, Louis. *For Marx.* Trans. Ben Brewster. London: Allen Lane, 1969.
Althusser, Louis, and Étienne Balibar. *Reading Capital.* Trans. Ben Brewster. London: New Left Books, 1970.
Aly, Götz. *Hitlers Volksstaat. Raub, Rassenkrieg und nationaler Sozialismus.* Frankfurt am Main: Fischer, 2005.
Ambrose, Stephen F. When the Americans Came Back to Europe. *International Herald Tribune*, 20 May 1997.
Archibold, Randal C. Cuba's Imprint on Haiti. *International Herald Tribune*, 9 November 2011.
Arendt, Hannah. *Crises of the Republic.* San Diego, New York and London: Harcourt Brace Jovanovich, 1972.
———. *On Revolution* (1963). London: Penguin, 2006.
Arrighi, Giovanni. *The Long Twentieth Century: Money, Power, and the Origins of Our Times.* London and New York: Verso, 1994.
———. *Adam Smith in Beijing: Lineages of the Twenty-First Century.* London and New York: Verso, 2007.
Badiou, Alain. *The Century.* Trans. Alberto Toscano. Cambridge: Polity Press, 2007.

Bebel, August. *Die Frau und der Sozialismus* (1879), 60th ed. Berlin: Dietz, 1964.

Benjamin, Walter. Moscow. In *One-Way Street and Other Writings*, trans. Edmund Jephcott and Kingsley Shorter. London: Verso, 1985.

Bentham, Jeremy. *The Works*. Ed. John Bowring, 11 vols. Edinburgh: Tait, 1838–43.

Berelovich, A. L'Occidente, o l'utopia di un mondo normale. *Europa/Europe*, no. 1 (1993).

Bernstein, Eduard. Der Sozialismus und die Kolonialfrage. *Sozialistische Monatshefte* (1900), 549–62.

Best, Geoffrey. The Militarization of Western Society, 1870–1914. In *The Militarization of the Western World*, ed. J.R. Gillis. New Brunswick and London: Rutgers, 1989.

Bloch, Ernst. *Geist der Utopie* (1918). Frankfurt am Main: Suhrkamp, 1971.

Bocca, Giorgio. Dimenticare Hitler.... *La Repubblica*, 6 February 1992.

Boffa, Giuseppe. *L'ultima illusione. L'Occidente e la vittoria sul comunismo*. Bari: Laterza, 1997.

Bonanni, Andrea. Si apre la sfida al Congresso. Eltsin è pronto a ricorrere alle urne per contrastare l'opposizione. *Corriere della Sera*, 1 December 1992.

Bowring, Philip. Toward More Efficient State Capitalism, if Beijing Has its Way. *International Herald Tribune*, 9 November 1995.

Broué, Pierre. *La Rivoluzione perduta. Vita di Lev Trockij, 1879–1940*. Turin: Bollati Boringhieri, 1991.

Buckley, Kevin. *Panama: The Whole Story*. New York: Simon & Schuster, 1991.

Bukharin, N.I. Towards a Critique of the Economic Platform of the Opposition. In *Selected Writings on the State and the Transition to Socialism*, ed. and trans. Richard B. Day. Nottingham: Spokesman, 1982.

———. Concerning the New Economic Policy and Our Tasks. In *Selected Writings on the State and the Transition to Socialism*.

Burke, Edmund. *The Works: A New Edition*, 16 vols. London: Rivington, 1826.

Burton, Antoinette M. The White Woman's Burden: British Feminists and "The Indian Woman", 1865–1915. In *Western Women and Imperialism: Complicity and Resistance*, eds. N. Chaudhuri and M. Strobel. Bloomington and Indianapolis: Indiana University Press, 1992.

Buzan, Barry. New Patterns of Global Security in the Twenty-First Century. *International Affairs* 67, no. 3 (July 1991), 431–51.

Calhoun, John C. *Union and Liberty*. Ed. R.M. Lence. Indianapolis: Liberty Classics, 1992.

Callaway, Helen, and D.O. Helly. Crusader for Empire: Flora Shaw/Lady Lugard. In *Western Women and Imperialism: Complicity and Resistance*, eds. N. Chaudhuri and M. Strobel. Bloomington and Indianapolis: Indiana University Press, 1992.

Caretto, Ennio. A Mosca chiederò la testa di Castro. Bush annuncia le sue richieste per aiutare le riforme in URSS. *La Repubblica*, 19 July 1991.

———. L'ONU vuol punire la Libia. *La Repubblica*, 29–30 March 1992.
Carlyle, Thomas. *Latter-Day Pamphlets* (1850). Ed. M.K. Goldberg and J.P. Seigel. Ottawa: Canadian Federation for the Humanities, 1983.
Carr, E.H. *The Bolshevik Revolution 1917–1923* (1950–53), 3 vols. London and Basingstoke: Macmillan, 1978.
Castoriadis, Cornelius. La rivoluzione proletaria contro la burocrazia (French original in *Socialisme ou Barbarie*, no. 20, December 1956). *MicroMega* no. 9 (2006), 117–22.
Castro, Fidel. *Socialismo e comunismo: un processo unico*. Milan: Feltrinelli, 1969.
Césaire, Aimé. *Toussaint Louverture. La Révolution française et le problème colonial*. Paris: Présence Africaine, 1961.
Communist Party of China. *The Polemic on the General Line of the International Communist Movement*. Beijing: Foreign Languages Press, 1965.
Condorcet, Marie-Jean-Antoine. *Oeuvres* (1847). Eds. A. Condorcet O'Connor and M.F. Arago, reprint, Stuttgart and Bad Cannstatt: Frommann-Holzboog, 1968.
Constant, Benjamin. Principles of Politics Applicable to All Representative Governments (1815). In *Political Writings*, trans. and ed. Biancamaria Fontana. Cambridge: Cambridge University Press, 1988.
———. The Liberty of the Ancients Compared with that of the Moderns (1819). In *Political Writings*.
Corradini, Enrico. *Scritti e discorsi 1901–1914*. Ed. Lucia Strappini. Turin: Einaudi, 1980.
Croce, Benedetto. *Storia d'Italia dal 1871 al 1915* (1928). Bari: Laterza, 1967.
———. Preface to the 3rd edn. In *Materialismo storico ed economia marxistica* (1917). Bari: Laterza, 1973.
Cucurnia, Fiammetta. Mosca, tra furti e racket dilaga la baby-delinquenza. *La Repubblica*, 5 May 1993.
Dahrendorf, Ralf. *Class and Class Conflict in Industrial Society*. Stanford, CA: Stanford University Press, 1959.
———. *Per un nuovo liberalismo* (1987). Rome and Bari: Laterza, 1988.
———. *Reflections on the Revolution in Europe*. London: Chatto & Windus, 1990.
Davis, Mike. *Late Victorian Holocausts: El Nino Famines and the Making of the Third World*. London and New York: Verso, 2001.
De Gennaro, Ricardo. Paura a Torino. E gli impiegati vanno in corteo. *La Repubblica*, 16 January 1994.
Degras, Jane, ed. *The Communist International 1919–1943: Documents*, 3 vols. London, New York and Toronto: Oxford University Press, 1956–65.
Deng Xiaoping. *Selected Works*, 3 vols. Foreign Languages Press: Beijing, 1992–5.
Diaz, Furio. *Filosofia e politica nel Settecento francese*. Turin: Einaudi, 1962.
Dimitrov, Georgi. The Fascist Offensive and the Tasks of the Communist International (Report to the Seventh Congress of the Communist International,

2 August 1935). In *Selected Speeches and Articles*. London: Lawrence & Wishart, 1951.

Disraeli, Benjamin. *Sybil or the Two Nations* (1845). Ed. S.M. Smith. Oxford and New York: Oxford University Press, 1988.

Dostoevsky, Fyodor. *The Brothers Karamazov* (1879). Trans. Richard Pevear and Larissa Volokhonsky, New York and London: Everyman's Library, 1997.

Drescher, Seymour. *From Slavery to Freedom: Comparative Studies in the Rise and Fall of Atlantic Slavery*. London: Macmillan, 1999.

Dubois, Laurent. *Avengers of the New World: The Story of the Haitian Revolution*. Cambridge, MA and London: Belknap Press of Harvard University Press, 2004.

———. *Haiti: The Aftershocks of History*. New York: Metropolitan Books, 2012.

Duverger, Maurice. Mafia e inflazione uccidono la Russia. *Corriere della Sera*, 18 October 1993.

Enzensberger, Hans Magnus, ed. *Colloqui con Marx e Engels* (1973). Turin: Einaudi, 1977.

Fanon, Frantz. *A Dying Colonialism* (1959). Trans. Haakon Chevalier. New York: Grove Press, 1965.

———. *The Wretched of the Earth* (1961). Trans. Richard Philcox. New York: Grove Press, 2004.

Fauré, Charles, ed. *Les Déclarations des droits de l'homme de 1789*. Paris: Payot, 1988.

Ferguson, Niall. *Colossus: The Rise and Fall of the American Empire*. London: Penguin, 2005.

———. *The War of the World*. London: Penguin, 2006.

———. *Civilization: The West and the Rest*. London: Penguin, 2011.

Feuerbach, Ludwig. Die Naturwissenschaft und die Revolution (1850). In *Antrophologischer Materialismus. Ausgewählte Schriften*, ed. Alfred Schmidt, vol. 2. Frankfurt am Main and Vienna: Europäische Verlagsanstalt, 1967.

Figes, Orlando. *A People's Tragedy: The Russian Revolution, 1891–1924*. London: Pimlico, 1997.

Flores, Marcello. *L'immagine dell'URSS. L'Occidente e la Russia di Stalin (1927–1956)*. Milan: Il Saggiatore, 1990.

Franceschini, Enrico. Emergenza in Russia. Un milione alla fame, Eltsin corre ai ripari. *La Repubblica*, 17 October 1991a.

———. Mafia e donne in topless sulle rive del mar Nero. *La Repubblica*, 18–19 August 1991b.

Fraser, Nancy. Social Justice in the Age of Identity Politics: Redistribution, Recognition, and Participation. In *Redistribution or Recognition? A Political-Philosophical Exchange*, eds. Fraser and Axel Honneth. London and New York: Verso, 2003.

Frederick II, King of Prussia. *Oeuvres posthumes*, Vol. 20. *Correspondance de Monsieur d'Alembert avec Fréderic II Roi de Prusse.* Berlin, 1791.
Friedberg, A.L. Menace: Here Be Dragons—Is China a Military Threat? *The National Interest*, September–October 2009.
Fukuyama, Francis. The End of History? *The National Interest*, Summer 1989, 3–18.
Furet, François. *The Passing of an Illusion: The Idea of Communism in the Twentieth Century.* Trans. Deborah Furet. Chicago and London: University of Chicago Press, 1999.
Furet, François, and Denis Richet. *La Révolution française* (1963), new ed. Paris: Hachette, 1999.
Gadamer, Hans-Georg. *Truth and Method*, revised 2nd ed., trans. revised by Joel Weinsheimer and Donald G. Marshall. London and New York: Bloomsbury, 2004.
Goebbels, Joseph. *Tagebücher.* Ed. R.G. Reuth, Munich, and Zurich: Piper, 1992.
Goldstein, Andrea. *BRIC: Brasile, Russia, India, Cina alla guida dell'economia globale.* Bologna: Il Mulino, 2011.
Gramsci, Antonio. *Selections from the Prison Notebooks.* Ed. and trans. Quintin Hoare and Geoffrey Nowell Smith. London: Lawrence & Wishart, 1971.
———. *Quaderni del carcere.* Ed. Valentino Gerratana. Turin: Einaudi, 1975.
———. *Selections from Political Writings 1910–1920.* Ed. Quintin Hoare and trans. John Mathews. London: Lawrence & Wishart, 1977.
———. To the Central Committee of the Soviet Communist Party. In *Selections from Political Writings 1921–1926*, trans. and ed. Quintin Hoare. London: Lawrence & Wishart, 1978.
———. *Cronache Torinesi 1913–1917.* Ed. Sergio Capriologio. Turin: Einaudi, 1980.
———. *La Città future 1917–1918.* Ed. Sergio Capriologio. Turin: Einaudi, 1982.
———. *L'Ordine Nuovo 1919–1920.* Ed. Valentino Gerratana and Antonio A. Santucci, Turin: Einaudi, 1987.
Gras, Christian. *Alfred Rosmer et le mouvement révolutionnaire international.* Paris: Maspero, 1971.
Green, Thomas Hill. Lecture on Liberal Legislation and Freedom of Contract' (1881). In *Works*, ed. R.L. Nettleship, 3rd ed., 1891, vol. 3, reprint. London: Longmans Green, 1973.
Guevara, Ernesto Che. *Scritti, discorsi e diari di guerriglia 1959–1967.* Ed. Laura Gonsalez. Turin: Einaudi, 1969.
Guerrera, Francesco. Ascoltiamo quell'urlo in piazza. *La Stampa*, 2 October 2011.
Guillemin, Henri. *La première résurrection de la République.* Paris: Gallimard, 1967.

Gumplowicz, Ludwig. *Der Rassenkampf. Soziologische Untersuchungen.* Innsbruck: Wagner'sche Universitätshandlung, 1883.
Habermas, Jürgen. *Per la ricostruzione del materialismo storico* (1976). Milan: Etas, 1979.
———. *Theory of Communicative Action* (1981), 2 vols. Trans. Thomas A. McCarthy. Boston: Beacon Press, 1984–87.
———. *Communication and the Evolution of Society* (1976). Trans. Thomas A. McCarthy. Cambridge and Oxford: Polity Press/Basil Blackwell, 1991.
Hardt, Michael. La nuda vita sotto l'Impero. *Il Manifesto*, 15 May 1999.
Hardt, Michael, and Antonio Negri. *Empire.* Cambridge, MA and London: Harvard University Press, 2000.
———. *Multitude: War and Democracy in the Age of Empire.* London: Hamish Hamilton, 2005.
———. *Commonwealth.* Cambridge, MA and London: Harvard University Press, 2009.
Harvey, David. *The Enigma of Capital and the Crises of Capitalism.* London: Profile Books, 2010.
Hayek, F.A. von. *The Constitution of Liberty* (1960). Ed. Ronald Hamowy. Chicago and London: University of Chicago Press, 2011.
———. *Law, Legislation and Liberty* (1973–79). Abingdon: Routledge, 2013.
Hegel, G.W.F. *Vorlesungen über die Philosophie der Weltgeschichte.* Ed. Georg Lasson. Leipzig: Meiner, 1919–20.
———. *Berliner Schriften.* Ed. Johannes Hoffmeister. Hamburg: Meiner, 1956.
———. *Werke in zwanzig Bänden.* Ed. E. Moldenhauer and K.M. Michel. Frankfurt am Main: Suhrkamp, 1969–79.
———. *Jenaer Realphilosophie.* Ed. Johannes Hoffmeister. Hamburg: Meiner, 1969.
———. *Elements of the Philosophy of Right* (1821). Ed. Allen W. Wood and trans. H.B. Nisbet. Cambridge: Cambridge University Press, 1991.
Hennessy, Peter. *Never Again: Britain, 1945–1951.* New York: Pantheon, 1993.
Herzl, Theodor. Zionistisches Tagebuch. In *Briefe und Tagebücher*, ed. A. Bein et al. Berlin, Frankfurt am Main and Vienna: Propyläen, 1984–5.
Hildebrand, Klaus. *Vom Reich zum Weltreich. Hitler, NSDAP und kolonial Frage 1919–1945.* Munich: Fink, 1969.
Himmelfarb, Gertrude. *The Idea of Poverty: England in the Early Industrial Age.* New York: Vintage, 1985.
Himmler, Heinrich. *Geheimreden 1933 bis 1945.* Ed. B.F. Smith and A.F. Peterson. Berlin: Propyläen, 1974.
Hitler, Adolph. *Reden und Proklamationen 1932–1945.* Ed. Max Domarus. Munich: Süddeutscher Verlag, 1965.
———. *Mein Kampf* (1925–27). Trans. Ralph Mannheim. London: Pimlico, 1992.

Hoffmeister, Johannes, ed. *Dokumente zu Hegels Entwicklung.* Stuttgart: Frommann, 1936.
Holloway, John. *Change the World without Taking Power: The Meaning of Revolution Today.* London: Pluto Press, 2002.
Huntington, Samuel. *The Clash of Civilizations and the Remaking of World Order.* New York: Simon & Schuster, 1996.
Ikenberry, Gilford John. America's Imperial Ambition. *Foreign Affairs*, September–October 2002.
Jean, Carlo. "Guerre giuste" e "guerre ingiuste", ovvero i rischi del moralismo. *Limes: Rivista italiana di geopolitica*, no. 3 (June–August 1993).
Jessen, Jens. Unterwegs zur Plutokratie. *Die Zeit*, 1 September 2011.
Johnson, Paul. Colonialism's Back—and Not a Moment Too Soon. *New York Times Magazine*, 18 April 1993.
Judt, Tony. *Postwar: A History of Europe since 1945.* New York: Penguin, 2005.
Kant, Immanuel. *Gesammelte Schriften.* Ed. Academy of Sciences, Berlin and Leipzig, 1900.
Kaplan, R.D. A NATO Victory Can Bridge Europe's Growing Divide. *International Herald Tribune*, 8 April 1999.
Kautsky, Karl. *La dittatura del proletariato* (1918). Trans. Luciano Pellicani, 2nd ed. Milan: Sugarco, 1977.
Kolko, Gabriel. *Century of War: Politics, Conflict and Society since 1914.* New York: New Press, 1994.
Krastins, Valdis. Latvia's Past and Present. *International Herald Tribune*, 7 April 2000.
Laclau, Ernesto, and Chantal Mouffe. *Hegemony and Socialist Strategy: Towards a Radical Democratic Politics* (1985), 2nd ed. London and New York: Verso, 2001.
Lacouture, Jean. *Ho Chi Minh.* Trans. Peter Wiles. London: Allen Lane, 1968.
Lassalle, Ferdinand. Arbeiterprogramm' (1862-3). In *Reden und Schriften.* Leipzig: Reclam, 1987.
Le Bon. Gustave. In *The Crowd: A Study of the Popular Mind* (1895). New York: Dover, 2002.
Lenin, V.I. *Collected Works*, 47 vols. London: Lawrence & Wishart, 1960–78.
Livi, Roberto. La riforma di Raúl. *Il Manifesto*, 3 August 2010.
Locke, John. *The Reasonableness of Christianity as Delivered in the Scriptures.* London: Rivington, 1824.
——. *Political Writings.* Ed. David Wooton. London and New York: Penguin, 1993.
Losurdo, Domenic. *Democrazia o bonapartismo. Trionfo e decadenza del suffragio universale.* Turin: Bollati Boringhieri, 1993.
——. *Antonio Gramsci dal liberalismo al 'comunismo critico.* Rome: Gamberetti, 1997a.

———. *Hegel e la Germania. Filosofia e questione nazionale tra rivoluzione e reazione*. Milan: Guerini/Istituto Italiano per gli Studi Filosofici, 1997b.

———. *Heidegger and the Ideology of War: Community, Death and the West* (1991). Trans. Marella and Jon Morris. Amherst. NY: Humanity Books, 2001.

———. *Nietzsche, il ribelle aristocratico. Biografia intellettuale e bilancio critico*. Turin: Bollati Boringhieri, 2002.

———. *Hegel and the Freedom of the Moderns* (1992). Trans. Marella and Jon Morris. Durham, NC and London: Duke University Press, 2004.

———. *Il linguaggio dell'Impero. Lessico dell'ideologia americana*. Rome and Bari: Laterza, 2007.

———. *Stalin. Storia e critica di una leggenda nera*. Rome: Carocci, 2008.

———. *Liberalism: A Counter-History* (2005). Trans. Gregory Elliott, London and New York: Verso, 2011.

———. *Non-Violence: A History beyond the Myth*. Trans. Gregory Elliott. Lanham, MD: Lexington Books, 2015a.

———. *War and Revolution: Rethinking the 20th Century* (1996). Trans. Gregory Elliott, London and New York: Verso, 2015b.

Lukács, Georg. *History and Class Consciousness* (1922). Trans. Rodney Livingstone. London: Merlin Press, 1971.

———. *Ontologia dell'essere sociale* (1971). Trans. Alberto Scarponi. Rome: Riuniti, 1976–81.

Lu Xun. *Letteratura e sudore. Scritti dal 1925 al 1936*. Ed. A. Bujatti. Isola del Liri (Frosinone): Editrice Pisani, 2007.

Mackinder, H.J. The Geographical Pivot of History. *Geographical Journal* 23, no. 4 (1904), 421–37.

Mallaby, Sebastian. The Reluctant Imperialist. *Foreign Affairs* 81, no. 2 (March–April 2002), 2–7.

Mandeville, Bernard de. *The Fable of the Bees* (1705–14), 2 vols., ed. F.B. Kaye. Indianapolis: Liberty Classics, 1988.

Manning, Robert A. Getting China to Play by the World Trade Rules. *International Herald Tribune*, 9 January 1996.

Mao Tse-tung. *Selected Reading from the Works of Mao Tse-tung*. Beijing: Foreign Languages Press, 1967a.

———. *Selected Works*, 5 vols. Beijing: Foreign Languages Press, 1967b.

———. *On Diplomacy*. Beijing: Foreign Languages Press, 1998.

Martinetti, Cesare. Il Parlamento riabilita il vecchio rublo. *La Stampa*, 29 July 1993.

Marx, Karl. *Manuskripte über die polnische Frage (1863–4)*. Ed. W. Conze and D. Hertz-Eichenrode. S-Gravenhage: Mouton, 1961.

———. and Frederick Engels. *Collected Works*, 50 vols. London: Lawrence & Wishart, 1975–2004.

Marx-Aveling, Eleanor, and Edward Aveling. The Woman Question. *Marxism Today*, March 1972.
Mayer, Arno J. *Politics and Diplomacy of Peacemaking: Containment and Counterrevolution at Versailles, 1918–1919*. New York: Knopf, 1967.
———. *The Persistence of the Old Regime: Europe to the Great War* (1981). London and New York: Verso, 2010.
Mazower, Mark. *Hitler's Empire: How the Nazis Ruled Europe*. London: Penguin, 2009.
Mill, John Stuart. The Subjection of Women. In *Collected Works*, ed. J.M. Robson, vol. 21. Toronto and London: University of Toronto Press/Routledge & Kegan Paul, 1963–9.
———. *Utilitarianism, Liberty, Representative Government*. Ed. Harry B. Acton. London: Dent, 1972.
Misra, Amaresh. *War of Civilisations: India AD 1857*, 2 vols. New Delhi: Rupa, 2008.
Molnár, Miklos. *Marx, Engels et la politique internationale*. Paris: Gallimard, 1975.
Montesquieu, Charles-Louis. *The Spirit of the Laws* (1748). Ed. and trans. Anne M. Cohler, Basia C. Miller and Harold S. Stone. Cambridge: Cambridge University Press, 1989.
Mosse, George L. *Fallen Soldiers: Reshaping the Memory of the World Wars*. New York: Oxford University Press, 1994.
Myrdal, Gunnar. *An American Dilemma: The Negro Problem and Modern Democracy*. New York and London: Harper & Brothers, 1944.
Naím, Moisés. Mafia States: Organized Crime Takes Office. *Foreign Affairs*, May–June 2012, 100–11.
Nietzsche, Friedrich. *Sämtliche Werke, Kritische Studienausgabe*. Ed. Giorgio Colli and Mazzino Montinari. Munich: dtv-de Gruyter, 1988.
———. *Twilight of the Idols and the Anti-Christ*. Ed. Michael Tanner and trans. R.J. Hollingdale. London: Penguin, 1990.
———. *The Birth of Tragedy*. Ed. Michael Tanner and trans. Shaun Whiteside. London: Penguin, 1993.
———. *Daybreak: Thoughts on the Prejudices of Morality*. Ed. Maudemarie Clark and Brian Leiter. Cambridge: Cambridge University Press, 1997.
———. *Beyond Good and Evil/On the Genealogy of Morality*. Ed. Alan D. Shrift and Duncan Large and trans. Adrian Del Caro. Stanford, CA: Stanford University Press, 2014.
Noah, Timothy. *The Great Divergence: America's Growing Inequality and What We Can Do About It*. New York: Bloomsbury Press, 2012.
Nolte, Ernst. *Der europäische Bürgerkrieg 1917–1945. Nationalsozialismus und Bolschewismus*. Frankfurt am Main and Berlin: Ullstein, 1987.

Olusoga, David, and Casper W. Erichsen. *The Kaiser's Holocaust: Germany's Forgotten Genocide.* London: Faber & Faber, 2011.
Pasolini, Pier Paolo. Il genocido' (1974). In *Scritti corsari*, 3rd ed. Milan: Garzanti, 1981.
Piper, Ernst. *Alfred Rosenberg, Hitlers Chefideologe.* Munich: Blessing, 2005.
Pomeranz, Kenneth. *The Great Divergence: China, Europe, and the Making of the Modern World Economy.* Princeton and Woodstock: Princeton University Press, 2000.
Popper, Karl. *The Open Society and its Enemies*, 2 vols. London and New York: Routledge, 2003.
———. Io, il Papa e Gorbaciov. Interview with Barbara Spinelli, *La Stampa*, 9 April 1992a.
———. Kriege führen für den Frieden. Interview with Olaf Ihlau, *Der Spiegel*, 23 March 1992b.
Prashad, Vijay. *The Darker Nations: A People's History of the Third World.* New York: The New Press, 2007.
Preston, Paul. *The Spanish Civil War, 1936–39* (1986). London: Harper Perennial, 2006.
Proudhon, Pierre-Joseph. *La Pornocratie, ou les femmes dans le monde moderne.* Paris: Librairie Internationale, 1875.
R.E. Clinton: "Usammo i neri come cavie umane. Una vergogna americana". *Corriere della Sera*, 10 April 1997.
Reich, Robert B. When America's Rich Get Too Rich. *International Herald Tribune*, 5 September 2011.
Renan, Ernest. *Oeuvres complètes.* Ed. Henriette Psichari. Paris: Calmann-Lévy, 1947.
Renmin Ribao ('People's Daily'). *Once More on the Dictatorship of the Proletariat.* Beijing: Foreign Languages Press, 1956.
Roach, Stephen S. Transforming Economic Structure Risky but Vital Task of Nation's Future. *Global Times*, 15 November 2012.
Robespierre, Maximilien. *Oeuvres*, 10 vols. Paris: Presses Universitaires de France, 1950–67.
Rodinson, Maxime. *Muhammad.* Trans. Anne Carter. London: Allen Lane, 1971.
Rowan, C.T., and D.M. Mazie. Fame in America. *Selezione dal Reader's Digest*, March 1969, 99–104.
Scalfari, Eugenio. Al pettine i nodi di Reagan e Thatcher. *La Repubblica*, 26–27 January 1992.
Schlesinger, Jr. Arthur, ed. *History of United States Political Parties.* New York and London: Chelsea House & Bawker, 1973.
———. *The Cycles of American History.* Boston and New York: Houghton Mifflin, 1986.

———. Four Days with Fidel: A Havana Diary. *New York Review of Books*, 26 March 1992.

Schreiber, Gerhard. *La vendetta tedesca 1943–1945: le rappresaglie naziste in Italia* (1996). Milan: Mondadori, 2000.

Sieyès, Emmanuel-Joseph. *Écrits politiques*. Ed. Roberto Zapperi. Paris: Editions des archives contemporaines, 1985.

Sisci, Francesco. *La Differenza tra la Cina e il mondo. La rivoluzione degli anni ottanta*. Milan: Feltrinelli, 1994.

Sismondi, J.C.L. de. *Nuovi principi di economia politica e della ricchezza nei suoi rapporti con la popolazione* (1819–27). Ed. Piero Barucci. Milan: ISEDI, 1975.

Slotkin, Richard. *The Fatal Environment: The Myth of the Frontier in the Age of Industrialization 1800–1890* (1985). New York: Harper Perennial, 1994.

Smith, Adam. *An Inquiry into the Nature and Causes of the Wealth of Nations* (1775–6), 2 vols. Indianapolis: Liberty Classics, 1981.

———. *Lectures on Jurisprudence* (1762–3 and 1766). Indianapolis: Liberty Classics, 1982.

Snow, Edgar. *Red Star over China* (1938), new ed. New York: Grove Press/ Atlantic Monthly Press, 1994.

Soprani, Anne. *La Révolution et les femmes 1789–1796*. Paris: MA Éditions, 1988.

Spencer, Herbert. *The Principles of Ethics* (1879–93), 2 vols. Ed. T.R. Machan. Indianapolis: Liberty Classics, 1978.

———. The Proper Sphere of Government. In *The Man versus the State*. Indianapolis: Liberty Classics, 1981.

Spengler, Oswald. *The Hour of Decision* (1933). Trans. Charles Francis Atkinson. London: George Allen & Unwin, 1934.

Stalin, J. *Works* (1946–49), 13 vols. Moscow: Foreign Languages Publishing House, 1952–5.

———. *Problems of Leninism* (1952), 11th ed. Moscow: Foreign Languages Publishing House, 1953.

———. *Economic Problems of Socialism in the USSR* (1952). Beijing: Foreign Languages Press, 1972a.

———. *Marxism and Problems of Linguistics* (1951). Beijing: Foreign Languages Press, 1972b.

Stefanoni, Pablo. Bolivia a due dimensioni. *Il Manifesto*, 22 July 2006.

Stern, E. The Way Ahead for China: More Change, Sustainably. *International Herald Tribune*, 19 May 1994.

Taine, Hippolyte. *Le Origini della Francia contemporanea. L'antico regime* (1876). Milan: Adelphi, 1986.

Tawney, R.H. *Religion and the Rise of Capitalism: A Historical Study*. New York: Harcourt, Brace and Company, 1926.

Thurow, Lester. *Head to Head: The Coming Economic Battle among Japan, Europe and America*. New York: Morrow, 1992.

Tocqueville, Alexis de. *Oeuvres complètes*. Ed. Jacob-Peter Mayer. Paris: Gallimard, 1951.
———. *Democracy in America*. London: Everyman's Library, 1994.
Todorov, Tzvetan. La Guerra impossibile. *La Repubblica*, 26 June 2012.
Togliatti, Palmiro. *Opere*. Ed. Luciano Gruppi, vol. 5. Rome: Editori Riuniti, 1984.
Trotsky, Leon. *The Revolution Betrayed: What is the Soviet Union and Where is it Going?* (1936). Trans. Max Eastman, 5th ed. New York: Pathfinder Press, 1980.
Tucholsky, Kurt. Der Krieg und die deutsche Frau' (1927). In *Gesammelte Werke*, ed. M. Gerold-Tucholsky and F.J. Raddatz, vol. 5. Hamburg: Rowohlt, 1985.
Turone, Sergio. *Storia del sindacato in Italia (1943–1969)*. Rome and Bari: Laterza, 1973.
Tyler, P.E. Industrial Reform is under Assault in China. *International Herald Tribune*, 19 June 1995.
Vogel, Ezra. *Deng Xiaoping and the Transformation of China*. Cambridge, MA and London: Harvard University Press, 2011.
Weil, Simone. *Écrits de Londres et dernières lettres*. Paris: Gallimard, 1957.
———. *Écrits historiques et politiques*. Paris: Gallimard, 1960.
———. *Oeuvres complètes*. Ed. André A. Devaux and Florence de Lussy. Paris: Gallimard, 1989–91, Vol. II, *Écrits historiques et politiques*.
Wilkinson, William John. *Tory Democracy* (1925). New York: Octagon Books, 1980.
Wollstonecraft, Mary. *A Vindication of the Rights of Woman* (1792). London: Everyman's Library, 1992.
Woolf, Virginia. *A Room of One's Own and Three Guineas*. Ed. Morag Shiach. Oxford and New York: Oxford University Press, 2008.
Zinoviev, Aleksandr. *La Caduta dell' "impero del male". Saggio sulla tragedia della Russia*. Turin: Bollati Boringhieri, 1994.
Zizek, Slavoj. Mao Tse-tung, the Marxist Lord of Misrule. Introduction to Mao Zedong. In *On Practice and Contradiction*. London and New York: Verso, 2007.
———. *First as Tragedy, Then as Farce*. London and New York: Verso, 2009.
———. *Living in the End Times* (2010). London and New York: Verso, 2011.

Index[1]

A
Acton, J.E.E. Dalberg, Lord, 86
Adler, Georg, 118n20
Aeschylus, 38
Aguilera, Gonzalo, 315
Albert, Michel, 306n24
Albertini, Mario, 118n2
Alexander II, Czar of Russia, 109, 110
Allende, Salvador, 293
Althusser, Louis, 79, 80, 82
Aly, Götz, 173n70
Ambrose, Stephen F., 308n56
Annenkov, P.W., 229
Archibold, Randal C., 199n69
Arendt, Hannah, 75, 93, 190, 191, 269–75, 278, 311, 321
Aristophanes, 38
Arrighi, Giovanni, 198n56, 228n46, 266n16, 309n74
Aveling, Edward, 282

B
Badiou, Alain, 339
Bakunin, M. A., 5, 103
Bebel, August, 22, 73, 141
Beecher Stowe, Harriet, 24
Benjamin, Walter, 175, 188, 204, 216, 217, 236
Bentham, Jeremy, 30, 93
Berelovich, Alexis, 348
Bernstein, Eduard, 94, 139, 140, 143
Best, Geoffrey, 345n50
Bevin, Ernest, 280
Blanc, Louis, 132
Bloch, Ernst, 232
Bobbio, Norberto, 280
Bocca, Giorgio, 266n7
Boffa, Giuseppe, 266n21
Bogomolov, O.T., 259
Bolívar, Simon, 288
Bonanni, Andrea, 267n24
Bourbon dynasty, 263–5
Bowring, Philip, 309n83
Brecht, Bertolt, 239

[1] Note: Page number followed by "n" refers to endnotes

Brezhnev, L.I., 256, 263
Broué, Pierre, 173n81
Brown, John, 11, 109, 110
Brusilov, A.A., 152, 223
Buchanan, James, 125
Buckley, Kevin, 266n5
Bukharin, N.I., 183, 187, 190, 195, 213
Burke, Edmund, 77, 84, 263
Burton, Antoinette, 307n41
Bush, George Herbert, Sr., 251
Bush, George Walker, Jr., 251
Buzan, Barry, 253

C

Cabet, Ètienne, 104
Calhoun, John C., 37, 38, 61, 62, 68, 270
Callaway, Helen, 307n41
Caretto, Ennio, 266n8
Carlyle, Thomas, 32, 33, 112
Carr, E.H., 171n33, 196n15, 226n9, 246n21
Castoriadis, Cornelius, 332, 333
Castro, Fidel, 244, 251
Castro, Raul, 240
Catherine II, Empress of Russia, 36, 132, 133
Cavaignac, Louis Eugéne, 207
Césaire, Aimé, 308n65
Chávez Frías, Hugo Rafael, 38, 84
Che Guevara, Ernesto, 188
Cheney, Dick, 253
Chiang Kai-shek, 159
Cicero, 39
Condorcet, Marie-Jean-Antoine, 16, 76
Constant, Benjamin, 58, 204, 220
Constantine, Emperor of Rome, 38, 68

Corradini, Enrico, 154
Croce, Benedetto, 44, 46, 183
Cromwell, Oliver, 263
Cromwell, Richard, 265
Cucurnia, Fiammetta, 267n26

D

Dahrendorf, Ralf, 1, 2, 4, 262, 263, 275
D'Alembert, Jean-Baptiste, 34, 38
Dante, 38
Daumer, Georg Friedrich, 38, 40, 327
Davis, Mike, 70n16, 198n57, 346n66
de Balzac, Honoré, 38
de Cervantes, Miguel, 38
De Gennaro, Ricardo, 267n36
de Gobineau, Arthur, 28
de Gouges, Olympe, 16, 88
de Mandeville, Bernard, 323, 324
de Marmont, Auguste, 265
de Robespierre, Maximilien, 22, 77, 88, 89, 206, 262
de Sismondi, Jean Charles Léonard, 321, 323
de Tocqueville, Alexis, 27–31, 33, 54–6, 59, 207, 208, 324
Degras, Jane, 171n31, 173n85
Deng Xiaoping, 192, 195, 196, 215, 216, 222, 225, 235, 238, 244, 291, 295, 299, 301
Dessalines, Jean-Jacques, 286
Diaz, Furio, 136n42
Diderot, Denis, 35
Dimitrov, Georgi, 167
Diocletian, Emperor of Rome, 38
Disraeli, Benjamin, 28, 105, 106, 162, 282
Dostoevsky, Fyodor, 156
Drescher, Seymour, 49n77, 118n12
Dubois, Laurent, 96n7, 307n50
Duverger, Maurice, 266n22

INDEX 359

E
Engels, Friedrich, 4–12, 14–18, 22, 23, 28, 30, 32–46, 58, 61–9, 73–84, 86–90, 92–5, 103–16, 121–30, 132–4, 139, 141–3, 147, 149, 150, 154, 155, 161, 170, 178, 181, 204–6, 209–11, 213, 214, 219, 221, 224, 225, 230, 231, 234, 240, 261, 263, 277, 278, 282, 287, 290, 296, 312, 313, 326, 327, 337, 339–41
Enzensberger, Hans Magnus, 6n11, 47n17
Erichsen, Casper W., 173n72

F
Fanon, Frantz, 279, 284, 291
Fauré, Charles, 99n69
Ferguson, Niall, 4, 46, 296
Feuerbach, Ludwig, 51n131
Fichte, Johann Gottlieb, 230, 231, 233
Figes, Orlando, 171n41, 196n14, 226n5
Fitzhugh, George, 25, 26
Flores, Marcello, 196n1, 228n44
Foucault, Michel, 66, 69
Fourier, Charles, 16, 104
Franceschini, Enrico, 267n23
Franco, Francisco, 59, 108, 109, 164, 168, 315
Fraser, Nancy, 278
Frederick II, King of Prussia, 34, 38, 133
Frederick William IV, King of Prussia, 210
Friedberg, A.L., 266n17
Fukuyama, Francis, 249, 262
Furet, François, 196n6

G
Gadamer, Hans-Georg, 66, 67
Gaddafi, Muammar, 342
Galilei, Galileo, 68
Gandhi, Mohandas, 325, 326
Garbai, Alexander, 151
Garrison, William L., 36, 37
George V, King of Great Britain and Ireland, 260
Goebbels, Joseph, 166
Goldstein, Andrea, 309n86
Gorbachev, M.S., 244, 251, 257, 265
Göring, Hermann, 4, 164
Gramsci, Antonio, 117, 152, 166, 180, 181, 208, 210, 215, 219–21, 225, 226, 233, 261, 279, 289, 339
Green, Thomas Hill, 86
Grotius, Hugo, 84, 87, 89
Guerrera, Francesco, 309n77
Guillemin, Henri, 97n13
Guizot, François, 33
Gumplowicz, Ludwig, 28, 139, 164

H
Habermas, Jürgen, 2–4, 93, 275–8, 311
Hardinge, Charles, Lord, 260
Hardt, Michael, 333, 334
Harvey, David, 335–7
Havel, Vaclav, 338
Heath, Edward, 194, 295
Hegel, G.W.F., 30, 39, 40, 45, 46, 61, 66, 67, 78, 83, 86, 90–3, 95, 127, 184, 202, 210, 230, 231, 262, 263, 324, 333, 339
Helly, D.O., 307n41
Hennessy, Peter, 307n36
Herzen, A.I., 103
Herzl, Theodor, 154
Hildebrand, Klaus, 172n69
Himmelfarb, Gertrude, 98n55
Himmler, Heinrich, 162–4
Hitler, Adolph, 146, 161–4, 168, 294, 297, 303, 318

Ho Chi Minh, 279
Hobbes, Thomas, 40
Hoffmeister, Johannes, 72n61, 346n72
Holloway, John, 346n62
Hoover, Herbert, 289
Hugo, Gustav, 38
Huntington, Samuel P., 296
Hussein, Saddam, 251

I

Ikenberry, Gilford John, 266n18

J

Jardin, André, 118n11
Jean, Carlo, 266n19
Jefferson, Thomas, 87, 288
Jessen, Jens, 306n25
Johnson, Paul, 250
Judt, Tony, 267n40

K

Kant, Immanuel, 57, 67, 85, 202
Kaplan, R.D., 266n9
Kautsky, Karl, 133, 134, 201–3, 206
Kelsen, Hans, 234
Kennedy, John F., 290
Khrushchev, N.S., 185, 224, 241
Kipling, Rudyard, 254
Kissinger, Henry, 293
Kolko, Gabriel, 171n36
Kornilov, L.G., 144
Krastins, Valdis, 267n33
Kriege, Hermann, 326, 327
Kugelmann, Ludwig, 36
Kun, Béla, 151

L

Laclau, Ernesto, 171n30
Lacouture, Jean, 307n33

Lafargue, Laura, 94, 132
Lafargue, Paul, 39
Lassalle, Ferdinand, 118n5
Lazarevíc, Nicolas, 176, 177, 217, 304
Le Bon, Gustave, 28–30, 143, 144, 149
Le Chapelier, Isaac René Guy, 89
Leclerc, Charles, 286
Lenin, V.I., 116, 135, 139–49, 152, 154–8, 167, 169, 175–96, 217
Lincoln, Abraham, 23, 24, 26, 36, 74, 109, 125, 126, 131, 148, 313, 314
Linera, Garcia, 321
Liu Shaoqi, 194
Livi, Roberto, 246n38
Locke, John, 34, 85, 89
Longuet, Charles, 10, 11, 13, 19
Losurdo, Domenico, 2, 4, 6, 8, 10, 12, 14, 16, 18, 20, 22, 24, 26, 28, 30, 32, 34, 36, 38, 40, 42, 44, 46, 54, 56, 58, 60, 62, 64, 66, 68, 70, 74, 76, 78, 80, 82, 84, 86, 88, 90, 92, 94, 96, 102, 104, 106, 108, 110, 112, 114, 116, 122, 124, 126, 128, 130, 132, 134, 140, 142, 144, 146, 148, 150, 152, 154, 156, 158, 160, 162, 164, 166, 168, 170, 176, 178, 180, 182, 184, 186, 188, 190, 192, 194, 196, 202, 204, 206, 208, 210, 212, 214, 216, 218, 220, 222, 224, 226, 230, 232, 234, 236, 238, 240, 242, 244, 250, 252, 254, 256, 258, 260, 262, 264, 270, 272, 274, 276, 278, 280, 282, 284, 286, 288, 290, 292, 294, 296, 298, 300, 302, 304
L'Ouverture, Toussaint, 26, 75, 104, 270, 286, 287, 292, 336

Lu Xun, 164
Lukács, György, 231, 232
Lutwak, Edward, 290
Luxemburg, Rosa, 147
Lvov, G.E., 156

M
Mackinder, Halford, 296
Madison, James, 87
Mallaby, Sebastian, 266n10
Malouet, Pierre-Victor, 88
Manning, Robert A., 309n82
Manuel, Pierre, 77
Mao Zedong, 159, 188, 193, 214, 220, 241, 279, 291
Marat, Jean-Paul, 77
Martinetti, Cesare, 267n25
Marx Aveling, Eleanor, 97n19, 307n39
Marx, Jenny, 11, 36
Marx, Karl, 6n8, 47n1, 70n12, 96n3, 118n3, 135n1, 170n6, 196n11, 226n1, 245n1, 266n2, 267n32, 306n6, 344n2
Mayer, Arno J., 44
Mazie, D.M., 6n3
Mazower, Mark, 173n75
Menotti Serrati, Giacinto, 150
Mill, John Stuart, 16, 18, 29, 31, 55, 59
Misra, Amaresh, 346n69
Molnár, Miklos, 47n16
Monk, George, 265
Montesquieu, Charles-Louis de Secondat, Baron de La Bréde et de, 270
More, Thomas, 81, 272
Mosse, George L., 52n158
Mouffe, Chantal, 171n30
Muhammad, 327, 328

Mussolini, Benito, 166, 252, 284
Myrdal, Gunnar, 3

N
Naím, Moisés, 267n30
Napoleon I, Emperor of France, 206
Napoleon III, Emperor of France, 106, 123, 207, 208
Negri, Antonio, 333, 334
Nicholas I, Czar of Russia, 34, 122
Nietzsche, Friedrich, 18, 25, 30, 31, 33, 38, 60–2, 66–9, 93, 220, 270
Nkrumah, Kwame, 293
Noah, Timothy, 309n76
Nolte, Ernst, 144

O
Olusoga, David, 173n72
Owen, Robert, 273

P
Pareto, Vilfredo, 45, 149
Pascal, Pierre, 176–8, 181, 218
Pasolini, Pier Paolo, 325
Pelletier, Madeleine, 175
Phillips, Wendell, 36, 37, 126
Pilsudski, Józef, 151
Piper, Ernst, 173n74
Plato, 321
Pomeranz, Kenneth, 70n15, 198n58
Popper, Karl, 45, 46, 250
Prashad, Vijay, 308n67
Preston, Paul, 344n13
Proudhon, Pierre-Joseph, 11, 35, 101, 102, 104, 106, 123, 132, 255, 330, 331

R
Radek, Karl, 152
Reagan, Ronald, 250
Reich, Robert, B., 4, 46, 162–6, 191, 209, 277, 294, 303, 315, 316, 318, 320, 321, 332, 341
Renan, Ernest, 153
Rhodes, Cecil, 154, 161, 162
Richet, Denis, 196n13
Roach, Stephen, S., 309n87
Rodinson, Maxime, 345n49
Roosevelt, Franklin Delano, 259
Rostow, W.W., 290
Roth, Joseph, 182, 216
Rousseau, Jean-Jacques, 35, 263, 286
Rowan, C.T., 6n3
Ruge, Arnold, 58, 79

S
Saint-Simon, C.H. de Rouvroy, de Conte, 104
Scalfari, Eugenio, 266n6
Schlesinger, Arthur, Jr., 136n20, 247n53
Schoelcher, Victor, 104
Schreiber, Gerhard, 173n84
Senghor, Léopold, 326
Sieyés, Emmanuel Joseph, 77, 85
Sisci, Francesco, 246n36
Slotkin, Richard, 49n83
Smith, Adam, 84, 127, 148, 296, 328–30
Snow, Edgar, 158
Socrates, 67, 68
Soprani, Anne, 97n18
Spencer, Herbert, 42, 58, 86
Spengler, Oswald, 278
Stalin, J.V., 152, 157, 169, 184, 234, 236–8

Stefanoni, Pablo, 345n33
Stern, E., 309n82
Stirner, Max, 79
Stoddard, Lothrop, 287
Stuart dynasty, 16, 29, 264, 265
Sukarno, 293

T
Taine, Hippolyte, 29, 270
Talleyrand-Périgord, Charles-Maurice de, 265
Tawney, R.H., 96n11
Thurow, Lester, 267n29
Timur (Tamerlane), 81, 319
Tito, J.B., 244
Tkachov, P.N., 103
Todorov, Tzvetan, 346n75
Togliatti, Palmiro, 280
Trotsky, L.D., 1147, 150, 164, 165, 177, 179, 181, 184, 216, 226, 233, 235–7, 298
Truman, Harry S., 290
Tucholsky, Kurt, 328
Tukhachevsky, M.N., 150
Turone, Sergio, 6n2
Tyler, P.E., 309n83

V
Vogel, Ezra, 246n39
Voltaire, 35, 36
von Bismarck, Otto, 73–5, 102, 106, 209
von Clausewitz, Carl, 46
von Hayek, Friedrich, 259, 299
von Metternich, Klemens Wenzel, 121, 122
von Schiller, Friedrich, 39
von Tirpitz, Alfred, 45

W

Walker, William, 26, 153
Wallace, Mike, 301
Weil, Simone, 188, 325
Wilhelm II, Emperor of Germany, 22, 146, 189, 252
Wilkinson, William John, 118n18
Wilson, Woodrow, 289
Wollstonecraft, Mary, 17, 77
Woolf, Virginia, 90, 109, 110, 327

Y

Yeltsin, B.N., 265, 338

Z

Zasulich, Vera, 124
Zhou Enlai, 198
Zhou Enlai,
Zinoviev, Aleksandr, 150, 151
Zinoviev, G.E., 12, 13
Zizek, Slavoj, 285, 286, 288, 293, 294, 334

The manufacturer's authorised representative in the EU is Springer Nature Customer Service Centre GmbH, Europaplatz 3, 69115 Heidelberg, Germany. If you have any concerns regarding our products, please contact ProductSafety@springernature.com

Printed and bound by CPI Group (UK) Ltd, Croydon, CR0 4YY

10/03/2026

02069009-0008